DALE STEINREICH

ECONOMICS FOR EVERYDAY LIFE AND BEYOND

BOOK I: MICROECONOMICS

Auburn Academic Press (AAP)

ISBN (e-book): 979-8-9990989-0-0 (digital online)
           979-8-9990989-1-7 (electronic book text)
ISBN (hardcover): 979-8-9990989-2-4
ISBN (paperback): 979-8-9990989-3-1

Dedication

To Donna, at 93, and Sebastian, at 8, a most remarkable longevity for a raccoon.

PREFACE

This book came about through my own multiple frustrations using textbooks from large corporate publishers. After many years I have not been able to conclude anything else other than that these publishers really hate their customers: the college and university faculty and instructors who use their books to teach their classes and the students, parents, and financial aid and scholarship funds that ultimately pay for their books. This means one thing: market power, in the sense of too much of it.

Exorbitant prices have been a well-known issue (and of course another symptom of excessive market power). However, as an instructor, I have been shocked at some of the ill treatment to which I have been subjected. It includes, but is certainly not limited to, having questions and requests for assistance go completely ignored to curt or downright rude responses from publisher representatives. The most memorable so far was a response essentially saying, "Since your enrollments aren't that large, your issue is not that much a concern to us." Wow. Admittedly, my sections aren't hundreds of students in size, but they regularly reach twenty-five, which is not trivial.

What I am hoping this book delivers are explanations of microeconomic theory along with many examples and applications that are as accurate as they are lucid, and repeated demonstrations of the relevance of most if not all of the material to what we encounter in ordinary, everyday life. Accomplishing all of the aforementioned and at a price point that is a favorable outlier in juxtaposition to just about all the other microeconomics textbooks on the market would achieve most, if not all, of my goals. To be fair, I am aware of one other textbook which is lower in price than this one in at least a couple of its electronic forms. However, I have reviewed it and found that its substantial shortcomings outweigh its very few positive traits. It is an economic principle that you get what you pay for, no free lunch and all. My hope is that this book will prove to be the bigger "bang for the buck."

Pro Christo et Occidente,

Dale Steinreich, Ph.D.
Loveliest Village of the Plain
July 4, 2025

CONTENTS

Part I: Principles, Exchange, and Markets

Chapter 1: Nine Principles

1.0 Introduction

According to the *American Heritage Dictionary*, the term economy derives from **oikonomos** [*oikos* (house) + *nemein* (to manage)], the Greek word for household manager.[1]

oikonómos (οικονόμος) – the Greek word for household manager.

Everyone reading this book is a member of a household, thus the necessity of household management is universally understood. The first task is deciding who does what. Who will cook the meals? Who will wash and dry the laundry? Who will keep up with the bills and pay them? Who will feed the pets?

Countries of millions of people face the same "Who does what?" question. Who will grow the crops that will turn into household meals? Who will make the clothes that become household laundry? Who will work in the banks that facilitate the paying of bills? Who will breed the dogs and cats that become household pets?

These issues are important because lives depend on them. Just as when a household is dysfunctional, abusive, or neglectful, its members (especially children and the elderly) can unnecessarily suffer and even die, so can a nation suffer unnecessary hunger, disease, war, and death if resources are misallocated or wasted.

Disaster can come from mismanagement because all the earth's resources, like a household's, are scarce or limited in supply. **Scarcity** is the limited or finite supply of the world's resources. If scarcity did not exist, the earth's entire food supply could be grown in a single flowerpot. Not only would every person live in housing that is better than what they live in today, but the commodious mansion or condominium of his or her choice.

scarcity - the limited or finite supply of the world's resources.

Unfortunately, this is a fantasy because a full one hundred percent of the resources on the face of the earth are scarce. Students often tell the author that abundant resources such as air and water are not scarce, but this is mistaken. While there is a large supply of air and water on Earth, they are still finite and, thus, scarce. For any of us to consume more water, we must make do with less of something else: less food, less time doing other things, and so on.

In stark contrast to scarcity, a society's wants are unlimited. We would all like better clothing, housing, food, more money, more leisure time, and a more-beautiful-and-sexy significant other who wants to please us in every imaginable way. Not one of these desires is possible to fulfill without giving up something in return, hence the necessity of economics in providing insight into how the inescapable conflict between scare resources and unlimited wants is resolved. What is economics?

---

[1] *The American Heritage Dictionary*. Second College Edition. Houghton Mifflin, 1985, p. 437.

economics - the study of how scarce resources are allocated in a world of unlimited wants.

microeconomics – the study of economic decisions made at the individual, household, firm, and market level.

macroeconomics – the study of phenomena and issues at the level of an entire economy.

Economics is the study of how scarce resources are allocated in a world of unlimited wants.

Economics is usually divided into two subdisciplines, **microeconomics** and **macroeconomics**. Microeconomics is the study of economic decisions made at the individual, household, firm, and market level while macroeconomics is the study of phenomena and issues at the level of an entire economy.

The economic perspective is not instinctive to most people. It is a certain way of thinking that guides analyses of the world and its problems. To help the reader get into the groove of economic thinking, the following are nine principles that guide it.

1.1 Principle 1: Every action has a cost (tradeoff).

At one time or another you may have heard, "There ain't no such thing as a free lunch" (TANSTAAFL). Despite its poor grammar, this saying in the United States dates back at least to the 1940s and refers to the days of the Old-West saloon where if you purchased a glass of beer, you would receive a sandwich or be able to help yourself to a table of all-you-can-eat bread, meat, cheese, fruit, and the like.

ECONOMICS IN ACTION: Is There Such a Thing as a Free Breakfast?

Residence Inn Fort Myers at I-75 and Gulf Coast Town Center in Fort Myers, Florida (Marriott, Fair Use)

Residence Inn (a division of Marriott Hotels), in many of its locations, offers not only a "free" breakfast but evening socials where one can consume "free" beer, wine, and nachos. But are they really free? No. Like the "free lunch" provided by American saloons in the late 1800s to early 1900s, they are only meant to be consumed by guests who stay at the hotel for at least one night. Is there ever a problem with non-guests mooching food and beverages during the hotel's breakfast and evening-social hours? Yes, but hotel management can request a room number, key card, voucher, or other proof of current stay. Anyone who cannot prove his or her status as a current guest or friend of one can be ordered to leave the premises. This doesn't mean that it's good business for hotel staff to aggressively police breakfast or evening gatherings and risk alienating paying guests. However, it is hotel guests who are ultimately paying for the food and beverages through their room rates. If too much mooching goes on and food and beverage supplies dwindle quickly, guests don't get the full value of their stay and go elsewhere. This means that repeat moochers will be identified and no longer allowed into the hotel.

Because we live in a world of scarcity, everything we do has a cost (or **tradeoff**) associated with it. A tradeoff is the trading away of something you want for something you want more (e.g., trading money for a good or service). Nothing is completely free: the saloon lunch isn't because you have to purchase a beer to get it. Let's say that you receive a $100 Walmart gift card for your birthday and you decide to redeem it for two shirts and two pairs of pants priced at $25 each. The clothing, while free in terms of $100 of money, will not be cost-free. Besides having to pay sales tax on the clothing, you'll have to expend resources to travel to Walmart, but even if a friend drives you for free, the entire trip will expend (trade away or trade off) one of your most precious resources: time. While you select the clothing, try it on, and wait at a checkout lane to complete your trip to the store, you will lose (trade off) a half hour or more that could have been used for earning income, studying (if you're a student), relaxing in leisure, etc.

tradeoff – the trading away of something you want for something you want more (e.g., trading money for a good or service).

ECONOMICS IN ACTION: Buy-One-Get-One-Free (BOGOF) Sales

Publix, consistently rated one of the U.S.'s best supermarket chains, each week features buy-one-get-one-free (BOGOF) sales on grocery items such as Ritz Crackers and Pepperidge Farm cookies. From Publix's standpoint, it's a great way to clear excess inventory. However, this two-for-the-price-of-one deal is the same thing as a 50% reduction in the price of one item and this is exactly how Publix checkout scanners treat the transaction. If gallons of milk are priced at $4 each before a BOGOF sale, the BOGOF sale reduces the price to $2 per gallon until the sale ends. If you purchase just 1 gallon, the BOGOF sale allows you to get that 1 gallon for $2. If you purchase 2 gallons, you are getting double the quantity for the same amount of money ($4) that would only get you 1 gallon before the sale began. Good deal? Absolutely. Was anything acquired for free? No.

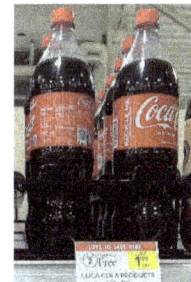

A Buy-One-Get-One-Free Sale on Coca-Cola at Publix (Reddit, Fair Use)

Hence, to get something of value, we must trade away or trade off something of value for it. Higher grades in college for most students require the sacrifice of more sleep and leisure time. Losing weight to look and feel better requires more effort in monitoring one's diet, sacrificing good tasting but unhealthy food, and spending more time exercising. To get a nicer looking date on Hinge or eHarmony, you have to dress better and look better, which requires time and money. There's no getting without giving.

Oikonomos reminds us that tradeoffs exist for societies as well as individuals. The Soviet Union, Pol Pot's Cambodia, Fidel Castro's Cuba, and today's North Korea and Venezuela are all examples of repressive military dictatorships. In these types of societies, scarce resources are primarily controlled by a powerful central government. Political and military leaders live in the best homes, eat the best food, have their children educated in the best schools, and otherwise exist in a *nomenklatura* (special class) in what are supposed to be societies without class distinctions ("people's republics").

14

guns-versus-butter tradeoff - the tradeoff that exists in society between government and consumer spending.

These aforementioned nations illustrate an extreme choice in a famous tradeoff in economics: the **guns-versus-butter tradeoff**, or the tradeoff that exists in society between government and consumer spending. These societies load up on "guns" (big militaries armed with tanks to nuclear missiles) while neglecting "butter," i.e., the basic staple goods and services that form a subsistence standard of living for the average citizen. In societies where there is greater political and economic choice, such as those in North America and Europe, the tradeoff is skewed toward more "butter" and fewer "guns."

1.2 Principle 2: The cost of something is everything that is given up to get it.

price - the number of currency units (e.g., dollars, pesos, or yen) that must be given up to obtain a good or service.

opportunity cost (full cost) – everything given up as the result of making a choice. It is equal to the explicit (money) costs plus implicit (non-money) costs of a good, service, or action.

This is a principle that ordinary people find confusing because they falsely assume that a good or service's **price** (the number of currency units [e.g., dollars, pesos, or yen] that must be given up to obtain a good or service) is its **full cost**, otherwise known as **opportunity cost**. Opportunity cost is everything given up as the result of making a choice. It is equal to the explicit (money) costs plus implicit (non-money) costs of a good, service, or action. Let's say that you are working a job and your employer gives you two unpaid weeks off during the summer. You have the choice of staying home and paying $1,000 to take a two-week long professional-development class at your workplace or paying $4,500 total for a two-week leisure trip to the Bahamas (with the $4,500 total broken down into $750 for roundtrip airfare, $1,400 for food, $2,100 for lodging, and $250 for ground transportation). Let's also say that, for now, you are leaning toward taking the class because you think that it will get you better job prospects and vacations in the future.

explicit costs - all of the money costs incurred as the result of taking an action.

implicit costs – all of the non-monetary costs incurred as the result of taking an action.

Back to price versus opportunity cost (full cost): why does the class's price of $1,000 not reflect the class's opportunity cost? The opportunity cost of the class includes not only the $1,000 tuition price but also the lost leisure, relaxation, and mental-health benefits gained from a trip to The Bahamas. These are costs as well even though they are not expressed in money terms. Taken together, monetary costs (**explicit costs**, or all of the money costs incurred as the result of taking an action) and non-monetary costs (**implicit costs**, or all of the non-monetary costs incurred as the result of taking an action) are part of the concept of opportunity cost, or everything given up as the result of making a choice:

$$opportunity\ cost = explicit\ costs + implicit\ costs.$$

Now the tricky part: are food and shelter a cost of the class as well? No. At home, you will eat

net cost – the difference in cost between alternative actions.

and seek shelter for $60 total per night ($25 in food + $35 in leased shelter) or $840 total for two weeks. If you take the Bahamian vacation, food and shelter become costs, but only to the extent that they exceed the costs of food and shelter at home. If in the Bahamas food is $100 per night and shelter is $150 per night, the total for food and shelter will run $3,500 for two weeks. This means that the **net cost**, the difference in cost between alternative actions, of the Bahamas trip in terms of food and shelter is ($3,500 - $840 =) $2,660.

Implicit costs? As mentioned earlier, the lost leisure and health benefits that come from taking a vacation. Working too much can sap a person's creativity, productivity, and immunity to colds and sickness. Long-term health problems (such as strain on your back and upper body) from sitting too much can develop as well. If physical and mental-health concerns now make the leisure trip look better, remember that there are implicit costs of the Bahamian trip: you delay picking up job skills and thus delay getting promoted or getting a better job.

Learning Economics: Mnemonics

A **mnemonic** is a pattern that helps a person more easily remember something, and thankfully there are many helpful ones for economics as we will see in this book. The first one is for opportunity cost.

> **mnemonic** – a pattern that helps a person more easily remember something.

Opportunity cost is | everything | given up | as the result of making a choice, where:

$$everything = explicit + implicit\ costs$$

and

$$given\ up = only\ what\ is\ truly\ given\ up\ (net\ cost)$$

Continuing with our Bahamas-trip example, everything truly given up is:

Explicit costs of the Bahamas trip:
airfare (not paid if you stay home, so definitely a pure cost) = $ 750
food (consumed if you stay home, so a net cost [difference in costs]) = $1,400 - $350 = $1,050
shelter (consumed if you stay home, so a net cost) = $2,100 - $490 = $1,610
ground transportation (consumed if you stay home,[2] so a net cost) = $250 - $14 = $ 236
                                                                    Total: $3,646

Implicit costs of the Bahamas trip:
lost income from development of work skills = $? Rough estimates can be made.
lost interest earned on savings of $3,646 = $? Rough estimates can be made here as well.

Two Lessons:
1. Prices and costs are not the same thing. Most laypersons would say that the $4,500 price tag of the Bahamas trip is its "cost," but the (explicit) costs of the trip are actually $854 lower at $3,646 (see total above).
2. Implicit costs are substantial but can be difficult to quantify. If you go on the trip and don't take the skills-development class, how much less is your value in the job market? If you go on the trip, how much money will you lose by not earning interest on the $3,646 explicit costs of the trip? These are just two implicit costs of going on the trip.

---

[2] Home transportation is assumed to be an owned bike with an explicit cost of maintenance and upkeep of $1 per day. For two weeks this amounts to a total of $14, which is subtracted from the $250 explicit cost of transportation in The Bahamas to arrive at the net explicit cost of transportation of $236 for the Bahamas trip.

All of these types of considerations show how complicated making truly informed and effective life choices can be. Costs, especially implicit ones, can be difficult to quantify and can vary widely across different individuals. The word "opportunity" in the term *opportunity cost* is an explicit reminder to consider implicit costs while weighing a decision because people are so prone to ignore them or ignore them until it's too late to reverse course on a decision.

CASE STUDY: Opportunity Cost in the Real World. For Deshaun Watson, More College or the NFL Draft?

By the end of his third season at Clemson University in early 2017, Clemson Tigers quarterback Deshaun Watson had led the Tigers to two national championship appearances. If he left Clemson for the 2017 National Football League (NFL) draft, he would almost certainly be picked early in the first round. Such talent commands a lucrative contract that can set up a person for a very comfortable life.

Deshaun Watson (Erik Drost, CC BY 2.0)

Watson's alternative to declaring for the draft was remaining at Clemson for another year. Although Watson had earned a Bachelor of Communications degree, he could have gotten a start on a graduate degree.

The problem is that astronomical opportunity costs made it difficult for Watson to spend a fourth year at Clemson taking more classes and playing more collegiate ball. One, he could have gotten seriously injured during another season of college football and jeopardized a career in the NFL. Second, any graduate classes he took wouldn't likely prepare him for a career with an income comparable to what he could earn playing in the NFL. Finally, it was extremely unlikely that the Tigers would return to the national championship and win it again. Given the rest of their talent, the Tigers had only one likely direction: down.

In short, from Watson's standpoint at the end of his third season with the Tigers, the explicit costs of remaining at Clemson were undoubtedly low while the implicit costs appeared toweringly huge. This was proven accurate when Watson entered the 2017 NFL draft, was drafted 12th overall by the Houston Texans, and signed a $13.84 million contract that included an $8.21 million signing bonus.[3] Watson earned a communications degree at Clemson University, but also earned a passing grade in terms of understanding the concept of opportunity cost.

---

[3] Patra, Kevin. "Deshaun Watson signs contract with Houston Texans." NFL.com. May 12, 2017. <https://archive.ph/qlrHO>

1.3 Principle 3: Rational economic decisions are made at the margin.

Rational in economics means tending to weigh the perceived costs and perceived benefits of an action before taking the action. **Margin** means "edge," and refers to the point at which a decision is made. For a profitable clothing store in mid-September, the decision is not whether to continue operating or go out of business. The business is profitable. The decision is also not whether to stock summer or fall clothes. By mid-September, fall clothing is arriving at the store in box after box while what is left of the summer clothing in inventory is not selling at all. At the margin or current point, the question is what to do with, for example, men's summer bathing suits. You can keep them at their summer price of $50 each or send most of them out the door in a 75-percent-off sale for $12.50 each. What do you do? If keeping them in inventory in the back of the store will cost more than $12.50 each, you have the sale. And this is why so often you see such steep price cuts (75 percent, even 90 percent) at the end of a season at clothing stores. From the store's perspective, getting something for end-of-season clothing is a lot better than getting nothing. The author, with a coupon, once got a nice shirt for a price of $0.00 at a Kohl's store at the end of a summer.

> **rational** – tending to weigh the perceived costs and perceived benefits of an action before taking the action.
>
> **margin** - the point at which a decision is made.

In American football, if a home team is losing by four points and is 15 yards from its opponent's goal on fourth down with only five seconds left in the game, if the team's objective is winning the game, the rational decision at the team's margin is not about whether to play the game or not play it. That ship sailed long ago. At the current margin, the decision is about what actions to take to win the game. A field goal for three points won't bring a victory. A successful run for a six-point touchdown against an opponent with a tough run defense seems unlikely. The best chance is a six-point touchdown pass, especially if passes have already been working well.

Now let's say that a pass is attempted, it falls incomplete, and the home team loses the game. Does that mean that the home team was economically irrational in making the choice it did? Not at all. It made the best choice to win at the margin, regardless of whether it succeeded or not. The team would have been irrational if it had kicked a three-point field goal since that action in no way would have accomplished its goal of winning the game.

So, is economically irrational behavior rare? It is, because, by definition, economics assumes that people are rational. This is not to be confused with saying that people rarely make wrong decisions. What rational in economics means is that *people usually weigh perceived costs and perceived benefits on some level before taking an action.* Should you brave heavy rain to take the trash to the curb tonight or wait until early tomorrow morning before you leave for work or school? You hate the rain, but hate much more the risk of missing this week's trash pickup.

marginal benefits - the additional benefits of taking an action.

marginal costs - the additional costs of taking an action.

rational choices - actions taken because the perceived marginal benefits are greater than the perceived marginal costs.

In all the preceding examples (clothing, football, trash), there was a comparison between **marginal benefits** and **marginal costs**. Marginal benefits are the additional benefits of taking an action while marginal costs are the additional costs of taking an action. Economically **rational choices** are actions taken because the perceived marginal benefits are greater than the perceived marginal costs. Continuing with our clothing store example from earlier in this section, the marginal benefits of the sale were $12.50 per bathing suit while the marginal costs were spending five minutes printing and posting a "75% Off Sale on Men's Bathing Suits" sign in the front window of the store. An easy decision. For the football game, the marginal benefit of throwing a pass was a good shot at victory. The marginal cost was rolling the dice for a possible injury to one or more players. Finally, for trash pickup, the marginal benefits of braving the rain to place the trash at the curb is the peace of mind that you definitely won't miss trash pickup and have excess trash stinking up your house for a week. That benefit, for most people, exceeds the low marginal cost of getting wet for a minute to make sure your trash is at the curb for pickup before next morning.

1.4 Principle 4: Incentives affect behavior.

incentive – a reward or punishment received for an action.

An **incentive** is a reward or punishment received for an action. Incentives are pervasive throughout everyday life for consumers, employees, and citizens, so it is no stunning revelation that they are effective. Earlier we discussed BOGOF sales. Publix supermarkets have them because they are very effective at quickly reducing excess inventory. Consumers enthusiastically participate in them because they like the "free" second item even if they do not have an urgent need for it.

At many firms, employees receive a bonus for reaching a certain sales or production target. Provided the target is realistic, the fact that it is challenging will usually be no obstacle to affecting behavior. The author's father managed a factory where, if the employees hit a certain production target with no worker injuries by November of each year, each employee received a coupon for a "free" Thanksgiving turkey at a local Kroger supermarket. What was interesting was how employees, even in February, were mindful of keeping production high and the workplace safe in order to receive their "free" Thanksgiving turkey nine months later! For the business, it was a bargain incentive.

In the world of driving, there are a ton of incentives. Speeding tickets are a penalty that has made drivers slow down. Laws against texting on a phone while driving have had a mixed effect because texting while driving is a hazardous behavior that is easier to conceal than speeding or drunken driving.

One stubborn reality that has repeatedly haunted politicians and policy makers is the **law of unintended consequences**. This law is the proposition that actions can trigger results that are undesirable or the opposite of those intended. The paradox of auto safety is a great example. In the 1950s, not all cars had seatbelts, and airbags did not become pervasive in cars until the 1990s. In 1965, attorney Ralph Nader published a book titled, *Unsafe at Any Speed: The Designed-In Dangers of the American Automobile*. After this, auto safety became a big issue in the U.S. media and federal government. A number of laws were enacted after the public was sold on them based on a plethora of predicted benefits. The problem? Nader was an attorney, not an economist, and overlooked the many unintended consequences of his "safety" proposals.

law of unintended consequences - the proposition that actions can trigger results that are undesirable or the opposite of those intended.

It seemed to be common sense that mandating seat belts (and later airbags) in cars and requiring their use improved safety for vehicle occupants. However, now strapped in behind seat belts and hundreds of pounds of metal, drivers drove *marginally* less carefully and took risks that they would not have taken before. The first evidence of this effect came in a famous 1975 study[4] conducted by University of Chicago economist Sam Peltzman. Peltzman found that while more auto safety regulation led to a smaller number of deaths per accident, it also led to a larger number of accidents. Contrary to what the media and politicians promised, driver deaths changed little. What just about no one foresaw was an increase in pedestrian deaths.

Sam Peltzman (University of Chicago, With Permission)

Why did more pedestrians die? While over a decade drivers became more and more cocooned behind seat belts, padded dashboards, and more metal, nothing changed for pedestrians. The greater number of accidents killed more of them. This was the law of unintended consequences at work.

Another unintended consequence of attempting to make just vehicle occupants safer was more distracted driving, especially after the spread of the smartphone around 2006. Even though every driver has heard horror stories of distracted drivers unintentionally killing pedestrians or occupants of other vehicles, anyone who spends a few minutes on today's roads will see myriad other drivers still texting, surfing the Web, Facebooking, and tweeting while behind the wheel of a speeding car. Why? Again, drivers feel relatively safe behind a seat belt, airbag, padded dashboard, steering wheel, and wall of metal in today's typical sedan or sport-utility vehicle (SUV). The thinking is, "I don't want to get into an accident, but even if I do, I should be okay." The number of fatal crashes on American roads hit its highest mark in an eight-year period ending in 2016 (34,439).[5] Since 2020, automobile deaths per 1 million inhabitants have risen in the U.S., Australia, France, Italy, and the United Kingdom.[6]

---

[4] Peltzman, Sam. "The Effects of Automobile Safety Regulation." *Journal of Political Economy* 83, no. 4 (1975): 677–725. http://www.jstor.org/stable/1830396.

[5] U.S. National Highway Traffic Safety Administration (NHTSA). "Traffic Safety Facts: 2016 Data." September 2018. <https://crashstats.nhtsa.dot.gov/Api/Public/Publication/812581>

[6] Organization for Economic Co-operation and Development (OECD). "OECD Data: Road Accidents." <https://web.archive.org/web/20230706145327/https://data.oecd.org/transport/road-accidents.htm>

One last example of unintended consequences in auto-safety regulation is the infamous case of Takata Corporation airbags in 2013. Defective airbags installed in millions of cars exploded shards of metal into drivers and passengers, badly injuring and even killing some of them. Because of rigid federal regulations, car owners were forbidden from using tutorials to quickly deactivate or remove these dangerous devices from their vehicles. Instead, they had to wait weeks to months on long waiting lists to have their airbags replaced at an authorized auto dealer.

ECONOMICS IN ACTION: The Value of a List—Is It in Not Forgetting Necessities or in Saving Time?

Organizational experts frequently advocate writing out a comprehensive list before doing anything from grocery shopping to leaving town for business or leisure. Most laypersons intuitively believe that the value of such lists is to not forget any important items. To be sure, remembering crucial items (phone chargers and cords, etc.) is important. Having to make a trip back to the grocery store is wasteful and unnecessary enough. A trip back home from a business or vacation trip while hundreds to thousands of miles from home is usually very impractical to impossible.

It's Really About Time

Forgetting needed items has a cost, but so does time, perhaps the scarcest resource for most people. What lists undoubtedly do is greatly speed up any task, saving half to two-thirds the amount of time taken without a list. This should come as no surprise, as rotely ticking down a list is much more efficient than having to repeatedly stop and think about what items you want to purchase at the store during your weekly visit to the grocery store or pack for a journey out of town. But the blessings of a list don't just stop with not forgetting essential items or going faster during recurrent tasks. The ritual of a list can also communicate what items you've regularly listed that you usually don't end up using or are not as necessary as you thought. This adds to efficiency by gradually shortening the list over time to only absolutely necessary items and leaving items at home that you first thought were necessary but experience showed were just the opposite.

Fastidious organization is costly, true, but the benefits it can confer over time can be enormous and well worth it to most people.

1.5 Principle 5: Trade and exchange make all parties better off.

division of labor – the dividing up of tasks among different members of a household, firm, or group to accomplish a goal.

Earlier in this chapter we discussed *oikonomos*, household management. Clearly trade and exchange inside the household make everyone better off. One person cooks, another collects all the dishes and washes them. One person goes grocery shopping each week and maintains adequate inventories of food items while another manages the household's finances and pays its bills on time. This **division of labor**, the dividing up of tasks among different members of a household, firm, or group to accomplish a goal allows the household to achieve all of its goals more efficiently and effectively than if one person has to undertake all the responsibilities alone.

So far, we've analyzed how members of a household trade with each other, but entire households trade with each other too, in terms of food, clothing, and just about all other goods and services. While some farmers can supply most of their household's food needs, they still have many other needs which will have to be fulfilled using external labor. If a farmer's house pipes are leaking and if he's good at growing and harvesting crops but not skilled in plumbing work, he will have to hire a plumber to repair his pipes. If he can locate a plumber who will fix his pipes in return for a bushel of wheat, then just like the members of a household who exchange services under one roof, both the farmer and plumber can benefit from exchanging services under different household roofs.

What's true for members of households and between households is also true for nations. The U.S. excels in producing large machinery, aircraft, chemicals, and now, after the shale-oil revolution, exporting oil and liquid natural gas. Asian countries excel in textiles, smaller manufactured goods, and electronics. Trade between the U.S. and Asian countries makes both sides better off. Asian airline and construction firms benefit from using Boeing airplanes, Caterpillar heavy machinery, and refined American oil. American consumers benefit from using Samsung Galaxy phones, LG televisions, and Toyota automobiles.

Trade between households and between countries provides more, varied, and higher-quality goods at lower prices. Why? This question is answered by our next principle.

1.6 Principle 6: The greater the level of competition among people, firms, industries, and countries, the better the economic outcomes.

The abandonment of pure socialism in Eastern Europe in 1989 and in the Soviet Union in 1991 marked a vast sea change—at least in thought—in the world about the superiority of the competitive **market** in allocating resources as opposed to centralized government planning. A market is a physical or virtual place where buyers and sellers meet to exchange goods and services directly or for money. Pure socialist **central planning** is the practice of a single government body deciding the main economic questions of a society: what will be produced, for whom, in what quantities, and at what prices. For a modern society comprised of millions of consumers demanding billions of goods and services, this is an impossible task.

market – a physical or virtual place where buyers and sellers meet to exchange goods and services directly or for money.

central planning - the practice of a single government body deciding the main economic questions of a society: what will be produced, for whom, in what quantities, and at what

While goods and services were low in posted price or even "free" at the point of sale, on average they were high in individual cost (in terms of the time spent in long lines to acquire them), artificially scarce, of questionable quality, and supplied erratically. Pulitzer Prize-winning *New York Times* reporter Hedrick Smith's famous account from inside the Soviet Union paints a vivid picture:

First, we needed textbooks for our children (who went to Russian schools) and found that the sixth-grade textbooks had run out. A bit later, we tried to find ballet shoes for our 11-year-old daughter, Laurie, only to discover that in this land of ballerinas, ballet shoes size 8 were unavailable in Moscow. Goods are produced to fill the Plan, not to sell. Sometimes the anomalies are baffling. Leningrad can be overstocked with cross-country skis and yet go several months without soap for washing dishes. In the Armenian capital of Yerevan, I found an ample supply of accordions but local people complained they had gone for weeks without ordinary kitchen spoons or tea samovars. I knew a Moscow family that spent a frantic month hunting for a child's potty while radios were a glut on the market. In Rostov, on a sweltering mid-90s day in June, the ice-cream stands were all closed by 2 P.M. and a tourist guide told me that it was because the whole area had run out of ice cream, a daily occurrence…The list of scarce items is practically endless…Traveling in the provinces I have also noticed the lack of such basic food items as meat. In cities like Nizhnevartovsk and Bratsk during winter, people had become so accustomed to the fact that the meat departments of food stores had simply shut down.[7]

monopoly - a single firm or government supplying a good, service, or societal governance for which there are no close substitutes.

Such severe coordination problems were the result of having a central-government **monopoly** in charge of allocating resources. (A monopoly is a single firm or government supplying a good, service, or societal governance for which there are no close substitutes.) Today's Cuba, North Korea, and Venezuela evince the same problems.

mixed economy - an economy composed of markets that range from competitive to substantially controlled by a government.

While the U.S. is often put forth as the economic opposite of pure socialist or communist central planning, it is in reality a **mixed economy**, an economy composed of markets that range from competitive to substantially controlled by a government.[8] In a mixed economy, there are sectors where, instead of a single government agency deciding all the economic questions, numerous firms and millions of consumers interact to decide what is supplied, how much, and at what price. These are competitive or near-competitive markets (barbeque sauce, generic computer parts, produce). On the other side of mixed economies is where there is anything from a single central planner (e.g., the Federal Reserve System, Tennessee Valley Authority, Veterans Administration health system) to heavy regulation that severely limits competition in an industry. A good example of the latter is U.S. health care, a cartel[9] where the U.S. state and federal governments have artificially restricted the number of physicians, surgeons, medical practices, hospitals, pharmacies, insurance firms, and drug companies. Hence, it's no surprise that U.S. health care is artificially scarce, exorbitantly expensive, and has legions of dissatisfied customers. This is the mixed economy, the typical economy of most modern countries that are a mix of free markets and industries that fiercely compete for profits and where the customer is king to cartels and monopolies protected from

---

[7] Smith, Hedrick. *The Russians*. Times Books, 1976.

[8] Notice that we did not use the pervasive but vague term, "capitalism." Coined by Louis Blanc in 1850, the term can refer to anything from competitive markets to government-business cartels (*fascism* in its original sense and *corporatism* in the modern sense). A term with so many different senses, some completely contradictory, loses all sensible meaning, which is why it will not be used in this book.

[9] This type of market structure will be discussed in much more detail later in this book in the chapters on industrial organization.

competition from governments where goods and services are artificially scarce, prices are high, and customer service is generally poor.

1.7 Principle 7: Markets work best when property rights are clearly defined and consistently enforced.

In the previous section, we explored the idea that competition produces better market outcomes. This is definitely true, but not the entire story. The Soviet, Eastern-European, and more recent Cuban, Venezuelan, and North-Korean experiences have shown that attempts to replicate market processes by central-planning boards has led to gross misallocation of goods and services: a roll of toilet paper in today's Venezuela is considered a luxury good.

So what, if anything, should governments do? One answer is to establish and enforce **property rights**, the freedom to exercise complete control over one's person and property.

property rights - the freedom to exercise complete control over one's person and property.

As can be readily seen from its definition, two practices that property rights outright forbid are **slavery** and **theft**. Slavery (a state of involuntary servitude of one person to another) is an obvious denial of self-ownership, and if the right to self-ownership or one's own person is not secure, then by extension neither is the right to own any other property. Theft, the acquisition of money or property through the use of illicit force (robbery), deception (fraud), or burglary (trespass and taking without permission) is another blatant violation of property rights among others.

slavery – a state of involuntary servitude of one person to another.

theft – the acquisition of money or property through the use of illicit force (robbery), deception (fraud), or burglary (trespass and taking without permission).

Markets do not function well if these property-rights violations are condoned and pervasive in a society. An entrepreneur will never invest hard-earned money to build a restaurant if her building can be vandalized and her business equipment stolen with little to no legal recourse. Investors will never build an aircraft factory in Venezuela if the plant will take a year and $100 million dollars to be built only for the plant and its output to be confiscated by Venezuela's government.

One view is that only governments in the form of local police, district attorneys, and a court system can efficiently enforce property rights. This seems convincing, as an all-powerful monopoly may seem to be an efficient adjudicator of disputes and enforcer of rights. Can a city have two or more private police departments and court systems enforcing laws? It could, and critics of such a system would certainly emphasize any potential shortcomings, including conflicts that arose between the different police and court authorities.

However, government monopolies are not without their shortcomings either. Many of them are entrusted with unlimited powers that in the wrong hands can be dangerous. It can be difficult to impossible for citizens to successfully sue police officers or their departments for false arrests, which can get an innocent citizen fired from his job and tarnish his reputation forever. The U.S. Drug Enforcement Agency (DEA) has repeatedly raided the wrong homes and businesses and seized the money and property of citizens who were eventually found to have no connection to illegal drugs. Victims have had to sometimes wait years to get their property returned, and some have never seen their property again because it went missing or was stolen.

eminent domain - the practice of acquiring land or property for public or private use.

And then there is **eminent domain**, the practice of acquiring land or property for public or private use. Under the traditional version, a state government can evict residents from and demolish their houses to expand a highway on the basis of "public need." In the newer version, a state government can evict residents from and demolish their houses to clear the way for a new shopping mall or hotel. While the former version has generally been tolerated by the American public, the latter—using eminent domain for the purpose of advancing commercial interests—has understandably been more controversial. Should a person be evicted from her house for the economic gain of a private developer and his investors? Regardless of one's particular answer to this latter question, eminent domain is definitely an issue of property rights and when their violation is acceptable.

1.8 Principle 8: The main determinant of a country's standard of living is its productivity.

productivity – units of production per worker per time period (day, month, quarter, year, etc.).

Since at least the 1700s and Adam Smith's *An Inquiry into the Nature and Causes of the Wealth of Nations*, economists have studied what made some countries rich and others poor. Why is the U.S. (where the average annual income is $80,300[10]) considered rich while Mexico (right next door where the average annual income is $12,100[11]) considered relatively poor? Why is Spain (where the average annual income is $32,180[12]) considered relatively prosperous compared to Morocco (again, right next door where the average annual income is $3,700[13]), which is considered very poor? One important factor is that the U.S. and Spain have higher **productivity**, i.e., higher units of production per worker per time period than their less-well-off neighbors. The higher the productivity of a country's workers, the higher that country's average standard of living.

Say's law - supply creates its own demand. In other words, in order to get you must first give.

This relationship should be common sense and is reflected in **Say's law**: Supply creates its own demand or, in order to get you must first give. When you *supply* a good or service, you earn an income that supports your *demand* for goods and services. As an individual becomes more productive, her income and standard of living rises. The same goes for a country's workers. As they become more productive over time, their incomes rise, and so does the average standard of living in their country.

---

[10] World Data. Average Income Around the World. <https://www.worlddata.info/average-income.php>

[11] Ibid

[12] Ibid

[13] Ibid

1.9 Principle 9: Prices rise when governments circulate too much money.

Inflation is a rise in the prices of all goods and services in an economy. It is a common mistake committed by students and members of the popular media to refer to a rise in the price of one product alone (e.g., gasoline) as "inflation." The price of gasoline can rise because of an increase in summer demand or Gulf-Coast refineries being shut down by a hurricane such as Katrina in 2005. Inflation, a rise in the price of *all* goods and services, is different because it is rooted in monetary instability. How do we know this? Because of what happens when inflation really takes off: money is much more plentiful. Everywhere it becomes worth less and less every day, and this causes prices to skyrocket.

> **inflation** – a rise in the prices of all goods and services in an economy. Otherwise known as a rise in an economy's price level.

In Berlin, Germany, in December of 1921, the price of a loaf of bread was 4 marks. By November 1923, that same loaf was priced at 201,000,000,000 marks.[14] Was this really inflation or just an increase in the price of bread? It was inflation because the prices of *all* other German goods and services had increased at about the same rate. In other words, in 23 months, Germany had experienced an approximate 5,024,999,999,900-percent (5 trillion percent) **hyperinflation**, an inflation rate of greater than 50 percent per month. The experience was not unique to Germany. From about 1921-1925, Austria, Hungary, and Poland all experienced similar hyperinflations.[15]

> **hyperinflation** - an inflation rate of greater than 50 percent per month.

What was propelling these massive inflations? A whopping surge in the circulation of the German, Austrian, Hungarian, and Polish currencies. In Germany, marks were everywhere and rapidly falling in **purchasing power**, i.e., how much in terms of goods and services a unit of currency can purchase. One funny story from the era is about a man on his way to a store with a wheelbarrow full of money to buy some food. He stops to break up a fight between two boys, turns around, and sees that he's been robbed. Of what? The item of real value: the wheelbarrow! On the sidewalk was left his big pile of money because it was worth so little that the thief didn't want it.

> **purchasing power** - how much in terms of goods and services a unit of currency can purchase.

1.10 Conclusion

This chapter introduced economics and nine principles of the discipline that shape its perspective and analysis of the world (see TABLE 1-1). With this new insight into the economic way of thinking, we will now move on to the appendix to this chapter, a review of graphs and other concepts. While the appendix to chapter 1 contains some remedial material, all readers should closely examine it to make sure that they fully understand all the material contained therein and thus be better prepared to fully understand all the material throughout the rest of this book. The

---

[14] White, Alan and Eric Hadley. *Germany 1918-1949*. Collins Educational, 1990.
[15] Sargent, Thomas J. "The End of Four Big Inflations," in Robert Hall, ed., *Inflation*. University of Chicago Press, 1983.

appendix to chapter 1 also provides previews of two upcoming models, the production possibilities frontier (PPF) and the demand curve, which most readers should find helpful.

TABLE 1-1: Nine Principles of Economics
1. Every action has a cost (tradeoff).
2. The cost of something is everything that is given up to get it.
3. Rational economic decisions are made at the margin.
4. Incentives affect behavior.
5. Trade and exchange make all parties better off.
6. The greater the level of competition among people, firms, and industries, the better the economic outcomes.
7. Markets work best when property rights are clearly defined and consistently enforced.
8. The main determinant of a nation's standard of living is its productivity.
9. Prices rise when governments circulate too much money.

1.11 Chapter Concepts

oikonomos
scarcity
economics
microeconomics
macroeconomics
tradeoff
guns-versus-butter tradeoff
price
opportunity cost (full cost)
explicit cost
implicit cost
net cost
mnemonic
rational
margin
marginal benefit
marginal cost
rational choice
incentive
law of unintended consequences
division of labor
market
central planning
monopoly
mixed economy
property rights
slavery

theft
eminent domain
productivity
Say's law
inflation
hyperinflation
purchasing power

1.12 Problems, Questions, and Discussion Topics (Items Requiring Examples are Marked with an Asterisk [*])

1. *oikonomos*

   A. What does it mean?

   B. How does a household resemble a nation's economy?

2. *A full _____ percent of the resources on the face of the earth are scarce.*

   A. Fill in the blank: _____.

   B. Explain:

3. macroeconomics (for an example, state and define a phenomenon that is studied in this discipline)*

4. "There ain't no such thing as a free lunch" (TANSTAAFL) (provide an example that demonstrates that nothing in life is really free)*.

5. At hotels such as Residence Inn,

   A. is there really such a thing as a free breakfast?

   B. Why or why not?

6. tradeoff*

7. In buy-one-get-one-free (BOGOF) sales such as those at Publix supermarkets,

   A. Is the second item really free?

   B. Why or why not?

8. guns-versus-butter tradeoff*

9. opportunity cost [full cost] (provide a quantitative example)*

10. implicit cost (provide an example of one created by reading this book and discussing this topic, i.e., explain your next highest-valued alternative to reading this book and discussing this topic)*

11. Marcus is taking a leisure trip to Hawaii. His travel agent tells him that on his all-inclusive tour of the islands, Marcus's food total will be $1,000. Having just completed a course in microeconomics, Marcus knows that $1,000 is not the true explicit cost of food for the time he will be on vacation. Provide a quantitative example of the microeconomic insight that Marcus is acknowledging.

12. Susan, a bartender, has two choices for Super Bowl Sunday. The first is going to a watch party with her fickle boyfriend Marcus and enjoying food and drinks with her friends. The second is working overtime at the bar for $40 per hour (double her normal wage) for six hours and losing Marcus, who has vowed to break up with Susan if she doesn't go to the watch party. What are Susan's total implicit costs of attending the party? What are Susan's implicit costs of going to work?

13. marginal cost (provide a quantitative example for a T-shirt factory)*

14. For Deshaun Watson, what was the main implicit cost of not entering the NFL draft in order to play college football for another year?

15. rational choices (provide a recent example of how you weighed perceived marginal benefits versus perceived marginal costs to arrive at a decision—some examples are whether to attend college, which college to attend, or whether to purchase a big-ticket item)*

16. incentive*

17. law of unintended consequences (provide an example of this in your life or the life of someone you know where you [he or she] made a choice anticipating one or more good results but were surprised by one or more negative or very negative results)*

18. Sam Peltzman (summarize his findings on the paradox of automobile safety [including his findings on driver versus pedestrian deaths], not his general biography)

19. For you, would the value of a pack list (for business or leisure) primarily lie in not forgetting important items or packing for your trip much faster? Support your answer by listing both the costs and benefits of your preference.

20. central planning (provide a current example of an economy operating on this type of macroeconomic organizational principle)*

21. mixed economy (provide a current example of an economy operating on this type of macroeconomic organizational principle)*

22. property rights*

23. eminent domain*

24. How is a nation's standard of living and its productivity related?

25. Say's law (provide an example from your life or the life of someone you know)*

26. *Prices rise when governments _____.*

    A. Fill in the blank: _____.

    B. Explain:

27. hyperinflation (provide a real-life example)*

28. purchasing power (provide a quantitative example)*

Appendix to Chapter 1: Review of Tables and Graphs

A.0 Introduction

On a publisher's conference call, the author of this book was made aware of one of the most depressing things imaginable: an economics professor at a large public university in the Northeastern U.S. teaches economics principles as essentially a course in math story problems. Depressing because this individual is not only a seriously flawed educator, but obviously has a gravely distorted understanding of economics. Economics is *not* a branch of mathematics and mathematics is a conceptual tool for enhancing economic insight in line with sound economic principles. To be sure, bad academics are found in many disciplines outside of economics. Not surprisingly, what many have in common is making mathematics an end in itself.

A.1 Four Types of Graphs

What is true for math is true for graphical illustrations (mathematics visualized) as well. Their purpose is to make evident patterns and trends through two- or three-dimensional imagery. A **pie chart** is one of the simplest graphical illustrations. It is a graphic form that displays a single variable broken down into two or more components. FIGURE A-1 is an example that many readers will have seen in personal money apps such as Quicken. It divides household spending into categories.

pie chart – a graphic form that displays a single variable broken down into two or more components.

FIGURE A-1: Total Household Spending Per Month (Dollars)

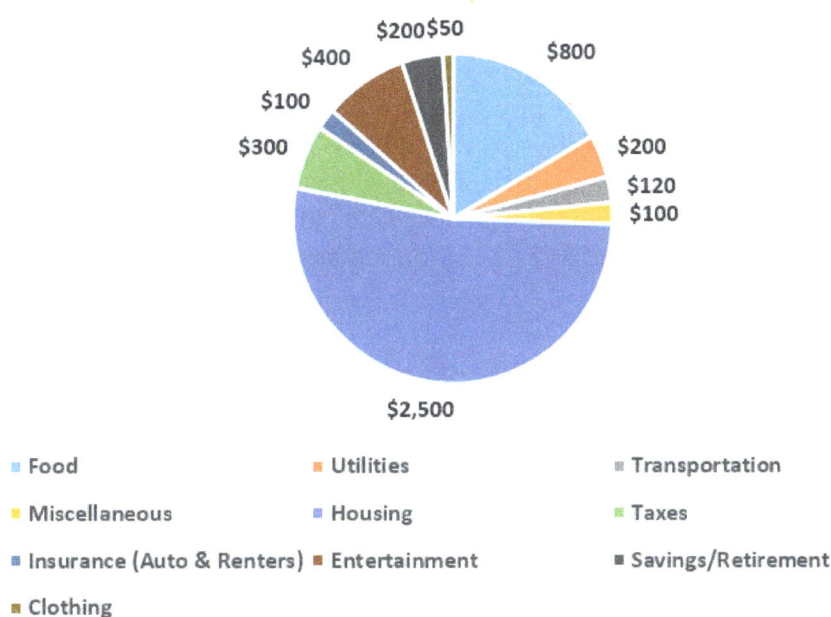

- Food
- Utilities
- Transportation
- Miscellaneous
- Housing
- Taxes
- Insurance (Auto & Renters)
- Entertainment
- Savings/Retirement
- Clothing

Pie charts of personal spending are helpful because they quickly clarify where an individual or household's money is going, what categories should be expanded (usually savings, as Americans generally save too little), and what pie slices should be reduced (e.g., wasteful electricity or

32

water consumption) or eliminated ("cutting the cord" on an exorbitantly priced cable-TV service).

bar chart – a graphic form utilizing bars to illustrate the magnitude of one or more variables.

The **bar chart** is a graphic form utilizing bars to illustrate the magnitude of one or more variables. FIGURE A-2 displays average total spending in households headed by single mothers and single fathers for 2016-2019 in thousands of dollars. Because of its form, notice how the bar chart is able to display two or more variables for each year or other category such as city or income.

FIGURE A-2: Average Total Spending in Single-Mother vs. Single-Father Households from 2016-2019 (Thousands of Dollars)

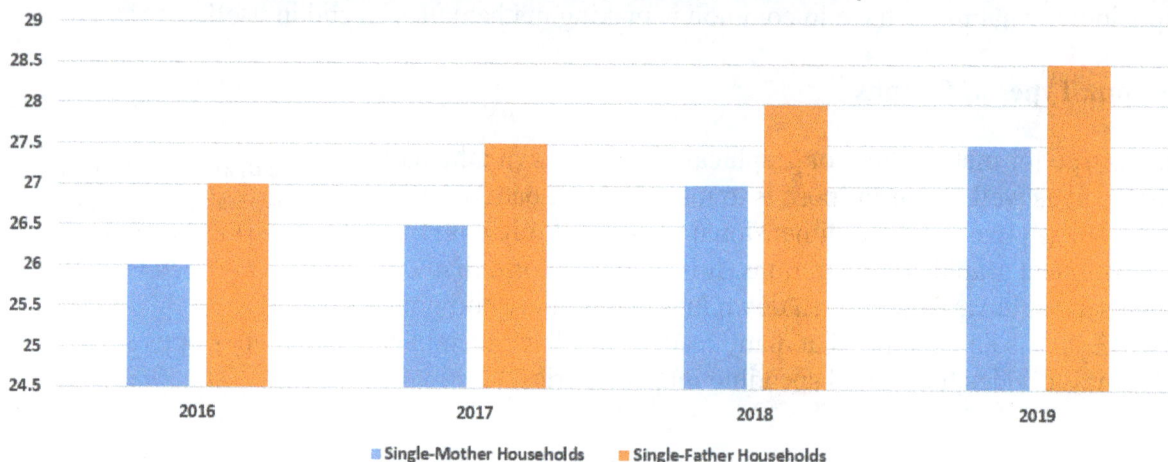

■ Single-Mother Households   ■ Single-Father Households

time-series graph – a graphic form that displays the level of one or more variables over time.

The **time-series graph** is so named because it is a graphic form that displays the level of one or more variables over time. FIGURE A-3 traces out the price of Microsoft stock from January 2, 1990 to January 5, 2015.[16] FIGURE A-3 demonstrates the value of graphs in economics and finance. What we can see in the figure is the unmistakable upward trend in Microsoft's stock price in a 25-year period that would have turned a $1,000 initial investment (961.5 shares) on January 2, 1990 into $45,057.69 on January 5, 2015 (ignoring any dividends paid).

---

[16] Source: Yahoo Finance (https://finance.yahoo.com/).

33

FIGURE A-3: Microsoft Stock Price 1990-2015 (Dollars per Share)

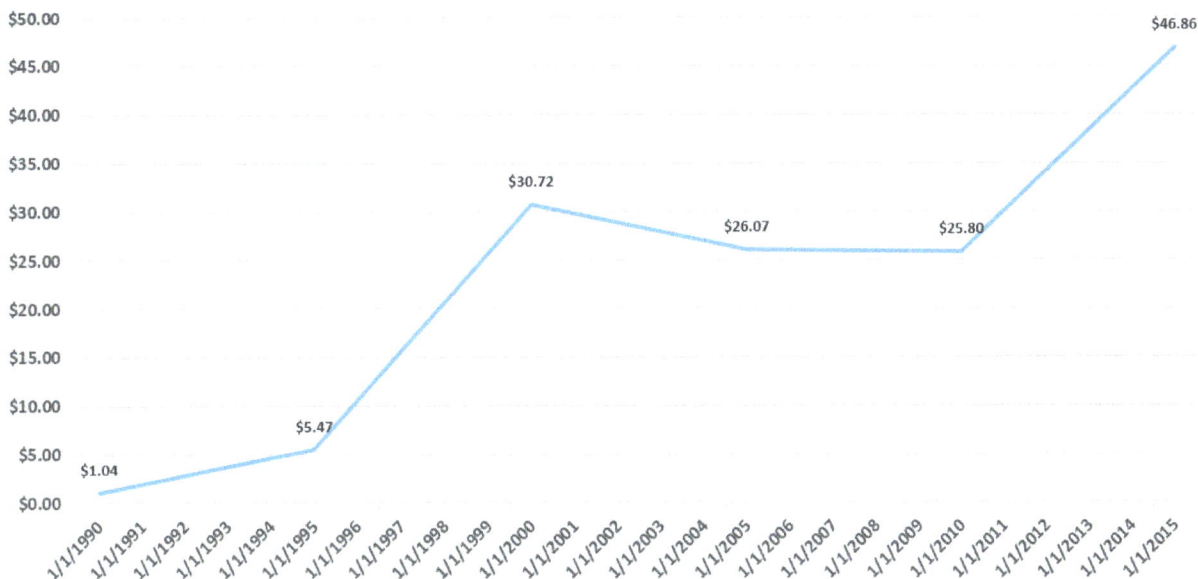

The **scatter plot** is a graphic form displaying the data points of two or more variables in coordinate space. Coordinate space (in the two-dimensional case we'll restrict ourselves to in this book) is a type of grid where points are located on the grid according to *x* and *y* coordinates (*x*, *y*), with the *x* variable measured on the horizontal axis of the grid and the *y* variable measured on the vertical axis of the grid. The point (0, 0) in *x-y* coordinate space is known as the **origin**.

scatter plot – a graphic form displaying the data points of two or more variables in coordinate space.

origin – the point (0, 0) in *x-y* coordinate space.

TABLE A-1 displays 14 (*x, y*) points that researchers collected in a survey to determine the relationship between household size (*x*) and average weekly grocery spending (*y*). FIGURE A-4 displays the 14 coordinate points listed in TABLE A-1 in *x-y* coordinate space. The points appear as if scattered on the page, hence the name scatter plot.

TABLE A-1: Average Weekly Grocery Spending in Dollars as a Function of Household Size

X (Household Size)	Y (Average Weekly Grocery Spending)
1	$50
1	$100
2	$100
2	$150
3	$150
3	$225
4	$250
4	$325
5	$350
5	$375
6	$350
6	$400
7	$400
7	$425

34

FIGURE A-4: Average Weekly Grocery Spending (in Dollars)

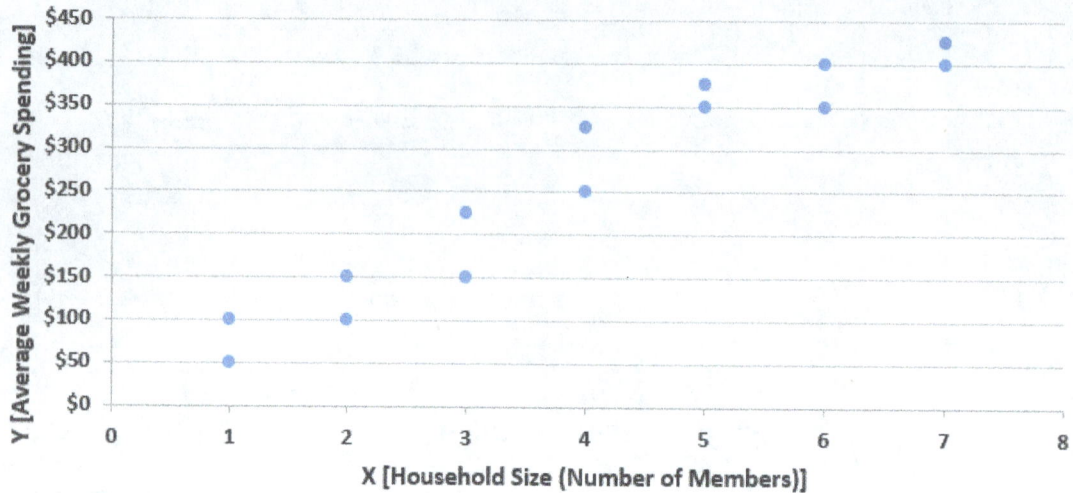

positive relationship (or positive correlation) – a causal relationship between two variables where when one increases the other increases, and when one decreases the other decreases.

trend line – a line in coordinate space displaying the overall trend in data points, be it positive, negative, or neither (a horizontal or vertical line).

Beginning at the origin (0, 0), the first (*x*, *y*) coordinate plotted is (1, $50), the fourteenth and last is (7, $425). What can be seen immediately in the plot is the apparent **positive relationship** between the two variables. A positive relationship or positive correlation is a causal relationship between two variables where when one increases the other increases, and when one decreases the other decreases. The relationship between the two variables in FIGURE A-4 makes sense: the larger the household, the more it will on average spend on groceries. FIGURE A-5 is identical to FIGURE A-4, but with a **trend line** inserted to emphasize the positive relationship between the two variables, household size and average weekly spending on groceries. A trend line is a line in coordinate space displaying the overall trend in data points, be it positive, negative, or neither (a horizontal or vertical line).

FIGURE A-5: Average Weekly Grocery Spending (in Dollars) with Trend Line

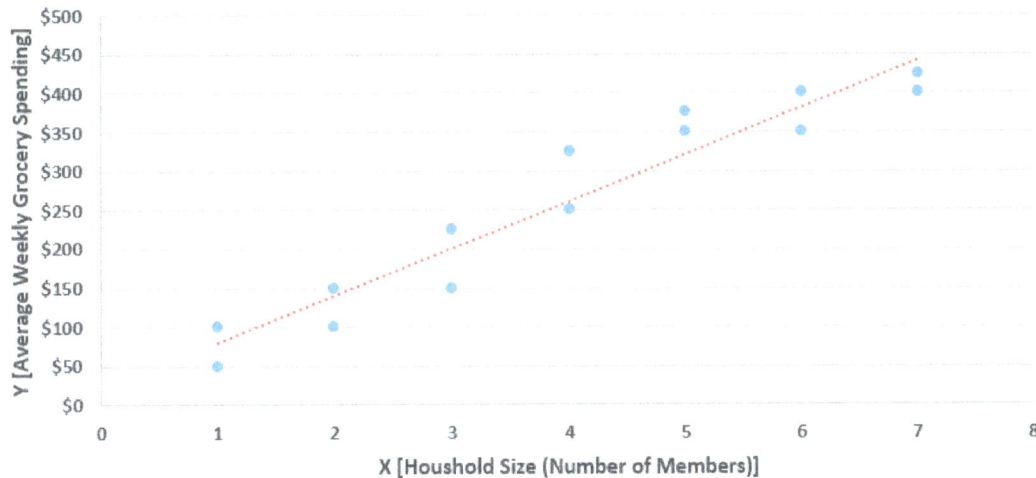

The opposite of a positive relationship is, of course, a **negative relationship** or negative correlation which is a causal relationship between two variables where when one increases the other decreases, and when one decreases the other increases. A negative relationship produces a downward-sloping scatter plot and trend line. When a scatter plot reveals no upward or downward flow of points between two variables and no trend line can be drawn, then there is **no relationship** between the two variables. The movement in one theoretically causes no movement in the other.

Some social scientists use a trend to estimate the value of one variable given the value of another variable. This is known as a **prediction** or **forecast**. In other words, for a given x in the data range, they believe they can predict a y using the trend line. Using FIGURE A-5, a researcher may claim that she can predict what a household will spend on groceries given its size. If a household has five members (x), its weekly grocery expenditures (y) should (from the position of the trend line in FIGURE A-5) come in at around $300. Thus, $300 is the forecast level of grocery spending.

negative relationship (or negative correlation) – a causal relationship between two variables where when one increases the other decreases, and when one decreases the other increases.

no relationship (or no correlation) – the state of relationship between two variables where the movement in one theoretically causes no movement in the other. The scatterplot of the two variables in question reveals no trend and therefore no trend line can be drawn.

prediction (forecast) – the use of a trend to estimate the value of one variable given the value of another variable.

Other social scientists are more skeptical of this methodology, noting that the world is complex and many factors other than just household size come into play to affect a household's average level of grocery spending.

A.2 A Model: The Production-Possibilities Frontier (PPF) (A Preview)

production-possibilities frontier (PPF) – a line or curve displaying the maximum various combinations of goods or services that can be produced by a person, firm, industry, or entire economy in a given period of time.

The **production-possibilities frontier (PPF)** is a model used in micro- and macroeconomics. It is a line or curve displaying the maximum various combinations of goods or services that can be produced by a person, firm, industry, or entire economy in a given period of time. FIGURE A-6 is a PPF for the famous island castaway, Robinson Crusoe.

FIGURE A-6: Crusoe's Daily PPF (PPF1)

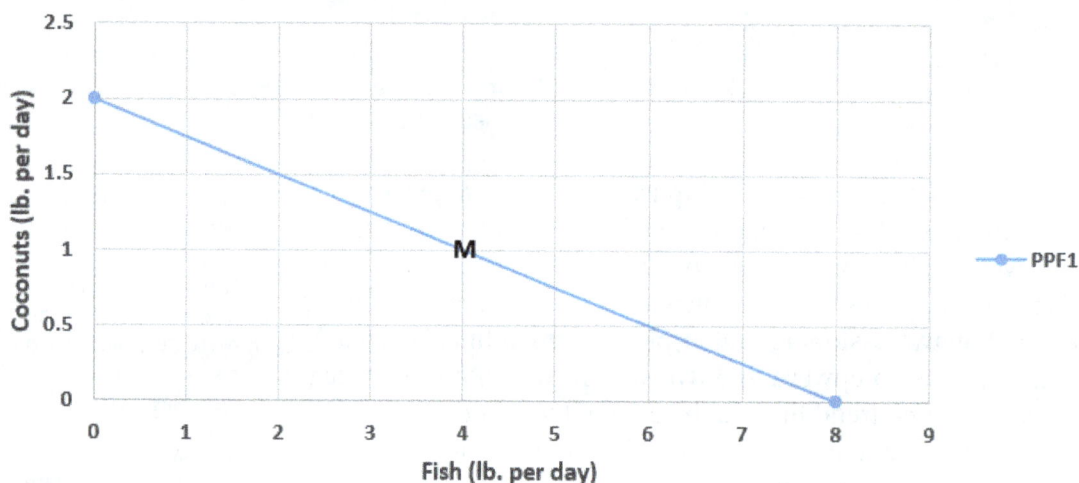

On his island each day, using his full ability and effort, Crusoe can catch a maximum of 8 pounds (lb.) of fish (8, 0), collect a maximum of 2 pounds (lb.) of coconuts (0, 2), or settle on some combination of both goods between those two endpoints on PPF1 such as 4 pounds of fish and 1 pound of coconuts (4, 1) or point *M*. Since Crusoe prefers balanced meals, he chooses this middle point on PPF1, (4, 1) or point *M*.

Notice that the PPF illustrated in FIGURE A-6 is a straight line. In chapter 2, the type of PPF that we will encounter will be an outward-bending curve [from the perspective of the origin, point (0, 0)]. This leads us to our next concept, slope.

A.2.1 Slope on the PPF

slope – in an *x-y* coordinate system, the change in the y variable divided by the change in the x variable, or, "rise" divided by "run."

The difference between straight-line PPFs and curved PPFs is their **slope**. In an *x-y* coordinate system, the slope is a change in the *y* variable divided by the change in the *x* variable, or, "rise" divided by "run." Straight-line PPFs have a constant (unchanging) slope while curved PPFs (see chapter 2) have changing slopes. The slope of PPF1 in FIGURE A-6 can be calculated from its endpoints [(8, 0), (0, 2)] as follows:

$$slope = \frac{"rise"}{"run"} = \frac{\Delta y}{\Delta x}$$

$$= \frac{y_1 - y_2}{x_1 - x_2}$$

$$= \frac{0 - 2}{8 - 0}$$

$$= \frac{-2}{8}$$

$$= \frac{-1}{4} = -0.25$$

where Δ = the change in the variable and (x_1, y_1), (x_2, y_2) are the two coordinate pairs between which the slope is being calculated. In other words, while we used the endpoints of the PPF to calculate a slope of -1/4 or -0.25, we could also have used any other points along the PPF such as (4, 1) and (2, 1.5):

$$= \frac{y_1 - y_2}{x_1 - x_2}$$

$$= \frac{1 - 1.5}{4 - 2}$$

$$= \frac{-0.5}{2} = -0.25$$

While we changed the coordinate points between which we calculated slope, we still arrived at the same answer with the same value sign, negative (-), which means that the PPF is downward sloping. A slope with no sign (implicitly positive [+]) means that the PPF is upward sloping like the trend line in FIGURE A-5.

A.2.2 Movement Along a Curve versus a Shift in a Curve

A **movement along a curve** is a change from one point (x_1, y_1) on a line or literal curve to another point (x_2, y_2) on the same line or curve. In the PPF in FIGURE A-6 (also seen in FIGURE A-7 as PPF1), we left Crusoe as he was catching 4 lb. of fish and gathering 1 lb. of coconuts per day. Let's say that he decides that he would rather catch 6 lb. of fish and gather 0.5 lb. of coconuts per day. Is this possible for him? Yes, and he moves rightward and downward along his fish-coconut PPF1 from point M (4, 1) to point N (6, 0.5) [see FIGURE A-7]. At either point, he is being efficient and producing his maximum output.

movement along a curve – a change from one point (x_1, y_1) on a line or literal curve to another point (x_2, y_2) on the same line or curve.

shift in a curve – a horizontal shift leftward or rightward of a line or literal curve in coordinate space.

A **shift in a curve** is a horizontal shift leftward or rightward of a line or literal curve in coordinate space.[17] Crusoe, one day while climbing a palm tree to harvest coconuts, falls and severely sprains his right ankle. For three weeks his output is cut in half. PPF2 in FIGURE A-7 is Crusoe's new (and lower) range of production possibilities. It lies below PPF1, Crusoe's pre-injury PPF copied over from FIGURE A-6.

FIGURE A-7: Crusoe's PPFs: Oringinal, Sprained Ankle, and Fishing Rod/Machete

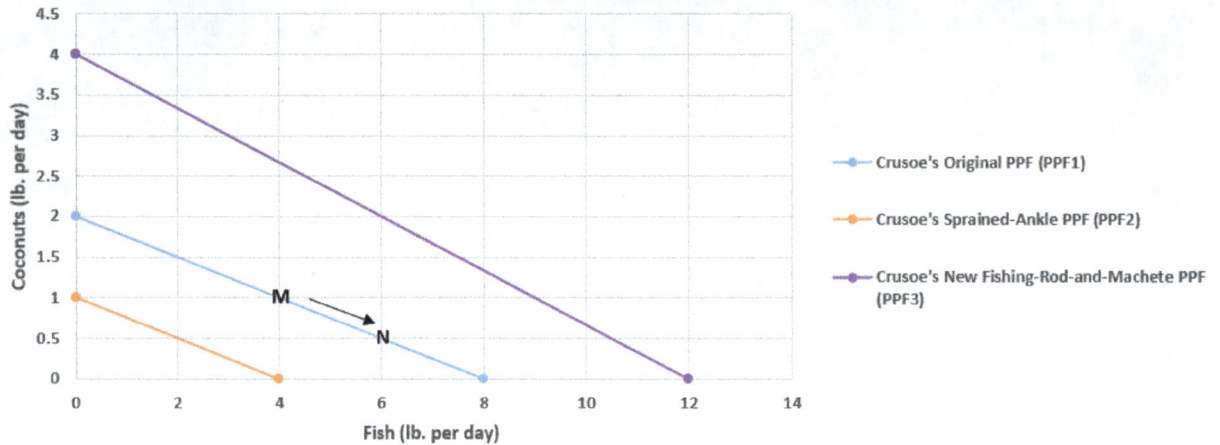

PPF2 shows Crusoe's new post-injury production possibilities: he can catch a maximum of 4 lb. of fish per day and gather 0 lb. of coconuts (4, 0); catch 0 lb. of fish and gather a maximum of 1 lb. of coconut per day (0, 1); or settle on any combination of fish and coconuts along PPF2 between those endpoints [e.g., a point such as (2, 0.5)]. Crusoe's injury is, in a way, a reduction in technology. If Crusoe were a firm, it would be like losing half of its assembly lines from a fire, explosion, or mechanical breakdown. Weather catastrophes and wars are also equivalent to technology reductions.

What about the opposite case where new technology boosts production? It shifts the PPF of the individual, firm, industry, or economy rightward. After Crusoe's right ankle heals, he returns to PPF1. After that, let's say that a small boat from a neighboring island comes ashore with items to trade. Crusoe trades a gold women's locket that he found in his ship's wreckage (for which he naturally has little use) for a machete and better fishing rod and fishing lures. The machete allows Crusoe to cut his way through heretofore impenetrable dense undergrowth, giving him access to new parts of the island with abundant coconuts that he could not reach before. The new and better fishing rod and fishing lures obviously allow him to catch more fish.

For Crusoe, the new technology produces PPF3 in FIGURE A-7, which now allows him to catch a maximum of 12 lb. of fish and gather 0 lb. of coconuts per day (12, 0), catch 0 lb. of fish but gather a maximum of 4 lb. of coconuts per day (0, 4), or settle on any combination of fish and coconuts somewhere on PPF3 in between those two endpoints [e.g., point (6, 2)].

---

[17] The movement-along-a-curve-versus-shift-in-a-curve distinction applies to lines as well as literal curves. It is a convention in economics literature to refer to both lines and curves as "curves," and this book will follow that convention. While this may seem sloppy, it is technically correct in that lines are "straight curves."

A.3 Another Model: The Demand Curve (A Preview)

In the previous section we saw what a movement along a curve versus a shift in a curve both looked like in terms of the PPF. Let's now look at the movement-along-a-curve-versus-shift-in-a-curve distinction through one last model, one that we will revisit in chapter 4, the demand curve. The first step in drawing a demand curve is, like the PPF, determining the coordinate points. Those are displayed in a **demand schedule**, a table that displays the relationship between the price of a good or service and the quantity demanded of that good or service.

demand schedule – a table that displays the relationship between the price of a good or service and the quantity demanded of that good or service.

Ray is a movie buff who is building a library of DVD movies. TABLE A-2 is Ray's monthly demand schedule for DVD movies he purchases from Amazon or other outlets given his income of $4,167 per month (about $50,000 per year). Notice that as price rises, Ray's quantity demanded of DVDs per month falls. At $25, Ray purchases only 2 DVDs per month and builds his library slowly. At $5, he purchases 6 DVDs per month and builds his library quickly. Like the PPF above, this pattern reflects a negative relationship between the two variables in the schedule, price and quantity demanded. This negative relationship is codified in the **law of demand**: there is an inverse relationship between the price of a good or service and the quantity demanded of that good or service.

law of demand – the proposition that there is an inverse relationship between the price of a good or service and the quantity demanded of that good or service.

TABLE A-2: Ray's Demand Schedule for DVD Movies (Income = $4,167 Per Month or $50,000 Per Year)	
Price	Quantity Demanded Per Month
$5	6
$10	5
$15	4
$20	3
$25	2

From Ray's demand schedule we can draw his **demand curve** (D1) for DVDs as seen in FIGURE A-8. (Notice that it is a straight line and not literally a curve despite being called one.) A demand curve is a line or literal curve that displays the relationship between the price of a good or service and the quantity demanded of that good or service. It is the demand schedule graphed in price-quantity space.

demand curve – a line or literal curve that displays the relationship between the price of a good or service and the quantity demanded of that good or service. It is the demand schedule graphed in price-quantity space.

FIGURE A-8: Ray's Monthly Demand Curve for DVD Discs ($50,000 Income)

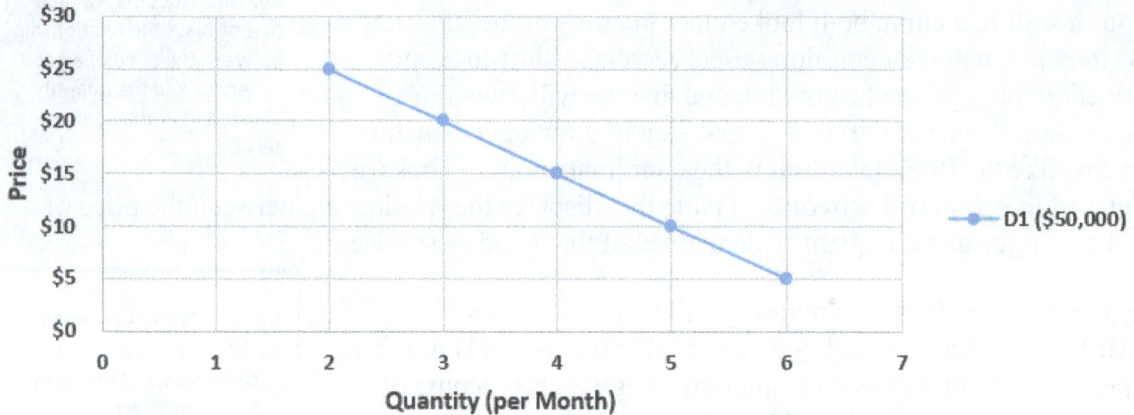

It is important to remember that price is being allowed to vary so that the demand curve can be traced out in price-quantity coordinate space. In FIGURE A-8, price starts out at $25 and is lowered in $5 increments to trace out the entire curve. Other factors that can affect demand (e.g., income, preferences, changes in related goods, etc.) are being held constant. Without these other variables being held constant, the curve shifts (fails to stay stationary as in FIGURE A-8) or even disappears. For example, if Ray gets a promotion at work and his income rises to $60,000 per year, the curve shifts rightward. TABLE A-3 becomes Ray's new demand schedule after his promotion at work and FIGURE A-9 illustrates the new demand curve (D2) generated by the new demand schedule.

TABLE A-3: Ray's Demand Schedule for DVD Movies (Income = $5,000 Per Month or $60,000 Per Year)	
Price	Quantity Demanded Per Month
$5	8
$10	7
$15	6
$20	5
$25	4

Notice the position of the new demand curve, D2, with respect to the old one, D1. Ray's quantity demanded of DVDs is higher at all price points. Ray formerly purchased 2 DVDs per month when they were priced at $25 each. With $10,000 more income, he purchases 4 DVDs per month when they are priced at $25 each. Ray formerly purchased 6 DVDs per month when they were priced at $5 each. After his work promotion, he purchases 8 DVDs per month when they are priced at $5 each.

Can the demand curve shift leftward? Yes. If, instead of getting a promotion, Ray (with demand curve D1) quit his job for a lower-paying one (at $40,000 per year) where he works mostly from home, his demand curve would shift leftward where he would demand lower quantities of DVDs at all price points (demand curve D3 in FIGURE A-9). And, as alluded to earlier, if Ray ever completely loses interest in building a DVD movie library, his demand for DVDs disappears.

FIGURE A-9: Ray's Demand Curves ($40,000; $50,000; $60,000 Income)

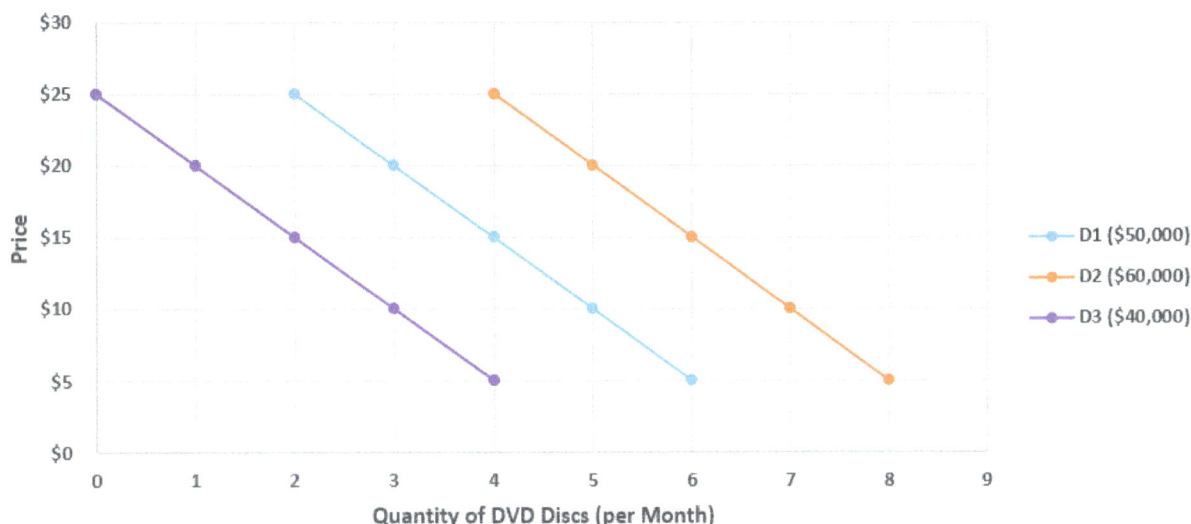

Once again, we see the distinction between a movement along a curve versus a shift of a curve. In the context of the demand curve, a **change in quantity demanded** (change in quantity demanded caused by a change in price) creates a movement along a demand curve while a **change in demand** is a rightward or leftward shift of the demand curve (increase or decrease in demand, respectively) caused by any factor other than price.

change in quantity demanded – a change in quantity demanded of a good or service caused by a change in the price of that good or service.

change in demand – a rightward or leftward shift of the demand curve illustrating a respective increase or decrease in demand.

The slope of the demand curve is the change in price divided by the change in quantity or

$$slope = \frac{\Delta y}{\Delta x}$$

$$= \frac{Price_1 - Price_2}{Quantity_1 - Quantity_2}$$

A.3.1 Practice Problems and Questions

1. Calculate the slope of demand curve *D1* in FIGURE A-9 using two coordinate points (*x, y*) on the curve. Write out all the steps you followed to arrive at your answer. What is the sign value (+ or -) of your answer and why?
2. In FIGURE A-9, demand curves *D2* and *D3* are parallel to demand curve *D1*. What does that suggest about their slopes compared to that of demand curve *D1*?

A.4 Conclusion

This appendix to chapter 1 reviewed four types of graphs and previewed two models (the production-possibilities frontier [PPF] and demand curve). Chapter 2 will examine the **scientific** methodology of economics, introduce a new model (the circular-flow diagram [CFD]), describe the role that assumptions play in constructing models, and explain why there are some areas of life where facts and sound analysis are often ignored when important decisions are made.

A.5 Chapter Concepts

pie chart
bar chart
time-series graph
scatter plot
origin
positive relationship
trend line
negative relationship
no relationship
prediction (forecast)
production-possibilities frontier (PPF)
slope
movement along a curve
shift in a curve
demand schedule
law of demand
demand curve
change in quantity demanded
change in demand

A.6 Problems, Questions, and Discussion Topics (Items Requiring Examples are Marked with an Asterisk [*])

1. The consumer price index (CPI) tracks goods in eight categories (housing [42%], transportation [17%], food and beverages [14%], health care [9%], education and communication [7%], recreation [6%], apparel [3%], and other goods and services [3%]). What would be the best graphic form (pie chart, bar chart, time-series graph, or scatter plot) for illustrating these data and why?

2. For punctuality and perfect attendance at his job over the past five years, Bob is awarded a one-ounce South African Krugerrand gold coin worth $4,500. Included with the coin is a table containing monthly price data for Krugerrand gold coins for the past five years. Bob wants to put this data in visual form. What would be the best graphic form (pie chart, bar chart, time-series graph, or scatter plot) for illustrating these data and why?

3. Meg notices that the more cups of coffee she drinks after dinner, the fewer the hours she is able to sleep that night until the next morning. If cups of coffee were the x variable and hours of sleep the y variable, how would the relationship between x and y best be

described:

A. positive, negative, or no relationship at all?

B. Why?

4. Four months ago, Gerald was so terrible at pickleball that his girlfriend Diane broke up with him after they lost a doubles game against another couple at a swanky resort. Since then, Gerald has practiced his serve on pickleball courts every day and has not hit a ball out of bounds over the last three weeks. If hours of practice were the x variable and the number of pickleball serves remaining in bounds were the y variable, how would the relationship between x and y best be described:

A. positive, negative, or no relationship at all?

B. Why?

5. Kurt has noticed that the more he works out at the gym, sometimes he gets better grades on his exams in his advanced-calculus class. However, since Kurt has been working out more and more, sometimes he does well on an exam and sometimes he doesn't. If hours of working out in the gym were the x variable and exam grades were the y variable, how would the relationship between x and y best be described:

A. positive, negative, or no relationship at all?

B. Would any trend line revealing the likely relationship between x and y be upward sloping, downward sloping, or neither?

6. With which graphic form (pie chart, bar chart, time-series graph, or scatter plot) can a trend line be used to show a positive or negative relationship between two variables?

7. For convenience, FIGURE A-5 from earlier in this chapter has been reproduced below. From the trend line in the figure, what could reasonably be predicted or forecast as the average weekly grocery spending for a family with seven members?

FIGURE A-5: Average Weekly Grocery Spending (in Dollars) with Trend Line

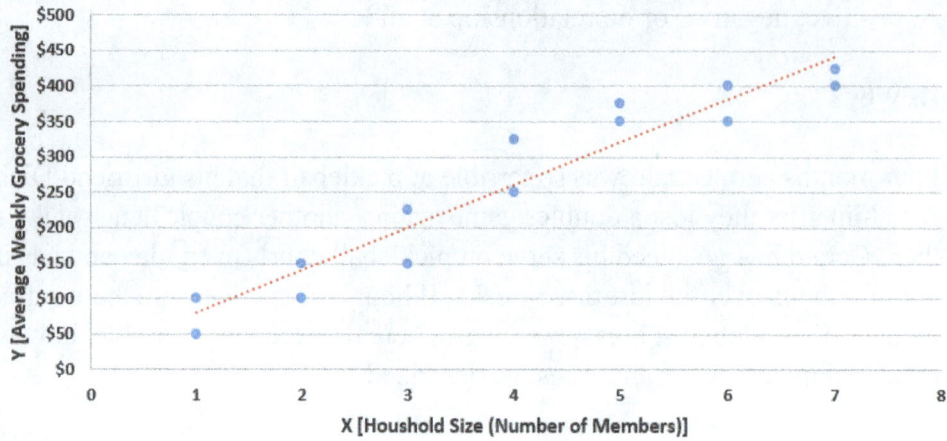

8. For convenience, FIGURE A-8 from earlier in this chapter has been reproduced below. What is the slope of Ray's demand curve in FIGURE A-8?

FIGURE A-8: Ray's Monthly Demand Curve for DVD Discs ($50,000 Income)

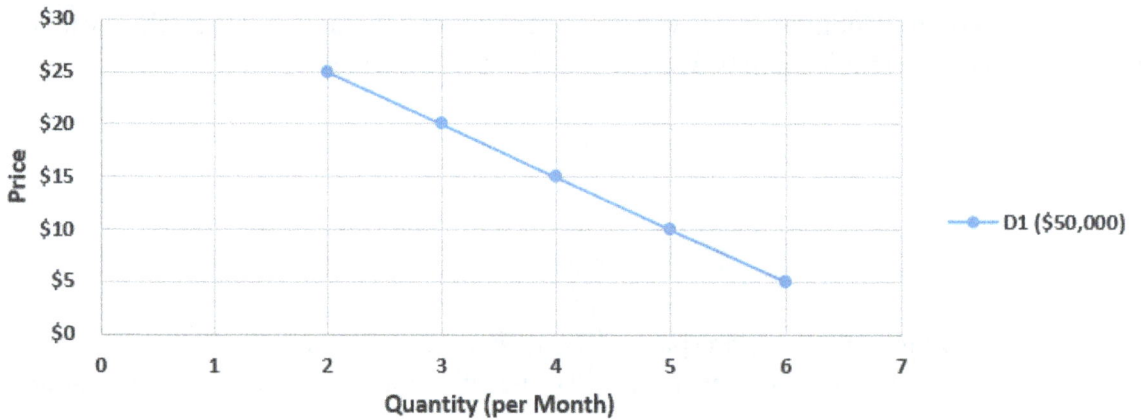

9. After moving from a large house to a small apartment, Ray abandons his project of building a DVD library and decides that, to save space in his new home, he wants his media (recorded TV shows and movies) all in digital format (MP4 or MOV files) on a few small, solid-state computer drives (SSDs). In terms of the demand-curve model, does this mean that Ray's demand for movies on DVD has moved along a curve or shifted?

10. Since the practice of vaping peaked in 2014, numerous public health messages have appeared in popular media to warn the public about vaping's potentially harmful effects on the human lungs, heart, and brain. After the appearance of these messages, both the prices and sales of some brands of e-cigarettes have

declined. In terms of the demand-curve model, does this mean that the demand for e-cigarettes has moved along a curve or shifted?

11.   After a recent cold snap in Florida, orange prices have risen. In terms of the demand-curve model, does this mean that the quantity demanded for oranges has moved along a curve or shifted?

Chapter 2: The Methodology of Science and Models

2.0 Introduction

Every area of human knowledge has its own terminology. This reflects that each discipline has its own unique concepts that it uses to analyze the world to make sense of it. Physicists explain our world through analysis of energy and mass. Chemists understand larger structures through the analysis of chemical compounds, and on a smaller level, atoms and their components. Economics encompasses a far more relevant arena of human experience for most people. Most people don't lose much on a personal level if they don't understand quantum mechanics, but they lose a lot more from poor money decisions that make them vulnerable to having insufficient funds not only for rare emergencies but bare subsistence in retirement.

While economics mastery can't promise that you'll become a multimillion or billionaire, it can just about guarantee that you'll be substantially better off in terms of making more informed and better choices on average. This begins with economic concepts and the recognition of their implications in real-world experience, past and present. Before that can be undertaken, the methodology of economics must be examined.

2.1 Is Economics a Science?

The introduction to this chapter discussed physics and chemistry as alternative disciplines to economics. Physics and chemistry, though, are hard sciences, meaning that their application of the **scientific method** (hypothesis, test of hypothesis [experiment], and acceptance or rejection of the hypothesis) involves testable predictions, repeatable controlled experiments, and objective results.

scientific method - the forming of a hypothesis about how some aspect of the world works, the testing of that hypothesis, and, based on the results of the test, acceptance or rejection of the hypothesis.

Economics, if it is a science, is not one in the same sense as physics or chemistry. For some questions, hypotheses can be formed, tests can be undertaken, and based on the results of these tests, hypotheses can be rejected. For example, the law of demand (discussed in the appendix to chapter 1) can be tested by experiment. A concession stand at a state fair can continually raise the price of its hamburgers over the course of a week and observe the quantities of burgers demanded. No doubt, far more burgers would be sold at a price point of $3.00 than $10.00. This is intuitive because it has been so abundantly confirmed. It has become common sense. Increase an action's costs, and you get less of it.

For other economic phenomena, analysis using the scientific method is more problematic. What causes economic depressions? Settling this question by setting up a massive experiment would entail a cost that is prohibitively steep. Millions of people would lose their jobs, thousands of firms would go out of business, many forever. Unlike the very small cost of observing a chemical reaction in a lab to test a chemistry hypothesis, the human toll would be too high.

To study economy-wide issues in economics such as inflation, unemployment, capital flight, and recessions, data from these recurring phenomena have to be examined, hypotheses formed, and as those phenomena continue to repeat in different economies at different times, different hypotheses are (ideally) accepted or rejected. As each boom, hyperinflation, and recession occurs, observation allows economists to learn more and more about their causal factors. While it would be preferable to not have to use this passive version of the scientific method, there is no other choice for very good reasons.

2.2 Models: What Are They Good For?

If the weather forecast calls for a 100 percent chance of rain the next evening and you plan to be outdoors during that time, you can make the reasonable assumption that you'll likely be getting wet without an umbrella or rainwear on.

Does this 100 percent forecast of rain absolutely guarantee that you will get wet if you go outdoors the next evening? No. Weather forecasts can be wrong because atmospheric conditions can quickly change that violate the assumptions that are part of the models used by meteorologists.

TABLE 2-1: Weekly Demand Schedule for LG Smart Phones

Price	Quantity Demanded (Per Week)
$50	500
$75	300
$100	100
$150	25
$200	0

The law of demand is the foundation of the economic model known as the demand curve, which we first saw in the appendix to chapter 1. TABLE 2-1 is a weekly demand schedule for LG smart phones with its corresponding demand curve illustrated in FIGURE 2-1. Note that in FIGURE 2-1, we have illustrated demand as a literal curve that more closely matches demand curves in the real world than the simplified straight-line demand curves that we first encountered in the appendix to chapter 1. In FIGURE 2-1, when the price of an LG basic smart phone falls from $100 to $75, the quantity sold at a particular big-box store will rise from approximately 100 to 300 per week.

FIGURE 2-1: Demand Curve for LG Smart Phones

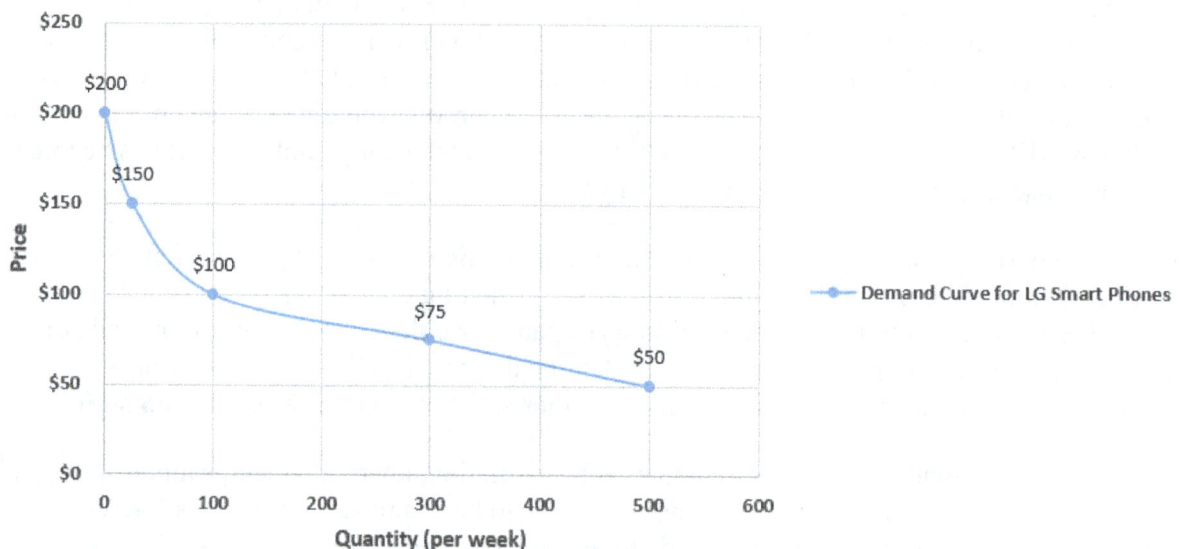

2.2a Assumptions: The Foundation of Models

An **assumption** is an acceptance of something to be true (without evidence) for the purpose of simplification. Assumptions are often unstated, but their implications show up in the structures of models. They are important because when an assumption doesn't hold, the predictions of a model can be slightly to severely inaccurate.

assumption - an acceptance of something to be true (without evidence) for the purpose of simplification.

What is the simple demand-curve model assuming? That increasing the quantity of phones by about 200 units is a possibility at the new lower price. For if this is not a possibility, the demand curve in FIGURE 2-1 cannot be extended to the new price point and stop somewhere between 100 and 300 phones. Also assumed is that the incomes of the cell-phone buyers illustrated by the curve stay relatively constant. If incomes are volatile, then the curve fails to stay stationary and ends up shifting right or left, which changes the quantities demanded. This is illustrated in FIGURE 2-2.

FIGURE 2-2: Demand Curves for LG Basic Smart Phones

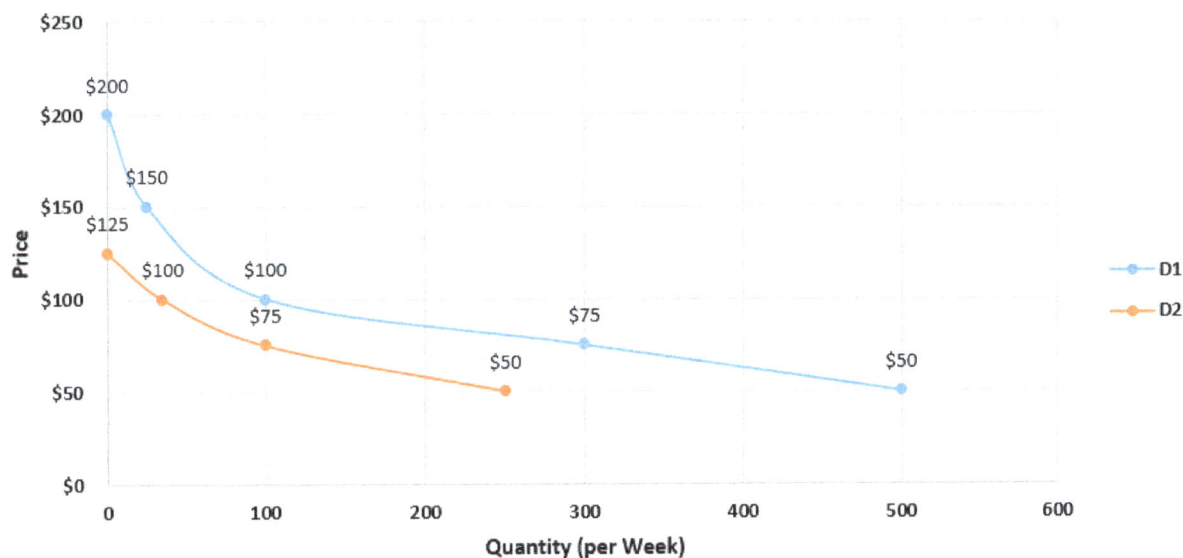

The original demand curve (*D1*) has shifted leftward because of a reduction in consumer income. On the new demand curve, *D2*, when the price of an LG basic smart phone falls from $100 to $75, the quantity sold at a particular big-box store will rise from approximately 35 to 100 per week. A reduction in income has greatly changed the range of quantities demanded (100 to 300 phones to 35 to 100) for the same fall in price ($100 to $75). In the real world, we could reasonably expect something like this to happen provided that all other demand factors besides income remain relatively constant.

2.3 The Circular-Flow Diagram (CFD)

circular-flow diagram (CFD) – a circular model of an economy that shows how money flows between households and firms as households exchange their labor for goods and services produced by firms.

goods and services markets – markets where households trade their money for goods and services produced by firms.

factor markets – markets where firms trade their money for labor services provided by households.

factors of production – every item that is used to produce a good or service; labor, capital (including land), and entrepreneurship.

labor - the human factor of production (workers and managers).

capital - the non-human factors of production (equipment, buildings, and land).

entrepreneurship – the effort and creativity expended in meeting the evolving economic needs and desires of a society.

One simple and abstract model of an economy is the **circular-flow diagram (CFD)**. The purpose of the diagram is to show how money flows between households and firms as households exchange their labor for goods and services produced by firms. The two categories of markets in the CFD are **goods and services markets** and **factor (factors of production) markets**. Goods and services markets in the simple CFD are where households trade their money for goods and services manufactured by firms. Factor markets in the simple CFD are where firms trade their money for labor services provided by households. **Factors of production** are **labor**, **capital**, and **entrepreneurship**. Labor, of course, is the human factor of production (workers and managers) while capital (not seen in the simple CFD) consists of the non-human factors of production (equipment, buildings, and land). Land is sometimes classified separately from capital, but this book doesn't follow that convention. Entrepreneurship is the effort and creativity expended in meeting the evolving economic needs and desires of a society.

The easiest part of the CFD to relate to is households, as everyone is part of a household if not a business. In FIGURE 2-3, starting in the Households square on the west side of the diagram, every household purchases and consumes goods and services. This action is represented by the two arrows seen between the Households square and the Goods-and-Services-Markets hexagon at the top of FIGURE 2-3, which includes firms such as grocery stores, mall stores, online merchants, and so on. The blue arrow leading from the Goods-and-Services-Markets hexagon to the Households square represents the flow of goods and services while the green arrow from Households to Goods and Services Markets represents the flow of dollars paid for the goods and services provided to households.

FIGURE 2-3: The Circular-Flow Diagram (CFD)

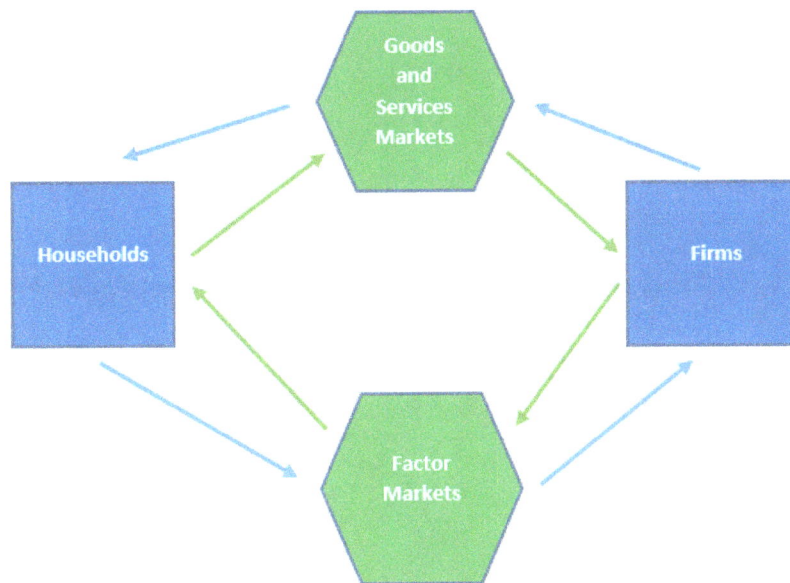

Where did the goods and services provided to households ultimately come from? Firms that produced them. These firms are represented by the Firms square on the east side of the CFD in FIGURE 2-3. Note the two arrows between the Firms square and the Goods-and-Services-Markets hexagon at the top of the CFD. Firms produce goods and services and sell them on the goods and services market. This action is represented by the blue arrow extending from the Firms square to the Goods-and-Services-Markets hexagon. The green arrow going in the reverse direction represents the flow of dollars from goods and services markets to firms as payment for the goods and services provided by firms.

So far so good, but we've only covered the top part of the CFD and thus have only told half the story of the diagram. Who produced the goods? Labor from households (represented by the Households square on the west side of the CFD) purchased in factor markets (represented by the Factor Markets hexagon on the bottom of the CFD). Factors of production (laborers from households) move from factor markets to business firms. This is represented by the blue arrow extending from the Factor-Markets hexagon to the Firms square in FIGURE 2-3. In return, those factors get paid for their services. This is represented by the green arrow extending from the Firms square to the Factor-Markets hexagon. Completing our "clockwise" journey around the diagram back to where we initially started (households) is the very last dual-sided transaction. These are the two arrows between the households square and factor-markets hexagon. The blue arrow is the supply of labor from households to factor markets. As you might have easily guessed, the green arrow from factor markets to households represents income from labor services supplied.

What the CFD does well is visually separate goods and services on the one hand from money on the other hand. This distinction is known as the **classical dichotomy**, or theoretical separation of **real variables** from **nominal variables**. Real variables are variables

classical dichotomy – the theoretical separation of real variables from nominal variables.

real variables - variables measured in physical units such as pounds or gallons.

nominal variables - variables measured in money units such as revenue or debt.

measured in physical units such as pounds, gallons, or tons. Nominal variables are variables measured in money units such as revenue, income, profit, or debt.

2.4 The Production-Possibilities Frontier (PPF) … Again

A little less abstract a model than the CFD is the production-possibilities frontier (PPF), which we first saw in the appendix for chapter 1. The central concepts of the PPF are efficiency and scarcity displayed in the tradeoffs between two goods or services.

FIGURE 2-4: Production-Possibilities Frontier (PPF) for Bakerville

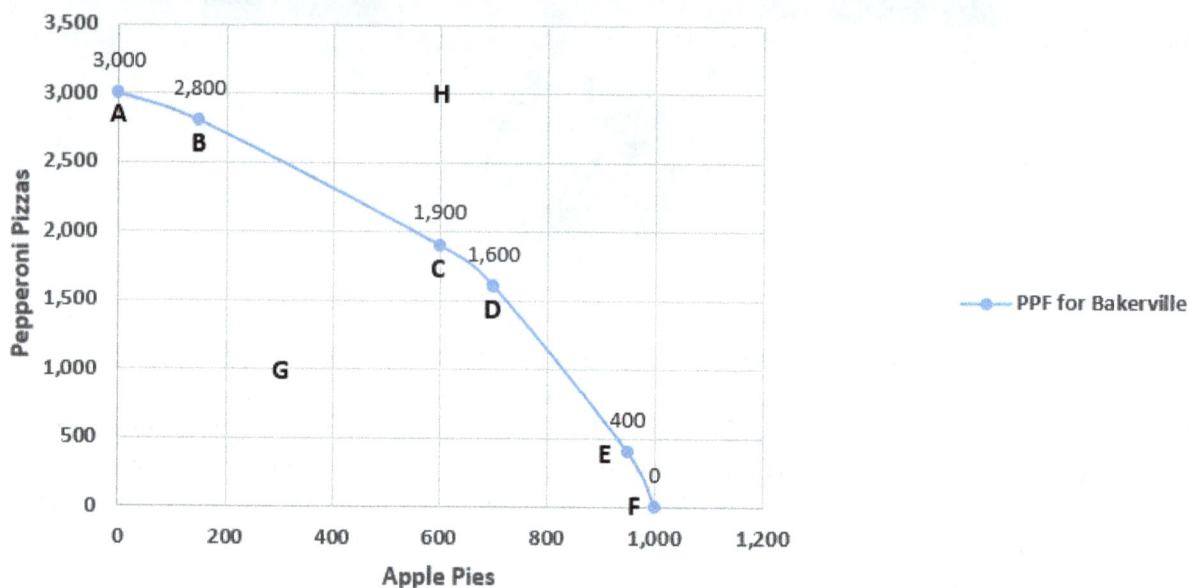

Bakerville is a town that produces two main products: apple pies and pepperoni pizzas. As can be seen in FIGURE 2-4, if the town's bakers, using the most up-to-date equipment, make only apple pies, their maximum output is 1,000 pies per week [point *F*, or coordinate (1,000; 0) on the graph in FIGURE 2-4]. If the town's bakers were to make only pepperoni pizzas, which are easier and less time consuming to make than apple pies, their maximum output would be 3,000 pizzas per week [point *A*, coordinate (0; 3,000) on the graph in FIGURE 2-4].

efficient – in production, getting the maximum output with the least waste in terms of materials, labor, and machinery. In the context of the PPF, any point on the PPF where, for all factors of production, maximum output is produced.

These two endpoints on the PPF (points *A* and *F*), while theoretically possible, are also improbable; the town will much more likely divide up its production between the two goods at points such as *B*, *C*, *D*, or *E* on the PPF because people prefer to produce and consume a variety of goods and services. These four points as well as points *A* and *F* and all others on the PPF are **efficient**. In other words, with efficient use of labor (everyone in the bakery is working and not standing idle) and with efficient use of technology (all space in the ovens is fully utilized to cook pies and pizzas), the PPF theoretically displays the maximum production of all the combinations of pies and pizzas that the town's bakers and capital can produce.

What about points under the PPF such as *G* (300 pies; 1,000 pizzas)? Obviously this represents an underemployment of Bakerville's labor or capital or both. Point *G* is known as a point that is **inefficient**, or a point where for all factors of production, maximum output is not produced. What could cause something like this? Let's say that 70 percent of Bakerville's commercial baking ovens are gas fueled and there is a natural disaster that affects energy infrastructure that takes a week to fix. This would be a **structurally induced inefficiency** or a production level below capacity because of a natural occurrence (e.g., tornado, hurricane, etc.). It would be short term in nature because the incentive for Bakerville's labor and bakeries is to get back into business as soon as possible to resume earning incomes and profits.

inefficient – in production, not getting the maximum output with the least waste in terms of materials, labor, and machinery. In the context of the PPF, any point below the PPF where for all factors of production, maximum output is not produced.

Another cause? Suppose that Bakerville's bakers are earning $15 per hour but its new mayor imposes a minimum wage of $45 per hour. For every baker employed, two are laid off and the production of pies and pizzas falls by about 70 percent. Such a **policy-induced inefficiency**, or production level below capacity because of government policy (high minimum wages, production limits, taxation, regulation, etc.) would not necessarily be short-term in nature because the new law is a political decision by the town's government. The town's politicians may quickly convene and agree that the new policy, while well intended, had unintended consequences. Or they may not. They may bicker in gridlock for possibly months to years and point *G* becomes a long-term reality as it does for years in strictly controlled economies such as Venezuela.

structurally induced inefficiency – a production level below capacity because of a natural occurrence (e.g., tornado, hurricane, lightning, earthquake, etc.).

policy-induced inefficiency – a production level below capacity because of government policy (minimum wages, production quotas, taxation, regulation, etc.).

This leaves us with only one point left to explain in FIGURE 2-4: point *H*. Point *H* is a production level known as **unattainable** or lying above the PPF that cannot be achieved with current labor and technology. Given natural scarcity, Bakerville, in a normal state of affairs with its given labor and technology, cannot produce coordinate *H* (600 pies; 3,000 pizzas).

unattainable – any point of production lying above the PPF that cannot be achieved with current labor and technology.

2.4a Opportunity Cost and Economic Growth on the Production-Possibilities Frontier (PPF)

Before closing out our discussion of the PPF, let's take a look at two more concepts that the PPF can illustrate. The first is opportunity cost (tradeoffs), which we first explored in chapter 1. The second is economic growth, which we'll examine in section 2.4c.

Returning to FIGURE 2-4, suppose that Bakerville starts off producing at point *C* (600 pies; 1,900 pizzas) on the PPF. The town's bakers then decide to move to point *D* (700 pies; 1,600 pizzas) on the PPF. What becomes evident is that even in a food-opolis such as Bakerville, there's still no such thing as a free lunch: from point *C*, to produce 100 more pies, Bakerville had to give up producing 300 pizzas. In other words, from point *C*, the opportunity cost of 100 more pies was 300 pizzas or 3 pizzas per pie. This is the concept of opportunity cost as illustrated on the PPF.

One last point: 3 pizzas per pie is just the opportunity cost of moving from point *C* to point *D*. Moving from, for example, point *D* (700 pies; 1,600 pizzas) to point *E* (950 pies, 400 pizzas) will involve a different and higher opportunity cost (4.8 pizzas per pie). Why?

2.4b Straight versus Curved PPFs

Before moving on to opportunity cost on the PPF, let's answer a question that may have entered some readers' minds. What is the difference between the PPF displayed in FIGURE 2-4 and the PPFs in FIGURES A-6 and A-7 that we examined in the appendix to chapter 1? Notice that in FIGURE 2-4, the PPF is concave (bowed outward) from the perspective of the origin of the graph [point (0, 0)]. Recall that the PPFs we saw in FIGURES A-6 and A-7 in the appendix to chapter 1 were straight lines, i.e., they had a constant slope, which means that there was a constant tradeoff between the products represented by the PPF.

The concave PPF in FIGURE 2-4 has an increasing slope all along its length, from Point *A* to Point *F*. In other words, the PPF's slope is much steeper at point *E* (950 pies, 400 pizzas) than point *B* (150 pies; 2,800 pizzas). This has implications for opportunity cost: if the slope of the PPF increases along the PPF, so does opportunity cost. Proof? Moving from point *C* (600 pies; 1,900 pizzas) to point *D* (700 pies; 1,600 pizzas), the slope of the PPF or opportunity cost per pie is 3 pizzas. Moving from point *E* (950 pies, 400 pizzas) to point *F* (1,000 pies, 0 pizzas), the slope of the PPF (400/50 = 8) or opportunity cost per pie is 8 pizzas. Clearly slope/opportunity cost rises steadily along the PPF in FIGURE 2-4 from Point *A* to Point *F*.

In summary, for a straight-line PPF, from its left endpoint to its right endpoint, slope and opportunity cost are constant. For a curved PPF, from its left endpoint to its right endpoint, slope and opportunity cost continuously increase.

2.4c Shifts of the PPF (Economic Growth)

A movement from one point to another along a PPF illustrates a change in current possibilities but not in all possibilities simultaneously. The latter would constitute a shift in the entire PPF itself. Why? From changes in technology. Let's say that pie-manufacturing technology does not change but a new pizza oven is released that utilizes combination-heating technology that cooks pizzas faster and more evenly. FIGURE 2-5 illustrates the difference the new technical know-how brings. *PPF1* is the old frontier which we first saw in FIGURE 2-4. *PPF2* is the new frontier made possible by the new pizza-baking technology. While 1,000 pies and 0 pizzas (point *F* or [1,000; 0]) are still a possibility (as on *PPF1*), what has changed is the production possibility of pizzas: 0 pies and 4,000 pizzas (0; 4,000) is the new left endpoint of Bakerville's PPF (point *A2*) seen on the new *PPF2*.

FIGURE 2-5: Upward-Rotation Shift of the PPF for Bakerville

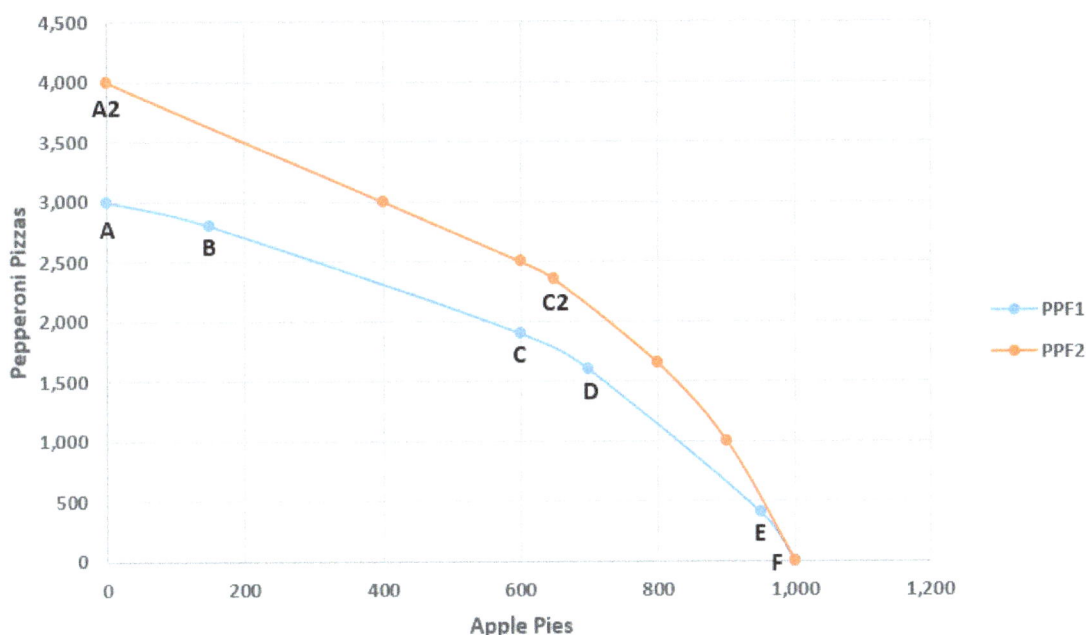

Even though only the pizza-manufacturing process was affected by a change in technology, notice that pie production (with the only exception of point *F*) has been affected as well. This can be most easily seen in a comparison of point *C* (600; 1,900) on *PPF1* to its new position on *PPF2*, point *C2* (650; 2,350). What is intuitive is that the new technology is producing 450 more pizzas at *C2* than *C*. What is counterintuitive is that we now have 50 more pies (600 previously, now 650). The new technology has freed up factors of production that are being used to produce more pies. This shows how important innovation is to the economy in that positive developments in one area can create positive developments in other areas. *The move from point C to point C2, as well as the shift in the entire PPF, represent the macroeconomic phenomenon of* **economic growth***, the increase in the amount of goods and services produced by an economy over a quarter or year.* Economic growth is not only represented by an upward rotation in the PPF (as seen in FIGURE 2-5) where the production possibilities of one product increase, but also a parallel outward shift in the PPF, a situation where the production possibilities of both products increase simultaneously (which we saw in FIGURE A-7 in the appendix to chapter 1).

> **economic growth** – an increase in the amount of goods and services produced by an economy over a quarter or year.

2.5 Microeconomics versus Macroeconomics

We first encountered this distinction in chapter 1. Why has economics traditionally been divided up into two levels? The standard answer is that microeconomics focuses on behavior at the individual, household, or market level while macroeconomics focuses on topics and issues at the level of an entire state or national economy.

This seems to make sense. Topics such as inflation, business cycles, and recessions or depressions seem to be economy-wide in nature. They undoubtedly affect households but seem to have few counterparts on the household level. While the concept of *oikonomos* in chapter 1 reminded us of how a household resembles an economy, some issues at the individual and household level such as who will be selected as a spouse or significant other and who will serve as the primary breadwinner seem to have little if any in the way of a counterpart on an economy-wide level.

It is also difficult to see how some issues and topics can be restricted to just one level or the other: price controls, savings, money, unemployment, and the effects of central-bank policy, to name just a few examples. Indeed, these examples underscore the fact that mastery of microeconomics comes first: Understanding changes in demand, supply, and markets is necessary for bringing insight into an economy's performance, whether it is healthy growth or malfunction.

While there seems to be justification for some separation (e.g., central-bank policy, business cycles, and international trade), sound macroeconomics unquestionably begins with sound microeconomics.

2.6 Positive Statements versus Normative Statements

Another important distinction is that between positive and normative statements, both of which economists and laypersons can make when discussing economic topics and issues.

positive statement – a statement that can be shown to be true or factual; a statement that is testable.

A **positive statement** is a statement that can be shown to be true or factual. In other words, it is "testable" in the sense that, at least theoretically, an experiment could be conducted to see whether it accurately describes the real world. It is important to keep in mind that because positive statements are testable doesn't mean that they have been tested or must be tested to be considered positive.

Example 1: *If we raise the price of Shell 87 octane gasoline from its current level (say, $3.00) per gallon to $15.00 per gallon, consumers will purchase less Shell gasoline than they are purchasing now.*

The statement in Example 1 above is definitely a positive statement because we can (not that we have to, but *can*) visit a Shell station and (station owners willing) raise the price of Shell 87 octane gasoline to $15.00 per gallon and watch the station's customers stop purchasing 87 octane gasoline from that station and patronize other stations instead.

normative statement – a statement that is a matter of opinion, cannot be shown to be true or factual, and is not testable.

A **normative statement** is a statement of opinion, and therefore cannot be shown to be true or factual and is not testable. Normative statements sometimes, but certainly not always, contain words such as "should" or "ought."

Example 2: *Strawberry ice cream tastes better than mint ice cream.*

The statement in Example 2 above is clearly a normative statement because it cannot be tested. Personally, the author agrees with the statement because he likes strawberry ice cream better than mint ice cream, but that's completely irrelevant. The author or anyone else's preferences for strawberry ice cream over mint ice cream hardly make the statement true or a fact because many other people prefer mint ice cream to strawberry ice cream. In other words, normative statements are subjective while positive statements can be (not are, but *can* be) factual (revealed to be true).

Why is this distinction important? Because most real-world discussions of economic topics and issues contain both types of statements. As an example, consider the following argument often made in U.S. popular media:

Statement A: *For individuals, U.S. health care is more costly than Canadian health care.*
Statement B: *Therefore, the U.S. should adopt a Canadian-style health-care system.*

For certain individuals, there is no question that *Statement A* can be true. A Canadian can visit a primary-care physician and pay no out-of-pocket expenses for the visit. However, in terms of opportunity costs, i.e., the higher tax rates and time costs that the Canadian system imposes on some Canadians, *Statement A* can also be untrue. Regardless, *Statement A* is a positive statement because it is testable. *Statement B* is normative because it cannot be tested and established as a fact. It is a conclusion or inference based on *Statement A*, which in some cases is true and other cases is false.

It is not that one type of statement is superior to the other; indeed, debate over economic issues, where these two types of statements most come into play, can be entertaining and fun. Mastering the positive-normative distinction is valuable because it can help separate facts from value judgments and better ensure that sound policy is based on facts which form a solid foundation for value judgments that can affect the well-being of millions of people.

2.7 Love, Personal Economics, and Politics: Why Facts and Sound Analysis Are Often Ignored

It is sometimes said that there are two areas of life where common sense is willfully ignored and emotion takes over: love and personal economics. In love, we have all known people who pursue a type of significant other whose traits have no bearing on the viability of happy, long-term relationships: the woman who thinks tall, good-looking men automatically make stable, faithful, and reliable husbands and fathers; the man who thinks ditzy but good-looking women will hold his interest and attraction for a lifetime; the woman who believes she can change a perennial bad boy into a prince through marriage, and on and on. These rational but often incorrect beliefs lead the shallow people who trust them into costly errors again and again until they wise up.

Personal economics is not very different. The principles delineated in chapter 1 of this book lay a broad but clear path on which to travel in making sound economic decisions in life. Real wealth is accumulated gradually over time *via* entrepreneurship and consistent, diversified savings. Nevertheless, people will come along in generation after generation pursuing quick riches through anything from day trading to casino gambling, refusing to heed the time-tested warnings that these paths are frequently ineffective to catastrophic. What almost always inevitably stops them is not suddenly wising up and seeing that these activities can never bring them stable steady incomes and wealth, but rather, like the drug addict who winds up in prison, losing all money to pursue them.

The political arena is often another universe of rational perversity because of the incentives that confront the politician. Most politicians are not interested in sound economic policy, but what gets votes and will help them win the next election. Thus, the politician will tend to pay greater attention to noisy activists and aggressive lobbyists who want various government protections or favors for their special-interest groups or industries: monopoly barriers to entry, quotas, tariffs, subsidies, special tax breaks, price supports, special fees, and so on. These all reduce competition and make consumers and society in general worse off. Indeed, they are often a transfer of wealth from consumers to producers. Regardless, they are attractive to politicians precisely because they benefit small but active, informed, and aggressive organized groups who are willing to generously donate to and lobby politicians who are willing to dole out generous special favors to special interests. These are the perverse incentives of many political systems.

2.8 Conclusion

This chapter began with the scientific methodology of economics, reviewed a model (the demand curve), reviewed and expanded on another model (the production-possibilities frontier [PPF]), introduced a new model (the circular-flow diagram [CFD]), and explained the role that assumptions play in constructing models. The chapter then introduced the distinction between positive and normative statements and explained why there are areas of life where facts and sound analysis are often ignored, and emotions carry the day when decisions are made. The next chapter begins an exploration of specialization and exchange.

2.9 Chapter Concepts

scientific method
assumption
circular-flow diagram (CFD)
goods and services markets
factor (factors of production) markets
factors of production
labor
capital
entrepreneurship
classical dichotomy
real variables
nominal variables
efficient
inefficient
structurally induced inefficiency
policy-induced inefficiency
unattainable
economic growth
positive statement
normative statement

2.10 Problems, Questions, and Discussion Topics (Items Requiring Examples are Marked with an Asterisk [*])

1. What are the three steps of the scientific method? Provide an example that includes all three steps*.

2. Why is economics not a "hard" science in the sense that chemistry and physics are? What are some of the potential problems of conducting experiments on entire modern economies composed of millions of consumers, firms, and workers?

3. With regard to assumptions,

    A. what are their purpose in economic modelling?

    B. Why are they important?

4. What is the purpose of the circular-flow diagram (CFD)?

5. What are the two types of factors of production? Provide an example of only one of these two factors that involves either you, someone you know, or something with which you have become familiar with in daily life*.

For convenience, FIGURE 2-3 from earlier in this chapter has been reproduced below. Please refer to it in answering topics 6, 7, 8, and 9 below.

FIGURE 2-3: The Circular-Flow Diagram (CFD)

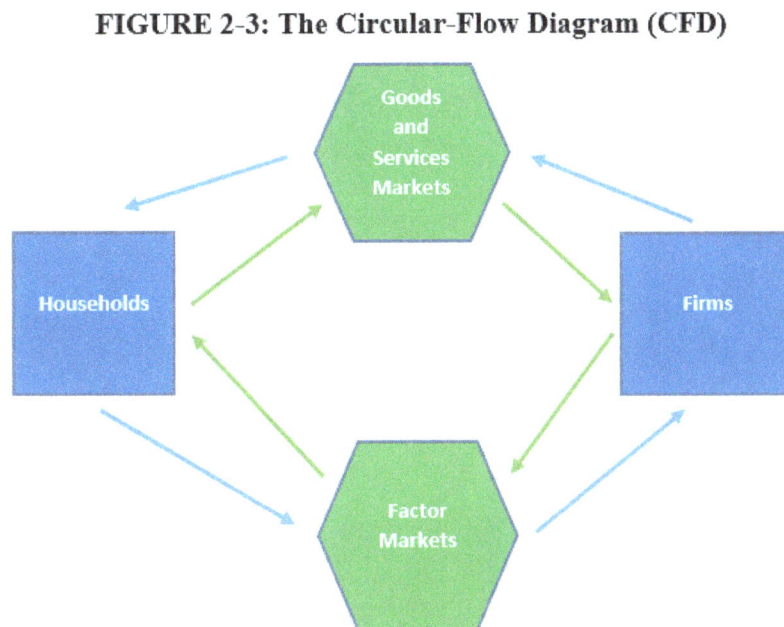

6. With the assistance of FIGURE 2-3, explain step-by-step how labor moves from Households to Firms (left to right) along the lower half of the CFD.

7. With the assistance of FIGURE 2-3, explain step-by-step how goods and services move from Firms to Households (right to left) along the upper half of the CFD.

8. Tangible goods and services follow a counterclockwise direction around the CFD. Following the blue arrows in the CFD in FIGURE 2-3, explain the path of goods and services in detail as they move from Households all the way back to Households.

9. In contrast to goods and services, money follows a clockwise direction around the CFD. Following the green arrows in the CFD in FIGURE 2-3, explain the path of money in detail as it moves from Firms all the way back to Firms.

10. classical dichotomy (define it, then provide examples of both sides of it)*

11. real variables versus nominal variables (define both but provide an example of only one and indicate which concept you are illustrating)*

12. FIGURE 2-6 contains the PPF for the town of Fryerville, which specializes in the manufacture of blueberry pancakes and apple crepes.

FIGURE 2-6: Production-Possibilities Frontier (PPF) for Fryerville

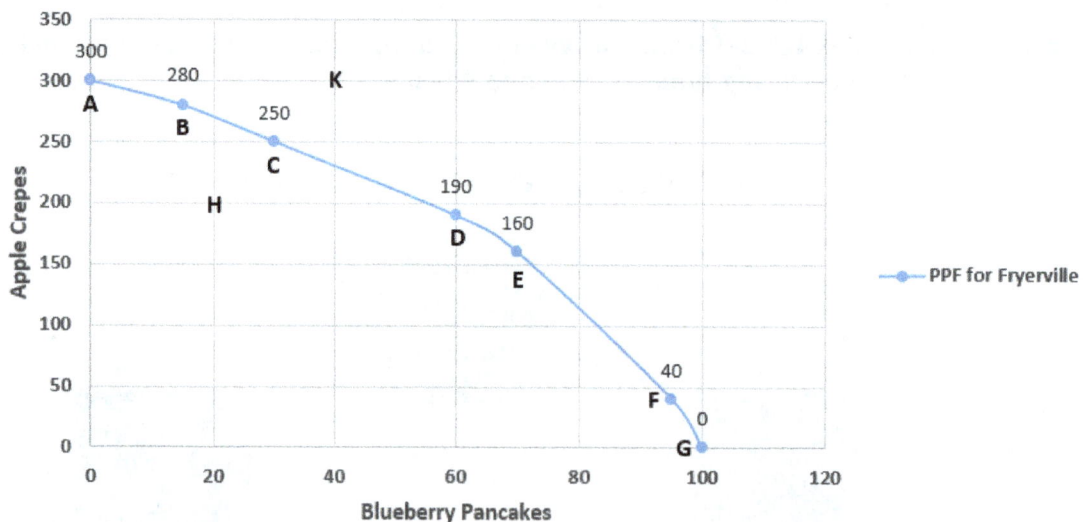

A. Name all points of efficiency, inefficiency, and unattainability for the PPF in FIGURE 2-6.

B. For the PPF in FIGURE 2-6, what is the opportunity cost of moving from point B (15, 280) to C (30, 250)? Point C (30, 250) to E (70, 160)? Point F (95, 40) to D (60, 190)? In what way does opportunity cost change across these three line segments (BC, CE, and FD) of the PPF in FIGURE 2-6?

13. policy-induced inefficiency (define and provide a quantitative example)*

14. *For a straight-line PPF, from left endpoint to right endpoint, slope and opportunity cost are _____. For a curved PPF, from left endpoint to right endpoint, slope and opportunity cost _____.*

   A. Fill in the blanks: _____ , _____ .

   B. Explain:

15. FIGURE 2-7 contains two PPFs for the town of Fryerville, which specializes in the manufacture of blueberry pancakes and apple crepes.

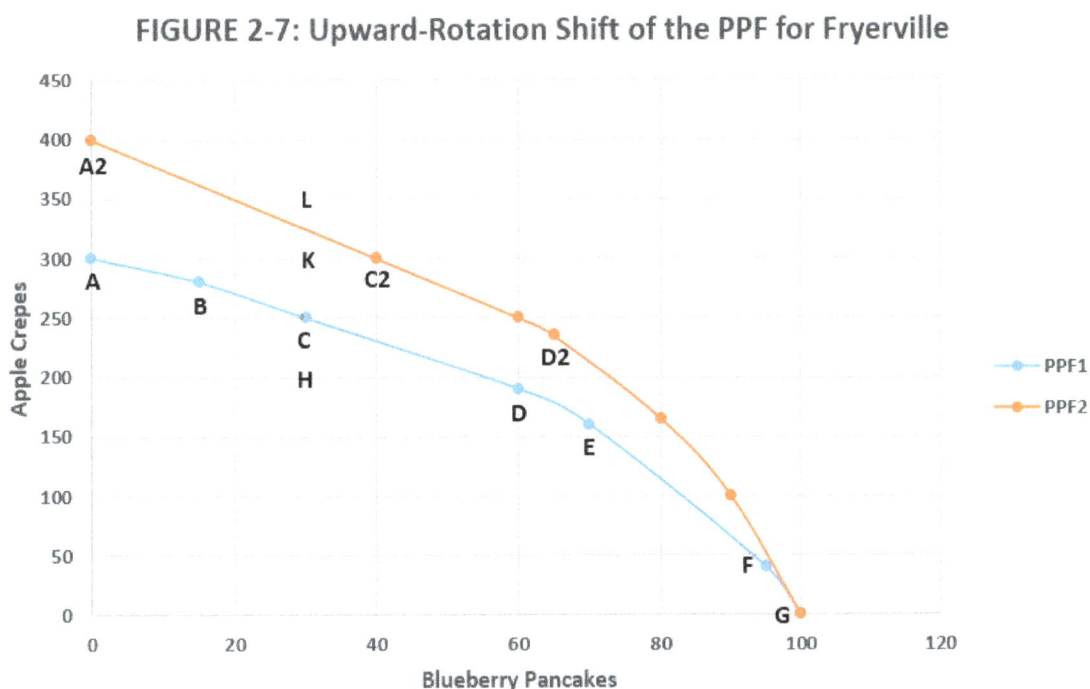

FIGURE 2-7: Upward-Rotation Shift of the PPF for Fryerville

   A. Name all points of efficiency, inefficiency, and unattainability for *PPF1* in FIGURE 2-7.

   B. Name all points of efficiency, inefficiency, and unattainability for *PPF2* in FIGURE 2-7.

   C. Why did the classification of points (efficient, inefficient, and unattainable) change from *PPF1* to *PPF2*?

   D. For *PPF2* in FIGURE 2-7, what is the opportunity cost of moving from point *A2* (0, 400) to *C2* (40, 300)? Point *C2* (40, 300) to *D2* (65, 235)? Point *G* (100, 0) to *D2* (65, 235)? In what way does opportunity cost change across line segments $\overline{A2C2}$, $\overline{C2D2}$, and $\overline{GD2}$ of *PPF2* in FIGURE 2-7?

16. *The shift in the entire PPF, represents the macroeconomic phenomenon of _____, the increase in all goods and services an economy produces each and every year.*

    A. Fill in the blank: _____.

    B. Explain:

17. What are some sound reasons justifying a distinction between microeconomics and macroeconomics? In what ways are these two subfields difficult to separate?

18. normative statement (define, provide an example)*

19. "The current national average price of gasoline is $4.50."

    A. Is this a positive or normative statement?

    B. Why?

20. "The current national average price of gasoline is too high."

    A. Is this a positive or normative statement?

    B. Why?

21. In the areas of love, personal economics, and politics, why are facts and sound analysis so often ignored?

Chapter 3: Specialization and Exchange

3.0 Introduction

Whether we are actively conscious of it or not, we engage in trade with countless people across the world every week. We purchase tomatoes from a local farmers market which received them from a farm a few miles away and grapes from a grocery store which imported them from Chile. We use smartphones and computers designed by Apple in the U.S. but assembled in China from parts manufactured in Korea and Taiwan.[18,19] This worldwide trade is both direct and indirect: some of the iPhone parts manufactured in Korea and Taiwan contain copper which came from Chile,[20] the same country supplying grapes to your local supermarket.

This is revolutionary. In the 1950s, an American and Taiwanese would only likely trade with each other through tourism: for example, if an American visited a shop in Taipei and purchased some goods. An American visiting Taiwan in the 1950s would almost certainly be a very wealthy one. Today, that is not necessarily the case. Tourism aside, most Americans will never set foot in Taiwan but will still trade with its residents through the purchase of everything from clothing to electronics.

There are mutual benefits from trade for both buyers and sellers, which is why it takes place and isn't limited to tangible goods. We are entertained or educated by YouTube videos uploaded from every continent on the globe, and the uploaders, if their subscriber base is large, are compensated through advertising. Trade takes place through traditional social institutions and at many levels: between spouses (e.g., companionship in marriage), friends, neighbors, church or synagogue members, customers and employees of local stores, and people who you will never meet or ever get to know across the world.

This chapter will demonstrate how trade benefits both buyers and sellers at the individual level and extend that conclusion to entire nations.

3.1 Exchange in a Simple Setting

To gain some insight, we have to leave the vast complexities of the current international environment and consider a land of two people who each mainly specialize in one good. Moses gathers manna on weekday mornings and Aaron gathers quail on weekday evenings. Moses bakes the manna into bread while Aaron boils the quail and serves it whole or in parts.

While Moses and Aaron could certainly survive on only the products from their own labor and never engage in trade, this is impractical. Bread made and baked in different ways makes great meals for a few days for Moses, but he desires more variety. He would love to get his hands on some of Aaron's quail meat to eat as is or in sandwiches. Quail cooked different ways makes

---

[18] Kabin, Benjamin. "Apple's iPhone: Designed in California But Manufactured Fast All Around the World (Infographic)." *Entrepreneur*. 11 September 2013. https://www.entrepreneur.com/article/228315

[19] Costello, Sam. "Where is the iPhone Made? It Takes a Village to Build an iPhone." *Lifewire*. 14 July 2018. https://www.lifewire.com/where-is-the-iphone-made-1999503

[20] "Chile." *The World Factbook*. CIA. https://www.cia.gov/library/publications/the-world-factbook/geos/ci.html

great meals for a few days for Aaron, but he too desires more variety. He would love to get his hands on some of Moses's bread to eat as is or to make sandwiches.

Trade happens if there is both a willingness and ability to trade. In the case of Moses and Aaron, both willingness and ability are clearly there. Willingness, because they each desire greater variety in their meals and ability because each produces valuable products desired by him and his potential trading partner.

3.2 Exchange in a Simple Model: The Straight-Line PPF Revisited

For further clarity, let's illustrate the production (and in this case, consumption) possibilities in the land of Moses and Aaron. Their production-possibilities frontier (PPF) schedules are found in TABLE 3-1 where Moses and Aaron completely specialize in one good and are about equally productive in their specialties.

3.2a Before Trade: Complete Specialization, Symmetric Proficiency

TABLE 3-1: Hourly and Daily Production of Manna and Quail		
Producer (specialty)	Hourly Production (Either Good) in Pounds (lb.)	Daily Production (Either Good) in Pounds (lb.)
Moses (manna)	1/4 lb. manna, 0 lb. quail	2 lb. manna, 0 lb. quail
Aaron (quail)	0 lb. manna, 1/4 lb. quail	0 lb. manna, 2 lb. quail

This yields the following PPFs in terms of daily production:[21]

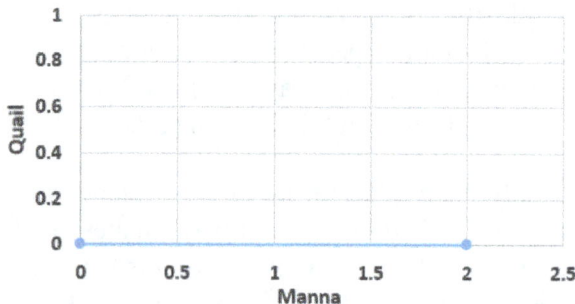

FIGURE 3-1A: Moses' PPF (Specialty: Manna)

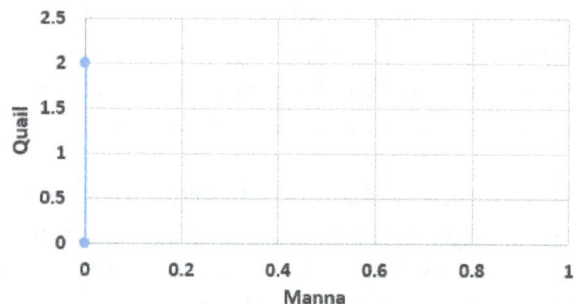

FIGURE 3-1B: Aaron's PPF (Specialty: Quail)

---

[21] Daily production means an 8-hour workday.

In this setting of complete specialization, the gains from trade are obvious and displayed in TABLE 3-2:

TABLE 3-2: Trade Potential for Moses and Aaron (Daily Production)				
	Moses (Specialty: Manna)		Aaron (Specialty: Quail)	
	Manna (lb.)	Quail (lb.)	Manna (lb.)	Quail (lb.)
4 No Trade	2	0	0	2
5 Trade				
6 Total Production	2	0	0	2
7 Production That Gets Traded	-1	0	0	-1
8 Production That Gets Consumed	1	+1 lb. of quail from Aaron *via* trade	+1 lb. of manna from Moses *via* trade	1
9 Net Gains from Trade	0	1 lb. of quail	1 lb. of manna	0

From row 4 of TABLE 3-2 (No Trade), we can see that under complete specialization and before trade, Moses gathers and consumes 2 pounds of manna and 0 pounds of quail daily while Aaron gathers and consumes 0 pounds of manna and 2 pounds of quail daily. In this scenario, after trade begins, Moses and Aaron maintain their current production (row 6 Total Production in TABLE 3-2): Moses continues gathering his maximum 2 pounds of manna per day while Aaron continues gathering his maximum 2 pounds of quail per day. Now that we know who is producing how much of what, we move to row 7 of TABLE 3-2 (Production That Gets Traded). Here we see, in the second cell of row 7, Moses trading away 1 of his 2 pounds of manna (-1) to Aaron and keeping 1 pound of manna for himself. Still in the same row (7 Production That Gets Traded) but in the fifth cell, we also see Aaron trading away 1 of his 2 pounds of quail (-1) to Moses and keeping 1 pound of quail for himself.

Now we move down to row 8 Production That Gets Consumed of TABLE 3-2. Row 8 demonstrates how both Moses and Aaron are better off after trade. Moses has the 1 pound of manna he gathered but didn't trade and 1 pound of quail (+1) he received from Aaron. Aaron has 1 pound of manna he received from Moses (+1) and 1 pound of quail he gathered but didn't trade. While it's true that they each are still consuming the same weight of food per day as they were before trade (2 lb.), they now have a more balanced consumption, which each greatly prefers.

The final row of TABLE 3-2 (row 9 Net Gains from Trade) illustrates the mutual gains from trade for both Moses and Aaron, which is one pound of a good that each never had before. Before trade (row 4 No Trade), Moses was consuming 2 pounds of manna and 0 pounds of quail per day while Aaron was consuming 0 pounds of manna and 2 pounds of quail per day. Row 9 Net Gains from Trade displays their individual gains from trade: Moses is now consuming 1 pound more quail per day than before trade while Aaron is now consuming 1 pound more manna per day than before trade. Again, while they each are still consuming the same daily weight of food (2 lb.) than before trade, they now have more balanced meals. Moses is very happy to receive 1 pound of quail in trade and isn't stuck with eating just manna while Aaron is giddy to get 1 pound of manna from trade and not being stuck with eating just quail all the time.

3.2b Before Trade: Less Specialization, Symmetric Proficiency

Where there is less specialization, gains from trade still exist but are less obvious. Let's look at a scenario where Moses can now gather quail but not as proficiently as he gathers manna and Aaron can now gather manna but not as proficiently as he usually gathers quail.

As can be seen in TABLE 3-3, Moses can gather 2 pounds of manna or half a pound of quail per day while Aaron can gather 2 pounds of quail or half a pound of manna per day. These individual production constraints create the PPFs found in FIGURES 3-2A and 3-2B. Should Moses and Aaron decide not to trade with each other, they will each choose the midpoint (M) on their PPFs in FIGURES 3-2A and 3-2B, where they are both maximizing their production of and preferred variety of both goods. For Moses, that is 1 pound of manna and a quarter pound of quail (M in FIGURE 3-2A) while for Aaron, it is 1 pound of quail and a quarter pound of manna (M in FIGURE 3-2B).

TABLE 3-3: Hourly and Daily Production of Manna and Quail		
Producer (specialty)	Hourly Production (Either Good) in Pounds (lb.)	Daily Production (Either Good) in Pounds (lb.)
Moses (manna)	1/4 lb. manna, 1/16 lb. quail	2 lb. manna, 1/2 lb. quail
Aaron (quail)	1/16 lb. manna, 1/4 lb. quail	1/2 lb. manna, 2 lb. quail

FIGURE 3-2A: Moses' PPF (Specialty: Manna)

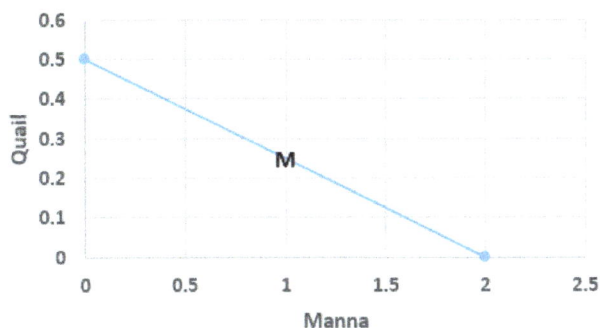

FIGURE 3-2B: Aaron's PPF (Specialty: Quail)

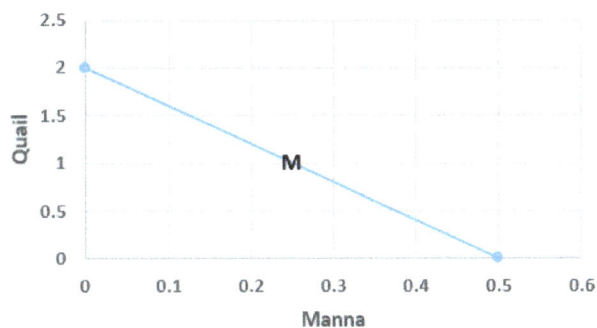

If Moses and Aaron trade, TABLE 3-4 displays what they gain. In this setting of less-than-complete specialization, the gains from trade are slightly less but still substantial.

TABLE 3-4: Trade Potential for Moses and Aaron (Daily Production)				
	Moses (Specialty: Manna)		**Aaron (Specialty: Quail)**	
	Manna (lb.)	**Quail (lb.)**	**Manna (lb.)**	**Quail (lb.)**
4 No Trade	1	1/4	1/4	1
5 Trade				
6 Total Production	2	0	0	2
7 Production That Gets Traded	-1	0	0	-1
8 Production That Gets Consumed	1	+1	+1	1
9 Net Gains from Trade	0	3/4	3/4	0

In TABLE 3-4, let's start at row 4 No Trade. Here we can see that under partial specialization and before trade, Moses gathers and consumes 1 pound of manna and a quarter pound of quail daily while Aaron gathers and consumes a quarter pound of manna and 1 pound of quail daily. In this scenario, right before trade begins, both Moses and Aaron maximize their gains from trade by maximizing their total specialized production. In row 6 Total Production in TABLE 3-4, we see Moses gathering his maximum 2 pounds of manna per day and no quail while Aaron gathers his maximum 2 pounds of quail per day and no manna. After trade begins, we see the mix of goods produced and consumed change. Row 7 Production That Gets Traded shows Moses trading 1 pound of manna (-1) to Aaron while keeping 1 pound of manna for himself and Aaron trading 1 pound of quail (-1) to Moses while keeping 1 pound of quail for himself.

Row 8 Production That Gets Consumed in TABLE 3-2 shows the condition of each after trade. Moses has the 1 pound of manna he gathered but didn't trade and the 1 pound of quail (+1) he received from Aaron. Aaron has the 1 pound of manna he received from Moses (+1) and the 1 pound of quail he gathered but didn't trade. Finally, from the last row of TABLE 3-4 (9 Net Gains from Trade), we see that trade has created mutual benefit for both Moses and Aaron. Prior to trade (row 4 No Trade), Moses was consuming 1 pound of manna and a quarter pound of quail per day while Aaron was consuming a quarter pound of manna and 1 pound of quail per day. Row 9 Net Gains from Trade displays their individual gains from trade: Moses is now consuming three quarters of a pound more quail per day than before trade while Aaron is now consuming three quarters of a pound more manna per day than before trade. Both are better off not only because each is now consuming more food per day (2 pounds instead of just one and a quarter pounds), trade has given each more balanced consumption.

3.2c Before Trade: Specialization and Asymmetric Proficiency

What about the case where there is not only specialization, but one party is more proficient in the production of both goods than the other?

Let's take the case of Robinson Crusoe and Friday on an island off the coast of South America. Crusoe lands on the island from a shipwreck while Friday, with Crusoe's help, escaped imprisonment by cannibals just before they intended to kill him. Crusoe is in his mid-forties, injured from the shipwreck, and does not have the energy of Friday, who is in his early twenties. Crusoe has become skilled at fishing on the island through experience but is still not so good at scaling the island's high palm trees to gather coconuts. Each week he can either catch 8 pounds of fish, gather 2 pounds of coconuts, or settle for a mix of the two goods. Friday, a native islander, is productive at fishing and gathering coconuts but gets bored fishing and prefers the thrill of scaling eighty-foot-high coconut palm trees. Each week Friday can catch 12 pounds of fish, gather 6 pounds of coconuts, or settle for a mix of the two goods. The PPF schedules for Crusoe and Friday are thus as follows:

TABLE 3-5: PPF Schedules for Crusoe and Friday	
	Weekly Production (Either Good) in Pounds (lb.)
Crusoe (fish, coconuts)	(8,0), (0,2), or any mix in between
Friday (fish, coconuts)	(12, 0), (0,6), or any mix in between

With these schedules, we derive the following weekly straight-line PPFs:

FIGURE 3-3A: Crusoe's PPF

FIGURE 3-3B: Friday's PPF

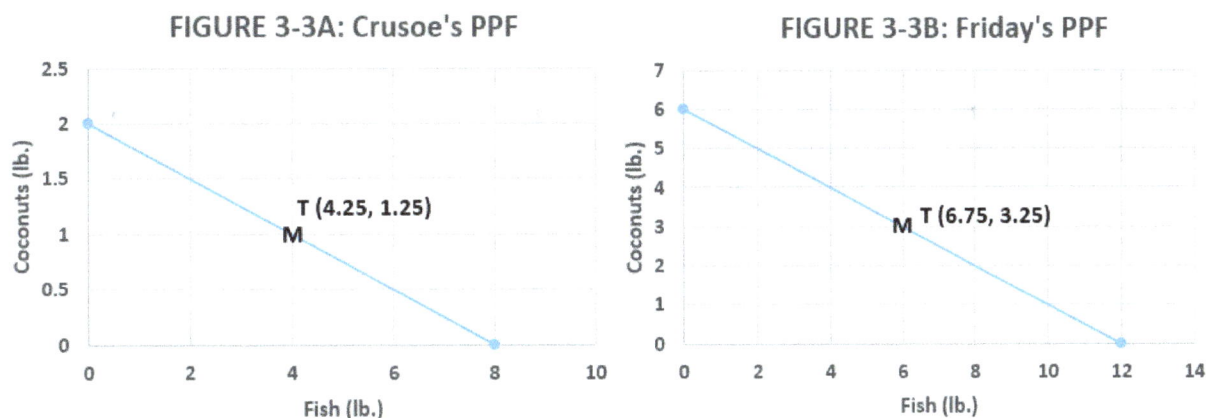

With no trade between them, Crusoe and Friday each choose a balanced bundle (M, for midpoint) on their PPFs. For Crusoe, that balanced bundle M is 4 pounds of fish and 1 pound of coconuts (4, 1). Friday's balanced no-trade bundle M is 6 pounds of fish and 3 pounds of coconuts (6, 3). (The meaning of point T in each graph will be explained later in this section of the chapter.) Can they both do better by trading with each other? Counterintuitively, yes.

TABLE 3-6: Trade Potential for Crusoe and Friday (from Weekly Production for Each)

	Crusoe		Friday	
	Fish	Coconuts	Fish	Coconuts
4 Production with No Trade (M)	4	1	6	3
5 Trade				
6 Production with Trade	8	0	3	4.5
7 Amounts Traded	Give 3.75	Receive 1.25	Receive 3.75	Give 1.25
8 Consumption After Trade (T)	4.25	1.25	6.75	3.25
9 Net Gains from Trade	+0.25	+0.25	+0.75	+0.25

As can be seen in TABLE 3-6 in row 4 Production with No Trade (M), Crusoe and Friday assume their midpoint (M) production levels prior to trade. Even though Friday can outproduce

Crusoe in procuring both goods, the motives to pursue trade are still substantial. With his injury, Crusoe is happy to completely specialize in fishing and give up climbing tall trees to collect coconuts while Friday is excited to dangle dangerously high above ground to harvest coconuts. Thus, each leans into greater specialization to maximize each of their grains from trade. In row 6 Production with Trade in TABLE 3-6, we see Crusoe downshift to catching fish full time and securing 8 pounds per week and 0 coconuts. In response, Friday cuts his fish production from 6 pounds to 3 pounds per week while boosting his coconut production from 3 pounds to 4.5 pounds per week.

Moving on to row 7, Amounts Traded in TABLE 3-6, we see that Crusoe trades 3.75 pounds of fish for 1.25 pounds of coconuts while Friday receives 3.75 pounds of fish in return for the 1.25 pounds of coconuts he gives to Crusoe. Row 8 Consumption After Trade (T) in TABLE 3-6 reveals that after trade, Crusoe now has 4.25 pounds of fish and 1.25 pounds of coconuts compared to 4 pounds of fish and 1 pound of coconuts before trade [see row 4 Production with No Trade (M)]. Friday now has 6.75 pounds of fish and 3.25 pounds of coconuts compared to his pre-trade consumption bundle of 6 pounds of fish and 3 pounds of coconuts [again, see row 4 Production with No Trade (M)].

Row 9, Net Gains from Trade, reveals the very interesting and counterintuitive results from trade, especially vis-à-vis Friday. Through trade, Crusoe gains 0.25 pounds of both goods while Friday gains 0.75 pounds of fish and 0.25 pounds of coconuts. What's interesting is that Friday, while more prolific at producing both goods, reaps the greater gains between the two trading partners.

Thus, Crusoe and Friday demonstrate that even when one party is significantly more productive in producing both goods, trade is still beneficial to both parties. They each end up with consumption bundles (T) that lie above their pre-trade PPFs illustrated in FIGURES 3-3A and 3-3B. Crusoe's post-trade bundle lies at point T (4.25, 1.25) in Figure 3-3A while Friday's post-trade bundle lies at point T (6.75, 3.25) in Figure 3-3B. Both of these points were unattainable before trade and are equivalent to a boost in technology or economic growth, which brings us to our Grand Point about trade in this chapter.

Grand Point: **As a result of specialization and trade, each party consumes more goods with no additional work done. Specialization and trade are thus like advanced technology such as faster computers or new machines that do more work without requiring more energy or fuel.**

CASE STUDY: "Made in the U.S.A."—What Does It Mean?

We drive Toyota cars assembled in Canada; we purchase Himalayan pink salt on Amazon that was mined in Pakistan and imported by the San Francisco Salt Company in Hayward, California; we are entertained or educated by YouTube videos uploaded from every continent on the globe. Yet there still exists this notion that there are "American" products, "Canadian" products, "Chinese" products, and so on.

This notion is not completely wrong, as there are still many products that accurately fall under these headings, especially services. A small barbecue restaurant in Alabama could sell entrees made of American pork (ribs, pulled pork, Brunswick stew), American beer and soft drinks, and desserts prepared in house (e.g., banana pudding). For automobiles and electronics today, though, the notion of only one country's citizens designing and manufacturing every part and completing the final assembly of a product seems farfetched. What we see instead is distinct specialization in the various parts of smart phones, laptop computers, tablets, and televisions. As discussed earlier with respect to the Apple iPhone, the product is designed in the U.S. but assembled in China from parts made in Korea and Taiwan. Some of the inputs (e.g., copper) used to make these parts come from still other countries around the globe (e.g., Chile).

No "Bright Line"

Made in U.S.A. is a label or standard for goods defined by the U.S. Federal Trade Commission (FTC), an agency of the U.S. federal government created in 1914. What does the label mean? With little thought, most U.S. consumers assume it's very straightforward: that every component part of a good is designed and manufactured in the U.S. and complete assembly of the final good takes place in the U.S. as well. This is incorrect.

The FTC standard for products regarded as made in U.S.A. is that "all or virtually all" of the final good is manufactured in the U.S. As you can imagine, the "virtually all" phrase in this definition is controversial and the FTC has admitted that no "bright line" exists to show when the "all or virtually all" requirement has been fulfilled.

Examples from a 1997 FTC proposal[22] highlight the problem. A bicycle could be considered U.S.-made if its final assembly is in the U.S. and 75 percent of its explicit costs are attributable to U.S. parts or labor. On the other hand, a toaster that has 75 percent of its costs sourced to the U.S. but a final assembly in Canada is considered a foreign (viz., Canadian) good.

Another problem is that not all goods entirely made in the U.S. carry the Made-in-U.S.A. label. Textiles, furs, and automobiles made in the U.S. must have labels stating where they were made ("country-of-origin" labels), but this requirement does not apply to many other goods.

One product that complies with the Made-in-U.S.A. standard is MyPillow pillows, made famous through TV advertisements. They are a one hundred percent American-made product from their foam filling and covering to their final assembly in Shakopee, Minnesota.

---

[22] "Examples of Applications: FTC Proposed Guides for the Use of U.S. Origin Claims." Federal Trade Commission. Washington: 5 May 1997. https://www.ftc.gov/news-events/press-releases/1997/05/examples-applications-ftc-proposes-new-standard-made-usa-claims

3.3 Absolute versus Comparative Advantage

absolute advantage – the advantage held by the individual, firm, or country that uses fewer inputs to produce a good or service than another individual, firm, or country.	**Absolute advantage** is the advantage held by the individual, firm, or country that uses fewer inputs to produce a good or service than another individual, firm, or country. Recall from TABLE 3-5 that in a week Crusoe can catch 8 fish or gather 2 coconuts while Friday can catch 12 fish or gather 6 coconuts.

Friday has the clear absolute advantage in both goods. Is this helpful? Not in this case. It doesn't definitively tell us who should specialize in what and trade for what, so let's move on to the second important concept in this section, comparative advantage.

comparative advantage – the advantage held by the individual, firm, or country that produces a good or service at a lower opportunity cost than another individual, firm, or country.	**Comparative advantage** is the advantage held by the individual, firm, or country that has the lower opportunity cost of producing a good or service than another individual, firm, or country. TABLE 3-7 displays the opportunity costs of fish and coconuts for Crusoe and Friday.

TABLE 3-7: Opportunity Cost for Crusoe and Friday in terms of Fish and Coconuts		
	Opportunity Cost of:	
	1 lb. of Fish	**1 lb. of Coconuts**
4 Crusoe [(8, 0)(0, 2)]	0.25 lb. of coconuts	4 lb. of fish
5 Friday [(12, 0)(0, 6)]	0.5 lb. of coconuts	2 lb. of fish

How did we derive these opportunity costs? From TABLE 3-5, we saw that Crusoe's weekly production was either 8 pounds of fish or 2 pounds of coconuts [(8, 0) or (0, 2)]. When we standardize to single pounds (by dividing both numbers by two), we get [(4, 0) or (0, 1)], which means that for the time it takes Crusoe to gather 1 pound of coconuts he could have caught 4 pounds of fish (see the third cell of row 4 of TABLE 3-7). As for Friday, from TABLE 3-5 we saw that his weekly production was either 12 pounds of fish or 6 pounds of coconuts [(12, 0) or (0, 6)]. When we standardize to a single pound of either good (by dividing both numbers by 6), we arrive at [(2, 0) or (0, 1)], which means that for the time it takes Friday to gather 1 pound of coconuts he could have caught 2 pounds of fish (see cell three, row 5 of TABLE 3-7).

Now that we have the opportunity cost of coconuts for each, deriving the opportunity cost of fish is easy and we can explain the remaining numbers in TABLE 3-7. If 1 pound of coconuts costs 4 pounds of fish for Crusoe (1:4), this means that (by dividing both sides by 4) 1 pound of fish costs 0.25 pounds of coconuts (or 1:4 = 1/4:1 = 0.25:1). This explains the result in cell two of row 4 of TABLE 3-7 (0.25). What about Friday? If 1 pound of coconuts costs 2 pounds of fish for Friday (1:2), this means that (by dividing both sides by two) 1 pound of fish costs 0.5 pounds of coconuts (or 1:2 = 1/2:1 = 0.5:1). This explains the result in cell two of row 5 in TABLE 3-7 (0.5).

Now that we have all of Crusoe and Friday's opportunity costs, we can determine each one's comparative advantage. Looking at the opportunity costs in TABLE 3-7, in terms of fish, Crusoe has a clear comparative advantage: 1 pound of fish costs him only 0.25 pounds of coconuts while for Friday 1 pound of fish costs him 0.5 pounds of coconuts. What about coconuts? The third cells of the last two rows of TABLE 3-7 are very clear in delivering an answer: 1 pound of coconuts costs Crusoe 4 pounds of fish while 1 pound of coconuts costs Friday only 2 pounds of fish.

Thus, comparative advantage gives us the clear answer that absolute advantage does not: Crusoe should be catching fish, Friday should be gathering coconuts, and the two of them should be trading with each other to maximize the abundance of both goods for each other.

3.4 The Exchange Rate of Goods

With the opportunity costs calculated in the previous section, the benefits of trade between Crusoe and Friday can now be further examined. Recall that in TABLE 3-6 (reproduced for convenience as TABLE 3-8), in trading with Friday, Crusoe received 1.25 pounds of coconuts in return for 3.75 pounds of fish (see row 7 Amounts Traded of TABLE 3-8).

TABLE 3-8: Trade Potential for Crusoe and Friday (from Weekly Production for Each)				
	Crusoe		Friday	
	Fish	Coconuts	Fish	Coconuts
4 Production with No Trade (M)	4	1	6	3
5 Trade				
6 Production with Trade	8	0	3	4.5
7 Amounts Traded	Give 3.75	Receive 1.25	Receive 3.75	Give 1.25
8 Consumption After Trade (T)	4.25	1.25	6.75	3.25
9 Net Gains from Trade	+0.25	+0.25	+0.75	+0.25

In other words, the price of 1 pound of coconuts for Crusoe is 3 pounds of fish (3.75 lb. fish/1.25 lb. coconuts = 3 lb. fish per 1 lb. coconuts). Friday received 3.75 pounds of fish in return for 1.25 pounds of coconuts. This means that the price of 1 pound of fish for Friday is 0.33 pounds of coconuts (1.25 lb. coconuts/3.75 lb. fish = 1/3 lb. or 0.33 lb. of coconuts per 1 lb. of fish). Either

exchange rate – the rate at which a good, service, or currency can be traded for another good, service, or currency.

way, the **exchange rate** (the rate at which a good, service, or currency can be traded for another good, service, or currency) is 3 to 1 (3:1) fish to coconuts. Coconuts are clearly the more valuable good, which makes sense since the island, with its limited land available for coconut growing, is so relatively small compared to the surrounding ocean teeming with fish.

Is the market a better deal for both sides? Yes, especially in light of opportunity costs. For Crusoe, to get 1 pound of coconut on the market, he gives up 3 pounds of fish. To get 1 pound of coconut through his own effort, he gives up 4 pounds of fish [see row 4 Production with No Trade (M) of TABLE 3-8]. The market is the better deal. For Friday, to get 1 pound of fish on the market he gives up 0.33 pounds of coconuts. To get 1 pound of fish by his own labor he gives up 0.5 pounds of coconuts [see row 4 Production with No Trade (M) of TABLE 3-8; 6/3 = 2/1 or 2 pounds of fish per 1 pound of coconuts = 1 pound of fish per 0.5 pounds of coconuts). Again, the market provides the better deal, which is why both Crusoe and Friday use it.

3.5 The Viable Price Range of Trade

Where trade can end between two parties in a very simple barter economy is when price exceeds or falls below a certain range, the **viable price range of trade**, or

viable price range of trade – the range of prices in which trade takes place.

range of prices in which trade takes place. Between Crusoe and Friday, the exchange rate or price of 1 pound of coconuts is 3 pounds of fish or $P_{coconuts\ (1\ lb.)}$ = 3 lbs. fish. This makes sense because it falls between Crusoe's opportunity cost of a pound of coconuts (4 lbs. of fish—see row 4 of TABLE 3-8) and Friday's opportunity cost of a pound of coconuts (2 lbs. of fish—see row 4 of TABLE 3-8).

Thus, Crusoe and Friday trade when $P_{coconuts\ (1\ lb.)}$ = 3 lbs. fish.

Taking this market price of coconuts and Crusoe and Friday's opportunity costs of coconuts, we get:

Friday's $OC_{coconuts\ (1\ lb.)}$ = 2 lbs. fish < $P_{coconuts\ (1\ lb.)}$ = 3 lbs. fish < Crusoe's $OC_{coconuts\ (1\ lb.)}$ = 4 lbs. fish.

The price of coconuts does not have to lie exactly in between the opportunity costs of coconuts for both parties for them to gain from trade, but it must be between 2 and 4 lb. of fish. What happens when price rises or falls outside that range?

If $P_{coconuts\ (1\ lb.)}$ = 2 lbs. fish, Crusoe would want to buy coconuts because their price would be below his opportunity cost but Friday may or may not trade because the market would offer no benefit to him with respect to his opportunity cost.

If $P_{coconuts\ (1\ lb.)}$ < 2 lbs. fish, both Crusoe and Friday would want to buy coconuts because the price would be below both of their respective opportunity costs of coconuts.

If $P_{coconuts\ (1\ lb.)}$ = 4 lbs. fish, Friday would want to sell coconuts because their price would be above his opportunity cost. Crusoe may or may not trade because the market would offer no benefit with respect to his opportunity cost of coconuts.

If $P_{coconuts\ (1\ lb.)}$ > 4 lbs. fish, both Crusoe and Friday would want to sell coconuts because the price would be above both of their respective opportunity costs of coconuts.

Trade between Crusoe and Friday ends when $P_{coconuts\ (1\ lb.)}$ < 2 lbs. fish or $P_{coconuts\ (1\ lb.)}$ > 4 lbs. fish. They cannot both be buyers of coconuts or sellers of fish nor can they both be sellers of coconuts or buyers of fish. This doesn't mean that trade doesn't continue; it goes on, but with an individual seller or firm from outside their small-island world.

Exchange that is mutually beneficial takes place when the price of coconuts resides between 2 and 4 pounds of fish. In this range, Friday sells coconuts to buy fish and Crusoe sells fish to buy coconuts because each is purchasing a good at a price lower than his respective opportunity cost. Each producer is specializing in producing the good for which he has a comparative advantage (lower opportunity cost) and both are better off with trade than without it.

ECONOMICS IN THE HOME: Should Kim Kardashian Do Her Own Housework or Hire Trish Haney?

Reality star Kim Kardashian is one of the most in-demand celebrities in the world. However, she has unyielding preferences about how she wants her house floors, furniture, mirrors, and counters cleaned. In terms of home services, Kim, like everyone else, wants honest help so that none of her priceless valuables gets stolen and sold on eBay.

Kim Kardashian (Glenn Francis, CC BY-SA 3.0)

It turns out that freewheeling housekeeper Trish Haney is available. Trish is a thorough cleaner on most days but sometimes late for work and does not always complete all of the tasks that her employers want done on certain days. However, despite her faults, Trish is honest and Kim greatly values this trait, so much that Kim is willing to pay a little extra for it. Should Kim clean her own house?

Kim's mansion in Hidden Hills, California is huge: 8 bedrooms, 10 bathrooms, and 15,667 square feet. Kim is energetic, obviously knows her own house very well, and while listening to music on her phone can vacuum, clean, and dust every room in 6 hours. Trish, in contrast, is a bit lazy, likes to watch TV while she works, misses a few small areas in some rooms, but usually finishes in 8 hours. In terms of just time, Kim clearly has the absolute advantage over Trish since she cleans her home in less time than Trish. So, Kim should clean her own home, problem solved, right? Not by a long shot.

Trish Haney (Grammnet, Fair Use)

In 6 hours, Kim could earn $2 million sitting for a photo shoot for two Web advertisements: one for Skims (Kim's clothing line) and the other for SKKN (Kim's beauty products line). Trish, in the span of an 8-hour workday earning $20 per hour, can clean Kim's house for $160. Given their extremely disparate income potential, between Kim and Trish, comparative advantage (lowest opportunity cost) is clearly held by Trish.

In conclusion, Kim should not clean her house but model for her two merchandise brands and hire Trish to clean her home. Both Kim and Trish will both be better off if Trish is paid anywhere from $160 up to around, but not equal to, $2 million.

3.6 Conclusion

This chapter began with an analysis of the benefits of trade for three simple pre-trade settings: complete specialization with symmetric proficiency, some specialization with symmetric proficiency, and specialization with asymmetric proficiency. Next, the concepts of absolute advantage, comparative advantage, exchange rates, and viable price range for trade were explored. The next chapter introduces demand, supply, and markets.

3.7 Chapter Concepts

absolute advantage
comparative advantage
exchange rate
viable price range of trade

3.8 Problems, Questions, and Discussion Topics (Items Requiring Examples are Marked with an Asterisk [*])

1. *As a result of _____, each party consumes more goods with no additional work done.*

    A. Fill in the blank: _____.

    B. Explain:

2. *Specialization and trade are thus like an _____ such as faster computers or new machines that do ____ work without requiring ____ energy or fuel.*

    A. Fill in the blanks: _____, _____, _____.

    B. Explain:

3. With regard to the Made in the U.S.A. standard,

    A. what do most consumers assume the standard means?

    B. In contrast, how does the U.S. Federal Trade Commission (FTC) define the standard?

4. The U.S. Federal Trade Commission (FTC) has admitted that no "bright line" exists to distinguish U.S.-made goods from foreign goods.

    A. Explain the bicycle and toaster examples that support this.

    B. What is the other problem with regard to which products are required to have "country-of-origin" labels?

5. absolute advantage (define, then provide a quantitative example and state which person, firm, or country in your example holds the absolute advantage)*

6. How are comparative advantage and opportunity cost related?

7. Why is the question of who trades for which goods answered by who has the comparative advantage rather than who has the absolute advantage?

8. exchange rate (define, then provide a quantitative example)*

9. Tarzan can either gather 10 pineapples or catch 1 fish per hour. Jane can gather 30 pineapples or catch 2 fish per hour. What is the opportunity cost of catching one fish for Tarzan? What is the cost of catching one fish for Jane? Who has the absolute advantage in catching fish? Who has the comparative advantage in catching fish?

10. The world's fastest typist can also competently perform brain surgery. Should she create all her documents or hire an assistant? (Explain in detail, no example is required. Hint: this is the Crusoe-Friday and Tarzan-Jane story all over again. Don't overthink it; just apply the same analysis.)

11. viable price range of trade (define, then provide a quantitative example)*

Topics 11 and 12 below refer to the chapter article, "ECONOMICS IN THE HOME: Should Kim Kardashian Do Her Own Housework or Hire Trish Haney?

12. When it comes to cleaning Kim Kardashian's home,

    A. who has the absolute advantage, Kim Kardashian or Trish Haney, and why?

    B. Who holds the comparative advantage, and why?

13. When it comes to cleaning Kim Kardashian's home,

    A. Should Kim Kardashian do her own housework or hire Trish Haney, and why?

    B. In both domestic and foreign trade relations, why should comparative advantage be the deciding factor on who should produce what rather than absolute advantage?

Chapter 4: Demand, Supply, and Markets

4.0 Introduction

This chapter will discuss the most important unit in economics: markets. Other than their structure (e.g., competition, monopoly, oligopoly, etc.), no other topic is more important in micro- or macroeconomics. It is also why students, to best understand the economics discipline, should take microeconomics (the small picture) before macroeconomics (the big picture). If one does not have a sufficient understanding of how a single market functions, how can one then understand how billions of them work inside a trillion-dollar economy of a large, modern nation?

4.1 Goods, Services, and the Competitive Market

A **product** is a good or service or both.[23] A **good** is a physical item for sale, for example: a cell phone. A **service** is an action performed for payment. For example, Martha pays Wesley's Garage $20 to fix her car's flat tire. As we saw in chapter 1, a **market** is a physical or virtual place where buyers and sellers meet to exchange goods and services directly or for money. It can be a checkout line at Walmart, a table at an upscale restaurant, a counter at a pawn shop or pizza parlor, or a page on Amazon.com.

> **product** – a good or service or both.
>
> **good** - a physical item for sale.
>
> **service** - an action performed for payment.
>
> **market** - a physical or virtual place where buyers and sellers meet to exchange goods and services directly or for money.

The particular type of market that will be analyzed in this chapter is **uniform competition** (otherwise known as "perfect" competition). This is a market where:

1. There are many buyers and sellers such that not a single buyer or seller can move the market's price either up or down. This makes each buyer and seller a **price taker**, or one of the numerous buyers or sellers active in uniformly competitive markets who, because of their large numbers, have no influence on market price and therefore must either "take" (accept) the market price and buy or sell the product or leave the market.
2. The goods or services being sold are uniform (nearly or exactly the same).
3. Individual sellers or firms are able to enter or exit the market at a low cost.

> **uniform competition** – a market structure with many buyers and sellers such that not a single buyer or seller can move the market's price up or down, a product that is uniform, and individual sellers or firms able to enter or exit the market at a low cost.
>
> **price taker** – one of the numerous buyers or sellers active in uniformly competitive markets who, because of their large numbers, have no influence on market price and therefore must either "take" (accept) the market price and buy or sell the product or leave the market.

Examples of uniformly competitive markets? Many economists believe agricultural commodities are sold in uniformly competitive markets. These include types of corn, soybeans, cotton, tobacco, wheat, lumber, fish, and rubber. These markets certainly have a large number of buyers and sellers. Are the goods uniform? At first it might not appear so as the category *fish* can include salmon to clams to octopuses. But inside the

---

[23] An example of a product that is both a good and service is delivery of a Domino's pizza, delivery being the service and the pizza being the good.

latter subcategories, for example, *salmon*, there is more uniformity: there are far fewer differences between Chinook, coho, and pink salmon than salmon and octopuses.

What about supermarket products? Barbeque sauce seems to be a pretty good candidate. There is certainly a large number of buyers and sellers. Uniformity? While there are white mayo-based sauces (for example, Gibson's, popular in Alabama) and yellow mustard-based sauces (for example, Maurice's, popular in South Carolina), they cater to smaller markets. Others are very spicy, still others pricey, but the vast majority are red, tomato-based, and appealing to most consumers because intense competition means smaller profit margins per unit, and making a sufficient total profit in a competitive market means moving high volume.

monopoly - a single firm or government supplying a good, service, or societal governance, for which there are no close substitutes.

price maker – an individual or firm with substantial market power because he/she/it has no or very few competitors.

market power – an individual or firm's ability to set the price of a product across a relatively wide range of potential prices because he/she/it has no or very few competitors.

To further drive the competition idea home, let's very briefly look at the opposite of competition: **monopoly**. As we saw in chapter 1, a monopoly is a single firm or government supplying a good, service, or societal governance, for which there are no close substitutes. In the case of a single non-governmental firm supplying a good or service, a monopoly is a market where the product has few or no close substitutes. Because a monopoly wields disproportionate power in setting its product's price, it is known as a **price maker**, or individual or firm with substantial **market power** because he/she/it has no or very few competitors. (Market power is an individual or firm's ability to set the price of a product across a relatively wide range of potential prices because he/she/it has no or very few competitors.) Water, electricity, trash-collection, and cable-television firms in most towns and cities are monopolies. While there are usually many buyers in these types of markets, again, in contrast to uniform competition, there is usually only one seller as opposed to many sellers and the products offered have no close substitutes.

Most markets in the real world are characterized by at least some competition. That is why it is most insightful to begin market analysis with the most competitive markets and work toward lesser and lesser degrees of competition.

4.2 The Individual Demand Schedule and Demand Curve

An **individual demand schedule** is a table that displays the quantity of a product that a consumer will purchase at different prices. Jay likes beef tacos and in TABLE 4-1 is his weekly demand schedule for them in the range of 0 to 6 dollars per taco. A graphical representation of a demand schedule is an **individual demand curve**, or a line or literal curve that displays the different quantities demanded of a product that a consumer will purchase at different prices. In FIGURE 4-1 is Jay's weekly demand curve for beef tacos based on his demand schedule. What is reflected by both the demand schedule and demand curve is the **law of demand**, which states that as a product rises in price, a lower quantity of that product will be purchased by consumers (with all other variables that influence demand besides price held constant).[24]

individual demand schedule – a table that displays the quantity of a product that a consumer will purchase at different prices.

individual demand curve – a line or literal curve that displays the different quantities demanded of a product that a consumer will purchase at different prices.

law of demand – as a product rises in price, a lower quantity of that product will be purchased by consumers (with all other variables that influence demand besides price held constant).

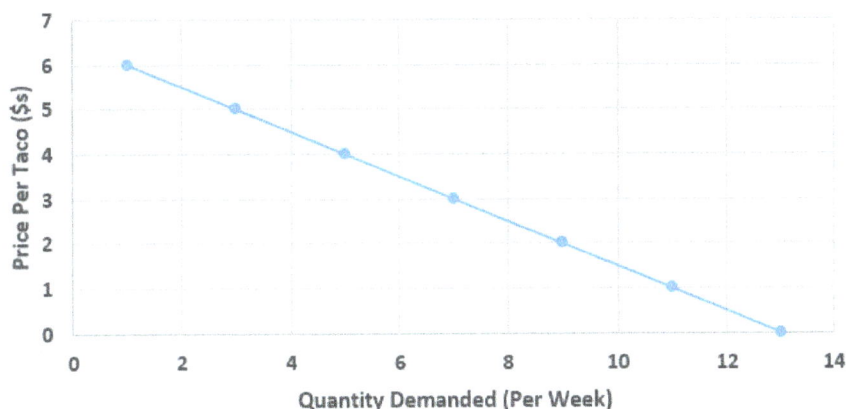

FIGURE 4-1: Jay's Weekly Demand Curve for Beef Tacos

TABLE 4-1 Jay's Weekly Demand Schedule for Beef Tacos	
Price Per Taco ($s)	Quantity Demanded (Per Week)
$0	13
$1	11
$2	9
$3	7
$4	5
$5	3
$6	1

As can be seen on Jay's demand curve for beef tacos, at a price of $0 per taco, when tacos are free, Jay accepts 13 tacos per week. When the price per taco rises to $1, Jay purchases 11 tacos per week. Finally, at a price of $6 per taco, Jay purchases only 1 taco per week.

---

[24] For these other demand variables besides price, see section 4.4. The six major ones—"shifters" of the demand curve—are income, the prices of related goods or services, tastes/preferences, expectations, the number of buyers in a market, and taxes/tariffs on the product.

4.3 The Market Demand Schedule and Demand Curve

market demand schedule – a table that displays the quantity of a product that two or more consumers will purchase at different prices.

The **market demand schedule** is a table that displays the quantity of a product that two or more consumers will purchase at different prices. Daisy likes beef tacos, but not as much as Jay. TABLE 4-2 displays the weekly demand schedules for beef tacos for Jay (copied from TABLE 4-1), Daisy, and the very small market demand composed of just Jay and Daisy combined. In other words, to derive the market quantities demanded in the fourth column of TABLE 4-2 [Market (Jay + Daisy)], Jay and Daisy's individual quantities demanded are horizontally summed to arrive at the total market quantity demanded at each price.

TABLE 4-2
Weekly Market Demand Schedule for Beef Tacos (Jay + Daisy)

Price	Quantity Demanded for Jay	Quantity Demanded for Daisy	Market (Jay + Daisy)
$0	13	8	13 + 8 = 21
$1	11	7	11 + 7 = 18
$2	9	6	9 + 6 = 15
$3	7	5	7 + 5 = 12
$4	5	4	5 + 4 = 9
$5	3	3	3 + 3 = 6
$6	1	2	1 + 2 = 3

From TABLE 4-2, one can see that when tacos are free ($0), Jay consumes 13, Daisy consumes 8, and thus the total market demand at a price of $0 is (13 + 8 =) 21. At a market price of $1 per taco, Jay purchases 11, Daisy purchases 7, and thus total market demand is (11 + 7 =) 18. Finally, at a price of $6 per taco, Jay purchases 1, Daisy purchases 2, and thus total market demand is 3.

market demand curve – a line or literal curve that displays the different quantities demanded of a product that consumers will purchase at different prices.

A graphical representation of the market demand schedule is the **market demand curve**, or a line or literal curve that displays the different quantities demanded of a product that consumers will purchase at different prices. In the rightmost graph of FIGURE 4-2 is the weekly market demand curve for beef tacos based on the market demand schedule in the fourth column of TABLE 4-2. The leftmost graph in FIGURE 4-2 is Jay's demand curve based on his demand-schedule data in the second column of TABLE 4-2 (copied from TABLE 4-1). The middle graph in FIGURE 4-2 is Daisy's weekly demand curve for beef tacos based on her demand-schedule data in the third column of TABLE 4-2. What FIGURE 4-2 reveals is that the weekly market demand curve for beef tacos is derived from the horizontal summation of both Jay and Daisy's weekly demand curves for beef tacos.

FIGURE 4-2:

Jay's Demand Curve   +   Daisy's Demand Curve   =   the Market Demand Curve

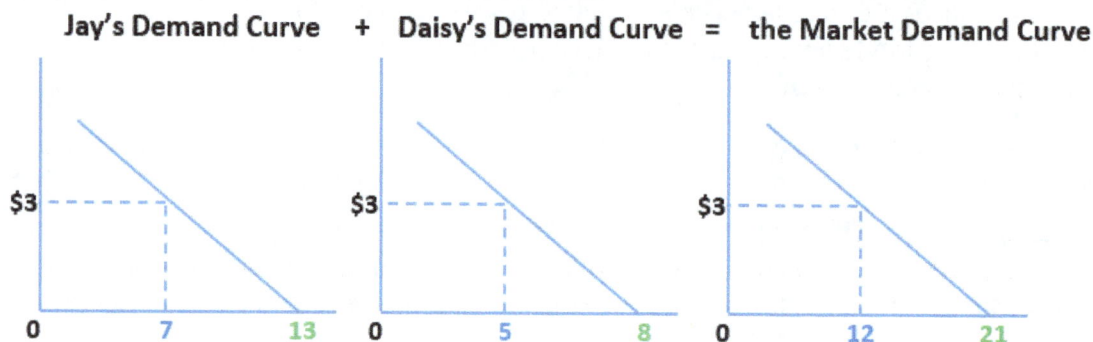

As can be seen in FIGURE 4-2 (based on TABLE 4-2), at a price of $3, Jay demands 7 tacos, Daisy demands 5 tacos, and therefore the market (composed of just Jay and Daisy) has a total quantity demanded of 12 tacos at price of $3. The quantity intercepts of Jay and Daisy's demand curves horizontally sum as well. At a price of $0, Jay demands 13 tacos, Daisy demands 8, so therefore, the total market quantity demanded at a price of $0 is (13 + 8 =) 21 tacos. What is reflected in both the market demand schedule and the market demand curve is the law of demand, which makes sense since, as we already learned, the law of demand influences individual demand schedules and curves, so it should only naturally affect market demands for goods and services as well.

4.4 Shifts in The Demand Curve: The Six Major Shifters

While viewing the demand-curve graphs in FIGURES 4-1 and 4-2, one could be excused for getting the mistaken idea that demand is always or almost always constant. This is known as the condition of **ceteris paribus** (Latin for "all other relevant factors or variables are

> **ceteris paribus** – a Latin phrase meaning, "all other relevant factors or variables are unchanged."

unchanged"). In fact, demand for goods and services changes all the time and there are many variables that can increase or decrease the demand for a particular product. And by the way, these are the "other variables constant" referred to in the law of demand: everything except price. Indeed, to graph a stationary demand curve, price is changing according to the law of demand but non-price variables are not. The six major variables that can shift the demand curve rightward or leftward (i.e., increase or decrease demand, respectively) are:

1. **Income.**
2. **Prices of related goods or services.**
3. **Tastes/Preferences.**
4. **Expectations.**
5. **Number of buyers in a market.**
6. **A tax on the good paid by buyers.**

1. Income. If a consumer's income rises, he or she has more money to spend on the goods and services he or she regularly purchases. Hence, it's not hard to imagine that if Jay's income rises, he will be purchasing more tacos—a good he strongly prefers—each week. The same goes for Daisy if her income rises. Not only will each of their demand curves shift rightward, the market demand curve will shift rightward. The reverse will occur for a fall in income. If Jay's income falls, so will his demand for tacos. Even if Daisy's income stays the same, the market demand for tacos will fall because Jay's demand (a component of market demand) fell.

What has been assumed so far is that tacos are what is known as a **normal good**. A normal good or service is a good or service for which demand rises if income rises. The opposite of a normal good is what is known as an **inferior good**. An inferior good or service is a good or service for which demand falls if income rises. While tacos are a normal good to most people, an example of an inferior good is ramen noodles. Many college students consume large quantities of

> **normal good** – a good or service for which demand rises if income rises.
>
> **inferior good** – a good or service for which demand falls if income rises.

ramen noodles because they are often very inexpensively priced. After many college students graduate and earn their first paycheck at their first job, they don't purchase ramen noodles again

84

for a long time. Subway transportation in New York City is another example. Low-income college students use it to get around the city while completing their college education. Students who have completed their education and begin working at a lucrative job begin using Uber or some other private mode of transportation more and avoid the subway more for both safety and convenience.

2. Prices of related goods and services. Another factor that exerts an influence on demand are the prices of related goods and services. Related goods and services come in two forms: **complements** and **substitutes**. Complements are goods or services for which an increase in the price of one good or service will decrease the demand for another good or service. Substitutes are goods or services for which an increase in the price of one good or service will increase the demand for another good or service.

Chicken tacos are usually considered a fairly close substitute for beef tacos. If the price of beef tacos increases relative to that of chicken tacos, other variables constant, the demand for chicken tacos will increase as consumers substitute chicken tacos for beef tacos. If the price of beef tacos falls relative to that of chicken tacos, other variables constant, the demand for chicken tacos will fall as consumers substitute beef tacos for chicken tacos.

What about complements? First, they are not to be confused with compliments ("You look really pretty today!"). The combination of peanut butter and jelly is a great example. When the price of peanut butter rises relative to that of jelly, the demand for jelly falls. Why? Because when the price of peanut butter rises, consumers purchase less peanut butter but also less jelly because the two goods are used together usually in constant ratios. Fewer purchases of peanut butter also mean few purchases of its consumption mate, jelly. The reverse occurs when the price of peanut butter falls relative to that of jelly. More peanut butter is purchased because its price has fallen and this in turn triggers an increase in demand for jelly.

Of course changes in the price of jelly can cause changes in the demand for peanut butter: an increase in the price of jelly can reduce the demand for peanut butter and a decrease in the price of jelly can increase the demand for peanut butter.

3. Tastes/Preferences. Tastes and preferences clearly play a role in creating demand for some goods and services. In the beef-tacos example we have been developing so far, Jay's stronger preference for tacos has placed his demand curve for tacos to the right of Daisy's. In other words, Jay's demand for tacos is higher than Daisy's across almost the entire range of prices except $5 (where they each demand 3 tacos) and $6 (where Daisy demands 2 tacos but Jay only demands 1). Of course demand patterns can change over time. As Jay gets older and he no longer has the ability to so facilely digest spicy beef, he may switch away from beef tacos to the healthier choices of fish or shrimp tacos or move away from Mexican food entirely. Daisy, during pregnancy with her first child, may increase her demand for tacos because of cravings. After her first child is born, Daisy may "go keto" and completely ditch tacos for steak or go vegetarian and ditch meat dishes altogether for health or lifestyle reasons.

Collective changes in tastes and preferences have played an obvious role in the decline of cigarette smoking in the U.S. since the 1960s. Some less obvious examples are wristwatches and sports bars. Many members of the Millennial (born 1981 to 1996) and Z (born 1997 to 2012) generations in the U.S. do not own wristwatches or patronize sports bars[25] and have applied for fewer driver licenses than previous generations. Many members of these generations see wristwatches and sports bars as redundant as they keep track of time and watch sports events on their phones. Many live close to their office jobs or work remotely in close-knit urban areas such that they frequently walk, bike, or use public buses or subways to get to work or shopping venues and thus have fewer reasons to own and drive an automobile.

Finally, a very vivid recent example involved the publication of a study[26, 27] linking the artificial sweetener erythritol to heart attacks and strokes. Suffice to say, this caused many consumers to immediately cease purchasing food and drinks containing erythritol.

4. Expectations. Like tastes and preferences, expectations are impossible to physically measure. Yet clearly, they influence demand. If a young apartment-dwelling couple has saved money, has good credit, but expects house prices and home-loan (mortgage) interest rates to significantly fall next year, the couple will rationally delay purchasing a house until next year. On the contrary, if the couple expects house prices and mortgage rates to markedly rise next year, the couple will rationally seek to purchase a house before next year. If either or both members of the married couple begin to fear loss of a job because of economic trouble at their employer or news of an approaching recession, the couple's plans to purchase a home may be completely abandoned indefinitely.

5. Number of buyers in a market. Unlike tastes or expectations, the number of consumers in a given area is much easier to directly measure. The daily demand for tap water in an average square block of Manhattan, New York (about 1.6 million population) will be many times that of Tifton, Georgia (about 17,000 population). The higher the number of consumers, the higher the market demand for goods and services. Even with our simple example of beef tacos, Jay plus Daisy's demand for tacos (the market demand curve) was higher in level than either Jay or Daisy's demand alone.

6. Taxes on products paid by buyers. A tax levied on a product paid by a buyer will reduce the demand for the product. Conversely, a reduction in tax on a product will increase the demand for the product. The market effects of taxes on products paid by buyers will be analyzed in much greater detail in chapter 6.

4.5 Demand Recap in Tables and Graphs

FIGURES 4-3 and 4-4 represent an increase (rightward shift) and decrease (leftward shift) in market demand, respectively. Any one of the six shifter variables changing by itself or changing

[25] Melore, Chris. "Sports Bars Going Extinct? 80% of Gen Z Watch Games on their Phone." StudyFinds. 24 June 2023. <https://studyfinds.org/sports-bars-gen-z-games-phone/>

[26] Witkowski, M., Nemet, I., Alamri, H. *et al.* The artificial sweetener erythritol and cardiovascular event risk. *Nat Med* 29, 710–718 (2023). https://doi.org/10.1038/s41591-023-02223-9

[27] "Artificial Sweetener Erythritol's Major Health Risks." healthessentials. Cleveland Clinic: 7 Mar. 2023. <https://health.clevelandclinic.org/erythritol/>

simultaneously with one or more of the other five shifter variables can produce these rightward or leftward shifts in demand. TABLE 4-3 displays all the shift variables and how they each increase demand for a good or service. In contrast, TABLE 4-4 displays all the shift variables and how they each decrease demand for a good or service. Again, notice that none of these shifters is the price variable. This is because changes in price allow us to create a demand schedule and with it, draw out the demand curve in price-quantity space on a graph while keeping all shift variables constant. Once drawn out, changes in the shift variables move the demand curve (demand) rightward or leftward.

FIGURE 4-3: An Increase in Demand

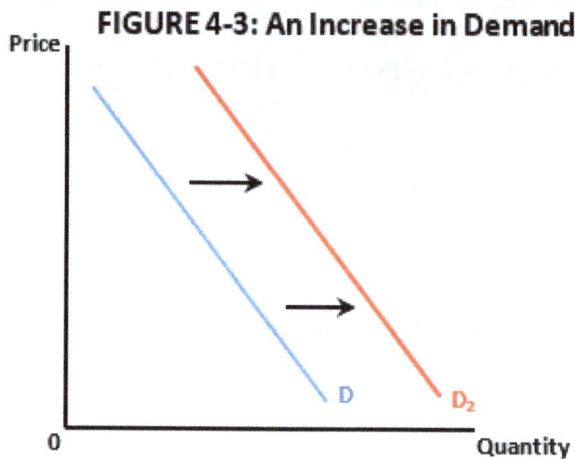

TABLE 4-3: How Changes in the Six Shifters Increase Demand as in FIGURE 4-3	
Factor	Demand rises when...
Income	income rises and the good is normal OR income falls and the good is inferior.
Prices of related goods or services	the price of a substitute increases OR the price of a complement falls.
Tastes/Preferences	tastes or preferences change in favor of the good or service.
Expectations	there are expectations that the product's price will rise in the future, hence the incentive is to buy the item today.
Number of buyers in a market	the number of buyers in a market increases.
Taxes on products paid by buyers	the tax rate falls.

FIGURE 4-4: A Decrease in Demand

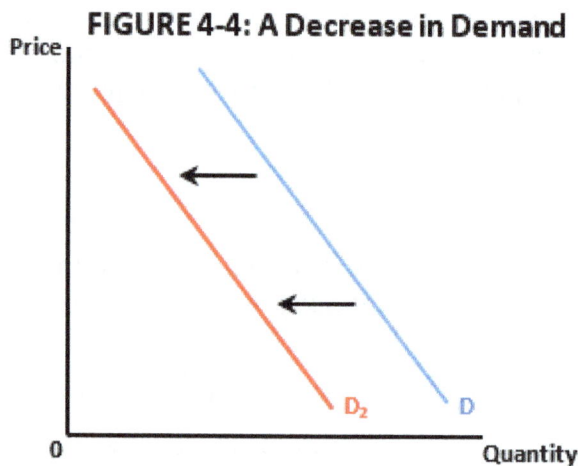

TABLE 4-4: How Changes in the Six Shifters Decrease Demand as in FIGURE 4-4	
Factor	Demand falls when...
Income	income falls and the good is normal OR income rises and the good is inferior.
Prices of related goods or services	the price of a substitute decreases OR the price of a complement rises.
Tastes/Preferences	tastes or preferences change against the good or service.
Expectations	there are expectations that the product's price will fall in the future, hence the incentive is to buy the item after its price falls in the future.
Number of buyers in a market	the number of buyers in a market declines.
Taxes on products paid by buyers	the tax rate rises.

4.6 The Individual Supply Schedule and Supply Curve

An **individual supply schedule** is a table that displays the different quantities supplied of a product by an individual or firm at different prices. Pierre's Taco Express produces beef tacos and TABLE 4-5 is its weekly supply schedule for beef tacos in the range of 0 to 6 dollars per taco. A graphical representation of an individual supply schedule is an **individual supply curve**, a line or literal curve that displays the different quantities supplied of a product by an individual or firm at different prices. In FIGURE 4-5 is Pierre's weekly supply curve for beef tacos based on his firm's supply schedule.

individual supply schedule – a table that displays the different quantities supplied of a product by an individual or firm at different prices.

individual supply curve – a line or literal curve that displays the different quantities supplied of a product by an individual or firm at different prices.

TABLE 4-5
Pierre's Weekly Supply Schedule for Beef Tacos

Price	Quantity Supplied
$0	0
$1	1
$2	2
$3	3
$4	4
$5	5
$6	6

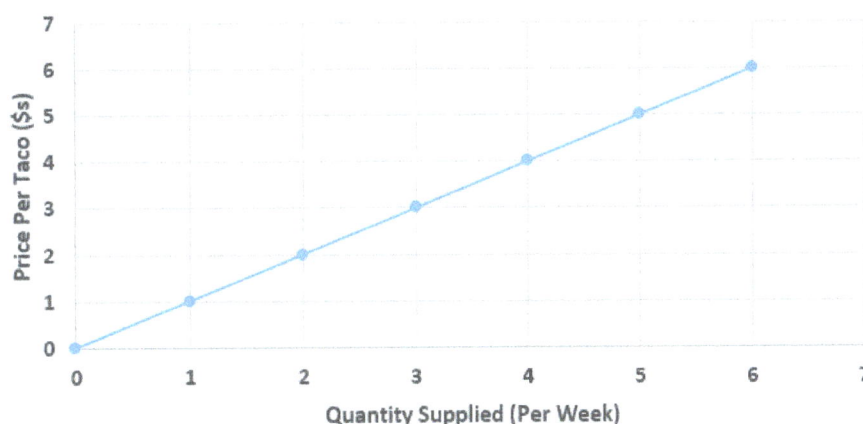

FIGURE 4-5: Pierre's Weekly Supply Curve for Beef Tacos

As can be seen in both Pierre's supply schedule and supply curve for beef tacos, at a price of $0 per taco, Pierre supplies 0 tacos per week. When the price per taco rises to $1, Pierre supplies 1 taco per week. At a price of $2 per taco, Pierre supplies 2 tacos per week. Finally, at a price of $6 per taco, Pierre supplies 6 tacos per week.

4.7 The Market Supply Schedule and Supply Curve

The **market supply schedule** is a table that displays the different quantities supplied of a product by two or more individuals or firms at different prices. Esmeralda (Pierre's former apprentice) has purchased a new taco truck and entered the industry as Pierre's newest competitor. TABLE 4-6 displays the weekly supply schedule

market supply schedule – a table that displays the different quantities supplied of a product by two or more individuals or firms at different prices.

for beef tacos for a very small market composed of just Pierre and Esmeralda. To derive the market quantities supplied in TABLE 4-6, Pierre and Esmeralda's individual quantities supplied are horizontally summed to arrive at the total market quantity supplied at each price.

TABLE 4-6 Weekly Market Supply Schedule for Beef Tacos (Pierre + Esmeralda)			
Price	Quantity Supplied by Pierre	Quantity Supplied by Esmeralda	Market (Pierre + Esmeralda)
$0	0	0	0 + 0 = 0
$1	1	0	1 + 0 = 1
$2	2	1	2 + 1 = 3
$3	3	3	3 + 3 = 6
$4	4	5	4 + 5 = 9
$5	5	7	5 + 7 = 12
$6	6	9	6 + 9 = 15

When tacos are $0 each, it should come as no surprise that 0 tacos are supplied to the market. At a price of $1 each, Pierre supplies 1 taco and Esmeralda supplies 0. At a price of $2, Pierre supplies 2 tacos and Esmeralda supplies 1. At $3, Pierre and Esmeralda each supply 3 tacos to the market. Finally, at a price of $6, Pierre supplies 6 tacos to the market while Esmeralda supplies 9.

market supply curve – a line or literal curve that displays the different quantities supplied of a product by two or more individuals or firms at different prices.

A graphical representation of the market supply schedule is the **market supply curve**, a line or literal curve that displays the different quantities supplied of a product by two or more individuals or firms at different prices. In the rightmost graph of FIGURE 4-6 is the weekly market supply curve for beef tacos based on the market supply schedule in the fourth column of TABLE 4-6. The leftmost graph in FIGURE 4-6 is Pierre's supply curve based on his supply-schedule data in the second column of TABLE 4-6 (copied from TABLE 4-5). The middle graph in FIGURE 4-6 is Esmeralda's weekly supply curve for beef tacos based on her supply-schedule data in the third column of TABLE 4-6. What FIGURE 4-6 reveals is that the weekly market supply curve for beef tacos is derived from the horizontal summation of both Pierre and Esmeralda's weekly supply curves for beef tacos.

FIGURE 4-6:

Pierre's Supply Curve + Esmeralda's Supply Curve = the Market Supply Curve

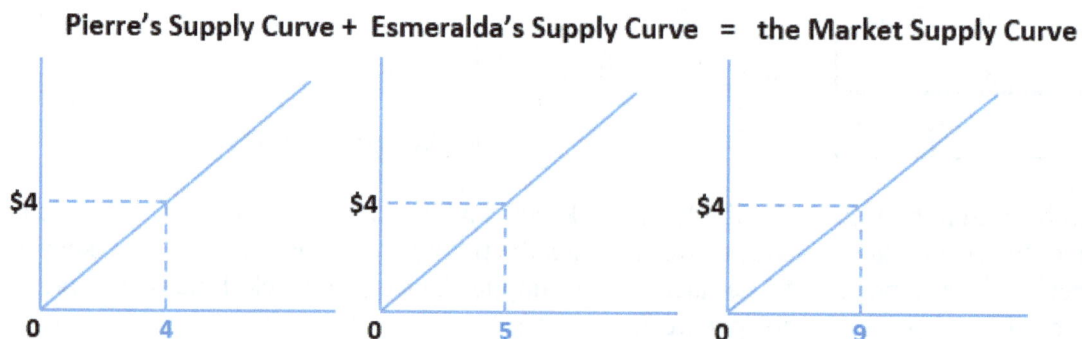

As can be seen in FIGURE 4-6, at a price of $4, Pierre supplies 4 tacos, Esmeralda supplies 5 tacos, and therefore the industry (composed of just Pierre and Esmeralda) has a total quantity supplied of 9 tacos at price of $4. The quantity intercepts of Pierre and Esmeralda's supply curves horizontally sum up as well. At a price of $0, Pierre supplies 0 tacos, Esmeralda supplies 0, so therefore, the total market quantity supplied at a price of $0 is (0 + 0 =) 0 tacos. It may be tempting at this point to think (as with demand) that what is reflected in both the market supply schedule and the market supply curve is a law of supply. However, as with individual market supply schedules and individual market supply curves, no such law exists.[28]

4.8 Shifts in The Supply Curve: The Six Major Shifters

Readers studying the supply-curve graphs above could, like demand, be excused for getting the mistaken impression that supplies of goods and services are always or almost always stationary. However, like demand, supplies for goods and services change all the time. While many different factors can increase or decrease the supply of a product, the five major ones are:

1. **Input prices.**
2. **Technology.**
3. **Expectations.**
4. **Number of suppliers.**
5. **Weather events.**
6. **Taxes on products paid by sellers.**

1. Input prices. A product **input** is simply anything used in the making of a product, i.e., a factor of production (labor, capital, or entrepreneurship), see chapter 2. If the price of an input used to manufacture a product rises, the supply of the product will fall. If the price of an input used to manufacture a product falls, the supply of the product will rise.

> **input** - anything used in the making of a product, i.e., a factor of production (labor, capital, or entrepreneurship).

If the price of beef, tortillas, or both rise, Pierre and Esmeralda will both supply fewer tacos to the market in the entire $0-to-$6 price range. In his individual supply schedule above, Pierre supplies 1 taco to the market for $1, 2 tacos to the market for $2, 3 tacos to the market for $3, …, all the way to 6 tacos to the market for $6. Let's say that just the price of beef rises and Pierre's response is to supply 0 tacos to the market for $1, only 1 taco to the market for $2, 2 tacos to the market for $3, …, all the way to only 5 tacos to the market for $6. What affects the supply schedule also affects the supply curve.

---

[28] Theoretically, a long-run supply curve can slope downward in the presence of "economies of scale." However, there is controversy over whether such economies really exist.

FIGURE 4-7: A Reduction in the Supply of Tacos Because of an Increase in the Price of Beef

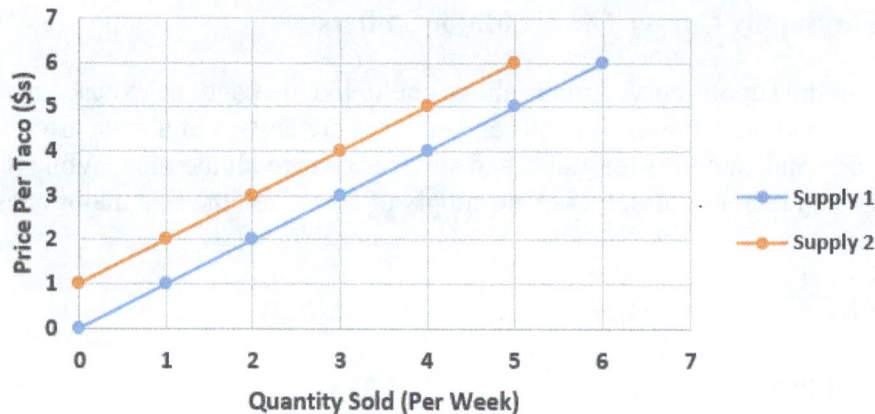

FIGURE 4-7 displays the old and new individual supply curves for Pierre. Pierre's supply curve before the rise in the price of beef was Supply 1 (reflecting his old supply schedule). The rise in the price of beef caused Pierre's individual supply curve to shift leftward and become Supply 2. Had the price of beef fallen, the opposite would have occurred: supply would have increased (the supply curve would have shifted rightward).

Another example is the production of aircraft and aluminum. Part of why aircraft are so expensive is the large quantity of aluminum and other expensive lightweight components that make up such a high proportion of aircraft airframes. If the prices of aluminum and other lightweight components heavily used in aircraft manufacturing increase, the supply of aircraft will, other variables constant, reasonably be expected to fall. If, on the other hand, the prices of aircraft components fall, the supply of aircraft will, other variables constant, reasonably be expected to rise.

2. Technology. Technological development increases the supply of goods and services. Let's say that Pierre purchases a new range which cooks beef much more evenly and quickly than his previous range such that he doubles his previous supply of tacos at each price. In other words, he now supplies 2 tacos for $1 (instead of just 1 taco), 4 tacos for $2 (instead of 2 tacos), etc. Obviously, the new technology will shift Pierre's supply curve to the right.

Where the real-world effects of this process have been the most obvious is of course on computers and consumer electronics. In 1976, a Sony Betamax video cassette player could be purchased for a retail price of approximately $1,200. Today, a consumer can purchase a far superior Sony DVD player for less than $50. The very first high-definition (HD) televisions were over $10,000 in price. Today, a consumer can purchase a superior 85-inch Ultra-High-Definition (UHD, twice the resolution of HD) television for less than $850. Computers and cell phones get better and cheaper every year with examples too numerous to list.

Is there such a thing as reverse technology? In other words, an "innovation" that puts technological knowledge in reverse and reduces product supplies? The closest two phenomena are wars and natural disasters. These can destroy infrastructure and capital in the short run, but recovery can be quick as it is very difficult to eradicate technological knowledge once it is acquired. Europe and Japan made quick recoveries after the end of World War II because capital and infrastructure was destroyed but technological knowledge was not forgotten.

3. Expectations. Like demand, expectations can work in favor of or against the supply of a product. Let's say that a vegan (someone who is opposed to dairy products) wins the presidency of Dessertica with the promise that right after her inauguration in two months' time she will ban ice cream. This would cause ice cream makers in Dessertica today to start reducing the supply of their product to the market, selling off capital before it loses more value and making plans to exit a soon-to-be-dead industry.

4. Number of suppliers. This is similar to the number of consumers on the demand side. When the number of suppliers in an industry increases, so does market supply and thus the market-supply curve shifts rightward. As we saw with Pierre and Esmeralda, when just Pierre occupied the supply side of the market, the overall market supply of beef tacos was lower. When Esmeralda joined the market, the market supply increased and the supply curve shifted rightward. If a third seller were to join the market in addition to Pierre and Esmeralda, the supply curve will shift further rightward. If any of the suppliers leaves the market, supply will decline and the market supply curve will shift leftward.

5. Weather events. This factor affects everything from crops to baseball games. If there is a sudden and unanticipated hard freeze (temperature at or below 28 degrees Fahrenheit for an extended duration) in north Florida and a large amount of the orange crop is ruined, the supply of oranges to the market will fall. If what appears to be dangerous thunderstorms move west from Long Island Sound into The Bronx, New York City, and hang around for long enough, the New York Yankees will not play a baseball game to avoid jeopardizing the safety of their fans or players. Fans who paid for tickets will not get their game supplied that day and will have to accept a rain check for a rescheduled or comparable game.

6. Taxes on products paid by sellers. A tax levied on a product paid by a seller will reduce the supply of the product. Conversely, a reduction in tax on a product will increase the supply of the product. The market effects of taxes on products paid by sellers will be analyzed in much greater detail in chapter 6.

4.9 Supply Recap in Tables and Graphs

FIGURES 4-8 and 4-9 represent an increase and decrease in market supply, respectively. TABLE 4-7 sums up the circumstance under which each of the six shifter factors increases supply while TABLE 4-8 sums up the circumstance under which each of the six shifter factors decreases supply.

FIGURE 4-8: An Increase in Supply

Price

Quantity

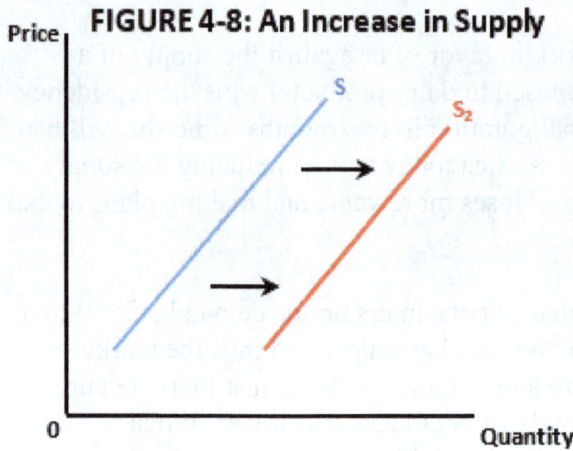

TABLE 4-7: How Changes in the Six Shifters Increase Supply as in FIGURE 4-8	
Factor	Supply rises when…
Input prices	input prices fall.
Technology	new technology is applied to production processes.
Expectations	there are expectations that the product's price will rise in the future.
Number of suppliers	the number of suppliers in a market increases.
Weather	weather conditions favor the purchase and consumption of the product.
Taxes on products paid by sellers	the tax rate falls.

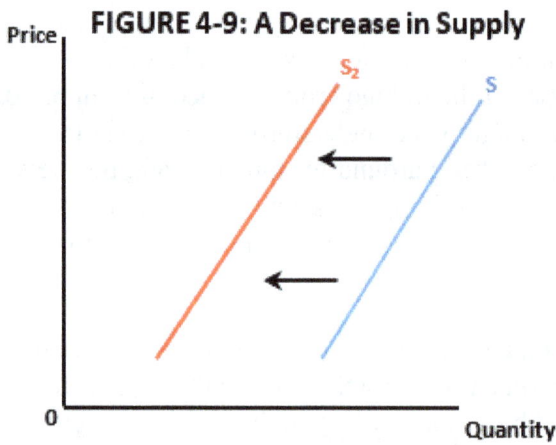

FIGURE 4-9: A Decrease in Supply

Price

Quantity

TABLE 4-8: How Changes in the Six Shifters Decrease Supply as in FIGURE 4-9	
Factor	Supply falls when…
Input prices	input prices rise.
Technology	there is a war or natural disaster that reduces production possibilities, at least in the short run.
Expectations	there are expectations that the product's price will fall in the future.
Number of suppliers	the number of suppliers in a market decreases.
Weather	weather conditions are unfavorable to the purchase and consumption of the product.
Taxes on products paid by sellers	the tax rate rises.

4.10 Equilibrium and Two Departures Therefrom

We might reasonably dispute whether it is the upper or the under blade of a pair of scissors that cuts a piece of paper, as whether value is governed by utility [demand] or cost of production [supply]—Alfred Marshall, *Principles of Economics*, 8th edition, London: Macmillan, 1920.

In the nineteenth century, economists argued among themselves about whether it was supply or demand that determined the prices of goods and services. Alfred Marshall settled the matter once and for all by pointing out that the argument was as silly as arguing whether it was the top or bottom blade of a pair of scissors that was responsible for cutting a piece of paper. Both demand and supply are involved in determining the price of a good or service. That insight can be seen in FIGURE 4-10, where we finally bring both demand and supply together in a full market.

FIGURE 4-10: The Weekly Market for Beef Tacos

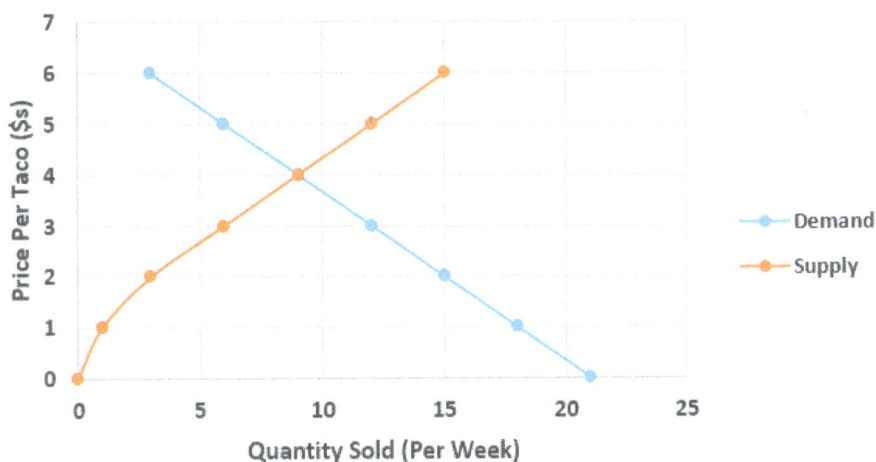

Where quantity demanded and quantity supplied are equal in a market is **equilibrium**, which outside of economics means a point at which opposing forces reach a balance. At the point of balance in a market lies the **equilibrium price** (the price in a market where quantity demanded and quantity supplied are equal) and **equilibrium quantity** (the quantity that will be sold in a market at its equilibrium price). For our small market for beef tacos, market equilibrium is at the equilibrium price of $4 per taco and the equilibrium quantity of 9 tacos per week. This equilibrium will prevail until:

> 1. the market's price temporarily or permanently moves above or below its equilibrium level OR

> 2. demand, supply, or both shift, and equilibrium then moves to another equilibrium price and equilibrium quantity.

Let's look at scenario 1 first.

4.10a Market Disequilibrium

Market disequilibrium comes in mainly two forms: a market price that is either above or below equilibrium temporarily or permanently.

1. A **shortage (excess demand)** is the difference between quantity demanded and quantity supplied in a market because the market price is below the equilibrium price. This is a source of great frustration with which you may have direct experience. You go to the store looking for your usual brand of paper towels and the shelf is bare. This was a common experience during the COVID-19 panic from 2020-2022, especially with items such as toilet paper, antiseptic wipes, alcohol, and even dog food, the latter making no sense other than being a pure panic purchase. Consumers working

equilibrium – where quantity demanded and quantity supplied are equal in a market. Graphically, this point is where the demand and supply curves intersect at a certain (equilibrium) price and (equilibrium) quantity.

equilibrium price – the price in a market where quantity demanded and quantity supplied are equal.

equilibrium quantity - the quantity that will be sold in a market at its equilibrium price.

shortage (excess demand) – the difference between quantity demanded and quantity supplied in a market because the market price is below the equilibrium price.

94

from home would use more toilet paper from their personal supply at home, but working remotely had nothing to do with needing more dog food.

In terms of our beef-tacos example in FIGURE 4-11, market price is at $3 rather than the equilibrium price of $4.

FIGURE 4-11: A Price Ceiling in the Weekly Market for Beef Tacos

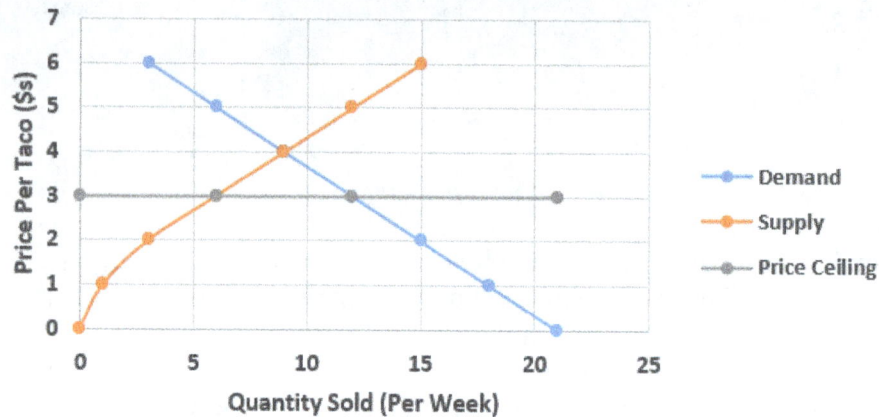

At $3, suppliers will bring 6 tacos to the market, but buyers will demand 12, twice as much. This creates a shortage or excess demand of 6 tacos per week. What does this situation incentivize? First, suppliers who start raising prices and bringing more tacos to the market are rewarded with earning another dollar per taco and charging the equilibrium price ($4). Another 3 tacos are brought to the market by suppliers. On the demand side of the market, 3 buyers who didn't especially value tacos, consumers who wanted them at $3 but not the market equilibrium price of $4, decide to leave the market. That leaves us with 9 buyers of tacos—demanders who really like tacos—being prioritized in getting the product while the indifferent exit. This is market efficiency and **market clearing**, or equilibrium price and equilibrium quantity prevailing in a market such that there is neither the presence of a market surplus nor shortage. Consumers who most value tacos get them and those who do not value them as much are incentivized to leave the market. There is no frustration, no lines of consumers waiting for a rationed product as under central planning, and no empty shelves.

market clearing – equilibrium price and equilibrium quantity prevailing in a market such that there is neither the presence of a market surplus nor shortage.

surplus (excess supply) – the difference between quantity supplied and quantity demanded in a market because the market price is above the equilibrium price.

2. A **surplus (excess supply)** is the difference between quantity supplied and quantity demanded in a market because the market price is above the equilibrium price. This is a source of frustration as well, but fewer people have direct experience with it. Many who do own small home-based businesses that sell items on eBay or Etsy. There were brisk sales after they first established their stores, but then sales fell and inventory began to pile up at home. After they dropped prices, sales rose again until all of the excess inventory was sold. That experience was a clue that their price could have been above market equilibrium for their product and they were losing sales to other suppliers.

Getting back to our beef-tacos example in FIGURE 4-12, market price is at $5 rather than the equilibrium price of $4.

FIGURE 4-12: A Price Floor in the Weekly Market for Beef Tacos

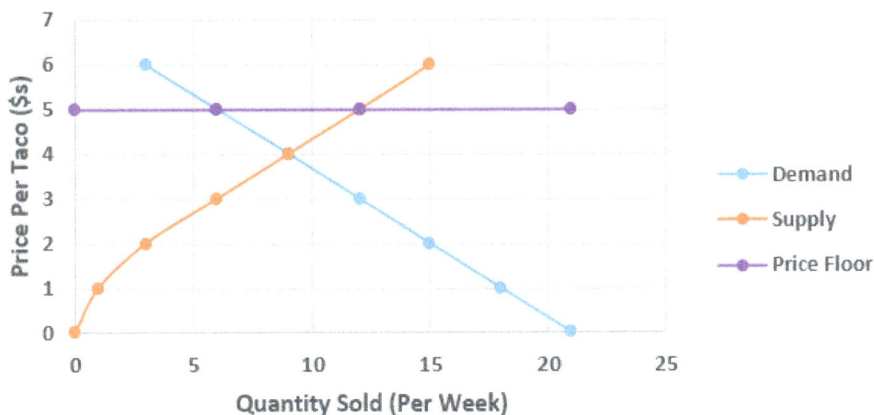

At $5 per taco, consumers only purchase 6 tacos per week while suppliers bring 12 tacos to the market, twice as many tacos as the number actually sold. This creates a surplus or excess supply of 6 tacos per week. What does this situation incentivize? First, suppliers who start reducing price and bringing fewer tacos to market, despite earning $1 less per taco, see more of their inventory go out the door in return for charging the equilibrium price. Another 3 tacos are sold instead of taking up space in store inventory. On the demand side of the market, 3 buyers who value tacos but couldn't afford the above-equilibrium price of $5 each now get the tacos they want at $4 each and don't have to consume the substitute good they find inferior (say, high-sodium, instant-ramen noodles). This is market efficiency and market clearing: with a return to market equilibrium ($4 per taco with 9 tacos demanded per week), we have 9 demanders who really like tacos getting their tacos, and their hunger satiated while tacos no longer sit unsold in inventory only to be later discarded as waste.[29]

---

[29] Actually, the discarding of unspoiled food is becoming less common as there are more private programs every year that collect unsold and unspoiled food items from grocery stores and restaurants and distribute them to low-income households and the homeless. Panera Bread operates its own such program.

Adam Smith (1723-1790) – Scottish philosopher and early economist who, drawing on prior oral teachings, produced one of the first comprehensive, formal discussions of economic theory in *An Inquiry into the Nature and Causes of the Wealth of Nations* (1776). He also is credited with creating the theory of absolute advantage.

invisible hand – a metaphor popularized by Scottish economist Adam Smith for describing how markets can direct the self-interest of different parties toward advancing the good of society.

Adam Smith (1723-1790)

Indeed, the tendencies of markets to revert to equilibrium once disturbed from it is an example of what famous Scottish economist **Adam Smith** (1723-1790) referred to as an "**invisible hand**" (a metaphor popularized by Scottish economist Adam Smith for describing how markets can direct the self-interest of different parties toward advancing the good of society). Market tendencies toward equilibrium are also an example of this book's Economics Principle Number 4: Incentives affect behavior (see chapter 1) at work.

In this section we analyzed two cases of temporary market disequilibrium. The permanent cases will be explored in chapter 6 (market intervention). Now let's move on to exploring how a shift in demand, supply, or both create a new equilibrium and thus a new equilibrium price and new equilibrium quantity in a market.

CASE STUDY: the Diamond-Water Paradox

diamond-water paradox – the mystery of the price of diamonds being many times that of water, despite the fact that water is essential for survival but diamonds are not.

One conundrum that economists struggled with in the early days of the economics discipline was the **diamond-water paradox**, the mystery of the price of diamonds being many times that of water, despite the fact that water is essential for survival but diamonds are not. Without water you could not live for more than a few days. It is essential to survival, but in most developed economies during normal times it is relatively cheap. In contrast, diamonds are completely inessential to survival, but they are very expensive and certainly so compared to water. Why are consumers willing to pay so much more for a diamond than a glass of water?

The key, as usual, is not in the total picture but in the marginal one (see economics principle number 3 in chapter 1, *Rational economic decisions are made at the margin*). Water certainly brings more total benefit than diamonds. If you run out of water, then diamonds become completely irrelevant. The key to the paradox lies at the margin. Right now, what is the benefit of a glass of water to you? Likely not very high. Water, while economically scarce (finite in supply) is still relatively plentiful and you can walk to a nearby tap to get more. Diamonds are a different story because they are much more naturally scarce than water and thus have a far higher *marginal benefit* than water either as jewelry or a store of value.

Thus, Alfred Marshall (see his statement at the beginning of section 4.10) was correct: Any price is determined by the forces of both supply and demand. Water has a relatively high demand but also an abundant supply. Diamonds have a relatively high demand but are supplied by nature at a relatively low level. *Ergo* (therefore), one high-quality diamond typically carries a much higher price than one gallon of water.

4.10b Shifting to a New Equilibrium

Obviously, looking at a graph of a full market, with both supply and demand curves present (e.g., FIGURE 4-12), in the presence of a shift in curves, a new equilibrium can appear anywhere in price-quantity space: above, below, to the right, to the left, and of course, northeast, southwest, etc. Exactly where the new equilibrium appears after a shift in demand, supply, or both depends on the market factors (shifters) that changed. Recall that for demand these are: income, prices of related goods and services, tastes/preferences, expectations, and the number of buyers in a market. Recall that for supply these are: input prices, technology, expectations, the number of suppliers, and weather events. When one or more of these demand or supply variables changes, the effects are felt through demand, supply, or both, and this causes demand, supply, or both to shift, which creates a new market equilibrium with a new equilibrium price and equilibrium quantity.

4.10b1 Single Shifts

This section will consider the effects of a single shift in either demand or supply.

1. An Increase in Demand.

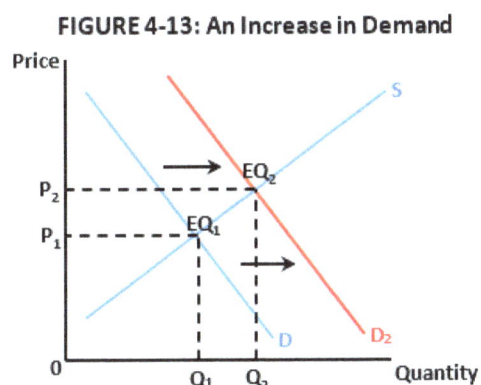

FIGURE 4-13: An Increase in Demand

In FIGURE 4-13, demand increases from D to D_2 while supply stays unchanged. Quantity increases from Q_1 to Q_2 while price increases from P_1 to P_2. Market equilibrium shifts from equilibrium one (EQ_1) at coordinate point (Q_1, P_1) to equilibrium two (EQ_2) at point (Q_2, P_2).

2. An Increase in Supply.

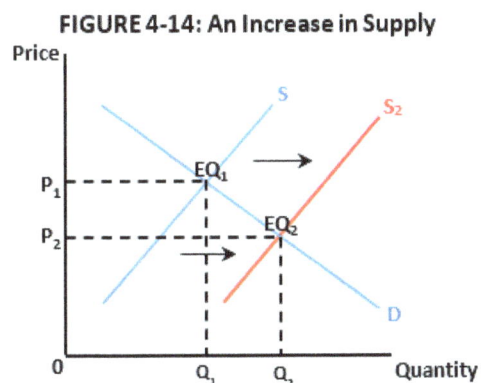

FIGURE 4-14: An Increase in Supply

In FIGURE 4-14, supply increases from S to S_2 while demand remains unchanged. Quantity increases from Q_1 to Q_2 while price decreases from P_1 to P_2. Market equilibrium shifts from equilibrium one (EQ_1) at point (Q_1, P_1) to equilibrium two (EQ_2) at (Q_2, P_2).

3. A Decrease in Demand.

FIGURE 4-15: A Decrease in Demand

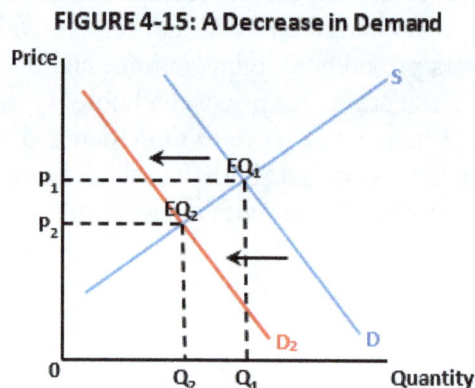

In FIGURE 4-15, demand decreases from D to D_2 while supply remains unchanged. Quantity decreases from Q_1 to Q_2 while price decreases from P_1 to P_2. Market equilibrium shifts from equilibrium one (EQ_1) at (Q_1, P_1) to equilibrium two (EQ_2) at (Q_2, P_2).

4. Reader Exercise: A Decrease in Supply.

FIGURE 4-16: A Decrease in Supply

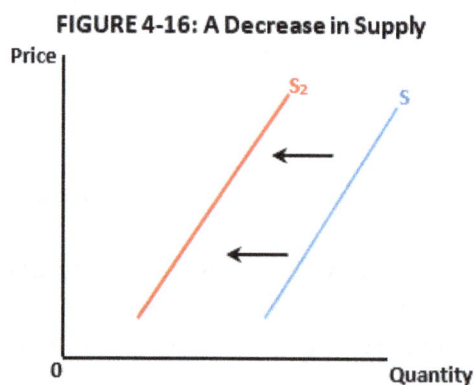

FIGURE 4-16 is an incomplete illustration of a market experiencing a decrease in supply. As a reader exercise, copy the graph axes and supply shift to a blank piece of paper, then draw in the non-shifting demand curve. Illustrate the changes in equilibrium quantity and price as market equilibrium shifts from one position to another.

4.10b2 Dual Shifts

This section will consider the effects of a single shift in both demand and supply. First, it will analyze the effects of both shifting in the same direction (an increase in both, then a decrease in both). Then it will analyze the effects of each shifting in the opposite direction of the other at different magnitudes.

1. An Increase in Both Demand and Supply (Shift in Demand > Shift in Supply).

FIGURE 4-17: An Increase in Both Demand and Supply
(Rightward Shift in Demand > Rightward Shift in Supply)

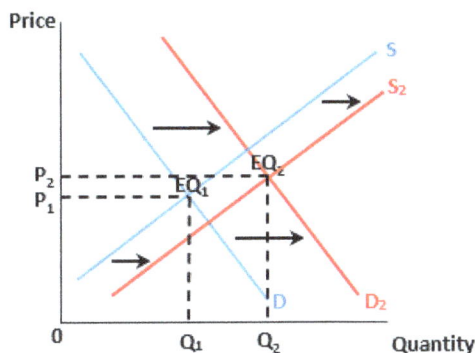

In FIGURE 4-17, demand increases from D to D_2 while supply increases from S to S_2. Quantity increases by a relatively large amount from Q_1 to Q_2 while price increases by a relatively small amount from P_1 to P_2. Market equilibrium shifts northeasterly from equilibrium one (EQ_1) at (Q_1, P_1) to equilibrium two (EQ_2) at (Q_2, P_2).

2. A Decrease in Both Demand and Supply (Shift in Demand < Shift in Supply).

FIGURE 4-18: A Decrease in Both Demand and Supply
(Leftward Shift in Demand < Leftward Shift in Supply)

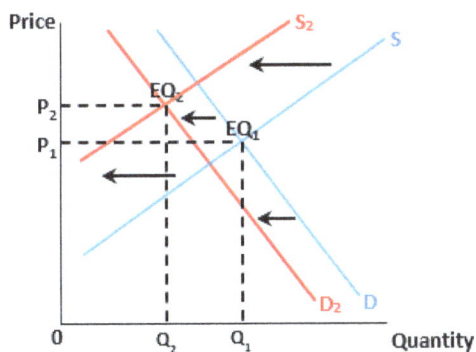

In FIGURE 4-18, demand decreases from D to D_2 while supply decreases from S to S_2. Quantity decreases by a relatively large amount from Q_1 to Q_2 while price increases by a relatively small amount from P_1 to P_2. Market equilibrium shifts northwesterly from equilibrium one (EQ_1) at (Q_1, P_1) to equilibrium two (EQ_2) at (Q_2, P_2).

3. An Increase in Demand and Decrease in Supply (Shift in Demand > Shift in Supply).

FIGURE 4-19: An Increase in Demand and Decrease in Supply
(Rightward Shift in Demand > Leftward Shift in Supply)

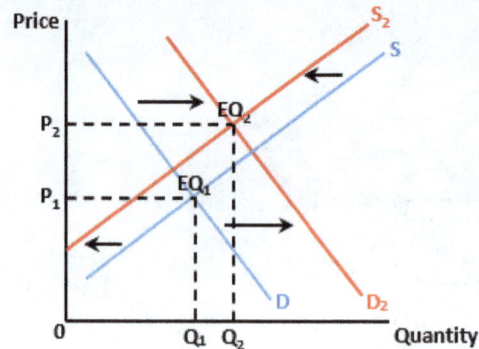

In FIGURE 4-19, demand increases from D to D_2 while supply decreases from S to S_2. Quantity increases by a relatively small amount from Q_1 to Q_2 while price increases by a relatively large amount from P_1 to P_2. Market equilibrium shifts steeply and northeasterly from equilibrium one (EQ_1) at (Q_1, P_1) to equilibrium two (EQ_2) at (Q_2, P_2).

4. Reader Exercise: A Decrease in Demand and Increase in Supply (Shift in Demand < Shift in Supply).

FIGURE 4-20: A Decrease in Demand and Increase in Supply
(Leftward Shift in Demand < Rightward Shift in Supply)

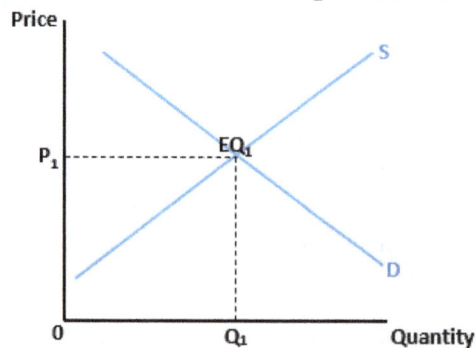

FIGURE 4-20 is an incomplete illustration of a market experiencing a decrease in demand and increase in supply with the decrease in demand being of lesser relative magnitude than the increase in supply. As a reader exercise, copy the graph axes and initial market equilibrium to a blank piece of paper, then draw in the shifting demand and supply curves. Illustrate the changes in quantity and price as market equilibrium shifts from one position to another. Note the compass direction of change (e.g., southeasterly, etc.) from one equilibrium to another.

4.10b3 Summary Table

TABLE 4-9: Effects on Price, Quantity, and Equilibrium Given a Shift in Demand, Supply, or Both

Demand	Supply	Effects on Price and Quantity	Equilibrium Moves
Increase	No change	↑Q, ↑P	Northeasterly (↗)
No change	Increase	↑Q, ↓P	Southeasterly (↘)
Decrease	No change	↓Q, ↓P	Southwesterly (↙)
No change	Decrease	↓Q, ↑P	Northwesterly (↖)
Increase	Increase	↑Q, ΔP depends on the size of the shifts relative to each other	Easterly (→), Northeasterly (↗), or Southeasterly (↘) (depending on the relative size of each shift)
Decrease	Decrease	↓Q, ΔP depends on the size of the shifts relative to each other	Westerly (←), Northwesterly (↖), or Southwesterly (↙) (depending on the relative size of each shift)
Increase	Decrease	↑P, ΔQ depends on the size of the shifts relative to each other	Northerly (↑), Northeasterly (↗), or Northwesterly (↖) (depending on the relative size of each shift)
Decrease	Increase	↓P, ΔQ depends on the size of the shifts relative to each other	Southerly (↓), Southeasterly (↘), or Southwesterly (↙) (depending on the relative size of each shift)

4.11 Market Analysis: A Methodology

Of course more shifts can occur in a market than two, and TABLE 4-9 does not imply otherwise. For simplicity, we have limited both the number of shifts and time period of analysis. For market analysis of real-world events, here is a helpful three-step method:

1. First determine and note which factors in the market have changed: demand, supply, or both?
2. Using a blank piece of paper, draw out the relative shifts in demand, supply, or both and their estimated magnitudes.
3. Do real-world data reflect the equilibrium changes drawn out in step 2? What has happened to market prices? Do they appear to have risen or fallen? What, to the extent that you can determine, has happened to quantities? Do they appear to have risen or fallen?

Now let's work through an example of a dual shift. We won't waste space on an example of a single shift as you'll see one in the first shift of the dual-shift example.

4.11a Example of a Dual Shift

Resuming where we left off in FIGURE 4-12, where we finally assembled a complete market, let's add one last round to our beef-taco example. Let's say that Jay and Daisy both receive wage increases at their jobs. Simultaneously, Pierre and Esmeralda both receive new and more efficient ranges that warm tortillas and cook beef faster than their old ranges. Let's bring in our three-step method to examine all the effects these two developments will have on the market:

1. Which factors in the market changed? Answer: First, the incomes of Jay and Daisy. Income is a demand factor and an increase in income will increase demand (shift the demand curve rightward). Second, technology developed such that Pierre and Esmeralda are now using more productive ranges. Technology is a supply factor, and better technology increases supply (shifts the supply curve rightward).

2. Using a blank piece of paper, draw out the relative shifts in demand, supply, or both and their estimated magnitudes. Answer: From our answers to question 1 above, demand has shifted rightward and so has supply as in FIGURE 4-21.

FIGURE 4-21: An Increase in Demand and Increase in Supply of Beef Tacos

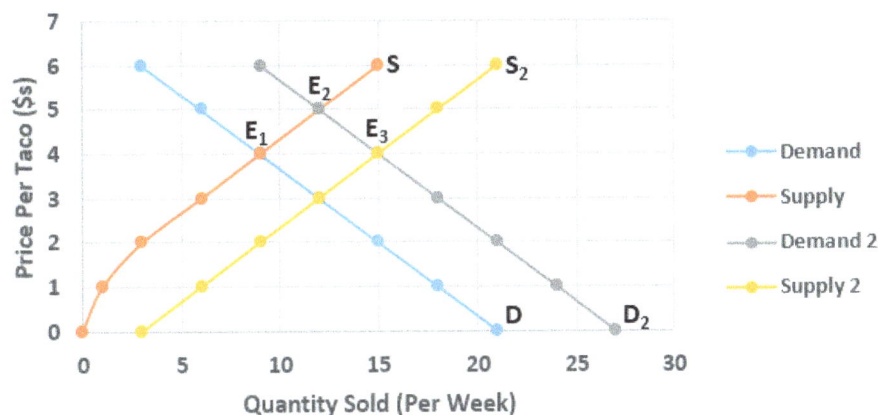

Recall that the initial market equilibrium first introduced in FIGURE 4-12 was 9 tacos selling at $4 each. That same equilibrium is replicated in FIGURE 4-21 at the intersection of Demand (D) and Supply (S) as equilibrium point E_1 (9, $4). Next, Jay and Daisy see their incomes increase. They can now buy more tacos across the $0-to-$6 range of prices, which means that demand increases (shifts rightward) to Demand 2 (D_2). This first shift in demand is a good example of a single shift to a new market equilibrium at the intersection of Demand 2 (D_2) and Supply (S) or equilibrium point E_2 (12, $5).

But as it turns out, another factor changes. Pierre and Esmeralda are using more advanced cooking technology. They can now bring more tacos to market across the entire $0 to $6 range of prices under consideration, which means that supply increases to Supply 2 (S_2). The dual shift is now complete with our market equilibrium having moved again to its final position at the intersection of Demand 2 (D_2) and Supply 2 (S_2) or the equilibrium point E_3 (15, $4).

By now you've probably noticed that, after the dual shift, we've ended up at the same market price we began with, $4. However, while price hasn't changed from equilibria E_1 (9, $4) to E_3 (15, $4), 6 more tacos (15 − 9 = 6) are being sold each week.

3. Do real-world data reflect the equilibrium changes drawn out in step 2? What has happened to market prices? Do they appear to have risen or fallen? What, to the extent that you can determine, has happened to quantities? Do they appear to have risen or fallen? Answer: These questions can only be answered by data provided by real-world markets. If the price of beef tacos has remained about the same and businesses are reporting more sales, then what we have assumed in drawing something that looks like FIGURE 4-21 on a piece of scrap paper could be a correct assessment of market changes. If real-world prices, quantities, or both have moved in the opposite direction from what we drew in FIGURE 4-21, then the market factors we thought changed did not in fact change or some other factors that we did not account for changed. We then have to gather more information and re-draw our graph. We have to pursue a process resembling the scientific method we studied in chapter 2: Form a hypothesis, seek real-world data, and with the real-world data either confirm the hypothesis or reject it and start over.

Finally: the exact proportional shifts that we saw in this example were not found in any case that we considered in any of our graphical dual-shift examples (FIGURES 4-17 to 4-19) but were left as a possibility in TABLE 4-9. Why? Because they are unlikely in any real-world scenario. However, the reader now knows that with such improbable shifts, price stays constant and market quantity increases or decreases depending on the specific shifts that take place.

ECONOMICS IN ACTION: Defend Price Gouging? This Book Won't

These days it seems almost obligatory for market-oriented economics textbooks to include a chapter section or application rationalizing **price gouging**, or the charging of abnormally high prices. A hurricane heads toward a coastal town. Residents evacuate, then return after the storm is gone only to discover that a gallon jug of water that sold for $1.50 before the hurricane struck is now selling for $7.50, five times the pre-hurricane price. The media scream bloody murder and outrage about "gouging" and "exploitation." Politicians, usually state attorneys general, do the same and vow to prosecute gougers for taking advantage of the tragedy. With demand high and inventories temporarily very low, how could prices not be way above their usual level?

> **price gouging** – the charging of abnormally high prices.

Of course the high prices make sense, and if the market is left alone for a few days, there will be a quick recovery as the high prices will attract a re-supply of water from multiple channels. This is exactly how prices function as a signaling mechanism in the real world. Making it a crime to sell water above the pre-hurricane level not only creates a large and unnecessary shortage where those who need the water the most don't get it, it prolongs the economic recovery. Persistent empty shelves are a sign of markets not being allowed to work, whether they are in Cuba or Florida.

It's not that free-market literature is incorrect on any of these aforementioned arguments. Gasoline selling for $7 a gallon in most areas of the U.S. except California would be a surprising anomaly, but a brief one that would guarantee that those still buying it need it the most. And no, it certainly would not be going only to the rich. Gasoline priced at $7 per gallon would be well worth it for someone in a medical emergency (where there are no ambulances or Ubers readily available) who only needed 1 or 2 gallons to take a friend or relative to the hospital quickly. And at that price the market would ensure that he or she got it without wasting precious time in a long line.

In terms of building materials, large chains such as Home Depot and Lowe's that can refresh their inventory faster can and do keep their prices the same as they were before a natural disaster occurs and thus reap good publicity for doing so that makes up for the losses incurred. The other painfully obvious point is, if you don't want to pay high prices after a disaster strikes, you make it a habit of keeping extra gasoline, food, water, flashlights, batteries, matches, candles, etc., on hand in case a power outage, tornado, earthquake, or hurricane strikes. And after a disaster occurs, don't be surprised if someone offers to buy some of your excess inventory at an above-market price. It makes sense.

Explaining the factors behind high prices is not excusing them. No one, including serious economists, likes paying higher prices regardless of the circumstances.

The problem is that popular media and politicians attack "gouging" in individual markets but rarely in perverse or unique *market structures*. Tablets of Tylenol sell for around 25 cents each in most drug stores. Yet hospitals have been known to charge Medicaid, Medicare, and private insurance $100 to $250 per tablet. Who pays this bill? We all do directly or indirectly, and yet the silence from popular media and politicians is deafening, never mind they are in a good position to help change such practices. (The U.S. medical cartel will be discussed in much more detail in chapter 11.)

Further: is a $3,000-front-row ticket to a Taylor Swift concert an instance of price gouging? Many of Ms. Swift's fans certainly don't think so and don't hesitate to pay such prices. Is Kansas City Chiefs quarterback Patrick Mahomes's average annual salary of $52.7 million an example of price gouging?[30] Especially when he could offer to play for much less and save Chiefs fans some money?

What is clear is that "price gouging" is often in the eye of the beholder and extends way beyond a few convenience stores charging $7.50 for a bottle of water after a hurricane strikes a coastal town. What is also clear is that the ignorance, hypocrisy, demagoguery, and double standards surrounding the issue in the media and among political leaders ensures that objective solutions will remain elusive for the foreseeable future, especially for consumers in dire need of a good or service who would greatly prefer paying an occasional exorbitant price than being faced with no good or service at all.

4.12 Conclusion

This has been a long chapter of intricate material. We slowly assembled a market by starting with the demands of consumers for a product in a certain range of prices and ending with the desires of suppliers to provide that product to the market in a certain range of prices. Where these opposing forces balanced, market equilibrium, an equilibrium price and quantity were established. We then looked at the effects of markets temporarily departing from equilibrium, particularly shortages and surpluses. Thankfully, consumer and producer incentives kick in to return markets quickly back to equilibrium to make these departures short-term phenomena in competitive markets. In chapter 6, we will see how certain government policies can make surpluses and shortages—and thus frustrations are among consumers and producers in many markets—permanent. Before that, however, we must cover the very important topic of the sensitivity of demand and supply.

4.13 Chapter Concepts

product
good
service
market
uniform competition
price taker
monopoly
price maker
market power
individual demand schedule
individual demand curve
law of demand
market demand schedule
market demand curve
ceteris paribus

---

[30] McKessy, Jack. "Patrick Mahomes Contract Details: How Chiefs QB's Deal Compares to Dak Prescott's." *USA Today*. 22 September 2024. <https://www.usatoday.com/story/sports/nfl/chiefs/2024/09/22/patrick-mahomes-chiefs-contract-value-length/75277543007/>

normal good
inferior good
complements
substitutes
individual supply schedule
individual supply curve
market supply schedule
market supply curve
input
equilibrium
equilibrium price
equilibrium quantity
shortage (excess demand)
market clearing
surplus (excess supply)
Adam Smith
invisible hand
diamond-water paradox
price gouging

4.14 Problems, Questions, and Discussion Topics (Items Requiring Examples are Marked with an Asterisk [*])

1. Three characteristics of a competitive market (name and define each, then provide an example of only one)*

2. price maker (define, provide an example)*

3. Premium organic peanut butter is selling at a local grocery store for $7 per jar with 20 jars sold per week. The store decides to hold a buy-one-get-one-free (BOGOF) sale of this peanut butter.

   A. What will likely be the response in quantity sold of this peanut butter?

   B. What law of economics is the basis for assuming this response?

4. Aaron has driven a used 1989 Toyota Corolla through high school, college, and graduate school. The car's current street value is about $550. After graduating with a master's degree in finance and securing a lucrative first-time job in the financial-services industry, Aaron ditches the 1989 Corolla for a new 2026 Lexus LS 500 priced at $99,900.

   A. In terms of normal versus inferior goods, what kind of good is the used 1989 Corolla? Support your answer in detail.

   B. In terms of normal versus inferior goods, what kind of good is the new 2026 Lexus? Support your answer in detail.

5. Since the prices of houses have recently risen in the small town of Podunk, New York, apartment vacancies have completely disappeared. This suggests that houses and apartments are what type of related goods:

   A. complements or substitutes?

   B. Why?

6. Since the average price of a new computer has risen about 20 percent, inkjet printer manufacturers have noticed that their sales have declined about 20 percent. This suggests that computers and printers are what type of related goods:

   A. complements or substitutes?

   B. Why?

7. Kickapoo High School football games are priced at $15 per ticket. However, even though the team has a winning 7-3 record, the stands are only 66 percent full for home games.

   A. What does this likely tell us about where the $15 ticket price is with respect to true market equilibrium?

   B. Is the current market for Kickapoo's games in a state of surplus or shortage?

8. Frequent Walmart customers often complain that popular items they can easily obtain from other stores at higher average prices frequently sell out at Walmart leaving an empty shelf.

   A. What does this likely tell us about where these items are priced with respect to true market equilibrium?

   B. Is the market for these items at Walmart in a state of surplus or shortage?

9. *The tendencies of markets to revert to equilibrium once disturbed from it and for individual self-interest to work through markets to the benefit of larger society is known as _____.*

   A. Fill in the blank: _____.

   B. Explain:

10. Adam Smith (1723-1790) is notable for, among several monumental contributions to economics, a book and a theory of trade. Name and briefly explain both

    A. the book:

B. and the theory of trade:

11. diamond-water paradox (define, then explain how the interaction of both supply and demand solves this paradox to explain why diamonds are relatively expensive and water is relatively cheap)

12. What other two products form a paradox similar to that of diamonds and water? How does the interaction of both supply and demand solve the paradox as to why one product is relatively expensive and the other is relatively cheap?

13. One criticism of Obamacare is that it increased demand (through insurance subsidies) but left supply unchanged (hint: see the scenario depicted in FIGURE 4-13 earlier in this chapter). If true, would this cause

A. market quantity to rise or fall?

B. market price (and hence health-care costs) to rise or fall?

14. Federal tax credits of up to $7,500 for new electric vehicles and $4,000 for used electric vehicles ended on September 30, 2025. The end of these subsidies has caused the demand for electric vehicles to fall with no change in supply (hint: see the scenario depicted in FIGURE 4-15 earlier in this chapter). If true, would this cause

A. market quantity to rise or fall?

B. market price to rise or fall?

15. Recently there has been an increase in the price of crystal, a component in the production of chandeliers. This will undoubtedly decrease the supply of chandeliers while leaving demand unchanged. These changes in supply and demand will cause

A. market quantity to rise or fall?

B. market price to rise or fall?

16. If demand and supply both increase in a market,

A. does market quantity unequivocally rise, unequivocally fall, or does it depend on the relative shifts in supply and demand, and why?

B. does market price unequivocally rise, unequivocally fall, or does it depend on the relative shifts in supply and demand, and why?

17. If demand increases and supply decreases in a market,

A. does market quantity unequivocally rise, unequivocally fall, or does it depend on the relative shifts in supply and demand, and why?

B. does market price unequivocally rise, unequivocally fall, or does it depend on the relative shifts in supply and demand, and why?

18. With regard to price gouging:

A. in what types of instances does it gain public notoriety and outrage?

B. In what types of instances does it get ignored?

Chapter 5: Sensitivity (Elasticity) of Demand and Supply

5.0 Introduction

Sensitivity (elasticity) is a topic that is interesting in part by some of the responses with which it is met. First, it seems to bring out of the woodwork at least two varieties of scoffers. The first is the undergraduate show-off who thinks that he knows far more about business than his business professor. The second and far less common is the empirical nihilist. The show-off usually has little in the way of real-world entrepreneurial experience in terms of having to set and change the price of a product with a large sales volume and worrying about how this will affect a company of more than fifty employees. If he has any work experience, it usually consists of menial, low-skill jobs such as a bagger, clerk, or manual laborer. He makes fun of the term elasticity and tells his friends that it's just another useless idea you have to endure in order to earn a business degree. Nothing could be further from the truth.

If one chooses to own or operate a small business, one of the most important decisions, especially given the behavior of your competitors, is where to set the price of your product and what circumstances day to day, week to week, month to month, or year to year, should move you to change the price of your product in reaction to any occurrence such as a new competitor in your industry, a repurposed good from another industry that now competes with your product, or an increase in economywide inflation.

Furthermore, if one has no interest in entrepreneurship but wants to live a life of minimal responsibility and just be an employee for a company on an assembly line or in a sales position, for which type of company would he or she almost certainly want to work? A company that makes a product for which it can raise the price and customers will still show up to demand the product, or a company that makes a product for which a slight rise in price can cause it to lose most of its customers? Most sensible people would choose the former.

Continuing with sensitivity's detractors, the empirical nihilist is more amusing than the undergraduate showoff. Sometimes he or she is nothing more than a mathphobe, frequently (but certainly not always) someone who struggles at math, and for that reason denigrates just about any and all use of it. While this is surely "throwing out the baby with the bathwater," there's definitely more than a grain of truth in the view that sensitivity can be taken too far. Some overenthusiastic economics graduate students and business consultants gather price and demand data, calculate sensitivity coefficients, forecast the effects of a price change, and end up thoroughly embarrassed and bewildered by the wildly wrong forecasts they make.

The wise practitioner proceeds between the two extremes of arrogant dilettante and dogmatic economic statistician. The successful real-world entrepreneur knows that lowering a product's price should increase sales to some extent, given the law of demand introduced in the last chapter. The results of a price decrease in a high, low, or moderate-growth economy can be roughly the same or very different. The entrepreneur may have run through a number of positive and negative scenarios on the back of several envelopes or in Microsoft Excel. What he or she knows more than anything is that they know nothing with perfect certainty. Pretending to know with even great certainty what the results will be of a business decision is what the wiser empirical skeptics soundly criticize.

5.1 Demand Sensitivity

In the previous chapter, we focused on the direction of change of quantity in response to a change in price. According to the law of demand, if the price of a good or service increases, then the quantity demanded of that good or service will decrease (keeping all other variables that influence demand—the demand-curve "shifters" such as income, the prices of related products, and preferences—constant). What was not discussed in the previous chapter was the issue of the varying degree of response of quantity demanded of different products to a change in their price. In other words, if price rises, how many fewer units of the product will be sold? This concept is the **price sensitivity of demand**, the percentage change in the quantity demanded of a product caused by a percentage change in the product's price.

price sensitivity of demand – the percentage change in the quantity demanded of a product caused by a percentage change in the product's price.

There are two major factors that affect the price sensitivity of demand of a product:

1. The availability of close substitute goods or services.

Goods and services with many close substitutes have a high price sensitivity of demand. As we saw earlier with beef tacos, if the price of beef rises, consumers can and will switch to chicken, pork, lamb, or fish. While not perfect, in a taco one or more of these beef replacements is a pretty acceptable substitute for most consumers. The greater the number of close substitutes for a product, the higher the price sensitivity of its demand. In contrast, gasoline and electricity are a good and service (respectively) for which each has few close substitutes. Thus, when the price of each is raised, the quantity demanded of each falls very little.

2. The portion of a consumer's total budget spent on a product.

Pillar Candles

Goods and services that make up a small portion of a consumer's budget are less sensitive. The reason? An item that is seldom purchased can double or triple in price without making a significant impact on a consumer's overall budget. For example, households purchase pillar candles in preparation for power outages. These items currently range in price from $7 to $10 each. Since they are used so infrequently, from power outages to holiday events, pillar candles can double in price with not a large reduction in their quantity sold. The total spending on these items as a portion of a consumer's total budget is still small, therefore they have a low price sensitivity of demand.

5.2 Calculating Price Sensitivity of Demand Coefficients: the Simple Formula

The **price sensitivity of demand coefficient (η)** is computed using the following formula, known as the **simple formula**:

$$Price\ sensitivity\ of\ demand\ coefficient\ (\eta) = \frac{Percentage\ change\ in\ quantity\ demanded}{Percentage\ change\ in\ price}$$

The right side of the equation above is read as, "the percentage change in quantity demanded caused by a percentage change in price." The resulting number (coefficient) is represented by the Greek letter *Eta* (η). For example, in Bakerville, the price of potatoes rose from $1.00 per potato to $1.50 per potato (a 50 percent increase) while the number of potatoes sold fell from 10,000 potatoes to 7,500 potatoes (a 25 percent decrease).

price sensitivity of demand coefficient (η) (simple formula) – the percentage change in quantity demanded divided by the percentage change in price.

$$Price\ sensitivity\ of\ demand\ coefficient\ (\eta) = \frac{-25\ percent}{+50\ percent} = -\frac{1}{2} = -0.5.$$

So, in Bakerville, the price sensitivity of demand coefficient is -0.5, meaning that the change in the quantity demanded is proportionately only half as large as the change in price. Because of the law of demand (which states that there is an inverse or negative relationship between price and quantity demanded), the price sensitivity of demand coefficient will always be negative. However, in applied economics, the usual custom is to drop the negative sign and report the coefficient as positive. For the example above, $\eta = 0.5$.

Because the quantity demanded of potatoes in Bakerville has a response proportionately half that of the change in price, we say that the price sensitivity of demand of potatoes in Bakerville is insensitive (or inelastic). Let's say that down the highway, in Butcherville, the price per potato had increased by 20 percent and this caused a drop in potato sales of 40 percent such that

$$\eta = \frac{-40\ percent}{+20\ percent} = -\frac{2}{1} = -2\ or\ 2\ (as\ usually\ reported).$$

Because the quantity demanded of potatoes in Butcherville has a response proportionately twice that of the change in price, we say that the price sensitivity of demand for potatoes in Butcherville is sensitive (or elastic).

Cool Mnemonic: Price Sensitivity (Elasticity) of Demand

As we saw in chapter 1, a mnemonic is a memory device, or something that makes remembering easier. What's an easy way to remember whether a sensitivity coefficient (η) falls in the insensitive or sensitive range? Just remember the word "is," and then insert the number one (1) between its letter *i* and its letter *s* just like this:

$$i^1 s$$

Therefore, if $\eta < 1$ in value, then the good or service has an *insensitive* (i) price sensitivity of demand. If $\eta > 1$, then the good or service has a *sensitive* (s) price sensitivity of demand. If $\eta = 1$, then the good or service has a *unit sensitive* price sensitivity of demand.

If you prefer the elastic-inelastic terminology, you can still use a mnemonic, but a less intuitive one. Just remember the Latin abbreviation "i.e.," for *id est*, usually translated into English as "that is." Then insert the number one (1) between its letter *i* and its letter *e* just like this:

$$i.^1 e.$$

Therefore, if $\eta < 1$ in value, then the good or service has an *inelastic* (i) elasticity of demand. If $\eta > 1$, then the good or service has an *elastic* (e) elasticity of demand. If $\eta = 1$, then the good or service has a *unit elastic* elasticity of demand.

The author of this book regards the elastic-inelastic terminology as vague and unintuitive, hence the use of the sensitive-insensitive terminology instead. Students intending to go on to major in economics or pursue graduate degrees in the discipline should be familiar with the elastic-inelastic terminology because, as awkward as it is, it is unfortunately and likely not going away anytime soon.

5.3 A More Than Slight Problem with Consistency

All of this seems good and well until you use the simple formula both ways. What do we mean by "both ways?" Our product is shampoo. Last week our product was selling for $4 per bottle and 120 units were sold. This week our firm had to raise the price of the product to $6 per bottle. Sales were 80 units. So, what is our sensitivity coefficient, η? From $4 to $6 is a 50-percent increase in price, while the drop from 120 units to 80 units is a (40/120 =) 33.3-percent decline. What is our η? It is

$$\eta = \frac{-33.3 \; percent}{+50 \; percent} = -0.67 \; or \; 0.67.$$

Wait a minute: what happens if we "go the other way?" Let's say that some of our ingredients drop in price and we can go back to selling our product for $4 per bottle again. So, last week our product was $6 per bottle but now we're back to $4. Sales go from 80 units back to 120. The coefficient (η) should stay the same, correct? Let's see if it does: \$6 to \$4 is a (2/6 = 1/3 =) 33.3-percent change in price while 80 to 120 units constitutes a (40/80 =) 50-percent increase in sales. So:

$$\eta = \frac{+50 \ percent}{-33.3 \ percent} = -1.5 \ or \ 1.5.$$

Whoa, 0.67 versus 1.5 is a serious discrepancy. Following our Cool Mnemonic (i^1s) in the boxed article above, we can see that our product is price insensitive ($\eta < 1$) for a rise in price but price sensitive ($\eta > 1$) for a fall in price. Talk about confusing! Thus, the midpoint formula.

5.4 The Midpoint Formula

A formula for computing price sensitivity of demand coefficients that are the same regardless of the direction of a price change (increase or decrease) is the **midpoint formula**. It is:

price sensitivity of demand coefficient (η) (midpoint formula) – the ratio of the change in quantity divided by average quantity to the change in price divided by average price.

$$Price \ sensitivity \ of \ demand \ coefficient \ (\eta) = \frac{(Q_2 - Q_1)/[(Q_2 + Q_1)/2]}{(P_2 - P_1)/[(P_2 + P_1)/2]}$$

with

P_1 = beginning price
P_2 = ending price
Q_1 = beginning quantity
Q_2 = ending quantity.

So, let's try this again using the price-quantity points from our previous example. For the price increase:

P_1 = \$4
P_2 = \$6
Q_1 = 120
Q_2 = 80

$$\eta = \frac{(Q_2 - Q_1)/[(Q_2 + Q_1)/2]}{(P_2 - P_1)/[(P_2 + P_1)/2]}$$

$$= \frac{(80-120)\big/[(80+120)/2]}{(6-4)\big/[(6+4)/2]}$$

$$= \frac{(-40)\big/[(200)/2]}{(2)\big/[(10)/2]}$$

$$= \frac{-40/100}{2/5}$$

$$= \left(\frac{-40}{100}\right)\left(\frac{5}{2}\right)$$

$$= \left(\frac{-200}{200}\right)$$

$$= -1 \; or \; 1 \; (unit \; sensitive)$$

Now, let's see what happens when we go the other way, i.e., use the numbers for a price decline:

$P_1 = \$6$
$P_2 = \$4$
$Q_1 = 80$
$Q_2 = 120$

$$Price\ sensitivity\ of\ demand\ coefficient\ (\eta) = \frac{(Q_2-Q_1)\big/[(Q_2+Q_1)/2]}{(P_2-P_1)\big/[(P_2+P_1)/2]}$$

$$\eta = \frac{(120-80)\big/[(120+80)/2]}{(4-6)\big/[(4+6)/2]}$$

$$= \frac{(40)\big/[(200)/2]}{(-2)\big/[(10)/2]}$$

$$= \frac{{}^{40}/_{100}}{{}^{-2}/_{5}}$$

$$= \left(\frac{40}{100}\right)\left(\frac{5}{-2}\right)$$

$$= \left(\frac{200}{-200}\right)$$

$$= -1 \ or \ 1 \ (unit \ sensitive)$$

Ergo (Latin for "therefore"), we get the same answer ($\eta = 1$) regardless of the price point with which we begin the calculation. While the mathematically inclined may enjoy such proofs, what is far more important is the practical and intuitive concept of price sensitivity of demand: changes in the price of a product will affect the sales of that product depending on the nature of the product, i.e., if it has many substitutes or makes up a substantial portion of consumer budgets. Forget expecting to have an exact and perfect forecast of a product's change in sales given a change in its price. A rough ballpark idea is often victory enough.

ECONOMICS IN ACTION: Some Price Sensitivity of Demand Coefficient Estimates ($\hat{\eta}$) from Studies

TABLE 5-1 contains demand-coefficient estimates for nine products. While it is beyond the scope of this boxed feature to evaluate the soundness of these estimates, none look far out of the ballpark or surprising. Salt makes up a small portion of the average consumer's budget; there are few substitutes for physician services; movies are an entertainment medium that are approximately unit sensitive; Cheerios cereal, Chevrolet automobiles, and Mountain Dew soda are specific goods with close substitutes; and fresh tomatoes have close substitutes in terms of tomatoes sold in cans or cartons.

TABLE 5-1: Price Sensitivity of Demand Coefficient Estimates ($\hat{\eta}$) for Some General and Specific Goods and Services

Product	Estimated Price Sensitivity of Demand Coefficient ($\hat{\eta}$)
Salt*	-0.1
Physician services*	-0.6
Movies*	-0.9
Housing (owner occupied, long run)*	-1.2
Restaurant meals*	-2.3
Cheerios**	-3.7
Chevrolet automobiles*	-4.0
Mountain Dew soda**	-4.4
Fresh tomatoes*	-4.6

*Gwartney, James D. et al. *Economics: Private and Public Choice*. Mason: South-Western Cengage, 2008.
**Mankiw, N. Gregory. *Principles of Microeconomics*. 9th ed. Stamford: Cengage Learning, 2021.

5.5 Price Sensitivity and How it Affects Demand

Price sensitivity has an obvious effect on demand because it defines the relationship between price and quantity demanded. FIGURE 5-1 illustrates five possible demands that can exist when the price sensitivity of demand changes. Displayed in FIGURE 5-1 are the cases in which $\eta = 0$, $\eta < 1$, $\eta = 1$, $\eta > 1$, and $\eta = \infty$.

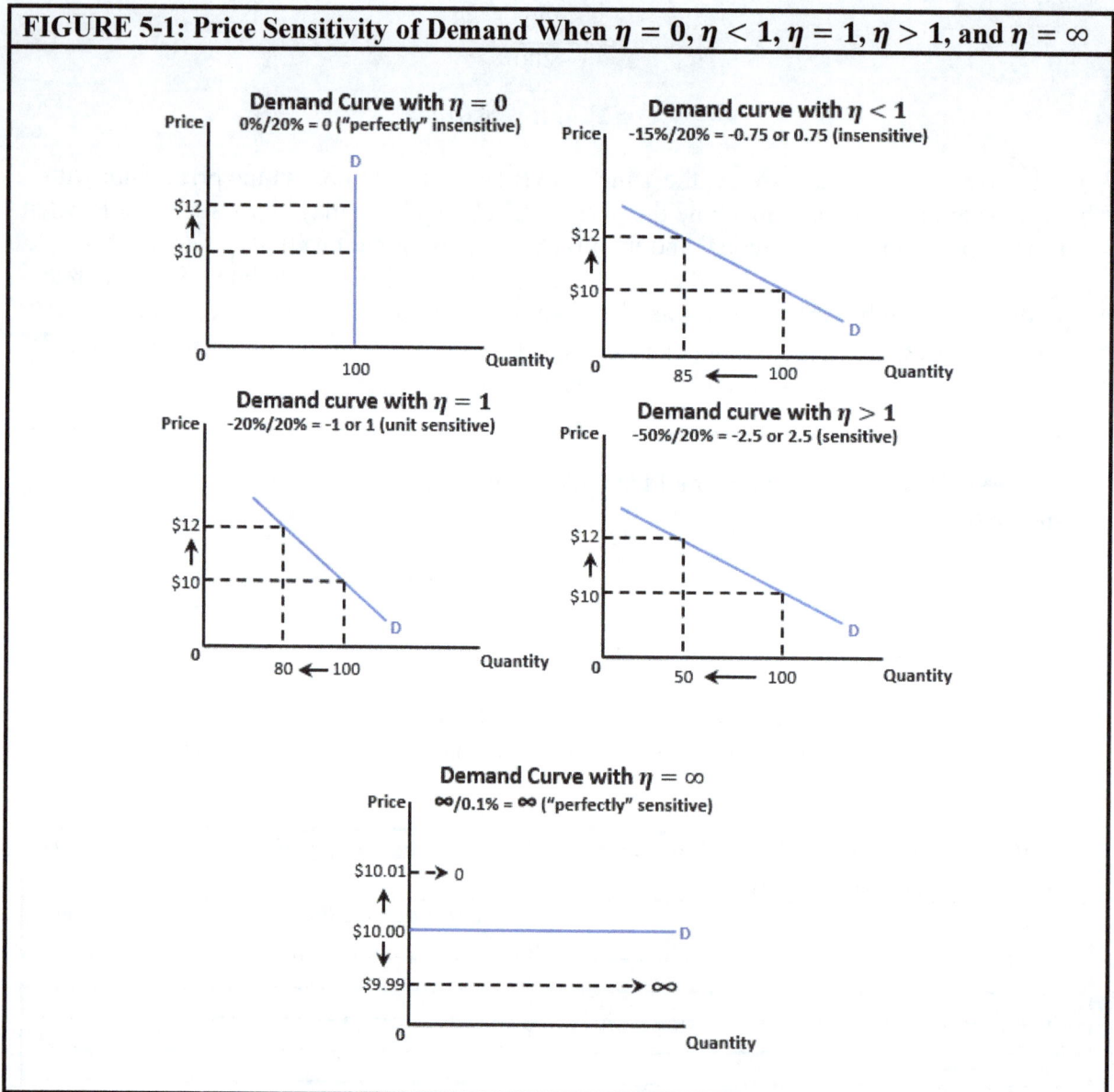

FIGURE 5-1: Price Sensitivity of Demand When $\eta = 0$, $\eta < 1$, $\eta = 1$, $\eta > 1$, and $\eta = \infty$

Not surprisingly, the two most confusing diagrams in FIGURE 5-1 are the first ($\eta = 0$) and the last ($\eta = \infty$). Zero price sensitivity of demand ($\eta = 0$) means that any increase in price will leave quantity demanded constant at, per our example in FIGURE 5-1, 100 units. It is an interesting theoretical scenario but not one with much relevance to the real world. Infinite price sensitivity of demand ($\eta = \infty$) means that at, per our example in FIGURE 5-1, any price above $10, including theoretically, $10.01, quantity demanded equals 0 and that at any price below

$10, including theoretically, $9.99, quantity demanded equals infinity. At the price of exactly $10, sales can be any quantity. "Perfect" price sensitivity of demand ($\eta = \infty$) is an interesting theoretical scenario but not one with much relevance to the real world. Far more important is the area between these two extremes where price sensitivity for consumer products in the real world falls in the insensitive to sensitive range.

Another Cool Mnemonic: Sensitivity and the Slope of Demand Curves

If you're having trouble remembering what a demand curve of zero or infinite price sensitivity of demand looks like, here are a couple things to remember. A zero sensitivity ($\eta = 0$) demand curve looks like the capital letter *I* (see the first graph in FIGURE 5-1). And that letter *I* stands for "insensitive." Once you remember that one item, then you know that an infinitely sensitive ($\eta = \infty$) demand curve is just the opposite of a vertical line resembling the capital letter *I*. It is a horizontal line and just like the horizon on an ocean at sunset, seems to extend into infinity. So, to recap, a perfectly price insensitive demand looks like a capital *I* (for "insensitive") and a perfectly price sensitive demand is the opposite: a flat line like the horizon on an ocean at sunset that seems to stretch into infinity.

A Mnemonic: an Ocean Horizon at Sunset

Final Note: it is a very common mistake for students to equate η (*Eta*, the sensitivity coefficient) with Δ (*Delta*, the **slope** of a line or the change in a variable). Recall from the appendix to chapter 1 that the slope of a line in an *x-y* coordinate system is the change in the *y* variable divided by the change in the *x* variable, or, "rise" divided by "run." Recall from earlier in this chapter that the price sensitivity of demand is the percentage change in quantity demanded caused by a percentage change in price. Slope (Δ) is a *ratio of units* while price sensitivity of demand (η) is a *ratio of proportions*. The two concepts are unquestionably similar but certainly not the same.

slope – in an *x-y* coordinate system, the change in the y variable divided by the change in the x variable, or, "rise" divided by "run."

5.6 Price Sensitivity of Demand and Total Revenue

We began this chapter by ridiculing a certain type of cynic: the showoff undergraduate (usually guy) who tells his friends that business professors know nothing about business; otherwise, they'd be in business and not teaching. (Meanwhile, left unexplained, is "Why is this guy taking classes from people that he claims know nothing? Wouldn't that be an uneconomic waste of time? Isn't he the one who is extremely confused?") If price sensitivity of demand has actual relevance in the business world, then it must have a relationship with sales revenue and (ultimately) profit. Does it in fact have this? It turns out that it in fact does and our cynic is wrong ... again. Let's define total revenue, then explore all three cases of sensitivity (insensitive, unit, and sensitive) to see how different types of demand affect revenue and profit.

total revenue (TR) - – the price of a product (P) times the quantity of that product sold (Q) or (P)(Q).

Total revenue (TR) is the price of a product (P) times the quantity of that product sold (Q) or (P)(Q). If the price of shampoo is $10 per bottle and 100 bottles are sold, then total revenue (P)(Q) = ($10)(100) = $1,000. Graphically, in relation to the demand curve, this will look like FIGURE 5-2:

FIGURE 5-2: Total Revenue (P)(Q) in Price-Quantity Space

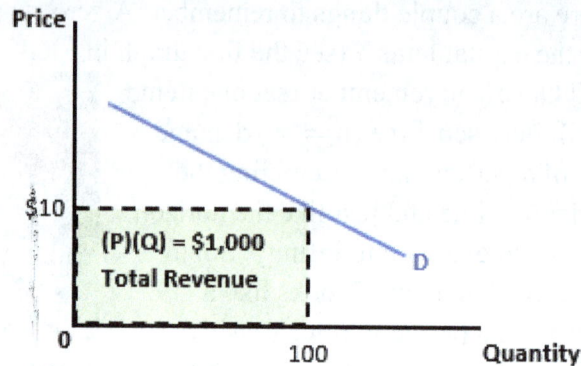

The height of the green total revenue box is $10 (P). Its length is 100 bottles (Q). Sales of 100 bottles at $10 each will produce a total revenue of $1,000. That's easy and obvious. The real question is, what happens under each of the three demand scenarios, i.e., insensitive, unit sensitive, and sensitive demands? FIGURE 5-3 has the answers.

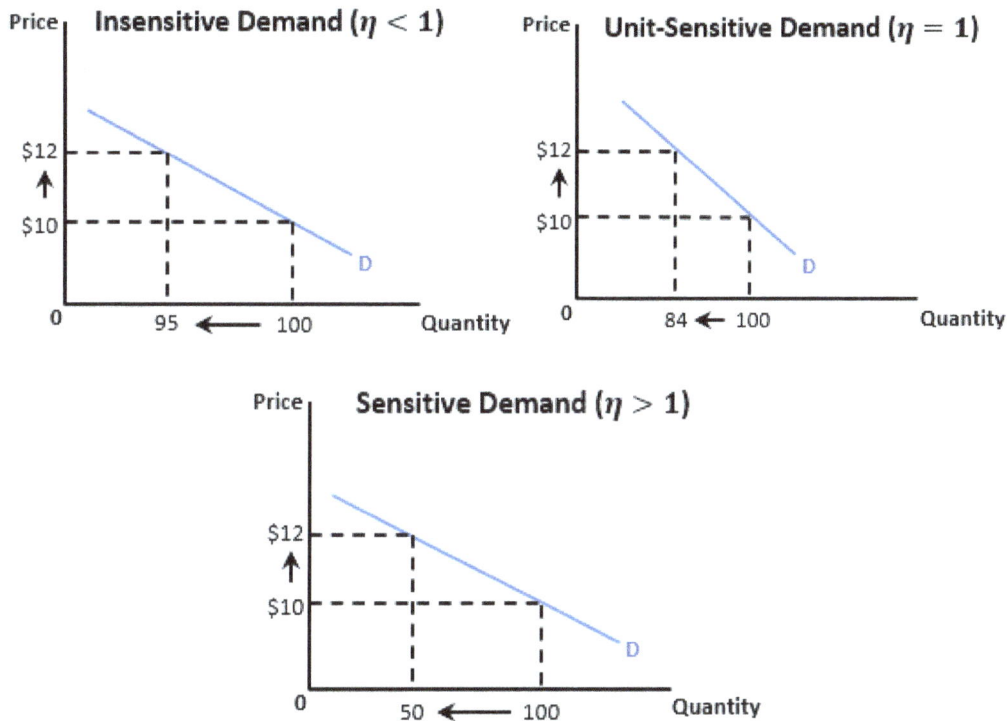

FIGURE 5-3: Price Sensitivity of Demand and Total Revenue When $\eta < 1$, $\eta = 1$, and $\eta > 1$

First Graph in FIGURE 5-3 (insensitive demand [$\eta < 1$]): total revenue goes from
TR_1 ($10)(100) = $1,000 to
TR_2 ($12)(95) = $1,140.
A price increase has increased total revenue.

Second Graph in FIGURE 5-3 (unit-sensitive demand [$\eta = 1$]): total revenue goes from
TR_1 ($10)(100) = $1,000 to
TR_2 ($12)(84) = $1,008
A price increase has slightly increased, slightly decreased, or kept total revenue the same.

Third Graph in FIGURE 5-3 (sensitive demand [$\eta > 1$]): total revenue goes from
TR_1 ($10)(100) = $1,000 to
TR_2 ($12)(50) = $600.
A price increase will cause total revenue to fall.

Three General Takeaways:
A. For insensitive demands, a price increase will increase total revenue.
B. For unit-sensitive demands, a price increase will slightly increase, slightly decrease, or leave total revenue unchanged.

C. For sensitive demands, a price increase will decrease total revenue.

5.7 Price Sensitivity of Demand and Total Revenue

TABLE 5-2 contains a demand schedule for bottles of shampoo for a particular market. FIGURE 5-4 illustrates the demand curve derived from the demand schedule in TABLE 5-2.

TABLE 5-2

Price ($)	Quantity	Total Revenue	% Δ P	% Δ Q	η	Sensitivity
0	10	0	-2	0.222222	-0.11111	insensitive
1	8	8	-0.66667	0.285714	-0.42857	insensitive
2	6	12	-0.4	0.4	-1	unit sensitive
3	4	12	-0.28571	0.666667	-2.33333	sensitive
4	2	8	-0.22222	2	-9	sensitive
5	0	0				

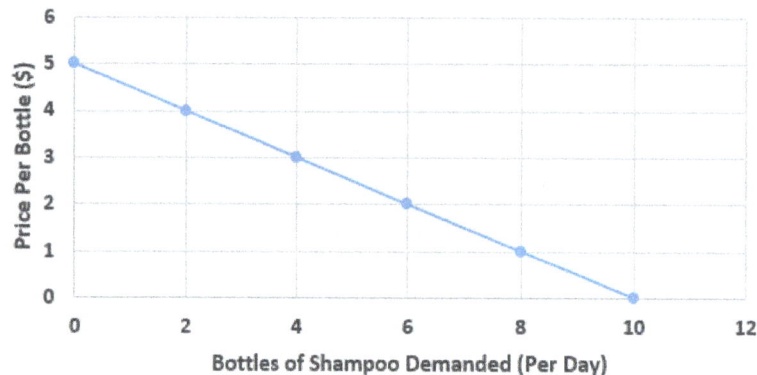

FIGURE 5-4: Price Sensitivity Along the Demand Curve

While the demand schedule and demand curve were covered in chapter 4 and the midpoint formula for calculating price-sensitivity-of-demand coefficients (η) was covered in section 5.4 of this chapter, what's new in TABLE 5-2 is the calculation of price-sensitivity-of-demand coefficients (η) using the midpoint formula at different points along the demand curve. Notice how they change (see column 6 [η] in TABLE 5-2) all along the curve, moving from insensitive in the range of $0 to $2 per bottle of shampoo to unit sensitive in the range of $2 to $3 per bottle to sensitive in the range of $3 to $5 per bottle.

This further reinforces the distinction between slope and price sensitivity of demand, despite the similarities between the two concepts. The demand curve illustrated in FIGURE 5-4 has a constant slope but nonconstant price sensitivity of demand. Because the demand curve illustrated in FIGURE 5-4 is a straight line, it has a constant slope of 0.5 (rise/run = -1/2 = -0.5 or 0.5). However, its price sensitivity of demand steadily increases all along the curve as price rises from $0 to $5 per bottle of shampoo.

5.8 Income and Cross-Price Sensitivity of Demand

Besides price sensitivity of demand, there is income sensitivity of demand and cross-price sensitivity of demand. **Income sensitivity of demand** is the percentage change in the quantity demanded of a product caused by a percentage change in income. The **income sensitivity of demand coefficient (α)** is computed via the simple formula as follows:

income sensitivity of demand - the percentage change in the quantity demanded of a product caused by a percentage change in income.

income sensitivity of demand coefficient (α) (simple formula) – the percentage change in quantity demanded of a product divided by the percentage change in a consumer's income.

$$Income\ sensitivity\ of\ demand\ coefficient\ (\alpha) = \frac{Percentage\ change\ in\ quantity\ demanded}{Percentage\ change\ in\ income}$$

Recall from chapter 4 the discussions about normal and inferior goods. Income sensitivity of demand has implications for such goods. As you may have guessed, normal goods have positive income sensitivities of demand while inferior goods have negative income sensitivities of demand. Toyota automobiles are an example of a normal good. If a consumer drives a Corolla (lower-priced model) and his or her income increases, he or she will be more receptive to upgrading to a Camry (mid-priced model). The income sensitivity of demand coefficient in this case (α) would be positive. Most college students, once they graduate and begin work, stop purchasing and consuming ramen noodles because they are (in terms of the preferences of most consumers) an inferior good. The income sensitivity of demand coefficient in this case would be negative. A higher income in many cases is a significant motivator to dump ramen noodles from one's grocery cart and purchase higher quality noodles instead.

cross-price sensitivity of demand - the percentage change in the quantity demanded of product B caused by a percentage change in the price of product A.

cross-price sensitivity of demand coefficient (β) (simple formula) – the percentage change in the quantity demanded of product B divided by the percentage change in the price of product A.

Cross-price sensitivity of demand is the percentage change in the quantity demanded of product B caused by a percentage change in the price of product A. The **cross-price sensitivity of demand coefficient (β)** is computed via the simple formula as follows:

$$Cross-price\ sensitivity\ of\ demand\ coefficient\ (\beta) = \frac{Percentage\ change\ in\ the\ quantity\ demanded\ of\ product\ B}{Percentage\ change\ in\ the\ price\ of\ product\ A}$$

Recall from chapter 4 the discussions about substitutes and complements. Cross-price sensitivity of demand has implications for such products. Let's start with substitutes: the price of beef tacos (good A) increases and this causes an increase in the quantity demanded of chicken tacos (good B). This brings about a positive cross-price sensitivity of demand coefficient, β. What about compliments? Let's try beef tacos and iced tea. The price of beef tacos (good A) increases and this causes a decrease in the quantity demanded of iced tea (good B). This brings about a negative cross-price sensitivity of demand coefficient, β. So, for substitutes, the cross-price sensitivity of demand coefficient is positive in value and for complements it is negative in value.

5.9 Price Sensitivity of Supply

price sensitivity of supply – the percentage change in the quantity supplied of a product caused by a percentage change in the product's price.

Just as there is a price sensitivity of demand, there is a price sensitivity of supply. The **price sensitivity of supply** is the percentage change in the quantity supplied of a product caused by a percentage change in the product's price. Like price sensitivity of demand, price sensitivity of supply is insensitive if the percentage change in quantity supplied is less than the percentage change in price and sensitive if the percentage change in quality supplied is greater than the percentage change in price.

The main factor that affects the price sensitivity of supply of a good or service is time horizon. In a short time period, say three months, producers of a good or service will be limited in terms of how much additional product they can produce in response to an increase in price. They will be limited by the capacity of their facility and the size of their workforce. Over a longer period of time, say, two years, they will have much more flexibility. They will be able to add new buildings to their facility, hire more labor, or relocate to a larger facility to handle the higher demand for their product. In terms of the industry, new firms will enter to compete with established firms. Over time, price sensitivity of supply will only go from less sensitive to more sensitive.

5.10 Calculating Price Sensitivity of Supply Coefficients: the Simple and Midpoint Formulas

The **price sensitivity of supply coefficient (γ)** is calculated using the simple formula as follows:

$$Price\ sensitivity\ of\ supply\ coefficient\ (\gamma) = \frac{Percentage\ change\ in\ quantity\ supplied}{Percentage\ change\ in\ price}$$

price sensitivity of supply coefficient (γ) (simple formula) – the percentage change in the quantity supplied divided by the percentage change in price.

The right side of the above equation is read as, "the percentage change in quantity supplied caused by a percentage change in price." The resulting number (coefficient) is represented by the Greek letter *Gamma* (γ). For example, in Bakerville, the price of potatoes rises from \$1.00 per potato to \$1.50 per potato (a 50 percent increase), which causes potato farmers to raise their harvest from 10,000 potatoes to 15,000 potatoes (a 50 percent increase).

$$Price\ sensitivity\ of\ supply\ coefficient\ (\gamma) = \frac{+50\ percent}{+50\ percent} = 1.$$

So, in Bakerville, the price sensitivity of supply coefficient (γ) is 1, meaning that the change in the quantity supplied is proportionately as large as the change in price. Because there is usually a positive relationship between price and quantity supplied (i.e., supply curves usually slope upward), the price sensitivity of supply coefficient (γ) will usually be positive in value. Hence there is no cause to worry about dropping a negative sign as there is with the price sensitivity of demand coefficient (η).[31]

Notice that we used the simple formula to calculate γ as a simple initial illustration. Obviously there is a midpoint version. Let's now use our data from Bakerfield in the midpoint formula and see how it compares with our initial answer using the simple formula:

$$Price\ sensitivity\ of\ supply\ coefficient\ (\gamma) = \frac{(Q_2 - Q_1)\Big/[(Q_2 + Q_1)/2]}{(P_2 - P_1)\Big/[(P_2 + P_1)/2]}$$

with

P_1 = beginning price
P_2 = ending price
Q_1 = beginning quantity
Q_2 = ending quantity.

So, let's try to calculate γ again, this time using the midpoint formula and the price-quantity points from our Bakerville example immediately above where:

price sensitivity of supply coefficient (γ) (midpoint formula) – the ratio of the change in quantity divided by average quantity to the change in price divided by average price.

P_1 = \$1.00
P_2 = \$1.50
Q_1 = 10,000
Q_2 = 15,000.

$$\gamma = \frac{(Q_2 - Q_1)\Big/[(Q_2 + Q_1)/2]}{(P_2 - P_1)\Big/[(P_2 + P_1)/2]}$$

$$= \frac{(15,000 - 10,000)\Big/[(15,000 + 10,000)/2]}{(1.50 - 1.00)\Big/[(1.50 + 1.00)/2]}$$

---

[31] Why do we write that supply curves "usually" slope upward? Because there's no law of supply as there is a law of demand. It turns out that, at least theoretically, the supply curve for an industry where the costs of production fall in the long run as output increases (a "decreasing-cost" industry) is downward sloping. Whether such a relationship exists in the real world is a whole other story.

$$= \frac{(5{,}000) \Big/ [(25{,}000)/2]}{(0.5) \Big/ [(2.50)/2]}$$

$$= \frac{5{,}000 \Big/ 12{,}500}{0.5 \Big/ 1.25}$$

$$= \left(\frac{5{,}000}{12{,}500}\right)\left(\frac{1.25}{0.5}\right)$$

$$= (0.4)(2.5)$$

$$= 1 \ (unit \ sensitive)$$

Reader Exercise: It will be left as an exercise for the reader to make the computation "in the opposite direction" (from P_1Q_1 to P_2Q_2) to prove that the midpoint formula produces the same answer ($\gamma = 1$). For the pattern to follow, see section 5.4 where we performed the same exercise but with data illustrating the price sensitivity of demand.

5.11 Price Sensitivity and How it Affects Supply

Price sensitivity has an obvious effect on supply because it describes the relationship between price and quantity supplied. FIGURE 5-5 illustrates five possible supplies that can exist when the price sensitivity of supply changes. Displayed in FIGURE 5-5 are the cases in which $\gamma = 0$, $\gamma < 1$, $\gamma = 1$, $\gamma > 1$, and $\gamma = \infty$.

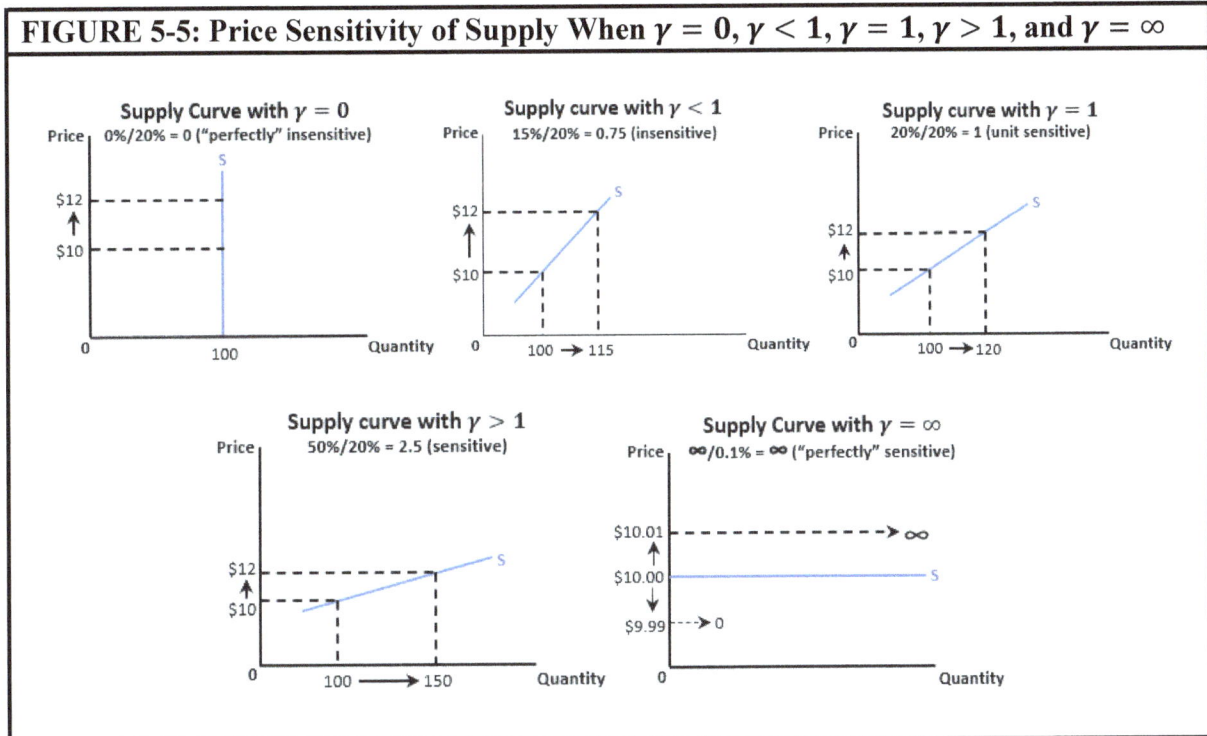

FIGURE 5-5: Price Sensitivity of Supply When $\gamma = 0$, $\gamma < 1$, $\gamma = 1$, $\gamma > 1$, and $\gamma = \infty$

Not surprisingly, as with price sensitivity of demand and FIGURE 5-1, the two most confusing diagrams in FIGURE 5-5 to students are usually the first ($\gamma = 0$) and last ($\gamma = \infty$). Zero price sensitivity of supply ($\gamma = 0$) means that any increase in price will leave quantity supplied constant at 100 units. It is an interesting theoretical scenario but not one with much relevance to the real world.[32] Infinite price sensitivity of supply ($\gamma = \infty$) means that if price rises to any level above $10, even just $10.01, quantity supplied rises to infinity and if price falls to any level below $10, even just $9.99, quantity supplied falls to zero. At the exact price of $10, quantity supplied can be with a wide range of quantities. While the three theoretical possibilities of quantity supplied in the $\gamma = \infty$ scenario are intriguing, they hold little relevance to the real world. Natural scarcity alone eliminates the possibility of infinite quantity supplied. Far more important are the areas between the two $\gamma = 0$ and $\gamma = \infty$ extremes where the price sensitivity of supply falls in the insensitive-to-sensitive range, which has relevance to the real world in which we all actually live.

5.12 Price Sensitivity of Supply and Total Revenue

TABLE 5-3 contains a supply schedule for bottles of shampoo for a particular market. FIGURE 5-6 illustrates the supply curve derived from the supply schedule contained in TABLE 5-3.

---

[32] At least one exception of course is individual stocks on the stock market. Common stock shares of individual companies are fixed in supply until the companies issue more stock.

TABLE 5-3

Price ($)	Quantity	Total Revenue	% Δ P	% Δ Q	γ	Sensitivity
1	0	0	-0.66667	-2	3	sensitive
2	4	8	-0.4	-0.4	1	unit sensitive
3	6	18	-0.5	-0.28571	0.571429	insensitive
5	8	40				

FIGURE 5-6: Price Sensitivity Along the Supply Curve

TABLE 5-3 displays price-sensitivity-of-supply coefficients (γ) using the midpoint formula at different points along the supply curve drawn in FIGURE 5-6. Notice how the γ values change (see column 6 in TABLE 5-3) all along the curve, moving from sensitive ($\gamma = 3$) in the range of $1 to $2 per bottle of shampoo to unit sensitive ($\gamma = 1$) in the range of $2 to $3 per bottle to sensitive ($\gamma \approx 0.57$) in the range of $3 to $5 per bottle.

Notice that the supply curve illustrated in FIGURE 5-6 has a varying slope but also varying price sensitivity of supply. While some markets are characterized by a varying price sensitivity of supply (as depicted above), others are not.

ECONOMICS IN ACTION: is Technology Good for Hunger but Bad for Farmers?

The answer to the question posed in the title of this case study depends on supply and demand (the topics of chapter 4), but also, more specifically ... the price sensitivity of farm crops. Where do we start? Wheat, corn, potatoes, soybeans? Why not wheat, since it is the basis for so many foods (bread, cereal, waffles, etc.)? Thus, we have the market for wheat in FIGURE 5-7.

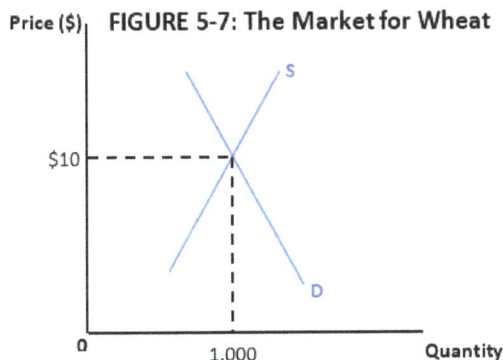

FIGURE 5-7: The Market for Wheat

Price per bushel is $10 with 1,000 units sold in this market. Suddenly, a new wheat seed is developed that has a higher yield and improved adaptability to adverse weather conditions. If the claims made about this new technology hold water, what effect does this have on our market?

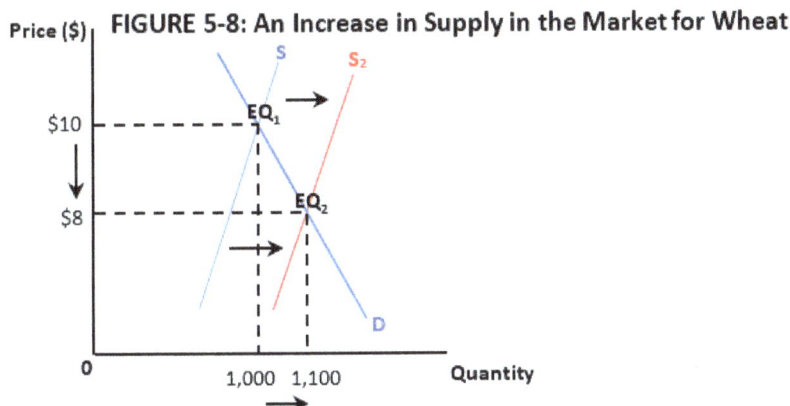

FIGURE 5-8: An Increase in Supply in the Market for Wheat

As can be seen in FIGURE 5-8, the new, more fertile, and durable seed increases supply from S to S_2 while demand remains constant. Equilibrium quantity increases from 1,000 to 1,100 bushels and price falls from $10 per bushel to $8 per bushel as the market moves from equilibrium one (EQ_1) to equilibrium two (EQ_2).

The key (with just a shift in supply but no shift in demand) is the price sensitivity of demand. The midpoint method puts the price sensitivity of demand coefficient at -0.43 or 0.43, which means that demand is insensitive. This is realistic for wheat because it has few close substitutes. From section 5.7, the first of our three takeaways is "For insensitive demands, a price increase will increase total revenue." Thus, a fall in price will decrease total revenue and, lo and behold, total revenue declines from ($10*1,000 bushels =) $10,000 to ($8*1,100 bushels =) $8,800. The new technology has lowered the price of wheat, helped decrease hunger, but made farmers economically worse off.

CASE STUDY: How Time and Technology Overthrew the Organization of the Petroleum Exporting Countries (OPEC)

The year 1973 saw the U.S. launch its first space station (Skylab), the Sears Tower in Chicago become the tallest building in the world, *The Godfather* win best picture, and an oil embargo implemented by the Organization of the Petroleum Exporting Countries (OPEC) cartel on October 17 against several countries for their support of the state of Israel. One of them was the United States. The effects felt were immediate.

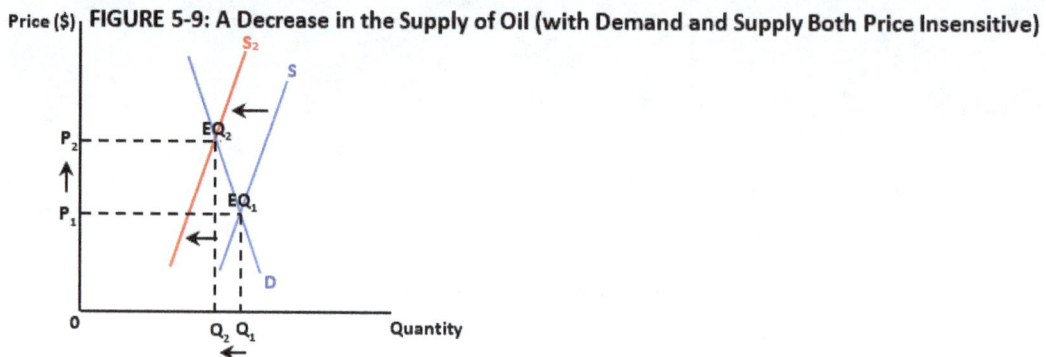

FIGURE 5-9: A Decrease in the Supply of Oil (with Demand and Supply Both Price Insensitive)

As in FIGURE 5-9, supply decreased from S to S_2 while demand remained relatively unchanged. Quantity decreased from Q_1 to Q_2 (because of price-insensitive demand) while price increased over 50 percent on world markets from 1973 to 1974, from P_1 to P_2. Market equilibrium shifted from equilibrium one (EQ_1) at (Q_1, P_1) to equilibrium two (EQ_2) at (Q_2, P_2). Recall from section 5.7 earlier in this chapter the three takeaways with respect to price insensitivity of demand and total revenue:

Three General Takeaways:
A. For insensitive demands, a price increase will increase total revenue.
B. For unit-sensitive demands, a price increase will slightly increase, slightly decrease, or leave total revenue unchanged.
C. For sensitive demands, a price increase will decrease total revenue.

Since the demand for oil (and its derivative, gasoline) is price insensitive, the substantial price increase by the cartel increased the total revenue of the cartel's members. The move was such a success among OPEC's members that the group returned five years later to double the price of oil from 1979 to 1981. Oil-consuming countries really felt the bite of this move and OPEC members once again reaped a huge stream of revenues. But then from 1982 to 1985 the price of oil started rapidly falling. By 1986, conflict among the cartel's members had grown so intense that its production restriction agreement fell apart and the price of oil fell by almost half. Four years later (1990), the price of oil (adjusted for inflation) was at the same level it was at in the early 1970s before OPEC began its production-tightening campaigns. So, what happened?

The supply of oil is insensitive in the short run because additional capacity takes time to create. Locating new deposits and extracting their contents takes time, but the sequential embargoes, by boosting the price of oil so significantly, caused non-OPEC nations to look to enter the oil business to score some of its very attractive and fat profits of the time. Demand is insensitive because for automobile owners, there are few close substitutes for oil (and its derivative, gasoline) in the short run. Thus, as FIGURE 5-9 shows, price rose substantially, quantity fell only slightly, and the total revenue of OPEC rose during the embargoes of 1973-1974 and 1979-1981.

But then the long run arrived, as it always does. After 1981, OPEC competitors, which had already been exploring for oil, brought new supply to the market. Russia expanded its operations, and supply as a whole became more sensitive. On the demand side, consumers in the U.S. carpooled more and increasingly abandoned large, not-so-reliable, gas-guzzling, V6- and V8-engine-powered American cars such as the Pontiac Grand Prix, Buick Regal, and Chevrolet Impala for smaller, reliable, fuel-efficient, four-cylinder Japanese cars such as the Honda Civic and Toyota Corolla.

FIGURE 5-10: A Decrease in the Supply of Oil (with Demand and Supply Both Price Sensitive)

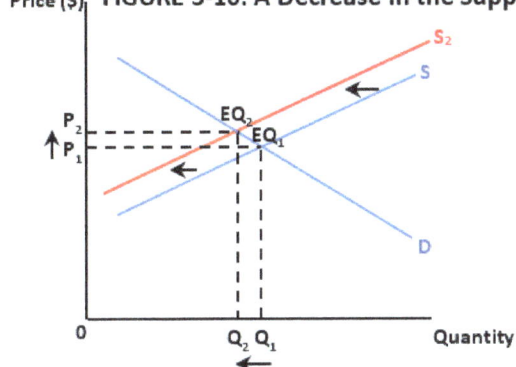

As can be seen in FIGURE 5-10, OPEC could now reduce barrel output by the same amount it did during its two previous successful embargoes, but this only raised price a small fraction of what it did before. From the third of our three takeaways with respect to price sensitivity of demand and total revenue, we know that for sensitive demands, a price increase will decrease total revenue. More competition for OPEC oil-producing nations and new technology producing reliable and fuel-efficient engines spelled the end of OPEC's market power. The oil-fracking revolution that came about later and substantially increased the supply of domestic oil weakened OPEC's market power even further.

ECONOMICS IN ACTION: the Counterproductive Economics of the "War on Drugs"

There are few malignant forces that eat away at the social fabric of a society as proficiently as the effects of illegal (and some legal) drugs. But one that might be its equal or near equal: the drug war. The war, especially as it has been more intensely waged since 1973 when U.S. President Richard Nixon created the U.S. Drug Enforcement Agency (DEA), has mainly consisted of attacks on black-market supplies. Why would this pose a problem?

There is no doubt that the demands for marijuana (where it is still recreationally illegal), heroin, and cocaine are very price insensitive, especially for addicts. (Interestingly, studies have found that the nicotine in legal cigarettes has been found to be just as addictive as illegal heroin, so besides dubious economics, the war has never had much logical consistency as well.) Supply is price insensitive because dealing illegal drugs on average entails the high costs of fines, prison sentences, and social stigma.

132

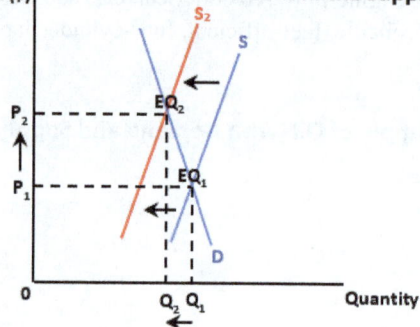

FIGURE 5-11: A Decrease in the Supply of Black-Market Heroin

As FIGURE 5-11 shows, drug raids on dealers and suppliers reduce supply from S to S_2. Thus, the market moves from equilibrium one (EQ_1) to equilibrium two (EQ_2) and thus sales fall only slightly from Q_1 to Q_2 while price rises substantially from P_1 to P_2.

The reason this has been dangerous is that substantially pushing up the street price of illegal drugs (with little effect on sales) has perversely led to an increased wave of crime. Users and addicts still want their fix, but now they have to rob, steal, and commit more burglaries to secure either money or goods they can sell for money to support their drug consumption. Responses to this secondary effect by politicians of different political leanings has made the problem worse. Many conservatives want an even more aggressive drug war to be waged while many progressives (e.g., former Los Angeles District Attorney George Gascon) favor reducing or even eliminating prosecution and penalties for most shoplifting, robbery, and burglary. The effect of such soft policies has predictably and recently led to not only many more property crimes being committed but an exodus of many retail businesses from many urban areas.

One proposed solution is more education and public-service campaigns to reduce demand in the black market for illegal drugs. FIGURE 5-12 illustrates the ideal in mind.

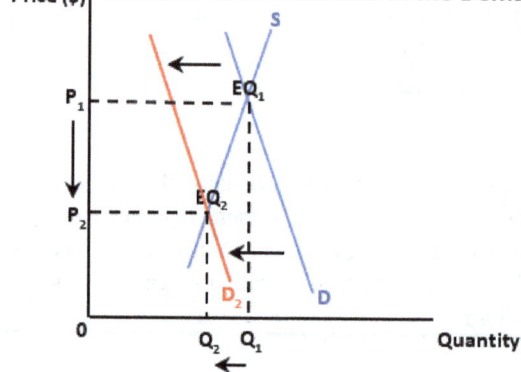

FIGURE 5-12: A Decrease in the Demand for Black-Market Heroin

Education and public-service campaigns inform and remind the public about the addictive qualities of heroin and other drugs and the physical and economic toll drugs can take on many lives. Through the demand factor of tastes/preferences, demand declines from D to $D2$ and the market moves from equilibrium one (EQ_1) at Q_1 and P_1 (where drug prices had been elevated from drug raids), to equilibrium two (EQ_2) at Q_2 and P_2. Sales have dropped slightly but prices have been reduced substantially. Ideally, education would be so effective that demand would decline to zero at all relevant prices (the demand curve would continually shift leftward until it completely shifted off the graph) and with no demand to service, supply would then disappear with the entire market.

Unfortunately, not only has the comparatively modest scenario delineated in FIGURE 5-12 not come close to happening, despite the best intentions, education at times has even perversely encouraged drug experimentation and regular use. One example is the film *Reefer Madness* (1936). Created to highlight the dangers of marijuana use, even some supporters of the drug war have conceded that it so dramatically overexaggerated the dangers of marijuana use as to help discredit the restrictive policies they favor.

Another example is the Drug Abuse Resistance Education (DARE) program started in 1983. Study after study (including one by the U.S. General Accounting Office [GAO]) concluded that over decades, DARE has had little effect on reducing the use of illegal drugs. Today, the program operates under a different name and emphasizes making better decisions.

No doubt drug education has been such a failure in part because so many who receive the "education" come to believe that addiction and its often-disastrous consequences will only befall someone else. This does not mean that education should be entirely abandoned, but it has to be designed with much more forethought than it currently is.

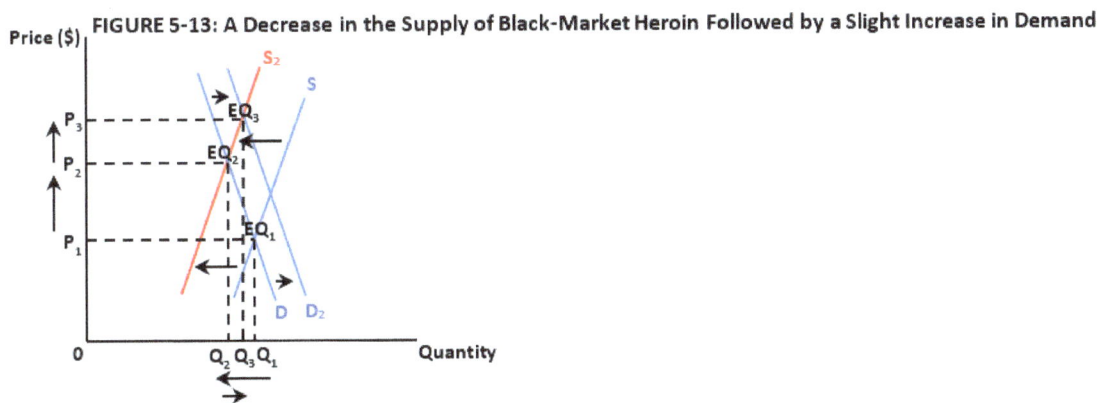

FIGURE 5-13: A Decrease in the Supply of Black-Market Heroin Followed by a Slight Increase in Demand

Otherwise, illegal-drug markets will remain where they are today, as in FIGURE 5-13 where the market begins at equilibrium one (EQ_1) with quantity at Q_1 and price at P_1 and as we saw previously, drug raids by law-enforcement authorities drive supply from S to S_2, moving the market from equilibrium one (EQ_1) to equilibrium two (EQ_2) with quantity at Q_2 and price at P_2. Finally, poorly constructed education fails to restrain demand or even perversely raises it, moving demand from D to $D2$ which in turn pushes the market from equilibrium two (EQ_2) to equilibrium three (EQ_3) with quantity at Q_3 and price at P_3. In the end, sales, moving from Q_1 down to Q_2 back up to Q_3, have fallen only slightly (on net) from the drug war but price has gone nowhere but continually up from P_1 to P_2 to P_3.

Further Reading

Thornton, Mark. *The Economics of Prohibition*. Salt Lake City: University of Utah Press, 1991. An in-depth study of the history, effects, and economics of alcohol, marijuana, and narcotics prohibition.

Woodhouse, Leighton. "How Weed Became the New Oxycontin." *Tablet*. August 30, 2022. < https://www.tabletmag.com/sections/news/articles/how-weed-became-new-oxycontin-marijuana-psychosis-addiction> How Big Tobacco and Big Pharma commandeered the industry in legal medicinal and recreational marijuana, making the plant much more potent, addictive, and psychosis-inducing.

5.13 Conclusion

Contrary to the scoffers, we see that the price sensitivity of demand and supply are essential concepts in business practice and social policy. Every successful entrepreneur has at least an intuitive feeling about how, given current business conditions, a raise or drop in the price of his or her product will affect the product's total revenue. This in turn, as we will learn later in chapter 7, has to affect profits [as profit (π) = total revenue (TR) – total cost (TC)], so of course it is a concept of crucial interest and importance to entrepreneurs and business firms. The three case studies in this chapter highlight the analytical importance of the price sensitivity of demand to understanding why the U.S. has seen fewer people working in farming over time, why the OPEC cartel has declined in market power since the early 1970s and 1980s, and why the War on Drugs is only increasing crime and drug addiction given current failed policies and approaches. As much as demand and supply sensitivity have practical use and value, one should not misuse them in a rote and hyper-empirical methodology. Price and sales data should lead no one to think that, with the midpoint formula, they can derive ultra-precise estimates of a product's sales given a product's price from today to the murky and constantly changing distant future. In chapter 4 we discussed the condition of *ceteris paribus* (Latin for "all other factors and variables are unchanged"). In the long run, all factors can change and one has to take as many of these into account as possible when trying to predict the effect of a change in price, income, or any other variable.

5.14 Chapter Concepts

price sensitivity of demand
price sensitivity of demand coefficient (η) (simple formula)
price sensitivity of demand coefficient (η) (midpoint formula)
slope
total revenue (TR)
income sensitivity of demand
income sensitivity of demand coefficient (α) (simple formula)
cross-price sensitivity of demand
cross-price sensitivity of demand coefficient (β) (simple formula)
price sensitivity of supply
price sensitivity of supply coefficient (γ) (simple formula)
price sensitivity of supply coefficient (γ) (midpoint formula)

5.15 Problems, Questions, and Discussion Topics (Items Requiring Examples are Marked with an Asterisk [*])

1. For its Christmas sale, Fast Eddy's Tire Shop reduces the price of its tires from $100 to $75 each to see its weekly demand rise from 1,000 to 1,500 tires.

   A. Using the simple formula, calculate the price sensitivity of demand coefficient (η).

   B. Does the price sensitivity of demand coefficient (η) suggest that Eddy's tires are price sensitive or insensitive?

2. For its Easter sale, Fast Eddy's Tire Shop reduces the price of its tires from $100 to $90 each to see its weekly demand rise from 1,000 to 1,050 tires.

   A. Using the midpoint formula, calculate the price sensitivity of demand coefficient (η).

   B. Does the price sensitivity of demand coefficient (η) suggest that Eddy's tires are price sensitive or insensitive?

3. In "ECONOMICS IN ACTION: Some Price Sensitivity of Demand Coefficient Estimates ($\hat{\eta}$) from Studies" and TABLE 5-1, there are price-sensitivity of demand estimates for nine products. Choose any two of the nine products and discuss how reasonable or off-the-mark you think each estimate ($\hat{\eta}$) is in light of

   A. the availability of close substitutes for each product and

   B. the portion of a consumer's budget spent on each product.

4. How is slope (Δ) different in concept from the price sensitivity of demand (η)?

5. For the month of December, Quiet Susan's Book Store sold 29 copies of Huckleberry Finn for $10.89 each. What is Quiet Susan's total revenue (TR) for Huckleberry Finn books for the month of December?

6. Sal's Potato Chips Incorporated notices that its recent price increase on its barbecue-flavored potato chips has caused its total revenue (TR) to fall. What does this indicate about the price sensitivity of demand of Sal's barbecue-flavored potato chips?

7. After Pharma-Monopoly Incorporated raises the price of its blood-pressure-lowering medication, Vampiria, from $1,000 per pill to $1,500 per pill, it sees its total revenue (TR) rise from $2 billion to $3 billion per year. What does this indicate about the price sensitivity of demand for Vampiria?

8. *As price steadily rises from 0 along a demand curve, price sensitivity of demand steadily goes from* _____ (insensitive, sensitive) *to* _____ (insensitive, sensitive).

   A. Fill in the blanks: _____, _____.

   B. Explain:

9. After graduating college with a master's degree in electrical engineering and finding a job at automaker Tesla, Andrea's income increases from $20,000 to $90,000 per year while her consumption of canned tuna drops from four cans per week to one can per week.

A. Calculate the income sensitivity of demand coefficient (α) using the simple formula.

B. What does the sign of α imply about what kind of good canned tuna is to Andrea?

10. The manager of Fast Eddy's Tire Shop notices that as the prices of new and used automobiles have on average increased 10 percent, sales of new automobile tires have dropped 20 percent.

A. Calculate the cross-price sensitivity of demand coefficient (β) using the simple formula.

B. What does the sign of β imply about what type of related goods (complements or substitutes) automobiles and automobile tires may be?

11. Antonio's Pizzeria every Friday evening was selling 20 calzones for $25 each. Since Antonio's competitor, Luigi's Ristorante, closed town from immigration violations last month, demand for Antonio's food has increased. Every Friday evening Antonio's is now selling 30 calzones for $30 each.

A. Calculate the price sensitivity of supply coefficient (γ) using the simple formula.

B. Does the price sensitivity of supply coefficient (γ) suggest that Antonio's calzones are price sensitive or insensitive?

12. *As price steadily rises from 0 along a supply curve, price sensitivity of supply steadily goes from* _____ (insensitive, sensitive) *to* _____ (insensitive, sensitive).

A. Fill in the blanks: _____, _____.

B. Explain:

13. How has technology been good for hunger but bad for farmers? (Hint: see FIGURE 5-8 and explain the process in detail.)

14. In the early 1970s, the Organization of the Petroleum Exporting Countries (OPEC) was the king of world oil markets. By the mid-1980s it had unthinkably been de-throned. What economic developments created this massive loss of market power? (Hint: see FIGURES 5-9 and 5-10 and explain the process in detail.)

15. Despite good intentions, how did anti-drug efforts steadily raise the prices of illegal drugs while only slightly reducing their sales? (Hint: see FIGURE 5-13 and explain the process in detail.)

Chapter 6: Market Intervention

6.0 Introduction

This chapter will examine market interventions and their effects, both intended and unintended. The two types of interventions that will be examined in detail are price controls and taxes. The price controls that will be discussed are price ceilings and price floors while the taxes that will be discussed are sales taxes.

6.1 Price Ceilings: Binding and Non-Binding

A **price ceiling** is a maximum price set on a good or service by a local, state, or national government. Price ceilings come in two varieties: binding and non-binding. A **binding price ceiling** is a price ceiling set below the equilibrium price of a market. It is the type of ceiling that has important effects on markets.

> **price ceiling** - a maximum price set on a good or service by a local, state, or national government.
>
> **binding price ceiling** – a price ceiling set below the equilibrium price of a market.

FIGURE 6-1 illustrates the two types of price ceilings. Graph A depicts a market with a binding price ceiling. Normally the market for this product (grilled-cheese sandwiches) clears at a price of $5 per unit with 100 units sold per day at Norm's Sandwiches, a small sandwich shop. While the public likes Norm's grilled-cheese sandwiches, so do many local politicians. So much so, in fact, that the politicians think that a way to improve Norm's grilled-cheese sandwiches would be to forbid their sale for any more than $3 per sandwich. Thus, the municipality imposes a price ceiling of $3 per grilled-cheese sandwich.

FIGURE 6-1: Two Types of Price Ceilings

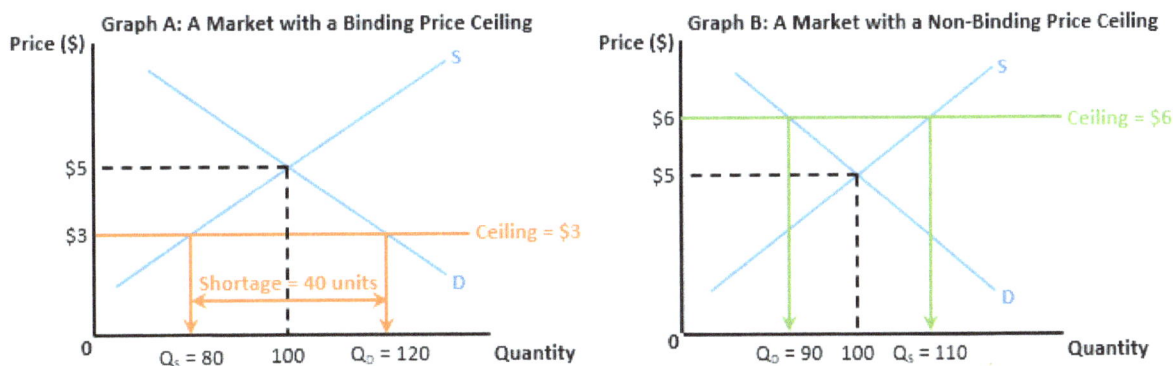

What are the effects of the ceiling? At $3 per sandwich, Norm's is willing to make and sell 80 sandwiches per day, so the quantity supplied per day falls to 80 ($Q_S = 80$ on the horizontal axis of the graph) from the free-market equilibrium quantity of 100. However, at the new lower ceiling price of $3 per sandwich, the quantity of sandwiches demanded increases to 120 ($Q_D = 120$). This new disparity between quantity demanded and quantity supplied ($Q_D - Q_S = 120 - 80 = 40$) is called a **shortage** (**excess demand**), or the difference between the quantity demanded and quantity supplied in a market because the market price is below the equilibrium price. A substantial amount of

> **shortage (excess demand)** – the difference between quantity demanded and quantity supplied in a market because the market price is below the equilibrium price.

frustration exists in the market illustrated in Graph A of FIGURE 6-1 because 120 sandwiches are demanded but only 80 are supplied and sold. In other words, if 1 sandwich per person is allocated, 1 out of every 3 consumers in this market is not receiving his or her desired meal.

In reaction to the price ceiling, let's say that consumer protests at city hall force the city to move its price ceiling up to $6 per sandwich. What are the effects of this new "ceiling?"

Graph B in FIGURE 6-1 (the same market as that depicted in Graph A) provides the answer. Price rises from the ceiling price of $3 per sandwich back to the market equilibrium price of $5 per sandwich, while quantity supplied rises from 80 back to the equilibrium quantity of 100 and quantity demanded falls from 120 to the equilibrium quantity of 100. In other words, the market returns to equilibrium because at prices below $5, quantity demanded is greater than quantity supplied, price is bid upward until quantity demanded equals quantity supplied at $5 per sandwich with 100 sandwiches sold. The market is said to "clear" at equilibrium because everyone who wants a sandwich gets one and is happy. There is no longer any frustration in the market in terms of a shortage.

But hold on: What about the new price "ceiling" of $6 and its effect on market quantities? The answer is that the new "ceiling" is irrelevant because it is situated above market equilibrium. The whole purpose of a true (binding) price ceiling is to prevent a market from reaching equilibrium and "clearing" by an upward adjustment of price. In fact, "non-binding price ceiling" is a misnomer because it is not a ceiling at all. It's no barrier to equilibrium, hence not a real price control. While the quantities where the new "ceiling" crosses the demand curve ($Q_D = 90$) and supply curve ($Q_S = 110$) are noted in Graph B for illustrative purposes, they are as irrelevant as the new $6 above-market-clearing price.

ECONOMICS IN ACTION: Why is Housing in Some Large Cities Artificially Scarce and Dilapidated?

Swedish economist Assar Lindbeck famously quipped that rent control is the fastest way to destroy a city besides bombing it. That's a dramatic statement, but what was Lindbeck getting at? **Rent control** is a maximum level of rent per month that a government will allow a landlord to charge tenants on a rental dwelling. In other words, it's a price ceiling, and usually a binding one. While this makes beginning economics students immediately imagine shortages in rental housing (and they are certainly on the right track), the policy also has many other effects that steadily increase in severity over time.

rent control - a maximum level of rent per month that a government will allow a landlord to charge tenants for a rental dwelling.

FIGURE 6-2 contrasts the effects of rent control over the short run versus the long run. In Graph A (the short run), the supply of housing is very price insensitive, with the supply curve almost completely vertical (as in the $\gamma = 0$ case in FIGURE 5-5 in chapter 5). As rents increase, it takes time to build new apartments and divide existing one-family homes or formerly non-residential commercial buildings into multi-family dwellings. Demand is insensitive as well, but not as much as supply. As rents rise, it takes time for households to find housing alternatives, which include acquiring a loan to purchase a house.

In Graph A of FIGURE 6-2, Mayberry implements a rent ceiling at $1,000 per month, or $500 below market-equilibrium rent. The quantity supplied of rental dwellings drops from 1,000 per month to 950 per month. Quantity demanded, however, jumps from 1,000 to 1,300. The rent ceiling produces a shortage of 350 units per month. Because of the insensitivity of both sides of the market (supply and demand), in the short run the main effect of rent control is a small shortage of rental dwellings.

FIGURE 6-2: Rent Control, The Long and Short of It

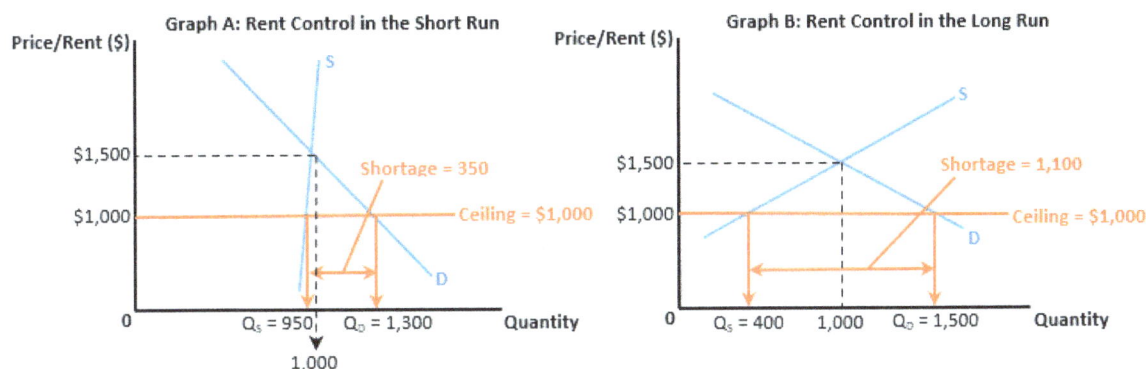

Graph B in FIGURE 6-2 gives a hint of the encroaching pathologies that appear in the long run. Supply becomes more price sensitive because more housing can be built as the market enters the long run. Demand becomes more price sensitive as well because it becomes easier for renters to move into or out of the city in the long run as leases expire. The first problem is that the shortage explodes 214 percent, from 350 to 1,100 units per month. This increase is made up of two components. In terms of quantity supplied, it is a reduction of 550 units (950 in the short run [see Q_S in Graph A] minus 400 in the long run [see Q_S in Graph B] as resources devoted to rental properties get increasingly diverted to uses that earn a market-equilibrium level return, such as turning rented apartments into condominiums that can be sold. In terms of quantity demanded, it is an increase of 200 units (from 1,300 in the short run [see Q_D in Graph A] to 1,500 in the long run [see Q_D in Graph B]) as prospective renters are lured into the city from the short run to long run by its below-market rents. As the market transitions from the short run to the long run, frustration, which is small to begin with, skyrockets as landlords want to supply housing, but not at the current rental rates, which are not profitable. Prospective renters, having heard about cheap housing in Mayberry, feverishly comb the town for a place to live at the prevailing (controlled) price, but find nothing. In summary, the effects of binding rent controls are as follows:

Short run: small shortage.
Long run:
1. Large shortage. Studies also show:
2. A deterioration in housing quality as routine and timely maintenance is abandoned.
3. Since equilibrium market price is no longer the allocation mechanism in the market, bribes and discrimination increase. Landlords accept secret payments to reserve newly vacant apartments for preferred tenants. Apartments become available for picturesque two-parent families and remain stubbornly unavailable for disfavored demographic groups.

Long-run effect number 2 above is what Assar Lindbeck was referring to when he compared the results of rent control to bombing.

CASE STUDY: What Caused the Long Lines at Gas Stations in the 1970s?

In chapter 5, we discussed the Organization of the Petroleum Exporting Countries (OPEC), a group of oil-producing countries that, in the early 1970s, successfully agreed to reduce its supply of oil to world markets in order to raise the price of oil and OPEC members' profits. This in turn increased the price of gasoline because oil is a major input in the production of gasoline. (Recall in chapter 4 our discussion about one of the factors that reduces market supply: an increase in the price of an input in the production of a product.)

FIGURE 6-3 contrasts the conditions of markets that are allowed to "clear" (i.e., reach equilibrium price and quantity) with those of markets in which binding price controls are implemented. In Graph A of FIGURE 6-3, the market in gasoline in Mayberry is in equilibrium at a price of $1 per gallon with 1,000 gallons sold per day. After OPEC cuts production of oil and raises its price, the supply of gasoline falls from S to S_2. The new equilibrium in Mayberry is at a price of $1.50 per gallon with 600 gallons sold per day. Even though the price per gallon of gasoline is 50 percent higher, there is no frustration in the market. Everyone who shows up at the gas station gets the amount of gas he or she desires and there are no lines at the gas pumps.

FIGURE 6-3: The Retail Market for Gasoline: Free versus Controlled

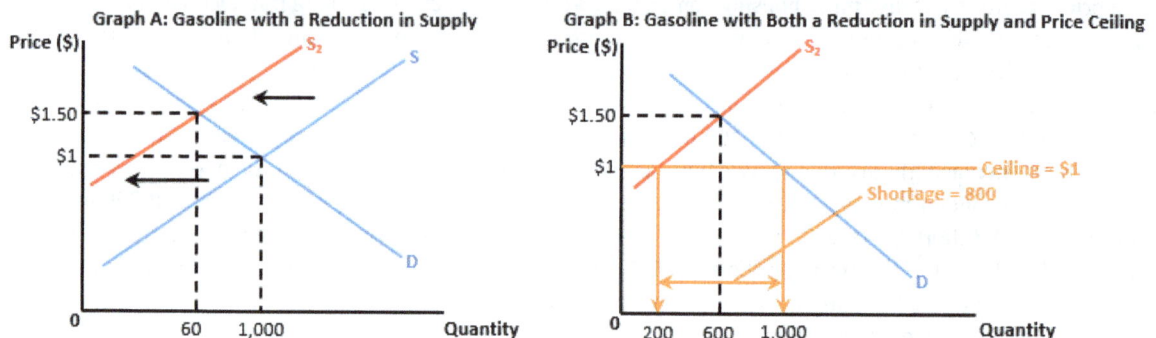

However, all is not copacetic in Mayberry. Mayor Floyd Pike and Deputy Barney Fife aren't happy with the new higher price of gasoline. They both agitate to have the city council enact a price ceiling at the old equilibrium price of $1 per gallon. Graph B illustrates the results. With the ceiling in place, quantity supplied is 200 gallons per day while quantity demanded is 1,000 gallons per day. The resulting shortage is (1,000 – 200 =) 800 gallons per day. There is now major frustration in Mayberry. There are now long lines of cars waiting for gasoline at each of Mayberry's gas stations.

This is essentially what happened in the U.S. in 1973. While Americans blamed OPEC for the long lines at gas stations because it reduced the supply of gasoline, economists blamed the price ceiling. Why? As Graph A of FIGURE 6-3 makes clear, ***reductions in supply don't cause shortages.*** While the American public was understandably unhappy with the increase in the price of gasoline, drivers who still wanted and needed to fill their tanks did so while others who didn't want to pay the higher price drove less and carpooled more.

What caused the long lines at gas stations—where drivers waited hours to purchase a restricted number of gallons of gasoline on odd- or even-numbered days—was the price ceiling. The underlying allocative problem was that in the long lines were not only drivers who really needed to purchase fuel (to get to a hospital for a medical emergency or get to work) but also panic buyers and neurotics who became overly fearful every time their fuel gauge fell just a little below the "F" (full) level. This was a substantial market distortion and misallocation of resources. The definitive proof of this was the almost instant disappearance of the long lines right after the price ceiling was repealed. Drivers who really needed and valued gasoline remained in the market, received quickly refilled fuel tanks, and paid the higher price while the nervous nellies turned around, drove home, and found something else in life to incessantly worry about.

6.2 Price Floors: Binding and Non-Binding

A **price floor** is a minimum price set on a good or service by a local, state, or national government. Price floors, like price ceilings, come in two varieties: binding and non-binding. A **binding price floor** is a price floor that is set above the equilibrium price of a market. As with price ceilings, binding price floors are the price controls that have important effects on markets.

price floor - a minimum price set on a good or service by a local, state, or national government.

binding price floor – a price floor that is set above the equilibrium price of a market.

FIGURE 6-4 illustrates two types of price floors. In Graph A, the market for this product (one brick[33] of salted butter) clears at a price of $5 per brick with 100 bricks sold per day in Appleton, Wisconsin. Wisconsin Dairy Farmers, however, would like the price to be $7 per brick and successfully lobby the Wisconsin state legislature to implement a price floor of $7 per brick of salted butter sold in the state.

Graph A in FIGURE 6-4 also shows the effects of the price floor: at $7 per brick, the quantity demanded per day in Appleton falls from 100 to 75 ($Q_D = 75$ on the horizontal axis of the graph) while the quantity supplied per day rises from 100 to 125 ($Q_S = 125$). This new disparity between quantity supplied and quantity demanded (Q_S - $Q_D = 125 - 75 = 50$) is called a **surplus (excess supply)**, or the difference between quantity supplied and quantity demanded in a market because the market price is above the equilibrium price. As with a binding price ceiling, frustration exists in this market because 125 bricks are supplied to the market daily but only 75 are sold. Unsold inventory is accumulating at the rate of 50 bricks per day.

surplus (excess supply) – the difference between quantity supplied and quantity demanded in a market because the market price is above the equilibrium price.

FIGURE 6-4: Two Types of Price Floors

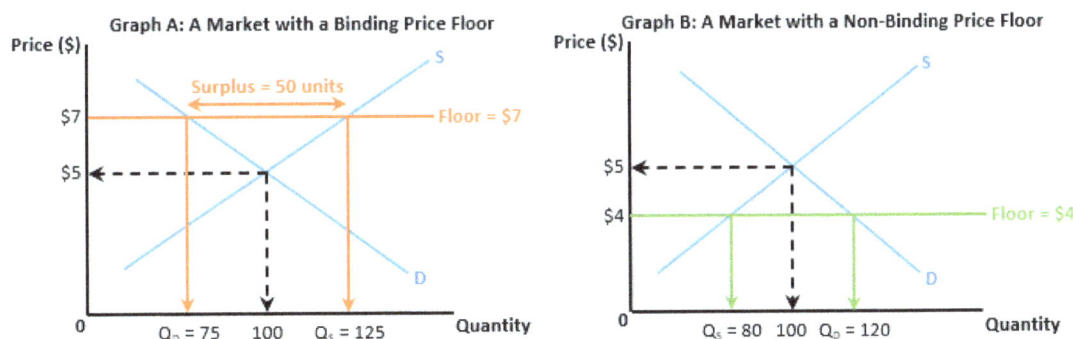

In reaction to the price floor, consumer groups and retail store owners counter-lobby the Wisconsin state legislature and demand that the price floor be repealed or reduced. The state legislature relents and moves the floor down to $4 per brick. What are the effects of this new "floor"?

Graph B in FIGURE 6-4 (the same market depicted in Graph A of FIGURE 6-4) provides the answer. Price falls from the floor price of $7 per brick back to the market equilibrium price of $5 per brick while quantity demanded rises from 75 bricks per day back to the equilibrium quantity

---

[33] One brick = one pound = four sticks = 2 cups of butter. The metric measures are 500 ml or 454 g per brick.

142

of 100 and quantity supplied falls from 125 bricks to the equilibrium quantity of 100. In other words, the market returns to equilibrium because at prices above $5, quantity supplied exceeds quantity demanded, price is bid downward until quantity supplied equals quantity demanded at $5 and 100 bricks of salted butter. The market clears at equilibrium where every brick of butter demanded is supplied and everyone is happy. There is no longer any frustration in this market.

What about the new price "floor" of $4 per brick and its effect on market quantities? The answer is that the new "floor" is irrelevant because it is situated below market equilibrium. The whole purpose of a true (binding) price floor is to prevent a market from reaching equilibrium by a downward adjustment of the market price. "Non-binding price floor" is a misnomer because it is not a floor at all. It's no barrier to equilibrium, hence not a real price control. While the quantities where the new "floor" crosses the supply curve ($Q_S = 80$) and demand curve ($Q_D = 120$) are noted in Graph B of FIGURE 6-4 for illustrative purposes, they are as irrelevant as the new $4 below-market-clearing price.

market-clearing price - the price where neither a shortage (excess demand) nor surplus (excess supply) exists in a market. It is the same thing as the equilibrium price.

Speaking of market clearing now (and in chapter 4 as well), and having now seen the adverse effects of binding price ceilings and floors, what is a market-clearing price? A **market-clearing price** is a price where neither a shortage (excess demand) nor surplus (excess supply) exists in a market. Shortages, surpluses, and frustration have all been "cleared" away. And yes, it is the same thing as the equilibrium price.

ECONOMICS IN ACTION: the Minimum Wage

The most famous (or infamous, depending on one's view) price floor is unquestionably the **minimum wage**, or

minimum wage – a price (wage) floor usually set for unskilled labor.

more precisely, minimum wage for unskilled labor. Graphs A and B of FIGURE 6-5 represent the weekly market for unskilled labor in the small town of Podunk, New York. In Graph A, the market is allowed to clear. At a wage rate of $10 per hour, 100 unskilled workers are hired. There is no frustration on either the demand or supply side of the market. Every employer of unskilled labor, when he or she has an open position of employment, is able to fill that position within a week's time.

FIGURE 6-5: The Market for Unskilled Labor: Free versus Controlled

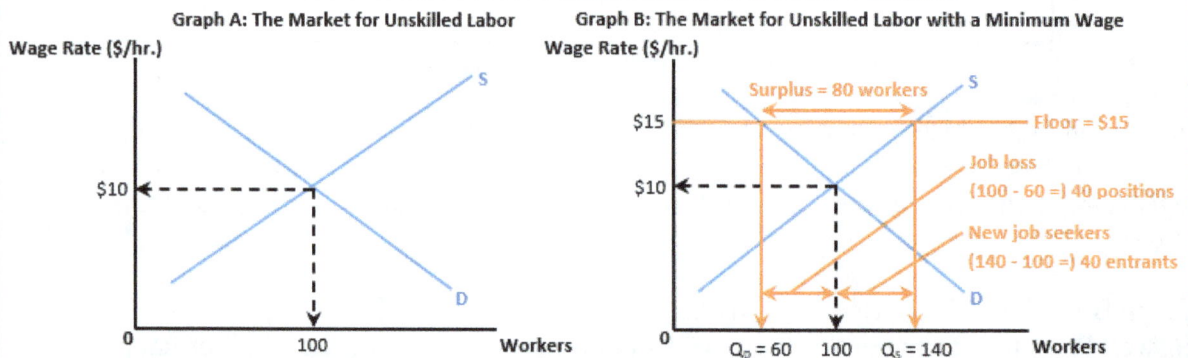

Officials in Tompkins County, in the county seat in the city of Ithaca, New York decide that the free-market wage for unskilled labor in Podunk is "unfair," and implement a minimum wage for Podunk of $15 per hour.

Graph B illustrates the effects of this new policy. At $15 per hour, the quantity of unskilled labor demanded in Podunk falls from 100 workers to 60 while the quantity of unskilled labor supplied rises from 100 to 140. This creates a market surplus of 80 workers per week.

This new surplus of 80 workers is deconstructed at the bottom of Graph B. Given the wage sensitivity of supply and demand in this particular market, below the old equilibrium quantity of 100 workers, the new $15 per hour minimum wage has led to a loss of $(100 - [Q_D = 60] =)$ 40 jobs for unskilled workers in Podunk. Above the old equilibrium quantity of 100 workers, the new $15 per hour minimum wage has lured $([Q_S = 140] - 100 =)$ 40 new job seekers into the labor market looking for work where (alongside the 40 workers who just lost their jobs) they find no work.

As is now obvious, the frustration in labor markets controlled by binding minimum wages is on the supply side, as low-income, unskilled workers look for employment, especially to feed their families and pay their bills, but no longer find it as easily as they once did. The situation becomes even worse when there is a large increase in unskilled workers from legal or illegal immigration. Immigration increases labor supply and drives wages down, which makes subsistence purchasing power increasingly difficult to acquire for low-income, unskilled workers in high-cost-of-living states such as California and New York. This is why so many economists despise the minimum wage. As an anti-poverty program, in terms of being counterproductive and anti-poor, it probably stands second only to throwing live grenades into housing projects.

6.3 Implicit Price Ceilings

By far, the most pervasive price ceiling, the **implicit price ceiling**, is a price ceiling set at no explicit price and effectively implemented by local or state "anti-gouging" or "fair-price" laws. These are so-called anti-gouging or "fair price" laws, and they produced large shortages of goods—from toilet paper to antiseptic wipes to diapers to even pet food—during the COVID-19 pandemic of 2020-2023.

implicit price ceiling – a price ceiling set at no explicit price and effectively implemented by local or state "anti-gouging" or "fair-price" laws.

Graph A in FIGURE 6-6 illustrates the market for toilet paper at Hy-Vee grocery store on East Sunshine Street in Springfield, Missouri in March of 2020 right before the beginning of the COVID-19 pandemic. The pre-pandemic price is $7 per 6-roll package (the unit most households purchase) with 50 units sold per day at this particular store. After the pandemic panic gets into full swing, demand surges by a large amount. If Hy-Vee is allowed to let prices follow market forces, the new short-term equilibrium that would be established is $17 per 6-roll package with 150 units sold per day. As we all know, this is not what happened.

What happened was that Hy-Vee, Walmart, Walgreens, and every other grocery, drug, and retail store that sold toilet paper kept their prices constant and store shelves quickly went completely bare for two weeks. Then store shelves were replenished, the supply was quickly snatched up in several hours, and store shelves went bare again for weeks. This process repeated throughout the rest of 2020 into 2021.

FIGURE 6-6: The Retail Market for Toilet Paper (6-Roll Packages): Free versus Implicitly Controlled

Graph A: An Increase in Demand

Price ($)

17

7

S

D_2

D

50   150

0

Quantity

Graph B: An Increase in Demand with an Implicit Price Ceiling

Price ($)

17

7

S

E_2

E_1 A   B

D_2

D

Effective Ceiling = $7

Shortage = 200 units

0

$Q_S = 50$ $Q_D = 250$

150

Quantity

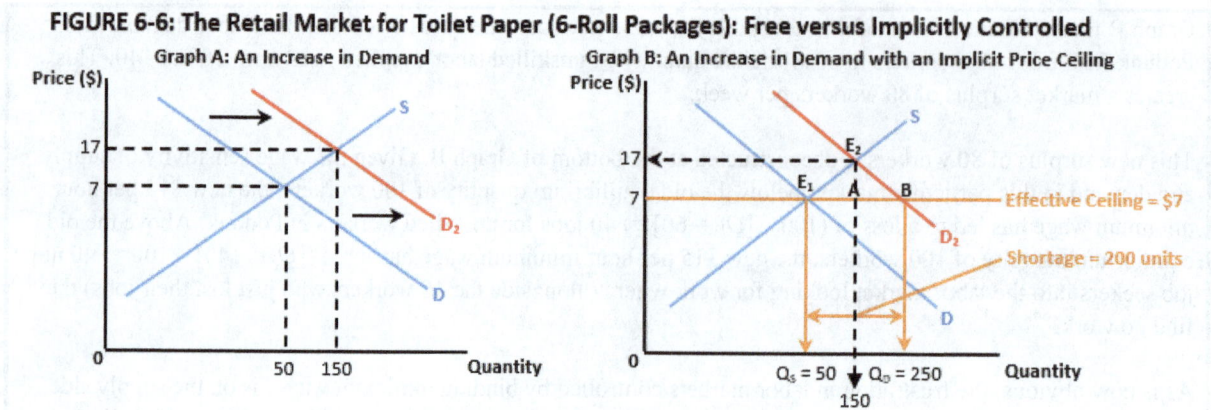

Graph B gives a snapshot of what happened. Hy-Vee keeps its price at $7 per unit to not run afoul of Missouri's anti-gouging law and state attorney general's office. This also keeps it out of hot water on social media platforms (such as Facebook, X, TikTok, YouTube, etc.) where cell-phone photos of a $17 price for a 6-roll package of toilet paper would spur calls to boycott Hy-Vee because of its "greed." (Never mind the greed of neurotic panic shoppers who already had shelves full of toilet paper and many other essentials at home but were continually panic-shopping for more because they thought the world was coming to an end. This exact behavior was making the situation worse, causing more bare shelves and more panic.)

At an effective ceiling of $7, the daily quantity supplied is 50 units but the daily quantity demanded, given the new panic-driven demand, jumps to 250 units. This disparity represents a large shortage of (250 - 50 =) 200 units per day. This is quadruple the normal pre-pandemic daily sales that were completely satisfied (50 units per day in Graph A). Similar to how we deconstructed the price-controlled labor market in Graph B of FIGURE 6-5, we can deconstruct the shortage in Graph B of FIGURE 6-6. At the pre-pandemic equilibrium of E_1 in Graph B of FIGURE 6-6, 50 units were sold daily. At the panic equilibrium of E_2 that was not allowed to happen, 150 units would have been sold daily and shelves would have remained as stocked as they were pre-pandemic. Point B in Graph B of FIGURE 6-6 represents the quantity demanded ($Q_D = 250$ units) in the controlled market.

The shortage along the price ceiling line at $7 per unit, from points E_1 to A to B, breaks down as follows. Obviously point E_1 represents the quantity supplied, so once those 50 units are gone, the shelves go bare and there is no longer any toilet paper in the store. The line segment from E_1 to A represents the consumers who really needed toilet paper and were willing to pay the new and higher equilibrium price to get it but were denied it and went home empty-handed. This is part of the harm of the implicit price control. Consumers who really needed the product such that they were willing to pay a substantially higher price for it did not get it.

Finally, the line segment from A to B represents all the consumers who did not really need toilet paper but were lured into the market by its artificially low price who were denied it and went home empty-handed. This is the second part of the harm of the implicit price control. Consumers who should not even have been out and about, especially helping spread the COVID-19 virus, were instead lured out of their homes by artificially low prices, which contributed to even more unnecessarily crowded streets, roads, and grocery-store aisles.

Interestingly, the notorious pandemic shortages even extended to pet food, which showed their completely panic-driven nature. Employees of businesses who were sent home to work remotely would obviously consume more residential toilet paper than normal, but not that much more than usual and certainly not enough to justify panic buying. However, no one was going to be feeding their pets more because of a pandemic. The shortage in pet foot and other pet items was proof that the early pandemic shortages were a pure panic phenomenon and another ramification of the extreme social damage caused by the implicit price ceilings on all manner of consumer goods.

Had market forces been allowed to work, store shelves would have stayed stocked and high prices would have lasted for several days before quickly adjusting back down to normal levels as supply chains would have had the time and incentive to reconnect. While high prices (including $17 for a six-roll pack of toilet paper) are no picnic for anyone, politicians effectively banning them made no one better off and just extended the misery of the pandemic. The irony is that high prices re-emerged with a vengeance after the pandemic in terms of 9.1 percent peak monthly inflation[34] and 19.4 percent cumulative inflation[35] as the result of, again, the ill-advised actions of politicians (see chapter 1, section 1.9, economics principle 9: prices rise when the government circulates too much money).

6.4 Sales Taxes

The most common sales tax is one that is a proportion of sales and collected by sellers on behalf of the government. The case we will explore is a per-sale tax. In terms of the product, we'll just stick with our chapter 5 example of bottles of shampoo.

6.4.1 A Sales Tax on Sellers

FIGURE 6-7 shows the market effects of a $1 tax per bottle of shampoo with sellers having to track sales and pay the tax revenue to the municipal government of Mayberry every month.

---

[34] CPI inflation for June 2022 (U.S. Bureau of Labor Statistics [BLS]). <https://www.bls.gov/opub/ted/2022/consumer-price-index-unchanged-over-the-month-up-8-5-percent-over-the-year-in-july-2022.htm>

[35] CPI 2021-2024 (U.S. Bureau of Labor Statistics [BLS]). <https://www.bls.gov/regions/mid-atlantic/data/consumerpriceindexhistorical_us_table.htm>

FIGURE 6-7: The Market for Shampoo with a Sales Tax on Sellers

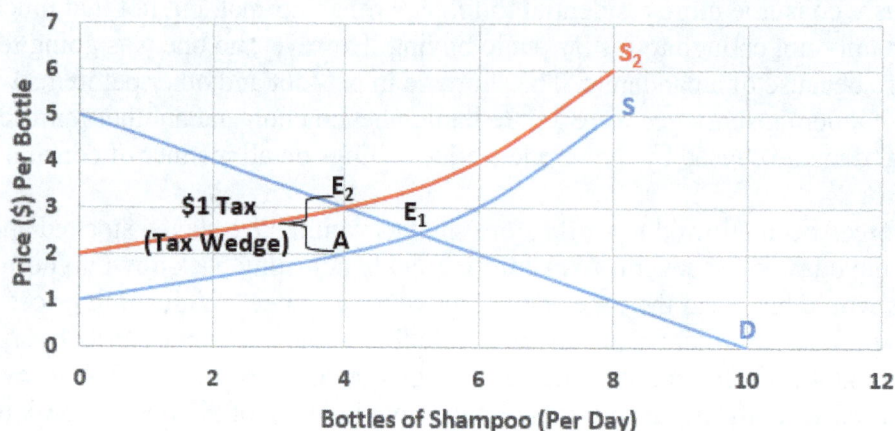

In the market displayed in FIGURE 6-7, we see the old (pre-tax) equilibrium E_1 (5, $2.50) and the new (post-tax) equilibrium E_2 (4, $3). Before the imposition of the tax, market price was $2.50 per bottle with 5 bottles sold per day. What effect does the levying of the $1-per-bottle tax have on the seller in this market? Chapter 4 already told us. One of the factors that can reduce

tax wedge – the difference between the price or wage demanders pay and the price or wage suppliers receive. It is equal to the size of the tax.

market supply is a tax on the goods being brought to market. In FIGURE 6-7, we see a reduction in supply where the curve shifts leftward by the amount of the tax, $1. The old equilibrium E_1 (5, $2.50) shifts to a new one, E_2 (4, $3). What we see formed by this change is a **tax wedge**, or difference between the price or wage demanders pay per unit and the price or wage suppliers receive per

unit. It is equal to the size of the tax. In FIGURE 6-7, the tax wedge is equal to the vertical difference between points E_2 and A or ($3 - $2 =) $1 or the new equilibrium price ($3) plus the tax ($1) or ($3 + $1 =) $4 minus the new equilibrium price ($3) or ($4 - $3 =) $1. Put another way, the tax wedge is also the difference between what demanders pay for the product after the imposition of the tax ($3) and what suppliers actually receive per bottle after the imposition of the tax ($2), or ($3 - $2 =) $1.

The triangle formed by points E_2, E_1, and A in this market after the levying of the tax is known as deadweight loss, or the loss to demanders and suppliers in a market caused by the imposition of a tax or control. (Deadweight loss will be further defined and discussed later in the chapter. It doesn't include the costs of complying with the tax in terms of, say, having to purchase a computer and accounting software and regularly having to remit the tax to the local government each month.) Consumers would normally purchase 5 bottles of shampoo per day, but after the tax they only purchase 4. The old equilibrium price of $2.50 is pushed up to $3, with consumers paying 50 cents of the $1 tax and sellers paying 50 cents. How the burden of a tax is divided in a

tax incidence – how the burden of a tax is divided in a market.

market is known as **tax incidence**, and in this (unlikely) case, half of the tax revenue is paid by buyers and half by sellers. Tax incidence depends on the price sensitivity of demand and supply in a market.

6.4.2 A Sales Tax on Buyers

In contrast to the market displayed in FIGURE 6-7, we now move to a tax on buyers. Such a tax would be easy to implement in the sense that at the cash register of each store, for card (credit or debit) transactions, the tax could be added to the amount charged or debited to each card. For cash transactions, the tax would be added to the final sale total. In the market displayed in FIGURE 6-8, we start at the old (pre-tax) equilibrium E_1 where price is $2.50 per bottle and quantity sold is 5 bottles per day. What are the market ramifications of levying a $1-per-bottle tax on buyers? Again, chapter 4 already told us. One of the factors that can reduce market demand is a tax on a good or service being sold.

FIGURE 6-8: The Market for Shampoo with a Sales Tax on Buyers

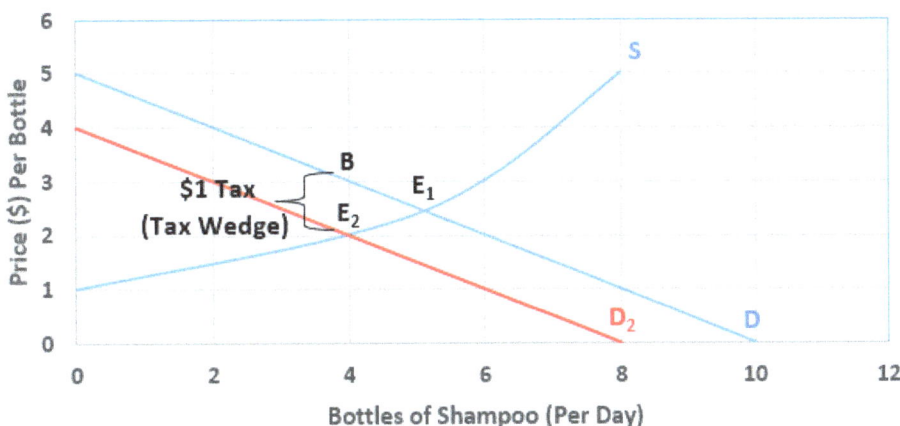

In FIGURE 6-8, we see a reduction in demand where the demand curve shifts leftward by the amount of the tax, $1. The old equilibrium E_1 (5, $2.50) shifts to a new one, E_2 (4, $2). The tax wedge is now the new equilibrium price ($2) plus the tax ($1) or:

$$tax\ wedge = (new\ equilibrium\ price + tax) - (new\ equilibrium\ price)$$

$$= (\$2 + \$1) - (\$2)$$

$$= \$3 - \$2$$

$$= \$1$$

This tax wedge is also the difference between what buyers now pay for the product after the tax (point E_2 in FIGURE 6-8) and what the sellers actually receive after the tax (point B in FIGURE 6-8).

The triangle formed by points B, E_1, and E_2 is the deadweight loss in this market from the imposition of the tax on buyers. Again, just as with the tax on sellers illustrated in FIGURE 6-7, consumers would normally purchase 5 bottles per day but after the tax purchase only 4. The old equilibrium price of $2.50 falls to $2, with consumers paying half (50 cents) of the $1 tax and sellers paying half (50 cents). The tax incidence in this (other unlikely) case ends up with half of the revenue paid by buyers and half paid by sellers. Again, the tax incidence depends on the price sensitivity of demand and supply, which is determined by the market, not politicians or tax authorities, no matter how much they try to skew the tax incidence one way or the other.

6.5 Payroll Taxes

payroll tax – a percentage of an employee's gross pay that can go to a local, state, or federal government to fund various programs.

A **payroll tax** is a percentage of an employee's gross (pre-tax) pay that can go to a local, state, or federal government to fund various programs. State and federal income taxes are obvious examples. Another well-known example is the Federal Insurance Contributions Act (FICA) tax, which is a federal payroll tax that funds the federal Social Security and Medicare programs. Unlike state and federal income taxes, FICA is a

bifurcated tax – a tax divided between two parties.

bifurcated tax, a tax divided between two parties. In the case of FICA, employees currently pay 6.2 percent of their gross pay to fund Social Security and 1.45 percent to fund Medicare for a total of 7.65 percent. However, that is not the whole story because employers also pay a 7.65 percent tax from their sales revenue. While at first this may look like a fair and even tax burden, it does not end up that way.

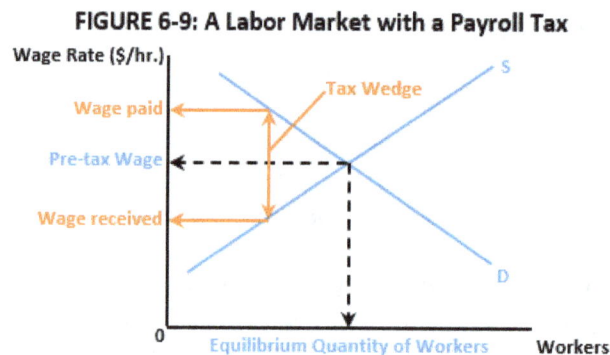

FIGURE 6-9: A Labor Market with a Payroll Tax

FIGURE 6-9 reveals the results. When a payroll tax is implemented, the wage paid by firms increases while the wage received by workers falls. The difference between these two wages is the tax wedge in this labor market. While there certainly is a sharing of the tax burden between workers and firms as intended, the actual division has absolutely nothing to do with what is stated in the law, "fair division of the burden" or otherwise. Nor would it make the slightest difference if the law called for firms to bear 100 percent of the burden or workers to bear 100 percent of the burden. Again, tax incidence depends on the price sensitivity of demand and supply as the next section of the chapter will conclusively demonstrate.

6.6 Tax Incidence and the Price Sensitivities of Demand and Supply

Now we get to how market forces divide the tax burden. FIGURE 6-10 displays two types of markets. In Graph A, the market has a price sensitive demand and price insensitive supply. As we saw previously, it doesn't matter whether the tax on a product or payroll (labor) is paid by buyers or sellers, and thus the curve that shifts as a result of who pays the tax (supply if sellers pay the tax and demand if buyers pay the tax) is irrelevant. That is why we won't even bother illustrating a shift to a new equilibrium: It isn't necessary.

In Graph A, we see the tax wedge that appears either way. If demand is price sensitive but supply is price insensitive as in Graph A, the portion of the tax paid by sellers is higher than that paid by buyers. This makes sense because the parties with higher price sensitivity, in this case consumers, have more options in terms of alternatives to the product and can therefore more easily leave the market. This is a product such as sockeye salmon. If the price rises substantially, consumers will exit this market and move to other markets such as chinook, coho, or pink salmon, or other fish such as tilapia or cod, or even non-fish food such as beef or pork. The side of the market with fewer options (in this case sellers), bears the burden of the tax.

FIGURE 6-10: How Market Forces Divide the Tax Burden

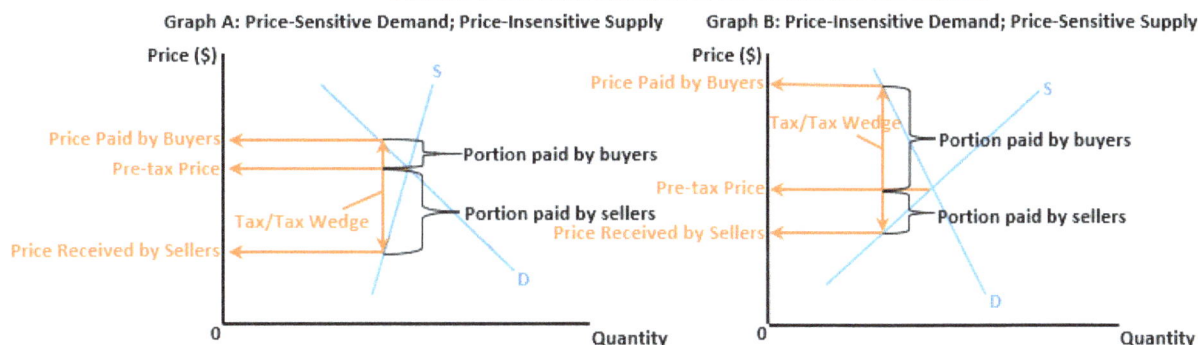

In Graph B of FIGURE 6-10, the market is characterized by a price-insensitive demand and price-sensitive supply. Given that it doesn't matter whether the tax on a product or payroll (labor) is paid by buyers or sellers, we won't bother with illustrating a shift to a new equilibrium in Graph B either. In Graph B, we see another tax wedge and can observe that if demand is price insensitive but supply is price sensitive, the portion of the tax paid by consumers is higher than that paid by sellers. This, like the situation in Graph A, too makes sense because the parties with higher price sensitivity, in this case, sellers, have more options in terms of alternatives to the product. This is a product such as gasoline. If the price rises substantially, consumers cannot so easily move to other options in the short run, even with electric vehicles which are still significantly more expensive than gasoline-powered vehicles. Sellers of gasoline can move to selling other necessities such as food or clothing. Again, the side of the market with fewer options (in this case buyers), bears the burden of the tax and that is what we see in Graph B of FIGURE 6-10.

Moral of the story: The side of the market that has higher price insensitivity (and can therefore less easily leave the market) bears more of the burden of a tax.

Going back to the payroll tax we saw in FIGURE 6-9, studies show that in most labor markets, the demand for labor is far more price sensitive than the supply of labor. Even though in FIGURE 6-9 we drew the tax wedge as if the burden of the payroll tax were even, this is not realistic. Workers mostly bear the burden of the payroll tax instead of firms. The effort of politicians to supposedly divide the burden evenly between firms and workers was mostly a failure.

6.7 Taxation and Deadweight Loss

Is market allocation of resources optimal? In chapter 1 we discussed central planning in nations such as the Soviet Union and North Korea. Could a human planner do better in allocating resources than markets? To answer these questions, we have to begin with concepts of economic well-being.

We begin with the demand curve, first introduced in chapter 4, which displays the number of goods and services demanded across a given range of prices. In chapter 4 we discussed willingness to pay as a crucial component of demand. Another way of thinking about demand curves is that their height represents the maximum willingness to pay for a product. In chapter 4 we also introduced the supply curve, which displays the number of goods and services supplied across a given range of prices. Another way of thinking about supply curves is that their height represents the minimum cost of bringing a product to the market.

consumer surplus (CS) – the value of a product to a consumer (as measured by the maximum willingness to pay) minus the price paid for the product.

This brings us to the concepts of consumer surplus, producer surplus, and total surplus. **Consumer surplus (CS)** is the value of a product to a consumer (as measured by the maximum willingness to pay) minus the price paid for the product:

$$Consumer\ suplus = value\ of\ the\ product - price\ paid\ for\ the\ product.$$

producer surplus (PS) - the price paid for a producer's product minus the minimum cost of bringing the producer's product to the market.

Producer surplus (PS) is the price paid for a producer's product minus the minimum cost of bringing the producer's product to the market:

$$Producer\ suplus = price\ paid\ for\ the\ product - cost\ of\ the\ product.$$

total surplus (TS) - consumer surplus (CS) plus producer surplus (PS) OR the value of the product minus the cost of the product.

Total surplus (TS) is consumer surplus (CS) plus producer surplus (PS) or:

$$Total\ surplus = (value\ of\ the\ product - price\ paid\ for\ the\ product) +$$
$$(price\ paid\ for\ the\ product - cost\ of\ the\ product).$$

Removing the parentheses on the right side of the equation gets us:

$$= value\ of\ the\ product - price\ paid\ for\ the\ product + price\ paid\ for\ the\ product -$$
$$cost\ of\ the\ product.$$

Since the middle two terms are inversions of each other, they cancel out so that we finally get:

$$= value\ of\ the\ product - cost\ of\ the\ product$$

So total surplus is equal to the value of the product (as measured by consumers' maximum willingness to pay for the product) minus the total maximum cost of producers to bring the product to the market. In this context (as opposed to that of the production possibilities frontier [PPF] in chapter 2), an allocation of resources is **efficient** if it maximizes total surplus in a market. This means that there is no frustration in the market. On the demand side, all of the consumers who value the product the most are able to purchase it. On the supply side, all of the producers who are able to produce the product at the lowest cost are producing and selling it.

efficient – in the context of market welfare or well-being, an allocation of resources that maximizes total surplus in a market.

All of these concepts so far covered in this section may seem frustratingly vague, but graphical analysis can help clear them up. FIGURE 6-11 shows consumer, producer, and total surplus at a market in equilibrium.

FIGURE 6-11: Consumer, Producer, and Total Surplus in a Uniformly Competitive Market

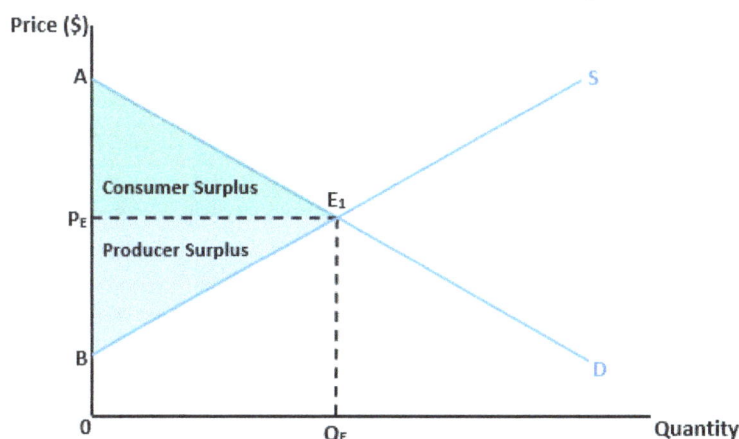

Recall that consumer surplus is the value of a product to a consumer (as measured by the maximum willingness to pay) minus the price paid for the product. The demand curve represents the maximum willingness to pay of individuals in a market. When we subtract equilibrium price (P_E) from the demand curve up to equilibrium quantity (Q_E), we get the light-green triangle area in FIGURE 6-11. The triangle ends at (Q_E) because consumers beyond that point do not value the product at equilibrium price or above, and hence they are not in the market. At least not until price declines.

Producer surplus is the price paid for a producer's product minus the minimum cost of bringing the producer's product to the market. Producers' cost is represented by the supply curve. When we subtract producer cost from equilibrium price (P_E) up to the equilibrium quantity (Q_E) prevailing in the market, we get the light-blue triangle area in FIGURE 6-11. The triangle ends at (Q_E) because the firms that could participate in the market beyond that point are not efficient enough to produce the product at equilibrium price or below and hence are not in the market. At least not until price rises.

Lastly, we have total surplus. Total surplus is consumer surplus plus producer surplus *or* the value of the product minus the cost of the product. In FIGURE 6-11 it is the triangle circumscribed by the points AE_1B. We can get this same triangle by adding the consumer and producer surplus triangles together or taking the value of the product (demand curve) and subtracting the cost of the product (supply curve) up to the market equilibrium quantity (Q_E) or E_1. Subtracting supply from demand up to (Q_E) or E_1 gets us the total-surplus triangle AE_1B.

6.7a Efficiency

The crucial question is, are markets like the one illustrated in FIGURE 6-11 efficient? What we have so far in FIGURE 6-11 is consumers who value the good more than its price purchasing the good. This is occurring along the demand curve from point A to point E_1. From point E_1 to the end of the demand curve (where the D label sits) represents consumers who currently don't value the good at its market price or above. On the supply side of the market what we have is suppliers who are producing the good at a cost less than or equal to the market price. This is occurring along the supply curve from point B to point E_1. From point E_1 to the end of the supply curve (where the S label is) represents suppliers who currently cannot produce the product at a cost equal to or below the market price.

This leads to three conclusions about market processes. In the absence of interference, markets:
1. Allocate products to consumers who value them most in terms of maximum willingness to pay for them at or above market price.
2. Allocate sales to individuals or firms which produce products at a cost equal to or below market price.
3. Produce the quantity of goods or services that maximize (producer surplus + consumer surplus =) total surplus.

While conclusions 1 and 2 above were demonstrated by FIGURE 6-11, conclusion 3 is demonstrated by FIGURE 6-12.

FIGURE 6-12: Maximization of Consumer, Producer, and Total Surplus in a Uniformly Competitive Market

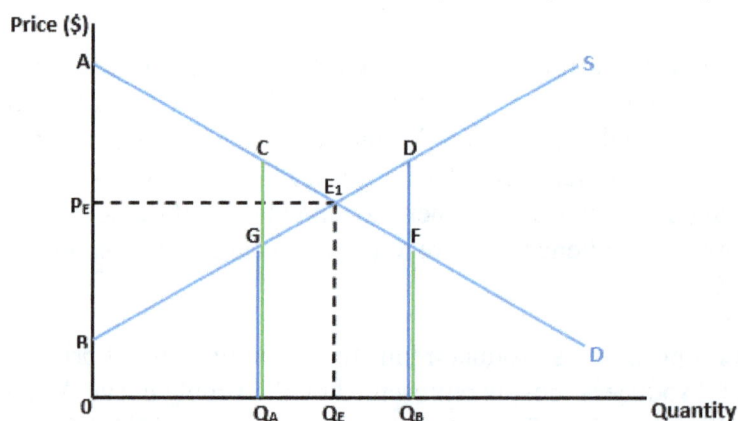

At quantities sold below equilibrium level Q_E, such as Q_A, the value of the product for the marginal demander at Q_A is the vertical line segment (from top to bottom) $\overline{CGQ_A}$, which is greater than the cost of the product to the marginal producer at Q_A (or vertical line segment $\overline{GQ_A}$). The difference between the two is vertical line segment $\overline{CG}$. Therefore, if the product's value to consumers is greater than its costs, then it only makes sense to increase quantity supplied and quantity demanded until the product's value equals its costs at equilibrium (E_1).

At quantities sold above equilibrium level Q_E, such as Q_B, the value of the product for the marginal demander at Q_B is the vertical line segment (from top to bottom) $\overline{FQ_B}$, which is less than the cost of the product to the marginal producer at Q_B (or vertical line segment $\overline{DFQ_B}$). The difference between the two is vertical line segment $\overline{DF}$. Therefore, if the product's value to consumers is less than its costs, then it only makes sense to decrease quantity supplied and quantity demanded until the product's value equals its costs at equilibrium (E_1).

Altogether, the three conclusions demonstrate that without outside interference, market allocations of goods and services are efficient at competitive market equilibrium (E_1) in that they maximize (consumer + producer =) total surplus. In other words, our planner is out of business before he or she even begins to draw up plans. Adam Smith's invisible hand has already done the incomparable and inimitable work. The central planner or central planning board, to match the performance of the market, has to not only be in possession of all of the costs of all potential suppliers, but the constantly changing valuations of all potential consumers. And this is not only for one market, but the billions of them in a modern market economy. Keep in mind that this is not a matter of having a fast-enough computer or rigorous-enough algorithm or software as some socialists and communists seem to believe. It's a matter, especially on the demand side, of reading hundreds of millions of minds every second of the day. This will never be possible and thus it's no small wonder that central planning is a disaster everywhere it has been repeatedly attempted.

None of this persuades politicians and regulators from trying to "improve markets." What this chapter has shown is that they usually do so anyway to various unintended consequences and the next Economics in Action application ("How the Middle Class Paid a Heavy Cost for a Luxury Tax on the Rich") is another example.

6.7b Tax Wedge and Tax Revenue

Recall that in section 6.6 on tax incidence, it matters not which side of the market is taxed (buyers or sellers). A tax on demanders reduces demand, raises the price of the product for demanders, reduces the price that suppliers receive for the product, and reduces market quantity. Similarly, a tax on suppliers reduces supply, raises the price of the product for demanders, reduces the price that suppliers receive for the product, and reduces market quantity. The tax burden falls not on who gets taxed but on the side of the market with the greatest price insensitivity. This will be conclusively demonstrated by the last figure (FIGURE 6-16) and the analysis accompanying it in this section.

Using the concepts of consumer, producer, and total surplus introduced earlier in this chapter, we will explain in more depth the market effects of taxes. In FIGURE 6-13 are illustrated the familiar concept of the tax wedge (in Graph A) and the new concept that we will derive from it, tax revenue (in Graph B).

154

FIGURE 6-13: The Tax Wedge and Tax

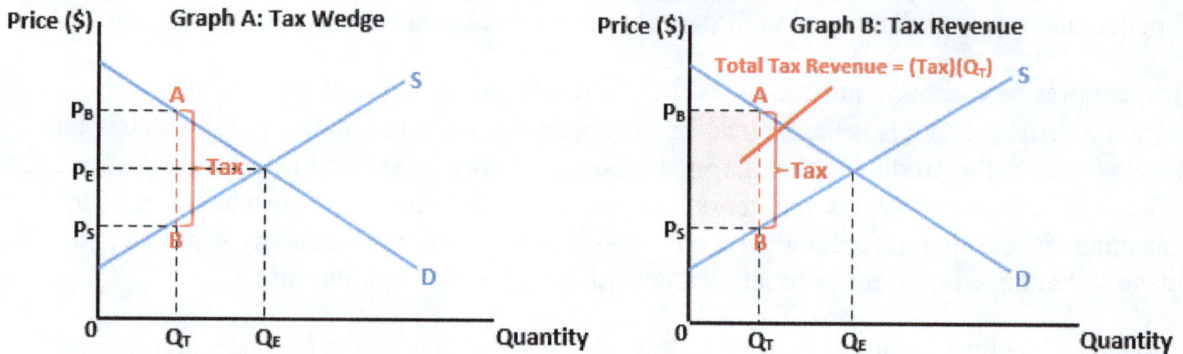

In Graph A of FIGURE 6-13, a tax is imposed on a market and either demand or supply declines by the size of the tax. That is, either the demand curve or the supply curve shifts leftward. (We won't illustrate a shift in either to keep the graphs above simple and uncluttered.) The size of the tax (tax wedge) is represented by dashed line segment $\overline{AB}$. Because of the imposition of the tax, market quantity falls from Q_E to Q_T, the latter being the quantity prevailing in the market after the tax is levied. Early in section 6.7 and in FIGURE 6-11 we introduced and graphically analyzed consumer surplus, producer surplus, and total surplus. Now we will add **tax revenue**,

tax revenue – the tax per product (*Tax*) times the quantity (Q_T) of the product sold, or (*Tax*)(Q_T).

or the tax per product (*Tax*) times the quantity (Q_T) of the product sold, or (*Tax*)(Q_T). In Graph B of FIGURE 6-13, the tax (tax wedge) is represented by dashed line segment $\overline{AB}$. When this is multiplied by the quantity of goods sold after the imposition of the tax (Q_T), the resulting sum is the total tax revenue to the government.

Now we will show not only the relationship, definitional and graphical, between consumer surplus, producer surplus, total surplus, and tax revenue. We will also bring in deadweight loss, first discussed in section 6.4.1.

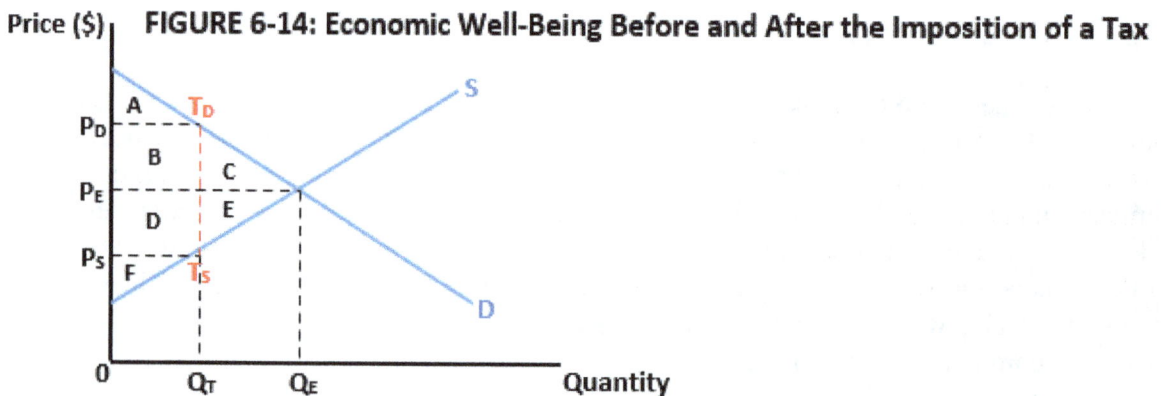

We begin with FIGURE 6-14. Before the imposition of the tax, the market produces and sells goods at the equilibrium quantity Q_E and equilibrium price P_E. Consumer surplus is the difference between maximum willingness to pay (value, or the demand curve) and actual market price paid (P_E), therefore, in FIGURE 6-14 it is triangle A plus square B plus triangle C. Producer surplus is the difference between the market price paid for the good to suppliers (P_E) and supplier costs (everything less than or equal to the supply curve), therefore, in FIGURE 6-14 it is square D plus triangle E plus triangle F. Total surplus is consumer surplus plus producer surplus, hence it is triangle A plus square B plus triangle C plus square D plus triangle E plus triangle F. Tax revenue is \$0 for this market since no tax has yet been imposed on it. Deadweight loss is also \$0 for this market since no tax, and therefore no market-quantity-reducing tax wedge, has yet been imposed on it.

After a tax is imposed on the market illustrated in FIGURE 6-14, all of our variables change. The tax is represented by dashed line segment $\overline{T_D T_S}$. Consumer surplus shrinks from areas $A + B + C$ to just triangle A. Producer surplus shrinks from areas $D + E + F$ to just triangle F. Total surplus shrinks from areas $A + B + C + D + E + F$, down to areas $A + B + D + F$. Tax revenue is square B plus square D. **Deadweight loss** (which we first encountered in section 6.4.1) we can now more precisely define as the decline in total surplus (loss to demanders and suppliers) in a market caused by the imposition of a tax or control. In FIGURE 6-14 it is triangle C + triangle E. Although the imposition of the tax gave the government

deadweight loss - the decline in total surplus (loss to demanders and suppliers) in a market caused by the imposition of a tax or control.

tax revenue from demanders and suppliers in the market, triangles $C + E$ were gained by no one. They are a pure loss. TABLE 6-1 summarizes the market changes illustrated in FIGURE 6-14.

TABLE 6-1
Summary of Market Effects Before versus After the Tax in FIGURE 6-14

Area	Before Tax	After Tax	Net Change (+ or -)
consumer surplus	A+B+C	A	-(B+C)
producer surplus	D+E+F	F	-(D+E)
total surplus	A+B+C+D+E+F	A+B+D+F	-(C+E)
tax revenue	zero	B + D	+(B+D)
deadweight loss	zero	C + E	+ (C+E)

Let's make four observations before closing out the chapter with one last application.

1. From FIGURE 6-14, we can see that the total losses to demanders and suppliers from the imposition of the tax (square B + triangle C + square D + triangle E) is greater than tax revenue (square B + square D).

2. Market quantity declines because price has been effectively raised for demanders and lowered for suppliers. With price raised to consumers, fewer consumers want to purchase the product and with price lowered for suppliers, fewer suppliers want to sell the product. The market has been moved from efficient to inefficient.

3. Taxes or other controls cause deadweight losses because they prevent a certain number of transactions taking place (everything from Q_T to Q_E in FIGURE 6-14) and gains from trade being

realized. In chapter 3 we discussed Kim Kardashian hiring happy-go-lucky housekeeper Trish Haney to clean Kim's house. Trish has another client, Helen, a working single mother who values Trish's work but who isn't near as rich as Kim Kardashian.

Trish (as with Kim) in the span of an 8-hour workday, earning $20 per hour, will clean Helen's house for $160. (Trish's opportunity cost of a workday is $120.) Helen views Trish's services as worth a maximum $200 per workday. Helen is thus realizing $40 of consumer surplus while Trish is realizing $40 of producer surplus. Together, total surplus is $80. So far so good, until the California legislature passes a $100 tax on cleaning firms. If Trish tries to pass off the entire tax on Helen, she'll have to raise her price to $260, which Helen will never agree to pay since Helen values Trish's cleanings at a maximum is $200. Trish cannot accept Helen's maximum price of $200 per workday since she'll be left with $100 after paying the tax while her opportunity cost is $120. The tax puts Trish out of business and leaves Helen at least temporarily, and maybe permanently, without cleaning services.

FIGURE 6-15 further and visually deconstructs what is happening.

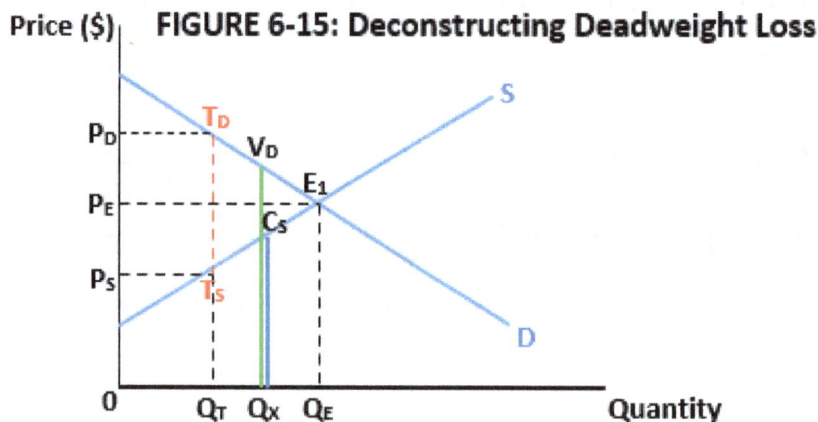

FIGURE 6-15: Deconstructing Deadweight Loss

After the imposition of the tax (dashed line segment $\overline{T_D T_S}$), market quantity rolls back from Q_E (the pre-tax equilibrium quantity) to Q_T (the new equilibrium quantity post-tax) and all transactions between Q_T and Q_E are lost. One among many is sale Q_X. For this lost exchange, the value of the product to demander X is line segment $\overline{V_D Q_X}$ whereas the cost to supplier X is line segment $\overline{C_S Q_X}$. The difference between them is V_D - C_S. This trade potential doesn't just disappear. A number of these transactions will still occur, just off the books in the underground economy.

4. The greater the price sensitivity of demand and supply, the greater the deadweight loss from the imposition of a tax. FIGURE 6-16 illustrates how the size of a deadweight loss can change with the price sensitivity of demand or supply. In Graph A, with demand very price insensitive and supply and the size of the tax constant, deadweight loss (the triangles A and B created by the red-dashed line connecting the demand and supply curves) is relatively small. In contrast, in Graph B, with demand very price sensitive and supply and the size of the tax constant, deadweight loss (again, triangles A and B) is relatively large, and much larger than it is in Graph A. In Graph C, with supply very price insensitive and demand and the size of the tax constant, deadweight loss is relatively small. In contrast, in Graph D, with supply very price sensitive and

demand and the size of the tax constant, deadweight loss is relatively large, and much larger than it is in Graph C.

FIGURE 6-16: How Deadweight Loss Varies in Size with the Price Sensitivity of Demand and Supply

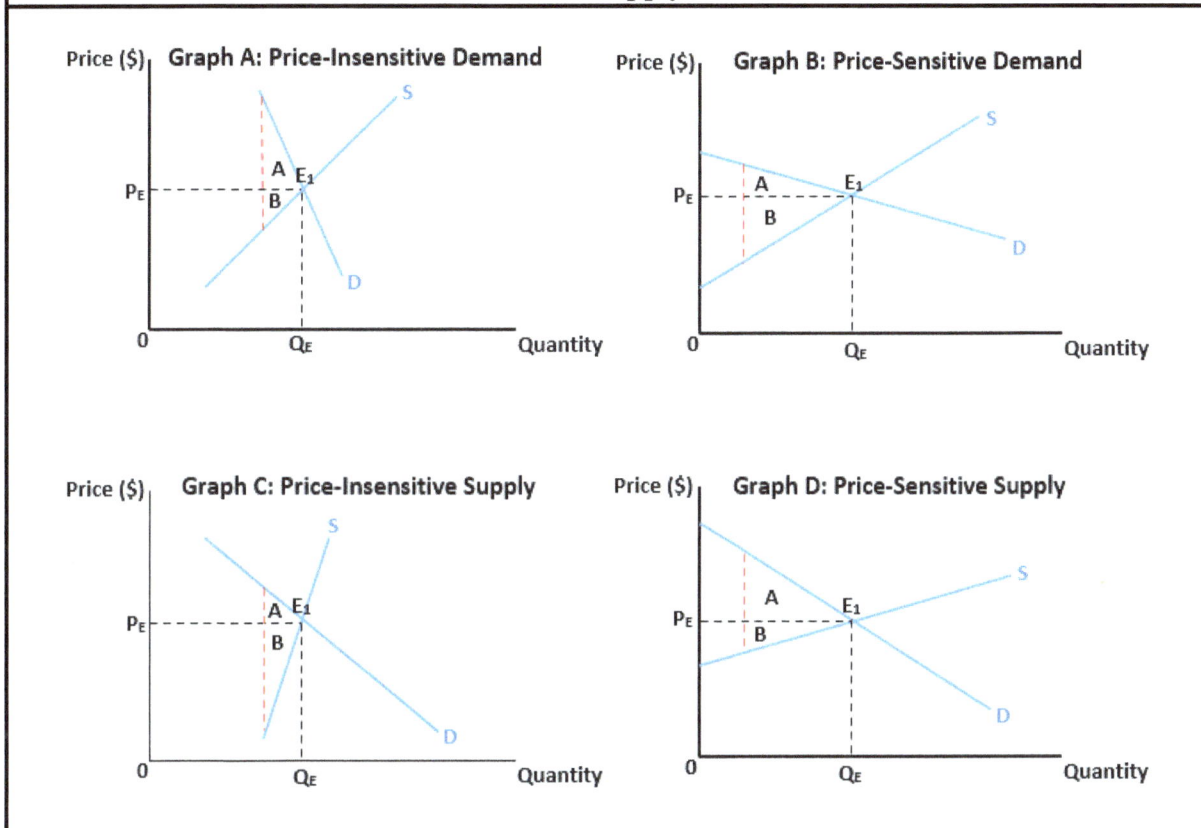

CASE STUDY: How the Middle Class Paid a High Cost for a Luxury Tax on the Rich

In 1990, members of Congress decided to impose a tax on various recreational items that the very rich typically purchase: yachts, pricey sports cars, private jets, and jewelry. To representatives and senators, the tax would be an easy way of earning a lot of revenue and would be targeted at the people who had the greatest ability to pay it: the very rich who were now finally going to "pay their fair share." Some economists warned that the law of unintended consequences (see chapter 1, section 1.4, economics principle 4: Incentives affect behavior) would likely come into play … and they were correct.

FIGURE 6-17 reveals where the problem lies. Luxury goods are a niche market. Demand is very price sensitive but supply is very price insensitive. Translation: buyers have lots of options but sellers don't. If you are very wealthy and have a net worth of, say, $50 to $100 million, there are many competitors for your recreational spending dollars. A new 105-foot Hatteras yacht priced at $15 million is just one among many alternatives. If you are a lower-middle-class line worker who molds yacht hulls at Hatteras, Incorporated, you do not have many options in the short run if the demand for yachts takes a nosedive. This is because your skills do not translate easily to any other industry. Ships are built much differently than automobiles and jet airplanes.

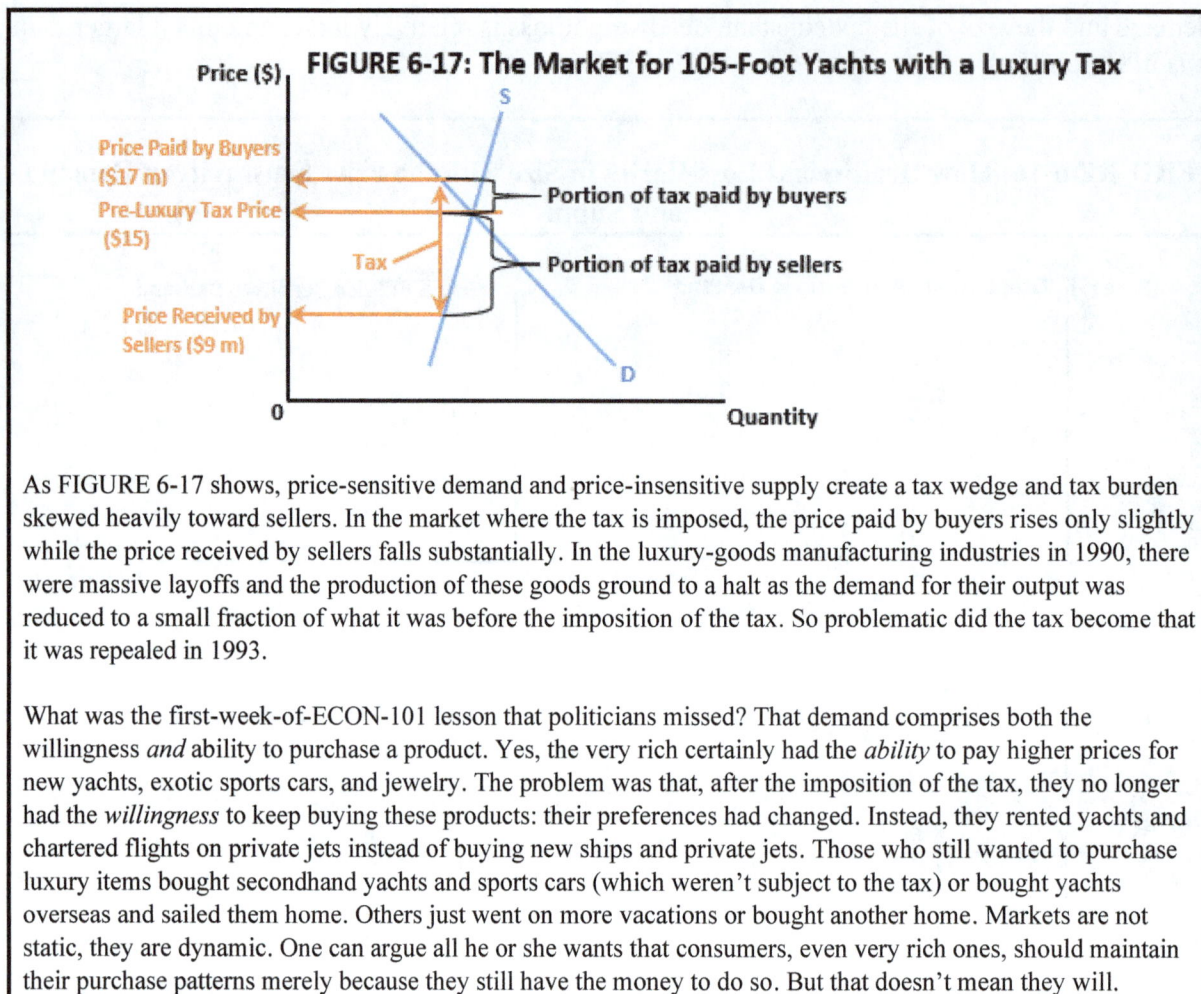

FIGURE 6-17: The Market for 105-Foot Yachts with a Luxury Tax

As FIGURE 6-17 shows, price-sensitive demand and price-insensitive supply create a tax wedge and tax burden skewed heavily toward sellers. In the market where the tax is imposed, the price paid by buyers rises only slightly while the price received by sellers falls substantially. In the luxury-goods manufacturing industries in 1990, there were massive layoffs and the production of these goods ground to a halt as the demand for their output was reduced to a small fraction of what it was before the imposition of the tax. So problematic did the tax become that it was repealed in 1993.

What was the first-week-of-ECON-101 lesson that politicians missed? That demand comprises both the willingness *and* ability to purchase a product. Yes, the very rich certainly had the *ability* to pay higher prices for new yachts, exotic sports cars, and jewelry. The problem was that, after the imposition of the tax, they no longer had the *willingness* to keep buying these products: their preferences had changed. Instead, they rented yachts and chartered flights on private jets instead of buying new ships and private jets. Those who still wanted to purchase luxury items bought secondhand yachts and sports cars (which weren't subject to the tax) or bought yachts overseas and sailed them home. Others just went on more vacations or bought another home. Markets are not static, they are dynamic. One can argue all he or she wants that consumers, even very rich ones, should maintain their purchase patterns merely because they still have the money to do so. But that doesn't mean they will.

6.8 Conclusion

In this chapter we examined the market effects of price controls and taxes. These effects include but are not limited to shortages, deterioration in the quality of housing, surpluses, job loss among unskilled workers, and deadweight loss. Having examined demand in chapters 4 and 5, starting in the next chapter we will move toward an analysis of the supply side of markets beginning with the topics of costs and production.

6.9 Chapter Concepts

price ceiling (binding and non-binding)
shortage (excess demand)
rent control
price floor (binding and non-binding)
surplus (excess supply)
market-clearing price
minimum wage
implicit price ceiling
tax wedge

tax incidence
payroll tax
bifurcated tax
consumer surplus (CS)
producer surplus (PS)
total surplus (TS)
efficient (in the context of total surplus, not the production-possibilities frontier [PPF])
tax revenue
deadweight loss

6.10 Problems, Questions, and Discussion Topics (Items Requiring Examples are Marked with an Asterisk [*])

1. *Price ceiling* versus *binding price ceiling* versus *equilibrium price*: how do these three concepts compare? Explain in sufficient detail.

2. How does a binding price ceiling create a shortage? Explain in sufficient detail.

3. Why is housing in some large cities artificially scarce and dilapidated? Explain in sufficient detail.

4. Name and define the four total (one short run plus three long run) effects of rent control.

5. Name and define the short-run versus long-run effects of rent control. Explain them in detail.

6. While Americans blamed OPEC for the long lines at gas stations in the 1970s,

   A. what did economists blame?

   B. Why?

7. *...reductions in supply don't cause _____.*

   A. Fill in the blank: _____.

   B. Explain:

8. *Price floor* versus *binding price floor* versus *equilibrium price*: how do these three concepts compare?

9. How does a binding price floor create a surplus?

10. market-clearing price*

11. How does a binding minimum wage increase unemployment in the market for unskilled labor? Explain in detail.

12. How did implicit price ceilings cause shortages among a wide range of essential products during the COVID-19 pandemic? Explain in detail.

13. *tax wedge* versus *tax incidence* (define both, then provide a quantitative example of only one)*

14. In what way is FICA a bifurcated tax? Provide a quantitative example.

15. *The side of the market that has higher price _____ (and can therefore _____ easily leave the market) bears more of the burden of a tax.*

    A. Fill in the blanks: _____, _____.

    B. Explain:

16. producer surplus (define, then provide a quantitative example)*

17. What are the three conclusions about market processes concerning efficiency? Explain each in sufficient detail.

18. If Josie's Boutique sells 175 packs of nine 12-inch taper candles per month and the tax per pack is $2, what is the monthly tax revenue from Josie's sales of taper candles?

19. deadweight loss (define, then provide a quantitative example)*

20. With respect to the 1990 luxury tax,

    A. How did the U.S. middle class end up paying a heavy cost for a luxury tax on the U.S. wealthy?

    B. What key roles did 1) the price sensitivity of demand and 2) the price sensitivity of supply in the luxury-goods markets each play in worsening the scale of the debacle?

PART II: INDUSTRIAL ORGANIZATION

Chapter 7: Revenue, Costs, Profit, and Production

7.0 Introduction

Up to this point we have built up the competitive market model and then shown in the previous chapter how government intervention in markets affects market outcomes. This chapter will explore revenue and costs in order to launch a four-chapter journey into industrial organization. That journey will begin with uniform competition, then move to monopoly, differentiated competition, and finally, oligopolies. However, before we can begin the odyssey of exploring different market structures, we must understand the cost structures that underlie each, and that begins with defining revenue and cost themselves.

7.1 Revenue, Costs, and Profit

Earlier in chapter 5 we saw that **total revenue (TR)** is the price of a product (P) times the quantity of that product sold (Q) or (P)(Q). **Total cost (TC)** is the sum of all of the costs of a firm in the making of its product. The difference between the former and latter is **economic profit (π)**:

$$economic\ profit\ (\pi) = total\ revenue\ (TR) - total\ cost\ (TC)$$

total revenue (TR) – the price of a product (P) times the quantity of that product sold (Q) or (P)(Q).

total cost (TC) - the sum of all of the costs of a firm in the making of its product. It is also equal to opportunity cost broken down into explicit costs plus implicit costs.

economic profit (π) – total revenue (TR) minus total cost (TC).

The assumed objective of all firms is the maximization of profit (π). In general, there is nothing socially harmful about maximizing profit in a naturally competitive environment.[36] Profit represents a positive incentive for adding value to raw materials by converting them into a final product that is useful and valuable to consumers.

To bring further clarity to our discussion, let's analyze the two terms on the right side of the equation above. Total revenue (TR) is the easiest term. As we saw earlier, it's just price (P) times quantity sold (Q):

$$TR = (P)(Q)$$

Total cost (TC), the sum of all of the costs of a firm in the making of its product, is a little more difficult, but what we're about to see should already be familiar:

$$TC = opportunity\ cost$$

where

$$opportunity\ cost = explicit\ costs + implicit\ costs.$$

---

[36] Government-protected cartels (such as the U.S. health-care system) and monopolies are another matter.

opportunity cost - the sum of all explicit and implicit costs.

explicit costs – all of the money costs incurred as the result of purchasing a good or service or taking an action. In the context of the firm, they are costs that consist of money paid for a firm's factors of production (capital, labor, and entrepreneurship).

implicit costs – all of the non-monetary costs incurred as the result of purchasing a good or service or taking an action. In the context of the firm, they are the costs that consist of forgone alternatives to a firm's production of its product.

So while **opportunity cost** is the sum of all explicit and implicit costs, recall from chapter 1 that **explicit costs** are all of the money costs incurred as the result of purchasing a good or service or taking an action. In the context of the firm, they are costs that consist of money paid for a firm's factors of production (capital, labor, and entrepreneurship). **Implicit costs** (from chapter 1) are all of the non-monetary costs incurred as the result of purchasing a good or service or taking an action. In the context of the firm, they are the costs that consist of forgone alternatives to a firm's production of its product. An example of an explicit cost is Ibex Computer Corporation paying workers to assemble computers. An example of Ibex's implicit costs is the return its owner could earn in the stock market if he did not own Ibex's capital, including the factory building, the machinery Ibex uses to manufacture computers, and the land the Ibex factory sits on. Let's say that this total cost of capital is $10 million and the stock market is providing savers with a 15 percent return. The implicit cost of Ibex capital is the forgoing of ($10 million times 15 percent or [$10,000,000][0.15] =) $1,500,000 or $1.5 million in stock returns to Ibex's owner.

The interesting thing about this implicit cost incurred by Ibex is that it does not appear on any of the firm's accounting statements. This is because accountants do not include implicit costs as a

accounting cost – the explicit costs of a firm's operation.

cost of doing business, just explicit costs. Therefore, **accounting cost** consists only of the explicit costs of a firm.

While explicit costs are important, they don't tell the full story of conducting business. Let's say that one day oil bubbles up on Ibex's factory property and it turns out that Ibex is sitting on a huge oil deposit worth untold millions of dollars. The story of whether Ibex continues in business is now all about implicit costs, not explicit ones (assuming it has had no recent trouble covering explicit costs). Balance sheets and income statements are worthless in terms of determining how the company should proceed given its recent oil discovery. Almost certainly, Ibex, at its current location, will cease operation. Whether the company will move and reopen at another location will be up to its current owner. If his oil riches are abundant enough, he may never resume his computer business again.

Because accountants ignore implicit costs, their conception of profit is different from that of economists. Again:

$$economic\ profit\ (\pi) = total\ revenue\ (TR) - total\ cost\ (TC)$$

$$= total\ revenue\ (TR) - (explicit\ costs + implicit\ costs)$$

Therefore, after setting implicit costs equal to 0,

$$Accounting\ profit\ (\rho) = total\ revenue\ (TR) - explicit\ costs.$$

Because **accounting profit** is total revenue minus explicit costs, it is going to be larger that economic profit. Let's say that Ibex Computer Corporation (before any discovery of oil on its property) has a yearly revenue of about $10 million, yearly explicit costs of $5 million, and yearly implicit costs of $1.5 million (recall the stock-market return above). This leaves the company with ($10 million revenue - $5 million explicit costs - $1.5 million implicit costs =) $3.5 million in economic profit. However, accounting profit ends up being ($10 million revenue - $5 million explicit costs =) $5 million. That $5 million accounting profit looks better on a firm's income statement than its economic profit of $3.5 million. However, the $3.5 million economic profit beats the $1.5 million implicit cost of the firm's operation, which is why Ibex's capital is being used to produce computers and not used to earn a return in the stock market.

accounting profit – total revenue (*TR*) minus explicit costs.

7.2 The Production Function and Cost Curve

A **production schedule** is a table that displays the different levels of **output** (units of product) that can be produced by a firm using different quantities of **inputs** (capital, labor, and entrepreneurship). A **production function** is a graphical representation of a production schedule in input-output space or, a line or curve that displays the relationship between the quantity of an input used to produce a product and the quantity of output of that product. Let's start with an example, The Paper Street Soap Company run by entrepreneur Tyler Durden. Before introducing some numbers, let's keep in mind that the following analysis takes place over the short run, a period of time during which Tyler can only increase his production level of soap bars by increasing the number of workers at the old abandoned house where his company is located. He can't expand the size of the house in the **short run**, only in the **long run** if his company is successful. (The short run is a period of time during which at least one factor of production (usually capital) cannot be changed while the long run is a period of time during which all factors of production can be changed.) The short run and long run are different lengths of time for different firms and industries. For Tyler and his young and hyper-enthusiastic workers, the short run is about three months.

production schedule – a table that displays the different levels of output that can be produced by a firm using different quantities of inputs.

output – units of product produced by a firm.

inputs – everything used to produce a product. The three main categories are capital, labor, and entrepreneurship.

production function - a graphical representation of a production schedule in input-output space or, a line or curve that displays the relationship between the quantity of an input used to produce a product and the quantity of output of that product.

short run – a period of time during which at least one factor of production (usually capital) cannot be changed.

long run - a period of time during which all factors of production can be changed.

Columns 1 and 2 of TABLE 7-1 contain Paper Street's production schedule. If Tyler has no workers, he produces no soap. After Tyler's friend Robert Paulsen joins the company, Paper Street now has 1 worker, therefore it produces 25 bars of soap per day. After Marla Singer joins the company, Paper Street now has 2 workers, therefore Paper Street's output rises to 50 bars of soap per day.

166

1	2	3	4	5	6
Workers	Output (bars of soap)	Marginal Product (MP)	Fixed Cost (FC) in $	Variable Cost (VC) in $	Total Cost (TC) = (FC + VC) in $
0	0	0	50	0	50
1	25	25	50	120	170
2	50	25	50	240	290
3	70	20	50	360	410
4	85	15	50	480	530
5	95	10	50	600	650
6	100	5	50	720	770

TABLE 7-1: Paper Street Soap Company (Production Schedule, MP, FC, VC, and TC)

marginal product (MP) - the additional units of product produced when another input is added to a production process.

Column 3 in TABLE 7-1 is **marginal product (MP)**, the additional units of product produced when another input is added to a production process. Before Robert Paulsen was hired, no soap was produced. After Robert joins Paper Street, 25 bars are produced, therefore, the marginal product of the first worker for Paper Street is 25 units. Then Marla Singer is hired, production rises by another 25 units, therefore the marginal product of the second worker is 25 units.

Brad Pitt as Tyler Durden (Unknown, Fair Use)

But notice what happens as more and more workers get hired up to and including the 6th worker. Marginal product steadily falls from a high of 25 bars to 5 bars from the addition of the 6th worker. Why does this happen? Because only so many workers can be accommodated in the old, abandoned house in which the company is located. Beyond the third worker, space begins to get tight as workers mix heated oil and lye and eventually pour the mixture into soap molds. By the time Charlie Dell (the 6th worker) joins the company, space is so tight that workers have to take care not to bump into each other and get scalded by hot soap. Charlie is so hindered in his productivity that he is only able to contribute 5 bars per day to total production.

7.3 Graphing the Production Function and Cost Curve

Paper Street Soap Company (Unknown, Fair Use)

Out of the production schedule in columns 1 and 2 in TABLE 7-1 we derive Paper Street's production function illustrated in FIGURE 7-1. On the horizontal axis is column 1, quantity of workers per day while the vertical axis represents Paper Street's output in bars of soap per day. Notice something very important about the production function illustrated in FIGURE 7-1: its slope (rise over run) at a particular point is also equal to marginal product (MP). TABLE 7-1 tells us that the marginal product for the first worker is 25 bars. It turns out that the slope of the production function for the first worker is ($\frac{25}{1}$ =) 25 bars per worker. What about the second worker, Marla? The slope is ($\frac{50}{2}$ =) 25 bars per worker again, exactly what TABLE 7-1 told us.

Thus, marginal product is both:
1. the additional units of output produced by adding an additional unit of input and
2. the slope of the production function at a *particular point*, not the entire curve because as we can see in FIGURE 7-1, the slope of the production function starts out steep (at the first worker) and steadily declines to where it is almost flat (at the sixth worker).

This characteristic of the production function (a steadily declining slope) is known as **diminishing marginal product**, or the decline in marginal product that occurs as more and more units of an input are added to a production process. The reason for this was discussed above: More and more workers in a fixed space creates crowding and beyond a certain point this increased crowding hampers production rather than increases it.

diminishing marginal product – the decline in marginal product that occurs as more and more units of an input are added to a production process.

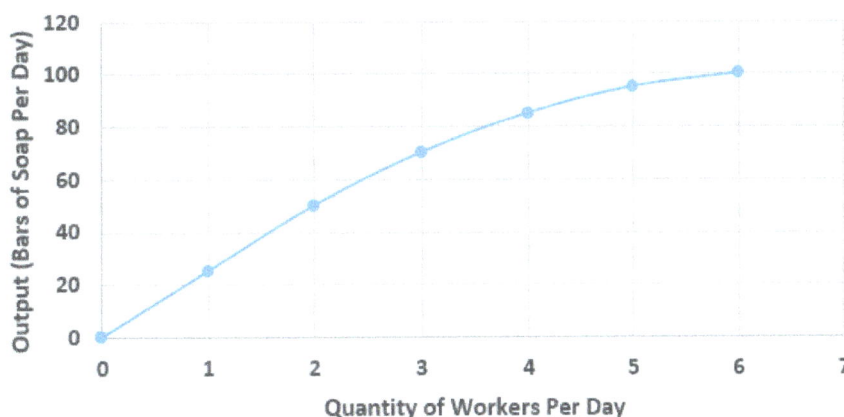

FIGURE 7-1: the Production Function for Paper Street Soap Company

Now let's finish TABLE 7-1 with a discussion about columns 4 to 6. Tyler rents the rickety, old, condemned, and abandoned house on the underground market for $1,500 per month, or $50 per day with utilities included. This sum of $50 per day is the total **fixed cost (FC)** of the firm. A fixed cost is a cost that does not change with the level of production. Rent, property taxes, and equipment rentals are examples. For Paper Street, rent doesn't change in the short run and Tyler has to pay it whether Paper Street remains in business or not. Failure to pay rent will eventually get Tyler evicted from his business and home (the rickety house in which he lives). Thus, in column 4 of TABLE 7-1, fixed cost is the same ($50) for every level of production, 0 to 100 bars of soap.

fixed cost (FC) – a cost that does not change with the level of production.

variable cost (VC) – a cost that changes with the level of production.

A **variable cost (VC)** is a cost that changes with the level of production. Labor and materials are examples, but for our Paper Street example we're ignoring materials to keep things simple. The cost of Paper Street's labor is $15 per hour or $120 per day per worker. If Tyler hires no one beyond Robert, his first worker, Paper Street's level of production stays at 25 bars and its labor cost is $120 per day. After Marla joins the company, production rises and labor cost also rises to $240 per day. Thus, in column 5 of TABLE 7-1, variable cost varies for each and every level of production.

total cost (TC) - the sum of all of the costs of a firm in the making of its product OR opportunity cost = explicit costs + implicit costs OR fixed cost (FC) + variable cost (VC).

Total cost (TC), which we first saw in section 7.1 (as the sum of all of the costs of a firm in the making of its product OR opportunity cost = explicit costs + implicit costs) can also be broken down into fixed cost (FC) plus variable cost (VC):

$$total\ cost\ (TC) = fixed\ cost\ (FC) + variable\ cost\ (VC).$$

For one worker, this ends up being TC = $50 FC + $120 VC = $170 per day (see column 6 in TABLE 7-1). After Marla comes on board, for two workers, TC = $50 FC + $240 VC = $290 per day (again, see column 6 in TABLE 7-1). Because total cost is comprised of fixed and variable components, in column 6 of TABLE 7-1 total cost varies for every level of production.

FIGURE 7-2 illustrates our TC curve. Duplicated right next to it for comparison purposes is FIGURE 7-1, the production function. Unlike the production function on the left, on the horizontal axis of the TC curve on the right is Paper Street's output in bars of soap per day while the vertical axis of the TC curve represents total cost per day. Do FIGURES 7-1 and 7-2 look eerily like flipped images of each other? Of course they do, because that's what they in fact are! The vertical axis of FIGURE 7-1 (output for the production function) is the horizontal axis of FIGURE 7-2 (output for the total-cost curve). The horizontal axis of FIGURE 7-1 (workers for the production function) is essentially the vertical axis of FIGURE 7-2 (workers in terms of their cost, added to fixed cost).

So, the total-cost curve in FIGURE 7-2 is just the production function in FIGURE 7-1 "flipped over" from hill shape to bowl shape. The total-cost curve is just the production function (output) in terms of all costs, fixed plus variable. Notice further that the production function has an intercept of zero (at x, y coordinates [0, 0], the origin point) while the total-cost curve has an intercept at $50 (at x, y coordinates [0, $50]) on the vertical axis of FIGURE 7-2. What is that? The fixed cost of $50 per day that has shifted the entire TC curve upward by its inclusion. If Tyler and company take a holiday and produce nothing, $50 per day rent still has to be paid on the dilapidated old house where soap is made.

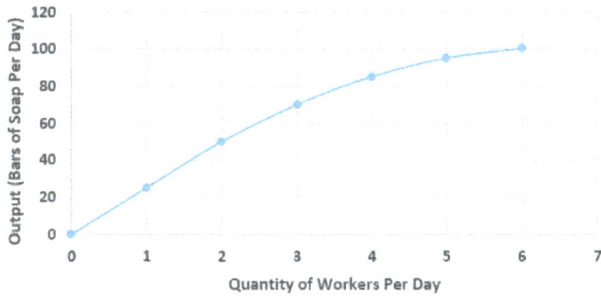

FIGURE 7-1: the Production Function for Paper Street Soap Company

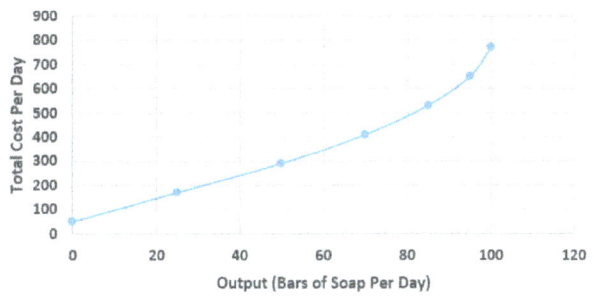

FIGURE 7-2: the Total-Cost (TC) Curve for Paper Street Soap Company

7.4 More Costs: Three Averages and a Marginal

Now we're going to add four new costs to those introduced in TABLE 7-1. Before panicking at the mention of four new costs, keep in mind that three are simple variations of ones we've already discussed and the fourth is pretty simple as well. They are average fixed cost (AFC), average variable cost (AVC), average total cost (ATC), and marginal cost (MC), which are all displayed in TABLE 7-2.

Columns 1-4 in TABLE 7-2 (Output, Fixed Cost, Variable Cost, and Total Cost) we already saw in TABLE 7-1 and subsequently discussed. So let's start with column 5 of TABLE 7-2 where **average-fixed cost (AFC)** is fixed cost divided by output. For example, for an output of 25 bars produced,

average-fixed cost (AFC) – fixed cost divided by output.

$$AFC = \frac{\$50 \ fixed \ cost}{25 \ bars \ of \ soap} = \$2 \ per \ bar.$$

TABLE 7-2: Paper Street Soap Company (Output, FC, VC, TC, AFC, AVC, ATC, MC)							
1	2	3	4	5	6	7	8
Output (bars of soap)	Fixed Cost (FC)*	Variable Cost (VC)*	Total Cost (TC)*	Average Fixed Cost (AFC)*	Average Variable Cost (AVC)*	Average Total Cost (ATC)*	Marginal Cost (MC)*^
0	50	0	50	NC	NC	NC	NC
25	50	120	170	2	4.80	6.8	6.8
50	50	240	290	1	4.80	5.8	5.8
70	50	360	410	0.71	5.14	5.857142857	5.857142857
85	50	480	530	0.59	5.65	6.235294118	6.235294118
95	50	600	650	0.53	6.32	6.842105263	6.842105263
100	50	720	770	0.50	7.20	7.7	7.7
*in $ units NC = not calculable (division by 0). ^slope = rise/run.							

average-variable cost (AVC) - variable cost divided by output.

In column 6 of TABLE 7-2 is **average-variable cost (AVC)**, which is variable cost divided by output. For example, for an output of 25 bars produced,

$$AVC = \frac{\$120 \ variable \ cost}{25 \ bars \ of \ soap} = \$4.80 \ per \ bar.$$

average-total cost (ATC) - total cost divided by output.

In column 7 of TABLE 7-2 is **average-total cost (ATC)**, which is total cost divided by output. For example, for an output of 25 bars produced,

$$ATC = \frac{\$170 \ total \ cost}{25 \ bars \ of \ soap} = \$6.80 \ per \ bar.$$

marginal cost (MC) - the change in total cost from producing one extra unit of output OR the slope of the total-cost curve at a particular point.

Last of all, in column 8 of TABLE 7-2 is **marginal cost (MC)**, which is both
1. the change in total cost from producing one extra unit of output or
2. the slope of the total-cost curve at a particular point (not the entire curve).

For example, for an output of 25 bars produced,

$$MC = slope = \frac{rise}{run} = \frac{\$170 \ total \ cost}{25 \ bars \ of \ soap} = \$6.80 \ per \ bar.$$

For 0 to 100 bars of output, what do these three average costs and one marginal cost look like on the same graph in cost-output space? FIGURE 7-3 displays all four costs plotted from the data in columns 5, 6, 7, and 8 of TABLE 7-2.

FIGURE 7-3: Paper Street Soap Company: AFC, AVC, ATC, MC

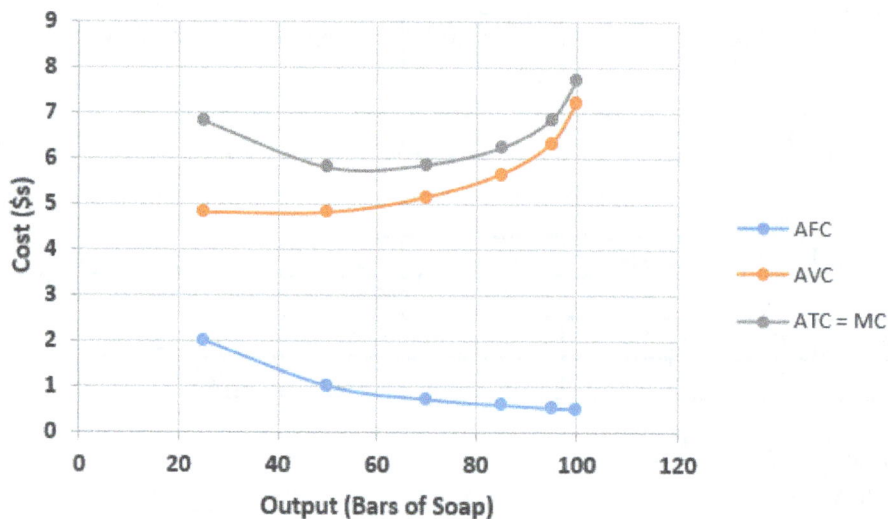

As can be seen in column 5 of TABLE 7-2, average fixed cost (AFC) steadily declines in value from $2 at 25 bars of soap to $0.50 at 100 bars. Hence, the blue ATC curve in FIGURE 7-3 plotted from the data in column 5 steadily declines from 25 bars of soap to 100 bars. Average variable cost (AVC) and average total cost (ATC) in contrast, steadily rise from 25 bars of soap produced to 100 bars. Notice that the last point on the orange AVC curve at 100 units of output almost touches the last point on the ATC curve at 100 units of output. In fact, both curves together form a horn shape, as output steadily increases from 25 units to 100. What does this steadily declining area of space between the two curves represent? Average fixed cost (AFC), which we already saw was steadily declining in the blue AFC curve.

Okay, so where is marginal cost (MC) on the graph? It turns out that the MC curve takes the exact same shape as the ATC curve in this particular case. Why? Because we used realistic hypothetical data to draw our curves. Thus, we had to calculate MC as a slope at a particular point (rise/run = total cost/output), which gave us the same exact calculation as that for ATC (total cost/output). Had we used discreet units of output (1, 2, 3, …, 100), we could have calculated exact changes in costs for every additional worker added. Because we used realistic increments (25, 50, 70…), we had to approximate slope with an actual average. Thus our MC curve is "stacked" on top of our ATC curve. Don't let this bother or confuse you. In the uniformly competitive model in the next chapter we'll see another stacking, but this time it will be the marginal revenue (MR) and demand curves of the firm.

7.5 Average Total Cost (ATC), Marginal Cost (MC), and Their Relationship

Before moving on to cost curves in the short run versus the long run and drawing this chapter to a close, we have to further examine the relationship between the average-total-cost (ATC) curve and the marginal-cost (MC) curve. We couldn't do that in the previous section because we used realistic data which contained an output variable that increased in large increments. In this section we will use an overall less realistic example but one with an output variable that increases in single-unit increments. This will separate the two curves and allow us to draw some important conclusions about their co-relationship.

Ellen Smith has a small proprietorship on Etsy.com known as Ellen's Bake Shop.[37] The Halloween-to-New-Year's-Day holiday season is her peak sales period of the year and she focuses on her award-winning gingerbread houses. TABLE 7-3 contains the output and cost data for her very small business. Ellen, with the help of her sister, can make up to 10 gingerbread houses per day (see column 1). Her fixed cost per day (in column 2) is $2. Variable cost (in column 3) ranges from $0 to $12 per day depending on output. Total cost (column 4) varies from $2 to $14 per day with output. Average-fixed cost, average-variable cost, and average-total cost are calculated the same way they were in TABLE 7-2 for the Paper Street Soap Company.

Marginal cost (MC), though, is different this time because we can now calculate marginal cost by observing the exact change in total cost per one-unit change in output instead of having to

---

[37] While many consumers may assume that "bakery" and "bake shop" are the same thing, bakeries make and sell a general range of baked goods from bread to pizza to cakes while bake shops specialize in baked sweets such as pies, cookies, and candy.

rely on computing a slope for every increment of output. For example, in column 8 of TABLE 7-3, we can see that the marginal cost of one gingerbread house produced per day is

$$total\ cost\ of\ house\ 1 - total\ cost\ of\ house\ 0 = \$2.30 - \$2 = \$0.30\ or\ 30\ cents.$$

The marginal cost to Ellen of producing a second gingerbread house (after already having produced the first one) is

$$total\ cost\ of\ house\ 2 - total\ cost\ of\ house\ 1 = \$2.80 - \$2.30 = \$0.50\ or\ 50\ cents.$$

And so on, down column 8 of TABLE 7-3 up to the maximum output level of 10 gingerbread houses per day.

TABLE 7-3: Ellen's Bake Shop (Output, FC, VC, TC, AFC, AVC, ATC, and MC)							
1	2	3	4	5	6	7	8
Output (gingerbread houses per day)	Fixed Cost (FC)*	Variable Cost (VC)*	Total Cost (TC)*	Average-Fixed Cost (AFC)*	Average-Variable Cost (AVC)*	Average-Total Cost (ATC)*	Marginal Cost (MC)*^
0	2	0	2	NC~	NC~	NC~	
1	2	0.3	2.3	2	0.3	2.3	0.3 (2.3-2)
2	2	0.8	2.8	1	0.4	1.4	0.5 (2.8-2.3)
3	2	1.5	3.5	0.666666667	0.5	1.166666667	0.7 (3.5-2.8)
4	2	2.4	4.4	0.5	0.6	1.1	0.9
5	2	3.5	5.5	0.4	0.7	1.1	1.1
6	2	4.8	6.8	0.333333333	0.8	1.133333333	1.3
7	2	6.3	8.3	0.285714286	0.9	1.185714286	1.5
8	2	8	10	0.25	1	1.25	1.7
9	2	9.9	11.9	0.222222222	1.1	1.322222222	1.9
10	2	12	14	0.2	1.2	1.4	2.1

*in $ units.
~NC = not calculable (division by 0).
^MC = change in total cost from one level of output to the next.

In FIGURE 7-4 are the three average cost curves (AFC, AVC, and ATC) and marginal cost (MC) curve plotted from the data in TABLE 7-3.

FIGURE 7-4: Average and Marginal-Cost Curves for Ellen's Bake Shop

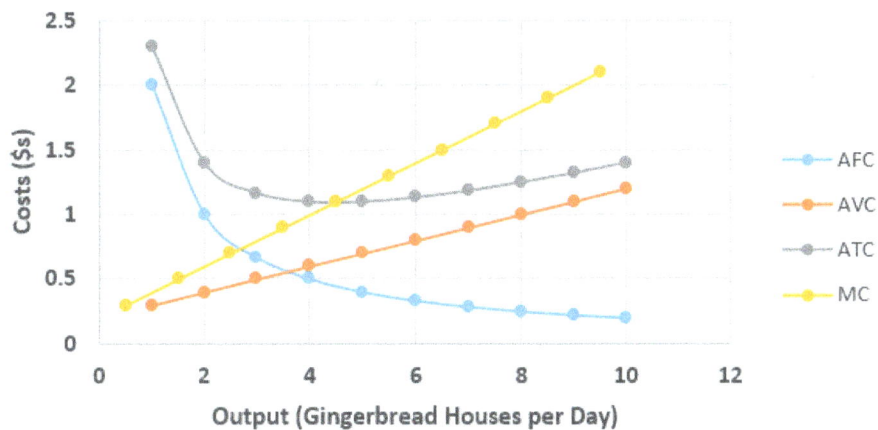

Looking at TABLE 7-3 and FIGURE 7-4, let's analyze three aspects of both:

1. **Marginal costs rise or eventually rise with the level of output.** We didn't see this in the Paper Street example where there was no distinction between MC and ATC, but here MC is clearly separated from ATC. This reflects the fact that with each additional gingerbread house produced, Ellen, her sister, and if need be, another worker joins the operation. Costs steadily rise as Ellen moves from producing one to two gingerbread houses per day all the way up to producing ten gingerbread houses per day. As she produces more and more houses, she has to squeeze more production out of a fixed eight-hour workday. To fully bake and decorate the tenth gingerbread house she has to race faster and faster around her small home kitchen in between two dough mixers, gingerbread-house molds, and a double oven. Thus, marginal costs steadily rise as illustrated in FIGURE 7-4.

Is a straight and upward-sloping line the only possibility for the shape of the MC curve? No, it can also appear as it does in FIGURE 7-5. This is the case of division of labor where multiple workers divide up tasks and experience a great boost in productivity at lower- to mid-levels of output. This is why costs, at first, fall and then start to rise as an increasing number of workers tries to accomplish greater and greater levels of output but with only a fixed level of capital (dough mixers, ovens, molds, etc.). The workers in a bakery start bumping into each other as they each have to navigate a small kitchen and race from its refrigerator to its dough mixers to its baking pans to its ovens to keep producing more and more baked goods.

FIGURE 7-5: Marginal Costs That Fall and Then Rise with Output

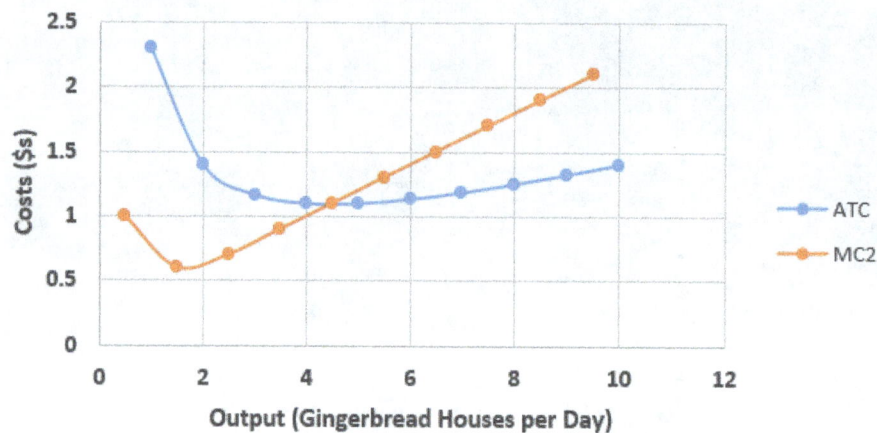

Regardless of whether the MC curve is accurately represented by a straight and upward-sloping line or a *J*-shaped curve like the orange MC curve illustrated in FIGURE 7-5, the point that we made at the beginning of this section still stands: marginal costs rise or eventually rise with the level of output.

2. **The average-total-cost (ATC) curve is U-shaped.** Why? Recall: average-total cost equals average-fixed cost plus average-variable cost. Remember that at low levels of output, fixed cost is being spread over very few units of output, so it starts off relatively high but steadily declines. You can see this pattern in both FIGURE 7-3 and FIGURE 7-4. And this is exactly why the average-total-cost curve starts off high and steadily declines. However, average-total cost, after hitting a low point begins rising again. Why is that the case? It is because variable cost begins rising because the marginal product of the workers is falling: it costs more and more to get Ellen and her two helpers to produce an additional gingerbread house from an increasingly cramped kitchen. At the lowest point on the average-total-cost curve, average-fixed cost and average-variable cost are both stable and at their lowest levels, therefore, so is average-total cost at its

> **efficient scale** - the level of output at which average-total cost (ATC) is at a minimum.

lowest level. In fact, this lowest point on the average-total-cost curve is known as **efficient scale**, the level of output at which average-total cost (ATC) is at a minimum.

3. **The marginal-cost curve intersects the average-total-cost curve at the average-total-cost curve's lowest point (efficient scale).** Why? Consider a college football wide receiver who has an average 40-yard-dash time of 4.5 seconds. To draw interest from pro-football scouts, he must get his time down to 4.48. In order to do that, his next sprint has to be less than 4.5 seconds and as close to 4.48 as possible. And the sprint after that has to fall within the same constraints, and so on. Any sprint below 4.5 seconds is going to push his average closer to 4.48 seconds while any sprint higher than 4.5 seconds is just going to raise his average above 4.5 seconds.

This shows how the marginal, whether it is the next gingerbread house baked or next sprint run, controls the average. When marginal cost is below average-total cost, average-total cost is falling. When marginal cost is above average-total cost, average-total cost is rising. When marginal cost is equal to average-total cost, average-total cost is constant (the slope of the average-total-cost curve is zero, which is true at its minimum level). The efficient-scale level where MC = ATC is $1.10 in TABLE 7-3 and FIGURE 7-4, and it occurs at either 4 or 5 gingerbread houses produced.

To conclude this section:
1. Marginal cost (MC) rises or eventually rises with the level of output.
2. The average-total-cost (ATC) curve is U-shaped.
3. The marginal-cost (MC) curve intersects the average-total-cost (ATC) curve at the average-total-cost (ATC) curve's lowest point (efficient scale).

7.6 The Long Run versus the Short Run

What every successful entrepreneur knows is that by the long run, all inputs are variable. When a firm wants to increase output in the short run, hiring more workers and increasing the number of shifts is usually the only way to go. Firms, from home businesses to factories, take time to add capital. This has implications for cost, and especially average-total cost (ATC). FIGURE 7-6 displays the ATC structure over the short and long runs for golf-cart factories. There are three short-run scenarios: ATC SR$_{SMALL}$ (a small factory in the short run that could be expanded to medium or large in the long run), ATC SR$_{MEDIUM}$ (a mid-sized factory that could be expanded to large or reduced to small in the long run), and ATC SR$_{LARGE}$ (a large factory that could be reduced to medium or small by the long run). ATC LR shows the path that can be traveled when any of the three short-run scenarios expires and the firm (depending on its short-run size) desires to build a larger facility or reduce the capacity of its current facility.

FIGURE 7-6: Average Total Cost: Short Run Versus Long Run

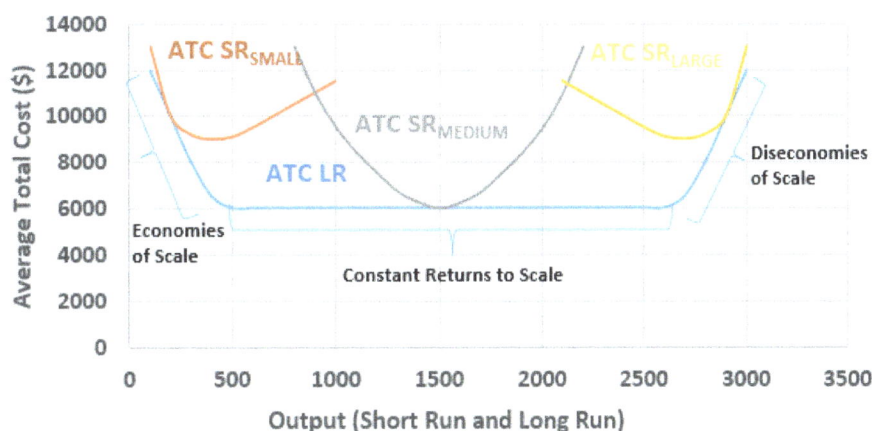

Let's start with ATC SR$_{SMALL}$: Kyle's Carts is a small factory producing 200 golf carts per week at an average-total cost (ATC) of $12,000 per cart. Kyle would like to increase output and reduce costs, but the problem is that along ATC SR$_{SMALL}$, he will be successful in the short run only up to about 700 carts where his ATC will be back to about where it is today, $12,000. At 800 carts, his ATC ($12,500) will be higher than it is now.

specialization – the process of each worker in an assembly process restricting him- or herself to specific and limited tasks to get more skilled and proficient at performing those tasks.

Why is the ATC SR$_{SMALL}$ curve U-shaped? As production increases inside the small facility, average-total cost (ATC) initially falls as Kyle and his four workers specialize in certain tasks on their assembly line. (**Specialization** is the process of each worker in an assembly process restricting him- or herself to specific and limited tasks to get more skilled and proficient at performing those tasks.)

However, the specialization at Kyle's Carts has its limits inside the small facility. As Kyle and his employees try to steadily increase output from their small manufactory, they start developing bottlenecks and getting in each other's way as they re-fresh each of the component stations on the line with new parts and move the incomplete product on to the next component station.

Golf Carts

economies of scale – the decline of long-run-average-total cost as output increases.

constant returns to scale – long-run-average-total cost remaining constant as output increases.

The only way to reduce costs substantially with higher output is to move to a larger facility. For Kyle, that will take a year, but once done, his new short-run ATC will be ATC SR$_{MEDIUM}$. With this new cost structure, he can produce 1,500 carts per week at an ATC of $8,000 per cart. The lowering of costs from $12,000 to $8,000 has come about because of a phenomenon known as **economies of scale**, or the decline of long-run-average-total cost (ATC LR) as output increases. This occurs because as Kyle moves his operation to a larger facility, workers spread out, more capital is added, and specialization reaps further gains not possible in the previous smaller facility.

Economies of scale is distinct from **constant returns to scale**, or long-run-average-total cost remaining constant as output increases. This stretch of the long-run ATC curve can be seen in FIGURE 7-6 extending from about 500 carts per week to about 2,600 carts. To produce 2,600 carts per week and enjoy constant returns to scale (keep his ATC at $8,000), Kyle will need to expand the size of his medium-sized facility and produce at the minimum ATC at this larger-than-medium-sized facility which would be represented by another U-shaped curve in FIGURE 7-6 between ATC SR$_{MEDIUM}$ and ATC SR$_{LARGE}$. Producing 2,600 carts per week at the medium-sized facility (ATC SR$_{MEDIUM}$) in the short run would come at too high an ATC. In fact, judging by FIGURE 7-6, it would be impossible.

Last of all, there are **diseconomies of scale**, or levels of increasing long-run average total cost as output increases. This stretch of the long-run ATC curve can be seen in FIGURE 7-6 extending from about 2,600 carts to 3,000 carts. This is the scenario where Kyle is producing his carts in a large factory at an output of about 2,900 carts per week. Long-run ATC is rising because of **coordination problems**, or barriers that arise that make managers less effective at keeping costs down. In a larger facility, Kyle cannot monitor his many more workers as closely as he could in the small- and medium-sized facilities. Outside of Kyle's watch, at high levels of output, Kyle's workers get tired quicker, take longer and more frequent breaks where they gossip, upload posts to Facebook and Instagram, and text their friends and spouses. This phenomenon is known as **shirking**, or the neglect of steady effort on a job. Thus, it costs more and more on average to continue raising output to higher and higher levels in even a large factory both in the short run (because of the size of the facility) and the long run (because of the inherent coordination problems associated with large and very large enterprises).

diseconomies of scale - levels of increasing long-run-average-total cost as output increases.

coordination problems - barriers that arise that make managers less effective at keeping costs down.

shirking – the neglect of steady effort on a job.

ECONOMICS IN ACTION: How to Decide What Upgrades to Make to Your Home

If you've gotten this far into the chapter, you probably feel overwhelmed with getting straight all the different costs and not too sure of their immediate practicality. So here is a very practical illustration from everyday life that can help you in making many different sound decisions and it only involves an easy application of marginal cost and marginal benefit (see chapter 1, economics principle number 3, *Rational economic decisions are made at the margin*).

Linda, after meeting with her realtor, is considering two upgrades to her house before putting it on the market. Linda's realtor friend Barbara told Linda that new carpeting and a new roof will make her house more attractive to potential buyers and the improvements will increase the house's value more than their cost. Linda's other friend Bob, a home appraiser, disagrees. New carpeting is $3,000 and a new roof is $6,000. According to Bob, new carpeting will raise the selling price of Linda's house by $2,500 and a new roof will raise the selling price of the house by $7,500.

Linda's four options are:
1. Replace the carpeting but not the roof.
2. Replace both.
3. Replace the roof but not the carpeting.
4. Replace neither.

Comparing the marginal benefit to the marginal cost for each upgrade, sound economics advises only one choice: option three, replace the roof but not the carpeting. Why? Let's go through the four options one by one:

1. If Linda replaces the carpeting but not the roof, she pays $3,000 but the house's value rises by only $2,500. Thus, Linda loses $500 after the house sells.
2. If Linda replaces the carpet and roof, she pays $9,000 for both upgrades, the house's value rises by $10,000, and thus Linda gains $1,000 from the sale of the house. This option (2) sounds good, but is it the best?
3. If Linda replaces the roof but not the carpeting, she pays $6,000 for a new roof, the house's value rises by $7,500, and thus Linda gains $1,500 from the sale of the house. This is the best option so far because it results in the greatest gains for Linda.

4. If Linda replaces neither the carpet nor the roof, the house's value does not rise at all. This option is the second-least-desirable alternative. While it's not the $500 loss of option 1, it's a gain of $0, which is far inferior to option 3, a gain of $1,500.

In conclusion, the economically soundest option is alternative three: replace the roof but not the carpeting since the marginal benefit of option three exceeds its marginal cost by the greatest amount of money among the four options.

CASE STUDY: from Adam Smith to Frederick Smith--Lessons on the Importance of Specialization

Adam Smith (1723-1790) was the first economist who, drawing on an oral body of knowledge, put into writing and formalized the economic knowledge of his time. One of his most important lessons is the benefits of specialization, dividing up all the tasks of the production process among various workers so that each one can gain experience and skill in a few tasks to speed up the entire production operation.

In chapter 1 (*Of the Division of Labour*) of book 1 of Smith's magnum opus *The Wealth of Nations* (1776), Smith describes the division of labor that occurred in pin factories in his day.

Adam Smith (1723-1790)

One man draws out the wire, another straightens it, a third cuts it, a fourth points it, a fifth grinds it at the top for receiving the head; to make the head requires two or three distinct operations...and the important business of making a pin is, in this manner, divided into about eighteen distinct operations...(Smith, p. 4).

Smith observes that one worker not familiar with the industry but using his or her full effort could probably end up making one pin per day but definitely not 20. A factory he personally observed employed ten workers which produced "upwards of forty-eight thousand pins in a day" (Smith, p. 5).

Henry Ford, founder of the Ford Motor Company, adapted the division of labor to a much more complex product than a pin: the automobile. While Ford Motor Company was not the first firm to use an assembly line to assemble a product, even automobiles, it certainly has been the most famous, inspiring other attempts to utilize specialization to boost production.

Frederick W. Smith (1944-2025)

In a paper for an economics class at Yale University, Frederick W. Smith (1944-2025) first outlined his idea of specialization applied to expedited shipping. In the most advanced version, jet airplanes, each with a specialty destination, would leave a central airport to fly to a specialty destination to pick up parcels and then return to the central airport to be unloaded, with all the parcels sorted according to their ultimate destination. Each airplane was then refilled with packages ultimately heading to each plane's specialty destination. The planes would again leave the central airport to fly to their specialty destination to unload all packages heading to that destination. Smith's version of specialization is applied every day at FedEx, formerly Federal Express, which he founded in 1971. FedEx's global air hub is at Memphis International Airport in Memphis, Tennessee, the city where Smith attended elementary school and high school.

Reference
Smith, Adam. *The Wealth of Nations*. Modern Library, 1994.

7.7 Conclusion

This chapter introduced revenue, cost, and economic profit but went into considerable detail about different costs in the short run and long run. Costs though, are only half the picture of what motivates firms to produce the levels of output that they produce. We will see the other half of that picture in the next chapter. TABLE 7-4 is a summary of the most important costs that we encountered in this chapter.

TABLE 7-4: Costs from Fixed to Marginal	
Type of Cost	**Verbal/Mathematical Definition**
fixed cost (FC)	Cost that doesn't change with the level of output produced.
variable cost (VC)	Cost that will vary or change with the level of output produced.
total cost (TC)	The sum of all of the costs of a firm OR opportunity cost = explicit costs + implicit costs OR fixed cost (FC) + variable cost (VC).
average fixed cost (AFC)	Fixed cost divided by output (AFC = FC/Q, where Q = output).
average variable cost (AVC)	Variable cost divided by output (AVC = VC/Q, where Q = output).
average total cost (ATC)	Total cost divided by output (ATC = TC/Q, where Q = output).
marginal cost (MC)	The change in total cost (TC) caused by a one-unit change in output. It can be determined by: 1. directly observing the change in total cost caused by a one-unit change in output OR 2. calculating the slope of the total-cost curve where MC = $\Delta TC/\Delta Q$ where Δ = change and Q = output.

7.8 Chapter Concepts

total revenue (TR)
total cost (TC)
economic profit (π)
opportunity cost
explicit costs
implicit costs
accounting cost
accounting profit
production schedule
output
inputs
production function
short run
long run
marginal product (MP)
diminishing marginal product
fixed cost (FC)
variable cost (VC)
total cost (TC)
average-fixed cost (AFC)
average-variable cost (AVC)
average-total cost (ATC)
marginal cost (MC)
efficient scale
specialization
economies of scale
constant returns to scale
diseconomies of scale
coordination problems
shirking

7.9 Problems, Questions, and Discussion Topics (Items Requiring Examples are Marked with an Asterisk [*])

1. For 2025, Top Shelf Sporting Goods's total revenue was $100 million, its explicit costs were $35 million, and its implicit costs were $60 million. Given these data for 2025,

   A. what was Top Shelf's economic profit (π)? Show all work used to arrive at your final answer.

   B. What was Top Shelf's accounting profit (ρ)? Show all work used to arrive at your final answer.

2. *short run* versus *long run* (define both concepts, then provide an example of only one using the narrative about the Paper Street Soap Company)*

3. production function (define, then provide a quantitative example)*

4. diminishing marginal product (define, then provide a quantitative example)*

Questions 5, 6, and 7 pertain to Fred's Buffalo Wings. The small, independent fast-food restaurant, open every day from 11 AM to 8 PM, has a fixed cost (rent) of $200 per day. Its variable cost is labor plus meals as follows. Labor is four workers per day each receiving $20 per hour with each worker's shift lasting nine hours per day. In terms of meals, Fred's sells 45 wing plates per day which cost $9 per plate (each plate = 10 wings at $0.50 each + sweet-potato fries at $2 + one fountain drink at $2).

5. Given the data for Fred's above,

   A. what is Fred's variable cost (VC) per day? Show all work used to arrive at your final answer.

   B. What is Fred's total cost (TC; fixed + variable) per day? Show all work used to arrive at your final answer.

6. Given the data for Fred's above,

   A. what is Fred's average fixed cost (AFC) per day?

   B. What is Fred's average variable cost (AVC) per day?

7. Given the data for Fred's above,

   A. What is Fred's average total cost (ATC) per day?

   B. For Fred's, given that the costs of all food items remain constant up to 59 wing plates per day, what is the marginal cost of producing a 46th wing plate?

8. What are the two ways of calculating marginal cost? Provide a quantitative example of only one.

9. In FIGURE 7-3, the marginal-cost curve of Paper Street Soap Company gets stacked onto its average-total cost curve. In contrast, in FIGURE 7-4, these two same curves are graphically distinct and separate for Ellen's Bake Shop. What difference between the two businesses led to this?

10. *Marginal costs* _____ *or* _____ *with the level of output.*

    A. Fill in the blanks: _____ , _____ .

B. Explain:

11. *The _____ curve is U-shaped.*

    A. Fill in the blank: _____.

    B. Explain:

12. efficient scale (define, then provide a quantitative example)*

13. *The marginal-cost curve intersects the _____ curve at the _____ curve's lowest point (_____).*

    A. Fill in the blanks: _____, _____, _____.

    B. Explain:

14. specialization*

15. Describe each of the following's role in causing diseconomies of scale:

    A. coordination problems

    B. shirking

16. After a decade of living in a townhome, you and your significant other decide that you are both ready to move to a house. Your seller's agent recommends replacing the laminate kitchen countertops with granite countertops and replacing the carpet flooring with hardwood to maximize the resale value of the townhouse. Local contractor estimates put the cost of new granite countertops at $5,000 and new hardwood flooring at $15,000. Local appraisers estimate that the new granite countertops will raise the townhome's selling price by $7,000 while the installation of hardwood flooring will add $13,000.

    A. Which renovations do you undertake: countertops, flooring, both, or neither?

    B. Why? Show all work used to arrive at your final answer.

17. Henry Ford and Frederick W. Smith each used production processes that utilized specialization to maximize productivity.

    A. Describe the specific process Henry Ford applied in automobile production.

    B. Describe the specific process Frederick W. Smith applied in package delivery.

Chapter 8: Uniform Competition

8.0 Introduction

In the previous chapter, we examined costs. Starting in this chapter, we take that knowledge to see how costs affect production and pricing in different market structures with increasing **market power** (the extent to which an individual seller or firm can control the market price of his/her/its product), from uniform competition (many sellers) all the way to monopoly (a single seller).

market power - an individual or firm's ability to set the price of a product across a relatively wide range of potential prices because he/she/it has no or very few competitors.

8.1 Uniform Competition Defined and Three Types of Revenue

As we saw in chapter 4, **uniform competition** (a.k.a., perfect competition) has three main features:

1. Many buyers and many sellers such that not a single buyer or seller can move the market's price either up or down. This makes each buyer and seller a **price taker**, or one of the numerous buyers or sellers active in uniformly competitive markets who, because of their large numbers, have no influence on market price and therefore must either "take" (accept) the market price and buy or sell the product or leave the market.
2. A product that is uniform (nearly or exactly the same from seller to seller), hence the name uniform competition. Example: 8.5" x 11" paper used by a photocopier or computer printer.
3. Individual sellers or firms are able to enter or exit the market at a low cost.

uniform competition – a market structure with many buyers and sellers such that not a single buyer or seller can move the market's price up or down, a product that is uniform, and individual sellers or firms able to enter or exit the market at a low cost.

price taker – one of the numerous buyers or sellers active in uniformly competitive markets who, because of their large numbers, have no influence on market price and therefore must either "take" (accept) the market price and buy or sell the product or leave the market.

The three uniformly competitive market attributes above affect revenue and therefore profit, which we saw in the last chapter was:

$$profit\ (\pi) = total\ revenue\ (TR) - total\ cost\ (TC)$$

The previous chapter defined total cost (TC) and chapter 5 defined total revenue (TR) as

$$total\ revenue\ (TR) = P\ X\ Q$$

where P is market price and Q is market quantity. Like average cost from the previous chapter, it only follows that average revenue (AR) is defined as total revenue (TR) divided by quantity (Q) or

$$average\ revenue\ (AR) = \frac{TR}{Q}$$

and like marginal cost (MC), marginal revenue (MR) is defined as

$$marginal\ revenue\ (MR) = \frac{\Delta TR}{\Delta Q}.$$

Guy's Guitar Picks is a business on Etsy that produces hand-crafted custom guitar picks. TABLE 8-1 displays Guy's daily production levels, price, and total-, average-, and marginal-revenue calculations.

TABLE 8-1: Guy's Guitar Picks (Q, P, TR, AR, and MR)				
1	2	3	4	5
Quantity (Q) of guitar picks	Price (P)	Total Revenue (TR = P X Q)	Average Revenue (AR = TR/Q)	Marginal Revenue (MR = $\Delta TR/\Delta Q$)
0	$10	$0	$0*	
1	$10	$10	$10	$10
2	$10	$20	$10	$10
3	$10	$30	$10	$10
4	$10	$40	$10	$10
5	$10	$50	$10	$10
6	$10	$60	$10	$10
7	$10	$70	$10	$10
8	$10	$80	$10	$10
9	$10	$90	$10	$10
10	$10	$100	$10	$10
*0/0 mathematically is known as an indeterminate form, but we will treat $0/0 as $0 of average revenue (AR).				

8.2 Maximization of Profit

This section is arguably the most important in this book. In it we will provide the critical answer that so many entrepreneurs want to know about their business: how much should I produce? Let's answer the question first for our current example. How many guitar picks should Guy produce per day such that he maximizes his profit? TABLE 8-2 provides the answer. To create TABLE 8-2, we kept the Quantity, Total Revenue, and Marginal Revenue variables from TABLE 8-1. These become column 1 (Quantity), column 2 (Total Revenue), and column 5 (Marginal Revenue) in TABLE 8-2. The new variables added for Guy's Guitar picks in TABLE 8-2 are Total Cost (column 3), Profit (column 4), Marginal Cost (column 6), and Change in Profit (column 7). These data will help answer Guy's question about how many units of product he needs to produce each day to maximize his profit.

TABLE 8-2: Guy's Guitar Picks (Q, TR, TC, π, MR, MC, and Δπ)						
1	2	3	4	5	6	7
Quantity (Q) of guitar picks	Total Revenue (*TR* = *P X Q*)	Total Cost (TC = FC + VC)	Profit (π = TR = TC)	Marginal Revenue (*MR* = Δ*TR*/Δ*Q*)	Marginal Cost MC (*MC* = Δ*TC*/Δ*Q*)	Change in Profit (Δπ = MR – MC)
0	$0	$10*	-$10			
1	$10	$15	-$5	$10	$5	$5
2	$20	$21	-$1	$10	$6	$4
3	$30	$28	$2	$10	$7	$3
4	$40	$36	$4	$10	$8	$2
5	$50	$45	$5	$10	$9	$1
6	$60	$55	$5	$10	$10	$0
7	$70	$66	$4	$10	$11	-$1
8	$80	$78	$2	$10	$12	-$2
9	$90	$91	-$1	$10	$13	-$3
10	$100	$105	-$5	$10	$14	-$4
*At a quantity of zero (0) guitar picks produced, this number is total fixed cost (or just fixed cost) for Guy's very small business.						

First, Guy can look at profit as the difference between Total Revenue (column 2) and Total Cost (column 3), which it certainly is, and this difference for different levels of production is found in Profit (column 4). Looking down the Profit (π) column (column 4), though, provides us with an ambiguous answer. Maximum profit is definitely at about $5, but this appears to occur at production levels of 5 and 6 guitar picks per day. The total cost and profit data (with their large increments between different levels of production, e.g., $0, $10, and $20) gave us an approximation, but not a precise-enough answer.

Let's take a look at the more continuous marginal data (with their zero- or one-unit increases between different levels of production, e.g., $5, $6, and $7) to see if they are more helpful. It turns out that they are. Moving from producing 0 guitar picks to 1 guitar pick provides us with an additional $10 in revenue (Marginal Revenue, column 5). It also adds only an additional $5 in cost (Marginal Cost, column 6). Thus, moving from a production level of 0 guitar picks to 1 guitar pick increases our profit by $5 (Change in Profit, column 7). So what do we do? We keep producing until we can no longer add to our profit. At a production level of 6 guitar picks per day, Marginal Revenue = $10 per day but Marginal Cost = $10 per day as well. This creates a Change in Profit equal to $0 per day.

In other words, we can no longer add to our profit beyond a production level of 6 guitar picks per day. If we produce 5 guitar picks per day, we can still add $1 to our profit. If we produce seven guitar picks per day, we lose $1 from our profit. We now have a clear and precise answer to our question: To maximize profit, Guy should produce 6 guitar picks per day.

8.3 Marginal Cost and Firm Supply

FIGURE 8-1 illustrates the uniformly competitive firm's cost and revenue structure and individual supply level graphically. First are the marginal-, average total-, and average-variable cost curves. We first saw these in the previous chapter, chapter 7. Notice how the average-total cost (ATC) curve falls, hits its lowest point, and then rises again as we move from 0 to higher and higher levels of output on the quantity axis. Notice also how the average-variable cost (AVC) curve does the same thing. In fact, the difference between the variables (ATC – AVC) is average-fixed cost (AFC). The marginal-cost (MC) curve rises steadily along the quantity axis and intersects the average-total cost (ATC) curve at its lowest point.

What has been new for this chapter has been revenue, and we see it graphically presented in FIGURE 8-1, specifically, marginal revenue (MR). Marginal revenue is equal to the price of the product and these two in turn are both equal to average revenue (demand) for the firm. (Average revenue is always equal to the price of the good, and average revenue, when drawn as a curve is the demand curve. Thus, the average-revenue curve and demand curve are the same thing.) The demand curve for the competitive firm is flat because it is a price taker. If the firm sells one unit or 10,000 units of its product, it must charge the same price per unit because it is only one among many firms in the market. If one firm raises the price of its product, even by a small amount, while all its competitors keep their price the same, the firm raising its price loses all or almost all of its sales.

FIGURE 8-1: The Uniformly Competitive Firm

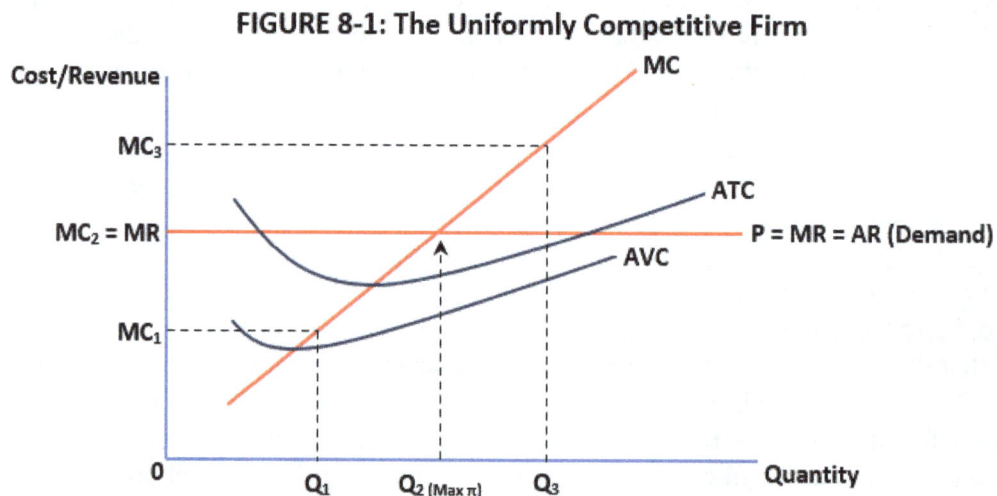

This picture of the competitive firm gives us the same answer as to how much the firm will supply as did TABLE 8-2: where marginal revenue (MR) = marginal cost (MC). That level of output is at $Q_{2\,(Max\,\pi)}$, the quantity where profit is maximized. Why? Because if production lies at Q_1, marginal revenue (MR) is at the level of the demand curve (P = MR = AR [demand]) while marginal cost sits at the level of MC_1. With marginal revenue greater than marginal cost (or MR > MC_1) at Q_1, the firm obviously should produce more units as long as each additional unit adds to revenue more than costs. It will only stop producing more when additions to revenue fail to exceed costs. That point arrives at $Q_{2\,(Max\,\pi)}$.

The opposite situation prevails at production level Q_3. Here, marginal cost lies at the level of MC_3 while marginal revenue is at the level of the demand curve ($P = MR = AR$ [demand]). With marginal cost exceeding marginal revenue ($MC_3 > MR$), the firm obviously should produce fewer units as long as each additional unit adds to cost more than it does to revenue. The firm will only stop producing fewer and fewer units when additions to cost fail to exceed additions to revenue. That point will be at $Q_{2 \, (Max \, \pi)}$.

This leads to a simple rule for not only competitive firms, but as we will see in the next three chapters, *all* types of firms:

Regardless of market structure (uniform competition, differentiated competition, oligopoly, or monopoly), all profit-maximizing firms produce at the profit-maximizing level of output where marginal cost (MC) equals marginal revenue (MR) or MC = MR.

What happens if the demand for the firm's product increases because of an increase in market (industry) demand? FIGURE 8-2 displays the results.

FIGURE 8-2: The Uniformly Competitive Firm with an Increase in Demand

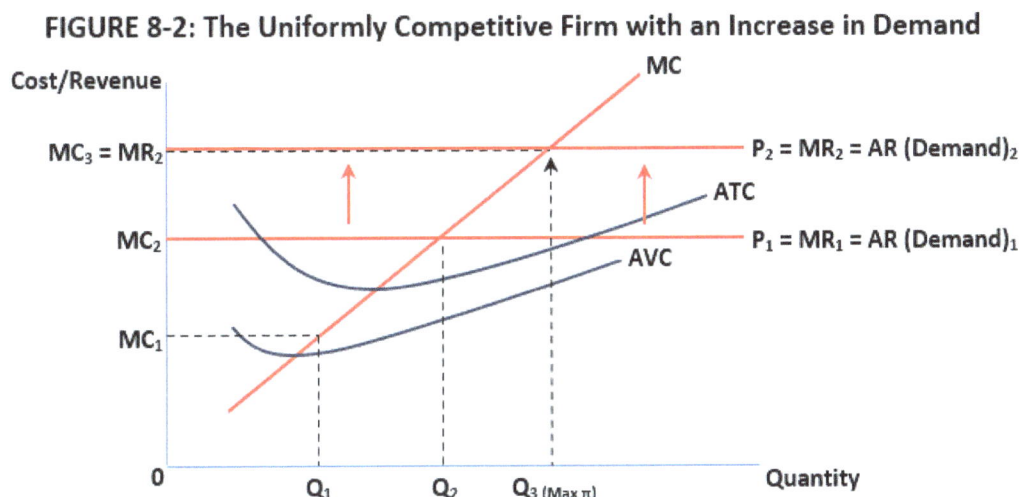

Demand rises vertically from $P_1 = MR_1 = AR$ (Demand)$_1$ to $P_2 = MR_2 = AR$ (Demand)$_2$. But this changes the profit-maximizing output for the firm. Q_2 is no longer the profit-maximizing level of output for the firm because marginal cost at Q_2 (MC_2) is now below the new marginal revenue (MR_2). The firm should now produce more output because each additional unit now adds more to revenue than cost. To what new level of output should the firm produce? Following our simple rule for profit maximation regardless of market structure, $Q_{3 \, (Max \, \pi)}$ where marginal cost is equal to marginal revenue (or $MC_3 = MR_2$). For if we go beyond that point, then marginal cost will exceed marginal revenue (MR_2) on each additional unit, and the firm will suffer marginal losses.

FIGURE 8-2 reveals how the uniformly competitive firm's demand curve can shift and change the firm's profit-maximizing output. What about the uniformly competitive firm's supply curve? Does it have one? Absolutely. In the market graphs in Chapter 4 we saw, for example, how shifts in the demand curve and changing equilibria traced out the supply curve for a market or how shifts in the supply curve and changing equilibria traced out the demand curve for a market. In a similar way, we see in FIGURE 8-2 how changing demand traces out the firm's supply curve:

188

the marginal-cost (MC) curve. As the uniformly competitive firm's demand curve rises or falls, the profit-maximizing output produced by the firm rises or falls (respectively) in line with the intersection of the firm's demand and marginal-cost (MC) curve.

This supports our second major conclusion of the chapter:

A uniformly competitive firm's marginal-cost (MC) curve displays the different quantities the uniformly competitive firm is willing and able to supply at different prices. Therefore, the uniformly competitive firm's marginal-cost (MC) curve is its supply curve.

8.4 The Stay Put, Shutdown, Exit, and Enter Rules

Thus far, we have been concerned with finding the profit-maximizing quantity of output that the uniformly competitive firm will produce: where marginal-cost (MC) equals marginal revenue (MR) or MC = MR. Again, MC = MR is the profit-maximizing level of output for *all* firms, regardless of the industrial organization of their industry (uniform competition to monopoly). However, a couple of important qualifications must now be added. FIGURE 8-1 and FIGURE 8-2 display competitive firms earning economic profits. There is no question that these two firms should continue operating. In FIGURE 8-2, market demand increased, and thus the firm's demand increased, and thus the firm's economic profits increased. But what if market demand, and thus firm demand, moved in the opposite direction: in other words, they fell? At what point should the firm stop producing temporarily or even leave the industry altogether? These are questions that many different firms in many different industries face every day. The answer lies in the extent to which demand has fallen.

1. STAY PUT. Again, FIGURES 8-1 and 8-2 displayed uniformly competitive firms earning positive economic profits. For a uniformly competitive industry, this situation will not last long, as free entry and exit (the third feature of uniformly competitive industries—see section 8.2) will provide the incentive for entrepreneurs and firms to enter a uniformly competitive industry to earn a piece of its limited profits. Entry will continue until total revenue (TR) is equal to total costs (TC) or

$$TR = TC$$

When we divide both sides by Q (output) we get:

$$\frac{TR}{Q} = \frac{TC}{Q}.$$

Recall that $TR = P*Q$ and $\frac{TC}{Q} = ATC$ (*average total cost*). Therefore:

$$\frac{P*Q}{Q} = ATC.$$

The Qs on the left side of the equation cancel each other out

$$\frac{P * Q}{Q} = ATC$$

so that we arrive at:

$$P = ATC \quad \textbf{Equation 8.1}$$

The importance of this last equation (8.1) will now be explained. FIGURE 8-3 shows a situation where the firm's condition is stable for both the short run and long run. This uniformly competitive firm produces at the level where profits are maximized, i.e., where marginal cost equals marginal revenue ($Q_{2 \text{ (Max } \pi)}$) where $P = MR = AR = MC_2$. So far so good, but notice also that Price (P) = Average Total Cost (ATC), see **Equation 8.1** above. In other words, the revenue coming in per unit (price) is covering the average total cost (ATC) per unit (average-fixed cost [AFC] plus average-variable cost [AVC]). With all costs covered, the firm is in good shape and should continue its production, i.e., "stay put," or even more precisely, the firm should **stay put** in the short run if revenue is equal to or greater than costs (as FIGURE 8-1, FIGURE 8-2, and FIGURE 8-3 show), thus, the stay-put rule is P ≥ ATC:

stay put – the continuance of a firm's production in the short run because price is greater than or equal to average-total cost (ATC).

stay-put rule – P ≥ ATC.

Stay-Put Rule: $P \geq ATC$.

FIGURE 8-3: The Uniformly Competitive Firm with All Costs Covered

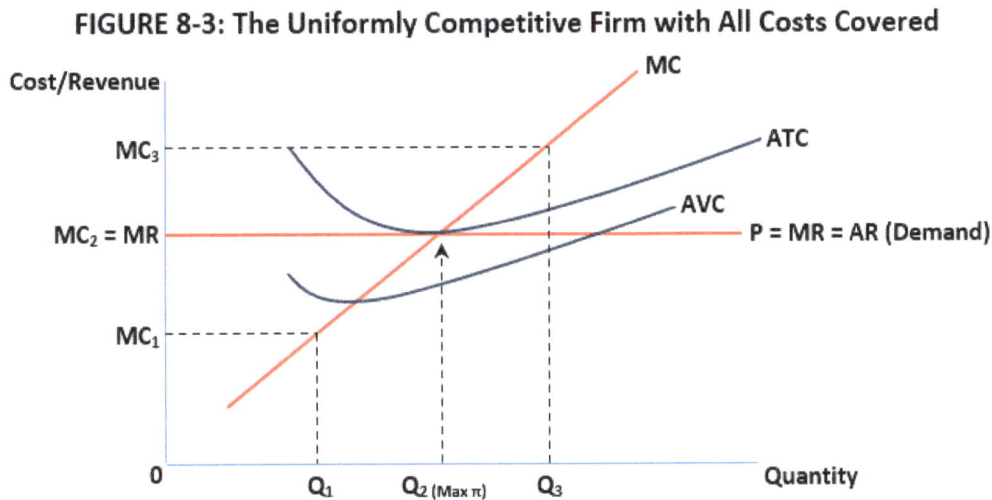

Tough decisions must be made when demand drops further. FIGURE 8-4 displays a firm in such a situation.

FIGURE 8-4: The Uniformly Competitive Firm with Only Variable Costs Covered

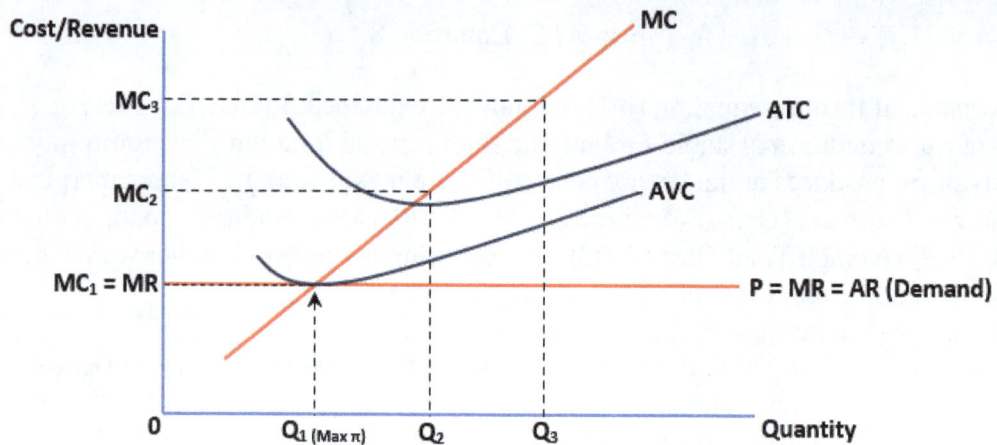

In FIGURE 8-4, a uniformly competitive firm has all of its variable costs covered but none of its fixed costs covered. The firm produces the profit-maximizing level of output where marginal cost (MC_1) equals marginal revenue (MR), or $Q_{1\ (Max\ \pi)}$ where $P = MR = AR = MC_1$. While $P = AVC$ at its lowest point at $Q_{1\ (Max\ \pi)}$, this is way below ATC (Average-Fixed Cost + Average-Variable Cost). While average-variable cost [and thus full variable cost or $P*Q_{1\ (Max\ \pi)}$] is covered, average fixed cost (and thus total fixed cost) is not being paid.

Clearly this means trouble for the long run but not the short run. Why? A small restaurant can get away with not paying its fixed cost (e.g., its rent or its mortgage payment) for a month or two or three before it gets evicted or foreclosed from its location. If it fails to pay its variable cost (i.e., its cooks, wait staff, bartender, and materials suppliers), it can no longer operate as its labor no longer comes in to work and it no longer has materials being supplied once labor and suppliers stop getting paid. Unlike banks or landlords, labor and materials suppliers are not bound by laws or bureaucratic red tape that force them to provide services without getting paid, regardless of the stated reason. With no cooks and waiters and ingredients to prepare meals, the restaurant cannot operate the way it can if it merely gets a month or two behind in paying its rent.

shutdown – a production level of zero in the short run because variable cost cannot be covered.

sunk cost – a cost that is incurred and irrecoverable.

2. SHUT DOWN. A **shutdown** is a production level of zero in the short run because variable cost cannot be covered. Fixed cost (such as rent or a mortgage payment) are not relevant in the short run because they are a **sunk cost**, or a cost that is incurred and irrecoverable. Missed rent or mortgage payments are sunk because they are still owed to a landlord or bank unless forgiven or foreclosed.

As we've seen, any business has to shut down if its total revenue (TR) fails to cover its variable costs (VC), or:

$$TR < VC.$$

When we divide both sides by Q (output) we get:

$$\frac{TR}{Q} < \frac{VC}{Q}$$

Recall that TR = P*Q and $\frac{VC}{Q} = AVC$ (*average variable cost*). Therefore:

$$\frac{P * Q}{Q} < AVC$$

After the Qs on the left side of the equation cancel each other out or

$$\frac{P * \cancel{Q}}{\cancel{Q}} < AVC,$$

we arrive at:

$$P < AVC.$$

Ergo, our shut-down rule is P < AVC or

Shut-down Rule: $P < AVC$.

shut-down rule – P < AVC.

In other words, if price (per unit) drops below average-variable cost (per unit) over the short run, the firm must shut down. As long as variable cost (labor and suppliers) is covered, then a product can be assembled and sold (e.g., everything from spaghetti-dinner entrées at a small Italian restaurant to bars of soap at Paper Street Soap Company). Landlords and banks (fixed cost) have no choice but exercise forbearance under the law. If business conditions get better quickly and demand increases such that fixed costs get covered again, then payments resume to landlords and banks and the landlords and banks cannot evict or foreclose the tenant or mortgage holder.

3. EXIT. Inevitably, the short run passes and the long run arrives. If our uniformly competitive firm is still at where it was in FIGURE 8-4 covering only variable costs but not fixed costs, or, even worse, its demand curve is even lower (a red flat line lying below the level of MC₁ = MR in FIGURE 8-4), it will be forced into an **exit**, or a closing of the firm by the long run because not all costs (fixed, variable, or both) are being covered. Exit becomes inevitable because of eviction, foreclosure, or a failure to pay some other non-rent, non-mortgage fixed cost. The long run has arrived, and every landlord or lender eventually gets his or her due. In fact, if any portion of a firm's total fixed cost is not being paid over the long run, the firm is forced to exit its industry. This leads to the exit rule: P < ATC or

exit – a closing of a firm by the long run because not all costs (fixed, variable, or both) are being covered.

exit rule - P < ATC.

Exit Rule: $P < ATC$.

This is a stricter rule than the shutdown rule, but then again, it must be. All costs must be covered by the long run as patience is at an absolute end for all creditors.

192

entrance – the act of a firm entering an industry because, at a minimum, it can cover all costs.

entrance rule - P ≥ ATC.

4. ENTRANCE. The easiest of the decision concepts in this chapter may be **entrance** (the act of a firm entering an industry because, at a minimum, it can cover all costs), especially since we just studied exit and the exit rule. The entrance rule is

Entrance Rule: $P \geq ATC$.

Notice that the entrance rule is the same as the stay-put rule. To enter an industry, a firm must have a minimum level of creditworthiness. It must be able to cover fixed cost first, otherwise it gets no location from which to sell a product (tangible good or intangible service). Then it must hire labor and purchase capital to supply its product, otherwise it's an empty storefront and has already entered short-run shutdown mode. Most new entering businesses are able to cover both fixed and variable costs early on. As we saw in this section, what happens later depends on what happens to the demand for the product.

CASE STUDY: Restaurants and Bars in a College Town During the Summer

Bow & Arrow (Google, Fair Use)

Bow & Arrow is a top-Google-reviewed barbecue restaurant in Auburn, Alabama. It serves Southwest-U.S.-style barbeque ranging from beef-brisket-and-cheddar tacos to spareribs. Every September, when the college football season is in full swing, its large dining rooms and full-service bar are packed with college students who attend nearby Auburn University and their families. This frenetic pace keeps up unrelentingly until the Christmas and New Year's Eve holidays in late December. Winter and spring months of the year are only slightly less busy.

However, after final exams end at the end of the school year the first week of every May, demand for the restaurant's food almost disappears as students, their families, and alumni head out of town for the very sultry months of summer. Most laypeople who don't work in the restaurant industry assume that, with demand reduced to a comparative trickle, the restaurant would naturally close. But they would be wrong.

First, the restaurant's mortgaged buildings and land are sunk costs in the short run (three weeks of May, June, July, and half of August). While the air-conditioning on a closed building can be turned way down, it, like the water, cannot be turned completely off.

Yes, demand greatly falls during the summer months, but so does staffing as college-student waiters, cooks, and bartenders leave town during the summer as well. Demand falls, but so does variable cost. With the necessary variable cost just covered, the restaurant stays open. A fraction of revenue is better than no revenue and the locals still get served good food when they want it.

CASE STUDY: Waterslides and Go-Carts in Coastal Towns in December

Almost 250 miles from Auburn, Alabama (see the case study above) by car, is the town of Gulf Shores, Alabama and an amusement park named The Track. Some of The Track's offerings include go-karts, bumper boats, spinning roller coasters, a merry-go-round, a miniature golf course, a small train, and arcade. During the summer season (mid-May to mid-August), The Track is a popular destination for families. However, from mid-August (the end of summer when children to college students return to school) until mid-March of the following year (spring break), demand substantially drops for The Track's rides and amusements. In fact, during the rainy

The Track (Google, Fair Use)

and cold months on the Gulf of America coast (November through February), traffic to the park drops to just about zero.

Unlike Bow & Arrow (see the case study above), the decision for The Track during these very slow months is to shut down. The very low demand experienced during the fall-to-winter months on the Gulf of America coast does not fully cover variable costs, therefore, the economically sound choice is to shut down. Ditto for nearby OWA outdoor waterpark, which is closed from early November to early March.

ECONOMICS IN ACTION: Taylor Swift, Dishwashers, and the Lesson of Sunk Costs

It's no secret that tickets to a Taylor Swift concert are pricey. After all, there's only one Taylor Swift in the world (very small supply) and she has millions of adoring followers (very high demand), sometimes referred to as "Swifties." For a sample of some price data, let's look at some seats for Ms. Swift's October 27, 2024 concert at Caesars Superdome in New Orleans, Louisiana. Very poor seats very high up in the stadium and to the rear of the stage (where the view of the artist was obstructed most of the time by the stage structure) sold for $1,915 each on StubHub. Excellent seats in row 9 of section N (on the floor of the stadium and on the front and left side of the stage within 15 feet of the artist) sold for $7,451 on StubHub. (Compare these prices to Shen Yun, which range from $150 to $1,000. Let's just say that this is good evidence that Shen Yun is nowhere near as in demand as Taylor Swift.)

**Taylor Swift
(iHeartRadioCA, CC BY 3.0)**

So what happens when very pricey Taylor Swift tickets are purchased and they turn out to be counterfeit? Regardless of the high sum paid, it becomes a sunk cost and irrelevant as to what to do next. Demand is both willingness *and* ability to pay. If either is missing, we don't have demand. What was paid and lost plays no factor in current demand. If an ardent Swift fan gets swindled but still wants to see her idol live in concert, she begs, borrows, or steals to come up with the money to pay for another (this time hopefully genuine) ticket, even in "nosebleed" seats where the view of the artist is poor or obstructed.

194

| fallacy of sunk costs – the mistaken idea that spent and irrecoverable costs should affect future decisions. | The same goes for any other decision in life, be it business strategy, investing, or even a consumption choice. Simple folk adages ("don't cry over spilt milk," "it's water under the bridge," "let bygones be bygones") accurately warn against falling prey to the **fallacy of sunk costs**, or the mistaken idea that spent and irrecoverable costs should affect future decisions. If you (like a certain |

economics author) purchase a stainless Frigidaire dishwasher for $500 and right after its warranty expires, the appliance's electronic control panel keeps failing again and again, you begin to search for a new and more reliable dishwasher.

You don't keep pouring money and time and parts into a repeatedly failing appliance, regardless of what you initially paid for it, even if it was $500. The $500 is a sunk cost and irrelevant. The relevant comparison is between the price of a new and reliable dishwasher today versus an endless stream of repairs on the old "lemon" dishwasher in terms of time and money over the coming years. In that comparison, the new and reliable dishwasher is the economically sound choice.

8.5 Total and Per-Unit Profit

Now that we've examined in detail why a firm stays put, shuts down, exits, or enters a uniformly competitive market, let's take a look at profit. Recall that profit (π) is equal to total revenue (TR) minus total costs (TC) or:

$$\pi = TR - TC.$$

When we divide both sides by Q (output) we get:

$$\frac{\pi}{Q} = \frac{TR}{Q} - \frac{TC}{Q}.$$

Recall that TR = P*Q and $\frac{TC}{Q} = ATC$ (*average total cost*). Therefore:

$$\frac{\pi}{Q} = \frac{P * Q}{Q} - ATC.$$

The Qs on the right side of the equation cancel each other out

$$\frac{\pi}{Q} = \frac{P * \cancel{Q}}{\cancel{Q}} - ATC$$

so that we arrive at

$$\frac{\pi}{Q} = P - ATC$$

which, after multiplying both sides of the equation by Q reduces to

$$\pi = (P - ATC)Q.$$

Next, we recycle FIGURE 8-1 and rename it FIGURE 8-5 for the sake of examining total and per-unit profit:

FIGURE 8-5: Total and Per-Unit Profit for the Uniformly Competitive Firm

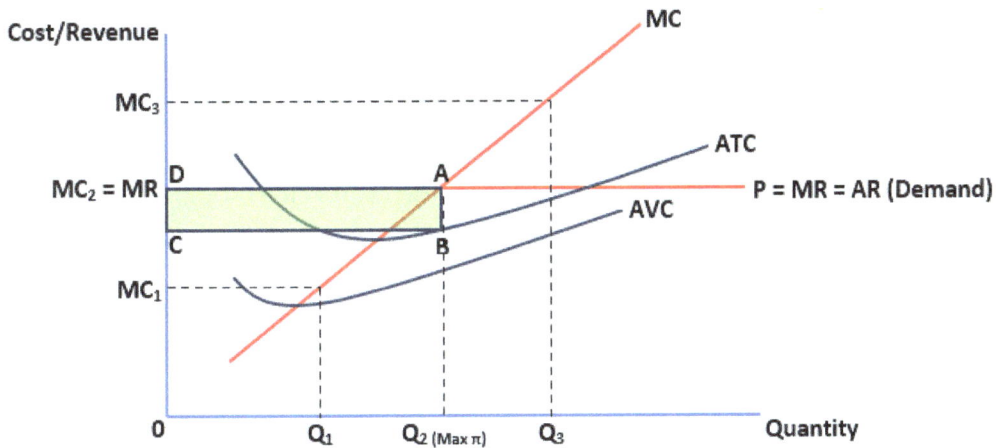

The green box in FIGURE 8-5 represents total economic profit in the short run for the uniformly competitive firm. The height of the box (seen at $Q_{2 (Max \pi)}$) is P – ATC (**per-unit profit**, or the amount of profit made for each unit of product sold. It is equivalent to the line segment AB or $\overline{AB}$. Total profit, though, as we found above is (P – ATC)Q (the total area of the profit box) or the entire rectangle ABCD. Thus, for FIGURE 8-5, (P – ATC)$Q_{2 (Max \pi)}$ gives us the **total profit** (total profit earned on all of the output sold) for the firm.

per-unit profit – the amount of profit made for each unit of product sold, or P – ATC.

total profit – the total profit earned on all of the output sold, or (P – ATC)(Q).

What about losses (negative profits)? Let's recycle FIGURE 8-4 and rename it FIGURE 8-6 for the sake of examining total and per-unit losses (negative profits):

FIGURE 8-6: Total and Per-Unit Losses for the Uniformly Competitive Firm

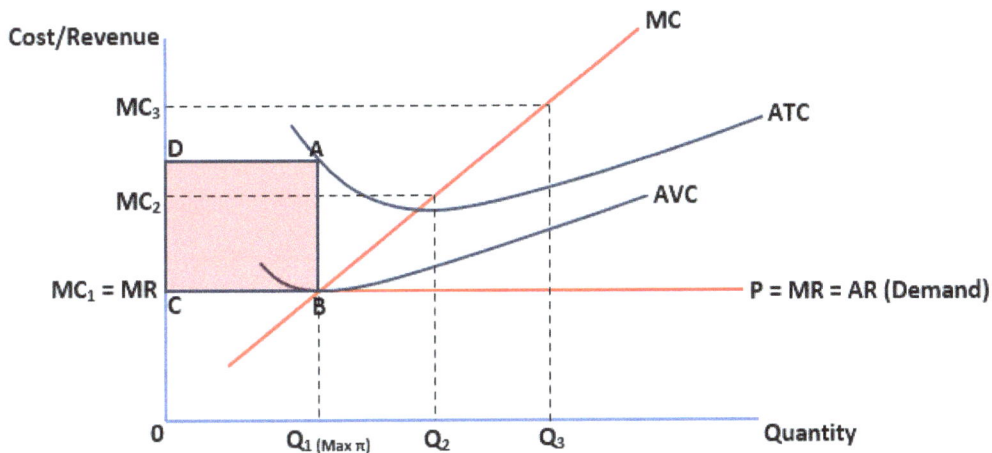

The light-red box in FIGURE 8-6 represents total (negative) economic profit in the short run for the uniformly competitive firm. The height of the box (line segment AB or $\overline{AB}$ seen at $Q_{1\ (Max\ \pi)}$)

per-unit loss (equal to P – ATC) - the loss on each unit sold that accrues to a firm producing at a price (P) less than average-total cost (ATC) per unit.

total loss (equal to [P – ATC][Q]) - the loss on all units sold that accrues to a firm producing at a price (P) less than average-total cost (ATC) per unit.

is P – ATC (**per-unit loss**), a calculation which will produce a negative value. Total profit, though, as we found above is (P – ATC)Q and is equal to the total area of the profit/loss box. Thus, (P – ATC)$Q_{1\ (Max\ \pi)}$ gives use a **total loss** (loss on all units sold) for the firm (represented by the entire light-red colored box) illustrated in FIGURE 8-6. Recall that the firm illustrated in FIGURE 8-6 is covering variable costs but not fixed costs, which means that we are seeing a snapshot of it in the short run. If the firm's situation does not change by the arrival of the long run (i.e., if the firm doesn't start covering all of its costs, fixed and variable, with demand shifting upward to at least the level of ATC (just below MC_2) on the Cost/Revenue axis of FIGURE 8-6), the firm will be forced to exit the market.

8.6 Production Summary for the Uniformly Competitive Firm

Before moving on to firm and market supply, let's summarize all production decisions at this point.

TABLE 8-3: Production Decisions for the Firm from Entrance to Operation to Shut Down to Exit			
	Question	**Verbal Answer**	**Mathematical Answer**
1	Should I enter the industry?	If price is greater than or equal to average-total cost, yes. If not, no.	P(demand) ≥ ATC; yes. P(demand) < ATC; no.
2	How much should be produced to maximize profit?	Increase or decrease production until price/marginal revenue is equal to marginal cost.	MR = MC.
3	Short run: should we stay in business?	Are fixed costs being covered? If not, yes. Are variable costs being covered? If so, yes. If variable costs are not being covered, shut down and wait until the long run to see if market conditions improve. If they do not improve, exit the market.	AVC ≤ P(demand) ≤ ATC; yes. P(demand) < AVC < ATC; no.
4	Long run: should we stay in business?	Are both fixed and variable costs being covered? If yes, stay in business. If not, exit the market.	P ≥ ATC; yes. P < ATC; no.

8.7 Firm Supply

Having now seen the entrance, stay-put, shut-down, and exit rules explicitly listed and precisely specified in TABLE 8-3, we can now trace out the individual short- and long-run supply curves for the firm. FIGURE 8-7 traces out the supply curve for the uniformly competitive firm in the short run.

FIGURE 8-7: The Short-Run Supply Curve of the Uniformly Competitive Firm

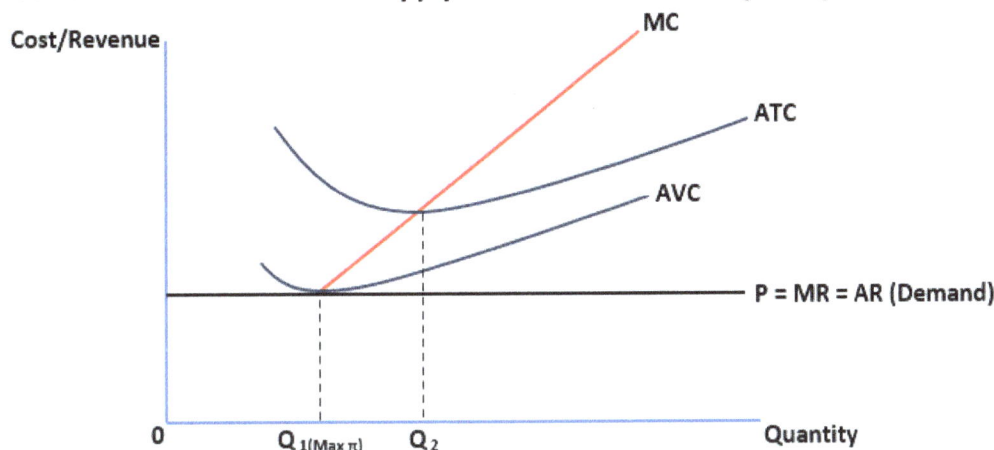

As can be seen in row 3 of TABLE 8-3, the profit-maximizing uniformly competitive firm operates in the short run if $AVC \leq P \leq ATC$ and shuts down if $P < AVC < ATC$. These rules trace out the firm's marginal-cost (MC) curve seen in FIGURE 8-7. If the $P = MR = AR$ (Demand) line falls below the lowest point on the AVC curve at $Q_{(Max \, \pi)}$ as illustrated in FIGURE 8-7, the firm shuts down. Thus every point below that is not a supply point and every point equal to or above that within a certain range is a supply point. As the $P = MR = AR$ (Demand) line rises, the profit-maximizing uniformly competitive firm's market conditions steadily improve, and if and when fixed costs get completely covered (at the lowest point on the ATC curve at Q_2), the firm is safe to continue operating by the arrival of the long run. If the $P = MR = AR$ (Demand) line rises above ATC, then the firm earns positive economic profits and is in good shape for the short run or long run. ***Therefore, the short-run supply curve for the profit-maximizing uniformly competitive firm is the portion of the firm's marginal-cost (MC) curve that lies above the lowest point on its average-variable cost (AVC) curve.*** This is represented by the entire red-colored MC curve illustrated in FIGURE 8-7.

Now we move to the long run when the patience of landlords, mortgage lenders, and all other creditors is at an end: All costs need to be covered.

FIGURE 8-8: The Long-Run Supply Curve of the Uniformly Competitive Firm

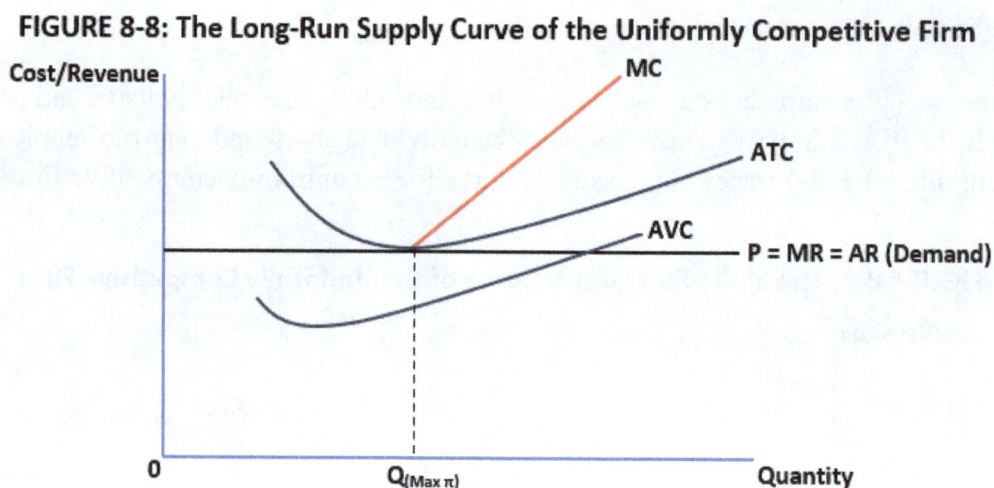

From row 4 of TABLE 8-3, the profit-maximizing uniformly competitive firm operates in the long run if P ≥ ATC and shuts down if P < ATC. These rules trace out the uniformly competitive firm's marginal-cost curve seen in FIGURE 8-8. If the P = MR = AR (Demand) line falls below the lowest point on the ATC curve at $Q_{(Max \pi)}$ as illustrated in FIGURE 8-8, the firm must exit the market. Thus every point below the ATC curve at $Q_{(Max \pi)}$ is not a supply point and every point equal to or above that within a certain range is a supply point. As the P = MR = AR (Demand) line rises, the profit-maximizing uniformly competitive firm begins earning positive economic profits and is in good shape for the long run. ***Therefore, the long-run supply curve for the profit-maximizing uniformly competitive firm is the portion of the firm's marginal-cost (MC) curve that lies above the lowest point on its average-total cost (ATC) curve.*** This is represented by the entire red-colored MC curve illustrated in FIGURE 8-8.

8.8 Market Supply

Now that we've seen the firm's supply curve, getting to the market should look familiar. Back in chapter 4, we summed individual supply curves horizontally to arrive at the market supply curve. We will do the same here but also introduce the differences between the short run and long run for the profit-maximizing uniformly competitive firm.

First, in the short run, we will treat the number of firms in an industry as a constant or fixed quantity. In FIGURE 8-9 are displayed the short-run firm supply curve and industry supply curve for the custom-made-guitar-pick industry. In graph (A) of FIGURE 8-9 is the supply curve for an individual firm. (We will use different numbers from the Guy's Guitar Picks example earlier in the chapter. Recall that Guy was earning profits of $5 per pick, which was good for simplicity of explanation but unrealistic, especially for the long run.) Each firm produces 4 guitar picks per day and there are 100 identical firms in the industry.

FIGURE 8-9: The Short-Run Firm and Market Supply

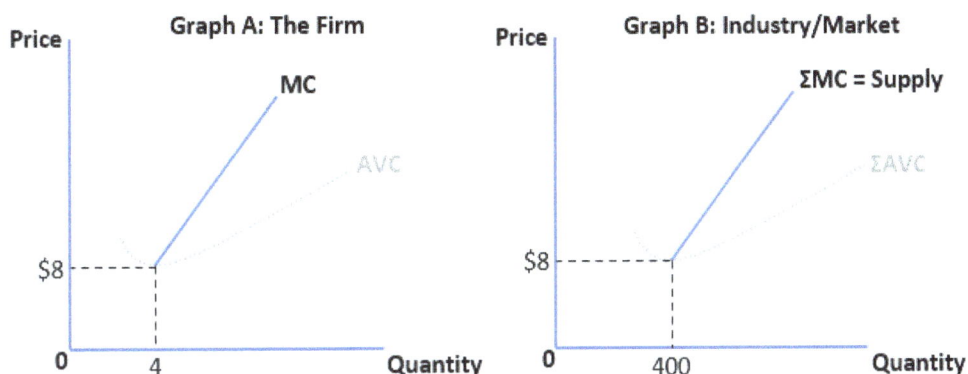

Graph A: The Firm

Price

MC

AVC

$8 - - - - - - -

0   4   Quantity

Graph B: Industry/Market

Price

ΣMC = Supply

ΣAVC

$8 - - - - - - -

0   400   Quantity

As can be seen in Graph A of FIGURE 8-9, each firm's supply curve is the portion of its marginal cost (MC) curve that is either equal to or above its average-variable cost (AVC) curve. All of the MC curves of the 100 identical firms in the industry horizontally sum up to the industry supply curve illustrated in Graph B of FIGURE 8-9. This is an industry just surviving the short run, as it is first producing the profit-maximizing quantity of picks where price = MC (400 picks per day) and then just covering all of its AVC at a price of $8 per pick.

Before we get to the long-run (when firms are now able to enter and exit the industry) and the uniformly competitive firm and industry supply curves, recall that:

$$profit\ (\pi) = (P - ATC)Q$$

In the long run, economic profit that firms earn will draw new firms to enter the industry while losses (negative profit) will drive incumbent (currently operating) firms out of the industry. When economics profit is zero, new firms neither enter nor incumbent firms exit; an equilibrium will be achieved. To get zero profit in the profit equation above, P must be equal to ATC. For example, for a price of $10 and an ATC = $10:

$$\pi = (10 - 10)Q$$

$$\pi = (0)Q$$

$$\pi = 0$$

When we couple the assumption of competitive profit maximization ($P = MC$) with this, P is not only equal to ATC at zero profit (π), but also MC, and this also means that ATC = MC.[38] So,

$$P = ATC = MC.$$

---

[38] This is known as the mathematical law of transitivity. If a = b and b = c, then a = c.

FIGURE 8-10: The Long-Run Firm and Market Supply

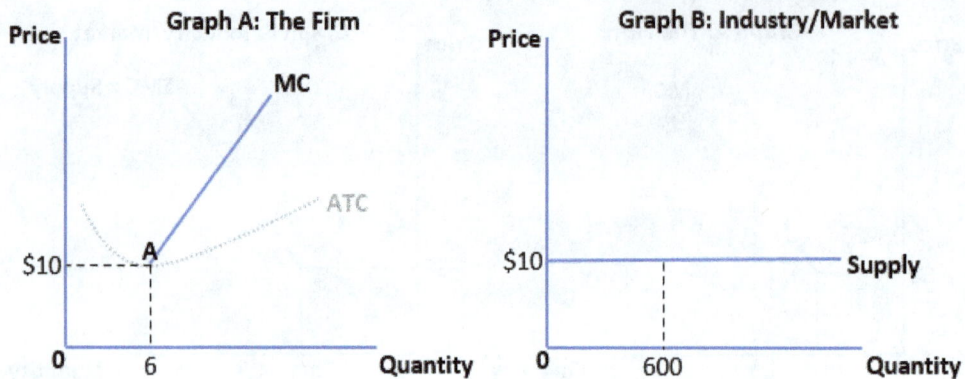

Graph A: The Firm

Graph B: Industry/Market

In Graph A of FIGURE 8-10 we can see exactly where the P = ATC = MC point is. It is the lowest point on the ATC curve where the dashed price line (at $10) intersects the ATC and MC curves, point A. Recall the concept of efficient scale that we encountered in the last chapter:

> **efficient scale** – the level of output at which average-total cost (ATC) is at a minimum.

efficient scale is the level of output at which average-total cost (ATC) is at a minimum. What all of this leads to is this conclusion: *for the profit-maximizing uniformly competitive industry in long run equilibrium where there is free and entry and exit, each firm will be operating at its efficient scale.*

This leads us to Graph B of FIGURE 8-10. With free entry and exit and zero economic profits, price (in this case, $10) is driven to efficient scale for all 100 firms. This traces out the infinitely price sensitive industry supply curve seen in Graph B of FIGURE 8-10. If price rises, positive economic profits are created, new firms enter the market, and industry production rises. If price falls, negative economic profits (losses) are created, incumbent firms exit the market, and industry production falls. A new equilibrium is reached where each firm is operating at efficient scale and all demand is satisfied at the new equilibrium price.

8.9 Economic Profit Explained

> **zero economic profit** – the condition of a firm where its opportunity costs are completely covered by its revenue (TR – TC = 0). It is also the condition in which the firm is earning the same maximum rate of return on its resources greater than or equal to that of its next highest-valued alternative.

How do competitive firms manage to stay in business if they earn **zero economic profit**, or opportunity costs are completely covered by revenue (TR – TC = 0)? To get an answer to this question, we once again have to return to the total-profit equation:

$$profit\ (\pi) = TR - TC$$

$$where\ TR\ = (P)(Q).$$

Total revenue (TR) is composed of objective quantities (P and Q) but TC is certainly not. Again, this is not the total cost from your accounting class or accounting textbook (comprised of only explicit costs), but opportunity cost (explicit costs + implicit costs). To get to zero profit in the long run, TR has to equal TC, which means that all money and opportunity costs must be covered. In other words, even under long-run zero economic profit, the owner of the firm is being compensated for forgoing their next highest valued opportunity (e.g., working in another job for someone else instead of running his or her own company). If this were not so, economic profit would be negative and there would be an exit from the industry.

8.10 Competitive Market Dynamics from Short Run to Long Run

Now that we have fully examined how firm supply is formed and how industry supply is derived from it, we now turn to how firms and industries respond to changes in demand. FIGURE 8-11 will help us track all the effects of an increase in firm demand in response to an increase in market demand. We first begin at Graph B: Industry/Market in Section 1 Long-Run Equilibrium in FIGURE 8-11 where price is P_1, quantity is Q_1, and market equilibrium is at E_1. Immediately to the left in Graph A is an illustration of the condition of each firm, where price is p_1, quantity is q_1, and firm equilibrium is at e_1.

All is well in the market in Graph B until a widely disseminated and read symposium interview in *Guitar Universe* magazine reveals that several prominent guitarists, playing in classical to jazz to rock bands, are now extolling the use of custom guitar picks. Since the publication of the interview, fans of the guitarists and guitar players are researching and buying custom guitar picks and incorporating them into their collections, practices, and performances. This (no surprise) causes an increase in market demand in the short-run custom guitar-pick market.

Thus in Graph D of section 2 of FIGURE 8-11, market demand increases from D_1 to D_2, which moves market equilibrium from point E_1 to point E_2, and thus market price from P_1 to P_2 and market quantity from Q_1 to Q_2. To the left in Graph C, in response to the increase in market demand, firm demand increases from d_1 to d_2. This moves each firm's equilibrium from point e_1 to point e_2 (since the firm's supply curve is its marginal-cost curve) and thus firm price moves from p_1 to p_2 while firm quantity moves from q_1 to q_2. The green box in Graph C represents the total profit now earned by the firm, which is positive since p_2 > ATC at q_2 and e_2. This profit doesn't draw new firms to the industry yet because we're still in the short run. By the arrival of the long run, it's a different story.

FIGURE 8-11: the Effects of an Increase in Market Demand from Short Run to Long Run

1. Long-Run Equilibrium

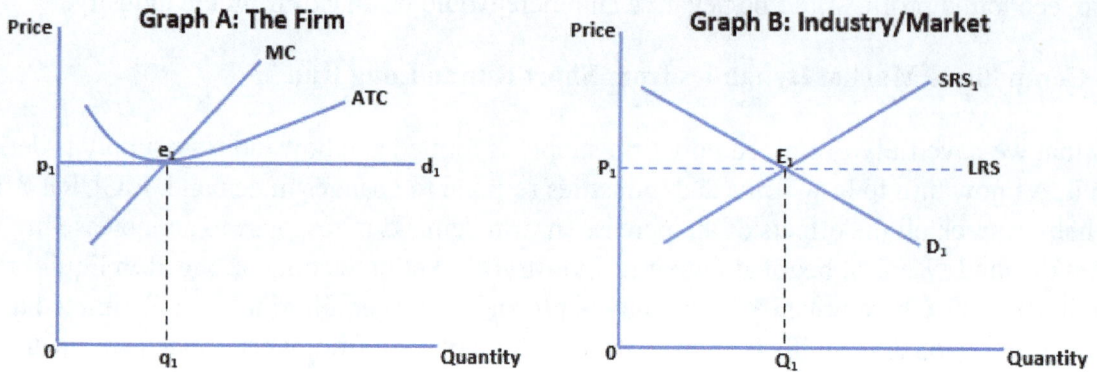

Graph A: The Firm

Graph B: Industry/Market

2. Short-Run Equilibrium

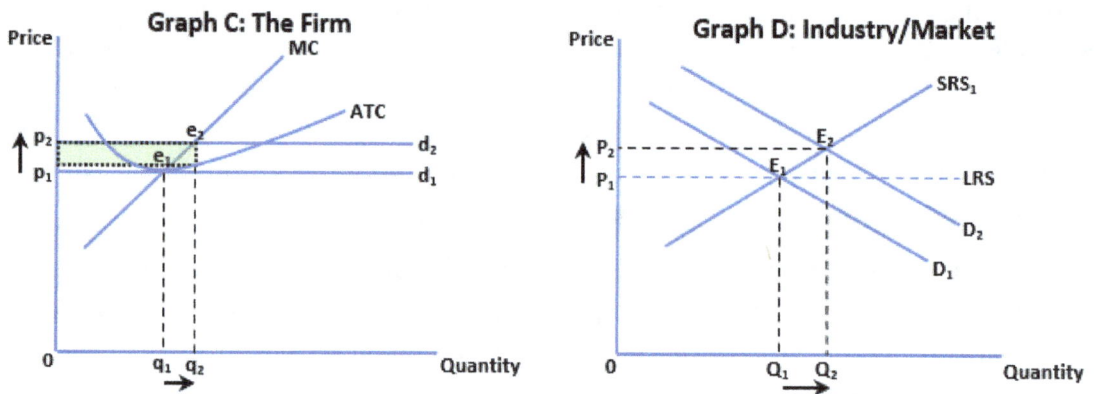

Graph C: The Firm

Graph D: Industry/Market

3. Long-Run Equilibrium

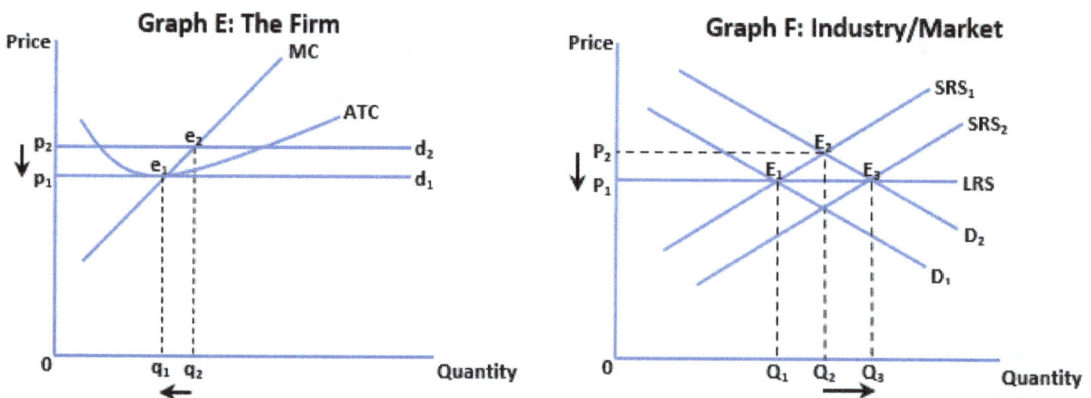

Graph E: The Firm

Graph F: Industry/Market

Now the long run arrives again, and we move to section 3 Long-Run Equilibrium of FIGURE 8-11. Because it's the long run, the presence of positive (greater than zero) economic profit drives new firms to the industry. (Recall that if losses were occurring, some firms would now be exiting the market instead of entering.) The action begins in Graph F where the entrance of new firms into the industry increases market supply from short-run supply curve S_1 to short-run supply curve S_2, which moves market equilibrium from point E_2 to point E_3, and thus market price from P_2 back down to P_1 and market quantity from Q_2 to Q_3.

On the firm level in Graph E, firm demand drops from d_2 back down to d_1 because of the entrance of the new firms, and this moves firm equilibrium from point e_2 back to point e_1. Thus firm price moves from p_2 back to p_1 with firm quantity moving from q_2 to q_1. The green total-profit box we saw in Graph C is now gone in Graph E because all firms are now earning zero economic profit because $p_2 = $ ATC at q_1 and e_1. Thus market price (in Graph F) has returned to its previous long-run level (P_1), firm price (in Graph E) has returned to its previous long-run level (p_1), and economic profit has returned to its previous long-run level ($\pi = 0$).

The only variable that has increased in magnitude is market quantity (in Graph F), which has steadily risen from Q_1 to Q_2 to Q_3. This movement in market quantity traces out the market's perfectly price sensitive long-run supply curve from long-run equilibrium E_1 to long-run equilibrium E_3. In contrast, firm quantity rises from q_1 to q_2 in Graph C while in Graph E that move completely reverses as firm quantity falls from q_2 to q_1 as new firms enter the market and each new firm grabs a share of industry output.

8.11 From Flat to Upward-Sloping Supply: Two Factors

One problem with the analysis illustrated by FIGURE 8-11 is that it is not very realistic, namely the infinitely price sensitive long-run market supply curve traced out in the last graph, Graph F. This is the result of the number of potential entrants that could theoretically enter the market in the case of an increase in demand. These new firms, it's assumed, all have the same cost structure as the incumbent firms. The end result is that the number of firms in the industry increases, total output in the industry steadily increases (from Q_1 to Q_2 to Q_3), but strangely, price stays unchanged or about the same.

Here are two problems with this scenario:

1. **Rising input costs.** As more firms enter an industry, the prices of scarce inputs rise. Capital products specific to producing guitar picks (lathes, types of plastics and wood, workshop space in towns and cities close to shipping firms) increase in price as the demand for them increases, even if entering the industry is of relatively low cost.

2. **Higher-cost new entrants.** Firms not currently in an industry are not there for a reason: their costs are not low enough and if they entered they would earn losses. Such a firm is known as a **marginal firm**, or a firm with the highest cost in an industry such that when demand falls it is the first to shut down in the short run if it cannot cover variable cost and the first to exit the industry by the long run if it cannot cover all of its costs. A firm that makes custom percussion mallets can re-tool some of its production to make guitar picks, but that won't be free, even if (after the retooling) entry into the custom-guitar-pick industry is a low-cost move. Many, if not most, incumbent firms, on the other hand, have the lowest costs. In order for new entrants to be attracted to the industry, their higher costs must receive compensation and that can only happen with an increase in demand and market price. This means that the new

marginal firm – a firm with the highest cost in an industry such that when demand falls it is the first to shut down in the short run if it cannot cover variable cost and the first to exit the industry by the long run if it cannot cover all of its costs. It can also be a firm just outside the industry that would enter if demand (and thus also price) rose, even by a relatively small magnitude.

marginal firms will just have all of their costs covered (earn zero economic profit) while incumbent firms will be rewarded with a positive economic profit.

In light of the above two factors, the long-run supply curve is still more price sensitive than the short-run supply curve albeit not as much as in Graph F of FIGURE 8-11. This can be seen in FIGURE 8-12.

FIGURE 8-12: the Effects of an Increase in Market Demand from Short Run to Long Run in the Presence of Rising Input Costs and High-Cost New Entrants

1. Long-Run Equilibrium

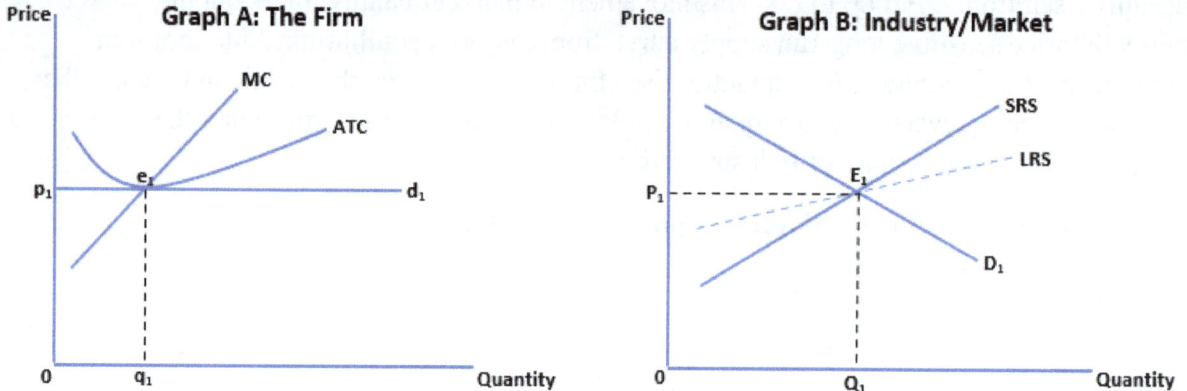

2. Short-Run Equilibrium

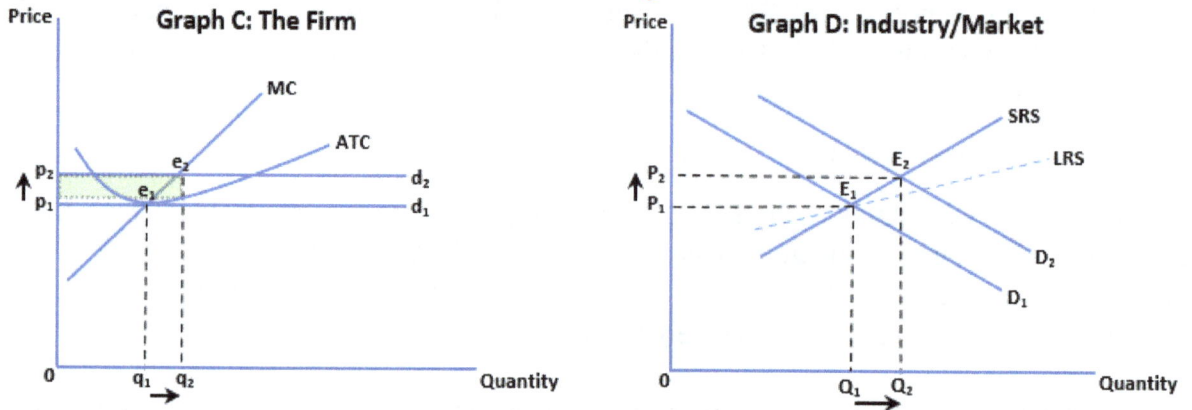

3. Long-Run Equilibrium

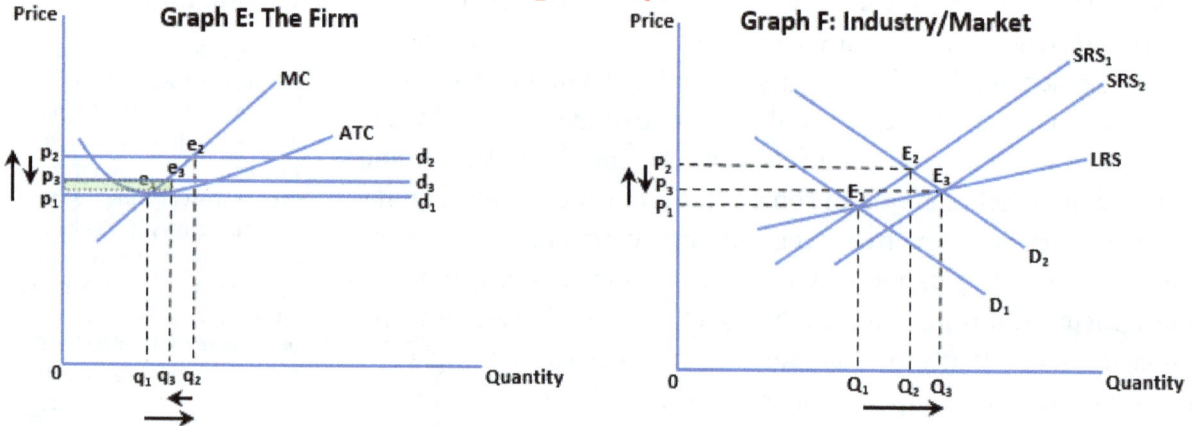

Incorporating our two factors into our analysis, in FIGURE 8-12 we begin at Graph B: Industry/Market where price is P_1, quantity is Q_1, and market equilibrium is at E_1. In Graph A is a picture of each firm, where price is p_1, quantity is q_1, and firm equilibrium is at e_1. Again, all is well until we get our surge in demand in the short-run for custom guitar picks. In Graph D of FIGURE 8-12, market demand increases from D_1 to D_2, which moves market equilibrium from point E_1 to point E_2, and thus market price from P_1 to P_2 and market quantity from Q_1 to Q_2. To the left in Graph C, each firm's demand increases from d_1 to d_2, which moves firm equilibrium from point e_1 to point e_2 and thus firm price moves from p_1 to p_2 while firm quantity moves from q_1 to q_2. The green box in Graph C is the total profit now earned by each firm, which is positive since $p_2 >$ ATC at q_2 and e_2. As in the previous scenario in section 8.10, this profit doesn't draw new firms into the industry yet because we're still in the short run.

Now the long run arrives and we move to Graph F, where the entrance of new firms into the industry increases market supply from short-run supply curve S_1 to short-run supply curve S_2. This moves market equilibrium from point E_2 to point E_3, and thus market price from P_2 to P_3 and market quantity from Q_2 to Q_3. On the firm level in Graph E, firm demand drops from d_2 to d_3 because of the entrance of new firms each picking up a portion of industry output, and this moves firm equilibrium from point e_2 to point e_3. Thus firm price moves from p_2 to p_3 with firm quantity moving from q_2 to q_3. The green total-profit box we saw in Graph C is now smaller in Graph E but has not disappeared like it did in Graph E in FIGURE 8-11 because now $p_3 >$ ATC at q_3 and e_3.

In summary, what the third section of FIGURE 8-12 (Graph E and Graph F) reveals is that when we adjust for rising input costs and the higher cost structure endemic to new entrants, our analysis shows that the final effects of an upward-sloping long run market supply curve are a higher final market price ($P_3 > P_1$) and higher final market quantity ($Q_3 > Q_1$) at final market equilibrium E_3. However, the final market quantity Q_3 is not as high as when the long-run market supply curve is perfectly price sensitive (completely flat) as in Graph F of FIGURE 8-11.

On the firm level in Graph E, firm demand drops from d_2 to the new level of d_3, not the initial firm demand level of d_1. The continued presence of the green total-profit box in the long run shows that firms can earn an economic profit even in the long run if a number of members have lower costs than the newest marginal entrants.

8.12 Conclusion

This chapter began with the concept of market power and ended with long-run market supply (both flat and upward sloping). In between was a detailed analysis of the uniformly competitive firm and how it is affected by its market. What we saw was that uniformly competitive firms are price takers and that they and their customers, because of their large numbers, have little power individually to move market quantities and prices. The next chapter about industrial organization in this book (chapter 9) analyzes the market structure known as monopoly. As we will see, firms that operate in that type of industry are the opposite of price takers. Leaving that extreme in terms of market power, we then move on to differentiated (or monopolistic) competition (chapter 10), a market structure whose firms have more market power than uniform competitors but much less than monopolies. Finally, we end our journey into the land of industrial organization with a chapter on oligopoly (chapter 11). As we'll see, the market power of oligopolistic firms is greater than that of differentiated competitors but less than that of monopolies.

8.13 Chapter Concepts

market power
uniform competition
price taker
stay put
stay-put rule
shutdown
sunk cost
shut-down rule
exit
exit rule
entrance
entrance rule
fallacy of sunk costs
per-unit profit
total profit
per-unit loss
total loss
efficient scale
zero economic profit
marginal firm

8.14 Problems, Questions, and Discussion Topics (Items Requiring Examples are Marked with an Asterisk [*])

1. From greatest to least, rank the following firms in terms of market power and explain the reasoning behind your rankings: Apple Incorporated, Five Guys, Little Italy (a local, independent pizzeria), Best Buy, Bobby's (the 9-year-old boy next door) neighborhood lemonade stand.

2. Three characteristics of a uniformly competitive industry (name and define each, then provide an example of only one)*

3. price taker (define, then provide an example)*

4. *Regardless of market structure (uniform competition, differentiated competition, oligopoly, or monopoly), all profit-maximizing firms produce at the profit-maximizing level of output where _____ equals _____ or _____ = _____.*

A. Fill in the blanks: _____, _____, _____, _____.

B. Explain:

5. *A uniformly competitive firm's _____ curve displays the different quantities the uniformly competitive firm is willing and able to supply at different prices. Therefore, the uniformly competitive firm's _____ curve is its _____ curve.*

   A. Fill in the blanks: _____, _____, _____.

   B. Explain:

6. Regarding the four different operational rules,

   A. how is shut down and the shutdown rule different from exit and the exit rule?

   B. Which of the four rules are the same and why?

7. Juanita's dream has been to quit working for the nasty and ill-tempered Paola of Paola's Hair and Nail Boutique and open her own salon. Juanita's sister Selena has promised to come on board as a stylist and her mother Enselma has agreed to purchase the furnishings and other materials to run the business. The only current sticking point is that Juanita still does not have the money to pay for even a first month of rent for the store location she wants. What should Juanita do?

8. Angel's Construction Company, which has been unable to pay its mortgage and property taxes on its building, has nevertheless continued remodeling kitchens and bathrooms. However, Angel's mortgage lender has just put his building into foreclosure and the county has placed a lien on his business property with forcible eviction occurring in 30 days.

   A. What is Angel's next action: stay put, shut down, or exit?

   B. Why?

9. Rick's Tires and Auto, after a rocky two years after opening, is now making all of its rent payments on time and completely covering all costs of inventory and labor (three tire technicians who plan to work at the shop for many years to come). After two new residential subdivisions began being settled across the road, his revenue, which surged and nosedived throughout the first two years, is now steady and growing.

   A. What should Rick do: stay put, shut down, or exit?

   B. Why or why not?

10. Tom's Home Painting, LLC, once a booming business, never fully recovered from the COVID-19 pandemic. While the shop moved into a large barn in back of the home Tom owns (i.e., he has no business rent or mortgage to pay), and he can cover the cost of inventory, he can no longer afford essential crew.

    A. What should Tom do: stay put, shut down, or exit?

    B. Why?

11. For Bow & Arrow Barbecue restaurant, when much of its usual demand disappears during the summer,

    A. is P < AVC? (I.e., is it forced to shut down?)

    B. Why or why not?

12. For The Track amusement park, when much of its usual demand disappears during November through February,

    A. is P < AVC? (I.e., is it forced to shut down?)

    B. Why or why not?

13. You and a friend go to your favorite restaurant for dinner after receiving a buy-one-meal-get-one-free coupon. However, just after arriving and while waiting for a table at the restaurant, you discover that the coupon expired two days ago.

    A. Should the costs (explicit and implicit [time]) of traveling to the restaurant determine whether you should still have dinner there?

    B. Why or why not?

14. For the uniform competitor in FIGURE 8-13,

FIGURE 8-13

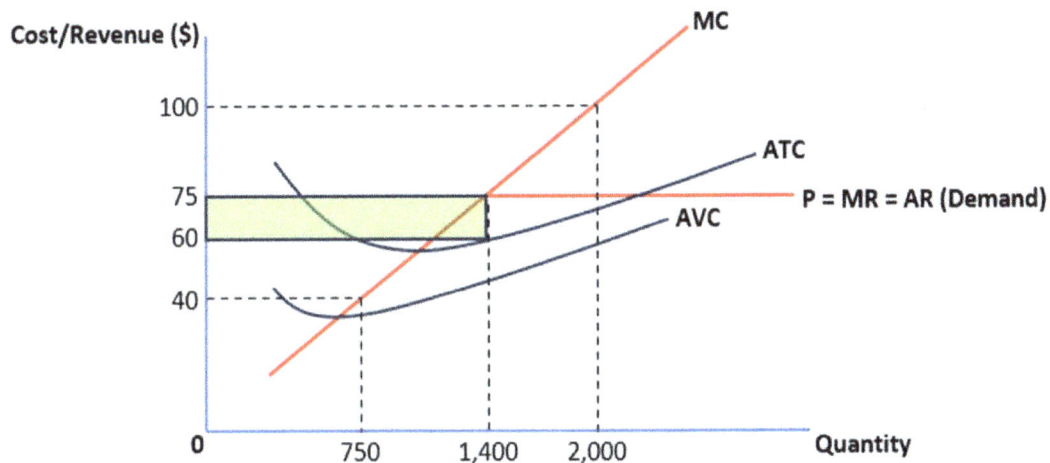

A. calculate per-unit profit or loss. Show all steps used to arrive at your final answer.

B. Calculate total profit or loss. Show all steps used to arrive at your final answer.

15. For the uniform competitor in FIGURE 8-14,

FIGURE 8-14

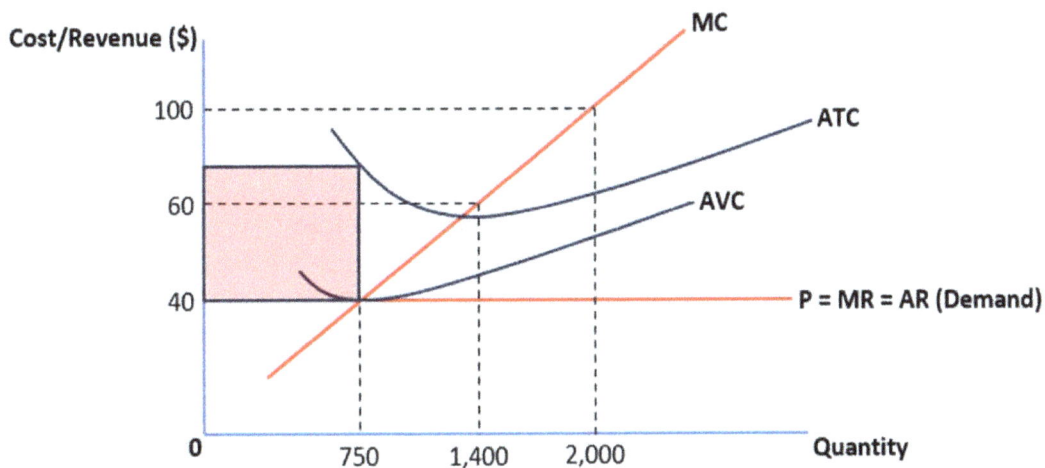

A. calculate per-unit profit or loss. Show all steps used to arrive at your final answer.

B. Calculate total profit or loss. Show all steps used to arrive at your final answer.

16. *Therefore, the short-run supply curve for the profit-maximizing uniformly competitive firm is the portion of the firm's _____ curve that lies above the lowest point on its _____ curve.*

A. Fill in the blanks: _____, _____.

B. Explain:

17. *Therefore, the long-run supply curve for the profit-maximizing uniformly competitive firm is the portion of the firm's _____ curve that lies above the lowest point on its _____ curve.*

    A. Fill in the blanks: _____, _____.

    B. Explain:

18. *...for the profit-maximizing uniformly competitive industry in long run equilibrium where there is free and entry and exit, each firm will be operating at _____.*

    A. Fill in the blank: _____.

    B. Explain:

19. Jan, a business owner who didn't major in business in college, has been told by a business consultant that her event-planning firm has a long-run economic profit of zero. On hearing this, Jan was distressed and thinking of at least temporarily shutting down her business.

    A. Should Jan be concerned or not?

    B. Why?

20. marginal firm (define, then provide a quantitative example)*

21. What are the effects of an increase in market demand from short run to long run in the presence of rising input costs and higher-cost new entrants for both a firm and the industry in which it operates? (Hint: see FIGURE 8-12.)

Chapter 9: Monopoly

9.0 Introduction

While in the previous chapter we analyzed industries with many firms selling uniform products with free entry and exit and many buyers of those products, we now analyze a market structure with almost the complete opposite characteristics: a single producer of a highly differentiated product for which there are no close substitutes. The only dimension of this new type of industry that remains the same is many buyers of the product. The implications of this market structure, **monopoly** (a single firm or government supplying a good, service, or societal governance for which there are no close substitutes) seem obvious: instead of a firm accepting market price (i.e., being a price taker) and maximizing profit by producing where market price is equal to marginal cost (P = MC), this very different market structure allows the firm to maximize profit by setting a price above marginal cost (P > MC). Because of this ability, the single firm in this market structure is known as a **price maker** (an individual or firm with substantial market power because he/she/it has no or very few competitors), i.e., it has **market power** (an individual or firm's ability to set the price of a product across a relatively wide range of potential prices because he/she/it has no or very few competitors).

> **monopoly** - a single firm or government supplying a good, service, or societal governance for which there are no close substitutes.
>
> **price maker** – an individual or firm with substantial market power because he/she/it has no or very few competitors.
>
> **market power** – an individual or firm's ability to set the price of a product across a relatively wide range of potential prices because he/she/it has no or very few competitors.

In fact, some degree of market power characterizes all of the remaining market structures we will analyze in this book (monopoly, monopolistic competition, and oligopoly). Some novice economics students define market power as "a firm's ability to charge whatever it wants for a product." In other words, if a firm wanted to charge $25 for a standard toothbrush, it would and presumably about the same number of buyers would continue to purchase the brush for such an exorbitant price. The problem is that such a firm, even with a little market power, would be so undercut in its market that its sales would dwindle to practically nothing, especially when at Walmart, standard Colgate toothbrushes now (March 2025) sell for $2.96 per four-pack ($0.74 each).

While even the most blatant monopolies (such as utility, water, trash pickup, cable-television, and wireless Internet carriers [e.g., T-Mobile] in some small towns) have substantial market power, they simply cannot charge "whatever they want." If a product or cost of living in a town gets too expensive, opportunity cost for consumers with limited incomes grows. Over time, more and more will eventually move out of town to other places with a lower cost of living. We have seen this occur increasingly since the 2020 COVID-19 pandemic with emigration from high-cost-of-living states such as California and New York to lower-cost-of-living states such as Texas and Georgia.

9.1 The Origin of Monopolies

The underlying long-term cause of a monopoly is a barrier to entry into an industry, usually provided by the government. In contrast to uniform competition, a number of firms over the long run may seek to enter a monopoly industry to acquire some of its abnormally high profits but a barrier prevents them from doing so. Barriers are thought to be of three types:

1. control of unique resources
2. economies of scale, and
3. government laws or regulations.

Current thinking is now focused much more on the third (government regulation and restrictions) than unique resources or economies of scale, but let's briefly consider all three.

1. Control of unique resources. Under competition, the product is uniform and therefore, with so many substitutes for consumers, price is forced to equal marginal cost (P = MC). Under one alleged form of monopoly, a single firm owns or controls a unique resource and can therefore price its product substantially above marginal cost.

The first example is that of a small town with just one water well. A farmer owns this well and therefore can charge a high price for water. The problem with this simple story is that this water monopoly's profits will not only induce the small town's stores to stock bottled water from outside sources but town residents to drill more water wells to compete with the monopoly. The competition from stores would be sufficient enough to keep the price of local well water down, but if alternative wells are successfully drilled, there goes the monopoly's significant market power. It's no coincidence that it's hard to find a real-life example that comes close to this fictional town with only one water well.

The second classic example is the British and South African diamond company, De Beers. This company in the late 1980s produced or sold approximately 90 percent of the diamonds in the world. While 90 percent is unquestionably a very high market share, the company was never a full monopoly and since the late 1980s has seen its control go nowhere but downhill. Indeed, by 2022, De Beers' market share had fallen to about 28 to 29 percent with Russia's ALROSA beating it slightly at 30 to 31 percent. The second problem the industry has had to deal with is the advance of technology. So many synthetic diamonds sold today so closely resemble natural ones that not even many seasoned experts can consistently tell the difference between the two anymore. Finally and ironically (as an alleged example of a monopoly that arose because of unique resources), De Beers was never a monopoly but an international cartel (two or more firms that attempt to behave as a monopoly in the short run) of diamond mines. As we will see later when we examine the market structure of cartels, the cartel form can exhibit substantial market power but also instability.

economies of scale - average total cost that steadily falls downward as output steadily rises above zero.

natural monopoly – market structure in which a single firm is able to supply a market at a lower cost than two or more firms.

2. Economies of scale. Another possible barrier to entry is **economies of scale**, or average total cost that steadily falls downward as output steadily rises above zero. A firm with such a cost structure is known as a **natural monopoly** or market structure in which a single firm is able to supply a market at a lower cost than two or more firms. This is illustrated in FIGURE 9-1. While the competitive ATC curve (ATC$_{Competition}$) falls and then rises as output steadily rises from zero to infinity, the ATC curve for a natural monopoly (ATC$_{Natural\ Monopoly}$) steadily falls as output steadily rises from zero to infinity.

FIGURE 9-1: Average-Total Cost of a Natural Monopoly

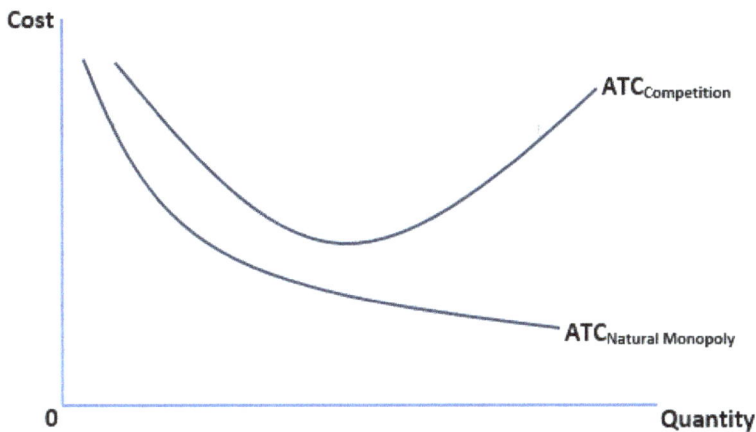

The alleged problem with *any* competition in this setting is that it will divide up the market with each firm producing its output at a higher average cost. FIGURE 9-2 reveals why this could allegedly occur.

FIGURE 9-2: A Natural Monopoly Market Structure with One versus Two Firms

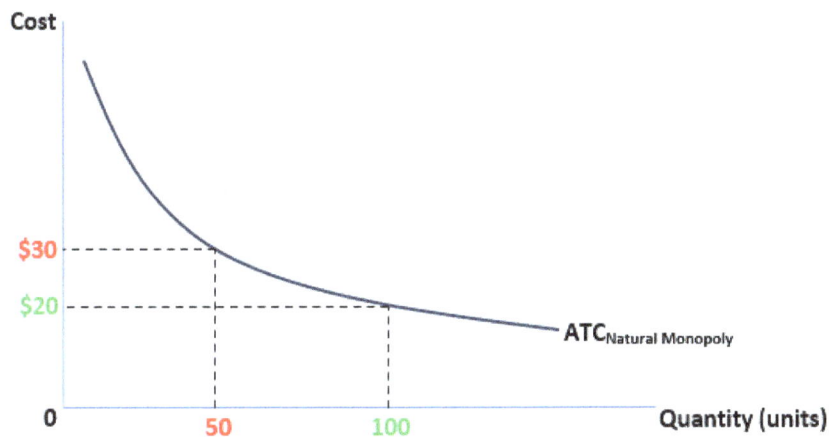

If the market is left a monopoly, then Firm A can produce 100 units per day at a cost of $20 per unit. If a second firm (Firm B) enters the market and production is exactly split in two between firms A and B, each firm produces 50 units, but at a cost of $30 per unit. That is, per-unit costs rise and thus market price rises if the industry moves away from a monopoly toward even the slightest degree of competition.

Supposed examples of this type of market structure in the real world seem to be rare and-or not-too convincing. The classic example is water distribution. At least in theory, one firm (usually a municipal government) can serve an entire town most efficiently. Unfortunately, proof of this theory has been scant to nonexistent. Studies of cable television show just the opposite. In Auburn, Alabama, two cable providers, Charter and Wide Open West (WOW!), compete for business through each firm's coaxial cables that run along utility poles in different residential subdivisions. Consumers who play one firm against the other are able to secure reliable, high-speed (300 Mbps) Internet price-locked service for approximately $35 per month (as of March 2025). So even one additional competitor can bring about substantial improvements in cost and

214

reliability. The average-total-cost curve does not slope steadily downward in this particular case as was alleged to be the case and used to argue (in front of city councils and courts) against adding a competitor to the market.

Another posited example is the so-called **club good**. A club good is a good characterized by **excludability** but not **rivalry** in consumption. Excludability is the property of a product whereby non-payers can be prevented from consuming a product while rivalry is the property of a product whereby consumption of a product by a person or group excludes all other persons or groups from consuming the same product. For example, if Enterprise Rent-A-Car has one pink Toyota Sienna minivan for rental, this item is characterized by both excludability and rivalry. If the Anderson family wants to rent the van but doesn't have a credit card, the family can be excluded from renting the van. If the Anderson family rents the van to drive to Disneyland for Labor Day weekend, the Brown family, which wanted to rent the same van for the same weekend, will not be able to rent the van.

A classic example of a club good is a two-lane bridge across a river. Cars can be prevented from crossing it by toll stations on each side, however, one car crossing the bridge doesn't prevent other cars driving across it. A high fixed cost of constructing the bridge coupled with a very small marginal cost of each additional driver implies a steadily falling average-total cost with higher and higher traffic, which implies a natural monopoly. However, more and more traffic, especially involving heavy vehicles such as 18-wheel tractor-trailer trucks, means more wear and tear on the bridge and higher costs, including repairs and maintenance. This does not imply a natural monopoly but rather an ATC curve that looks more like the competitive one ($ATC_{Competition}$) in FIGURE 9-1.

3. Government laws or regulations. The final type of barrier is that put in place by the monopoly over all monopolies: the government. In fact, one definition of **government** is the monopoly of legal force exercised over a given territory; the singular powers to create (legislative power), interpret (judicial power), and enforce (executive power) laws and regulations. In another fact, competition with governments is not only illegal, it is a specific crime usually punishable by death: treason.

Some of the first notable monopolies were those of the Roman Empire. During the emperorship of Tiberius (14 - 37 AD), exclusive rights were granted to senators and other prominent officials of the empire in the industries of grain, salt, marble, construction, and shipping. Another notable monopoly was the Salt Industry Commission (SIC) created by the Tang dynasty in China in 758. The SIC was a government agency responsible for selling the output of the government's salt monopoly and collecting the revenue from the government's salt tax.

The history of monopolies in England is rich. They began as a **charter** (an exclusive right to manufacture and sell a product in a given area) granted by the king or parliament to manufacture and sell certain goods such as salt and saltpeter (a key ingredient in gunpowder). After this, the exclusive rights covered shipping and in *quid pro quo* (trading something for something else) the company granted the charter usually had some seats on its board of directors occupied by members of the English royalty. The East India Company (EIC), founded in 1600, and the Dutch East India Company (DEIC), founded in 1602, are two examples. The royal charters granted to both firms allowed them to dominate the tea and spice trade, but EIC lasted much longer because while it was nominally private when it received its first charter, over time it functioned more and more as an arm of the British government until 1874, when the few private parts of it were eventually and officially dissolved into the government.

> **charter** - an exclusive right to manufacture and sell a product in a given area.

One form of government charter is a **patent** and another is a **copyright**. A patent is a license granting a specific individual or firm the exclusive right to manufacture and sell a certain, usually new and unique, product for a certain period of time. A copyright is an exclusive legal right granted to an author, composer, or other creator to print, publish, perform, and sell a written, musical, or other creative work for a certain period of time. Patents are a temporary monopoly intended to encourage innovations and technological development. Copyrights are a temporary monopoly intended to encourage authors, musicians, and software developers to continue to produce high-quality novels, movies, music, and software applications.

> **patent** - a license granting a specific individual or firm the exclusive right to manufacture and sell a certain, usually new and unique, product for a certain period of time.

> **copyright** - an exclusive legal right granted to an author, composer, or other creator to print, publish, perform, and sell a written, musical, or other creative work for a certain period of time.

Today, government laws or regulations (rather than control of unique resources or economies of scale) is now considered the most effective guarantor of a long-term monopoly.

While patents and copyrights are more short-term in nature, what outlives them are exclusive monopolies on such goods or services such as first- and third-class mail delivery (the U.S. Postal Service), money printing (the U.S. Bureau of Printing and Engraving), control of the money supply (the U.S. Federal Reserve system), and the sale of certain types of stock (NASDAQ).

Thus we can conclude that monopoly is a market structure with three main features:
1. Many buyers but one seller (a firm or government).
2. A highly differentiated product with no close substitutes, which means that each firm has substantial market power. Examples: electricity, water.
3. Barriers to entry in the short run and long run that include government charters, patents, and copyrights.

216

9.2 Monopoly Production and Pricing

Recall that in the previous chapter uniformly competitive firm demand was horizontal, or perfectly price sensitive (see Graph A in FIGURE 9-3). Why? Because the uniformly competitive firm is a **price taker**, or one of the numerous buyers or sellers active in uniformly competitive markets who, because of their large numbers, have no influence on market price and therefore must either "take" (accept) the market price and buy or sell the product or leave the market. If the firm increases its price by even a small amount, it loses all or nearly all of its business. A monopoly, on the other hand, is a single firm selling a product for which there are few, if any, close substitutes. Unlike a competitive firm, it is a price maker. If it raises the price of its product by even a small amount, unlike the uniformly competitive firm, it still retains most of its sales. Since the monopoly is the only firm in its industry, it *is* the market, so its demand curve is the market demand curve (see Graph B in FIGURE 9-3).

FIGURE 9-3: Demand Curves: Uniform Competition versus Monopoly

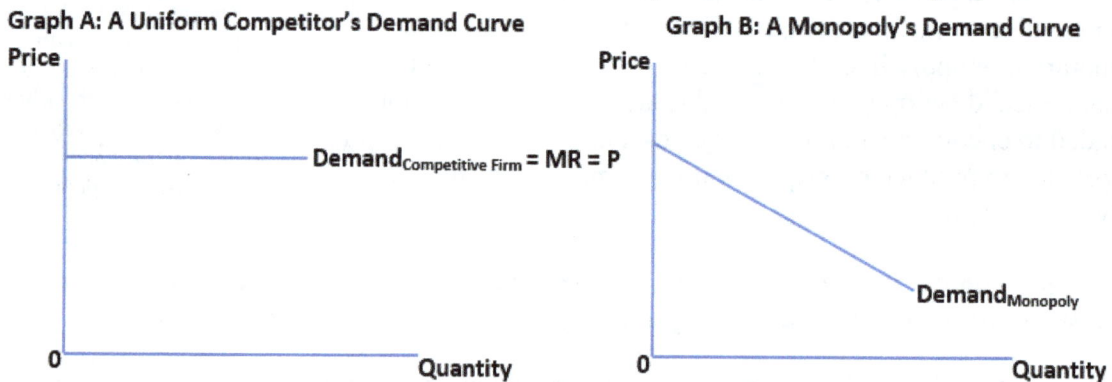

Graph A: A Uniform Competitor's Demand Curve

Graph B: A Monopoly's Demand Curve

Of course a different structure of demand means a different structure of revenue. Recall that for the uniformly competitive firm, demand, marginal revenue, and price were all equal (see the demand curve illustrated in Graph A of FIGURE 9-3). But how does revenue behave when the firm has market power as in Graph B of FIGURE 9-3? Let's see by way of example. Let's say that a new, patented drug that ends hair loss for men, HairEver, is brought to test market in Atlanta by TriPharma, Incorporated. TABLE 9-1 contains its demand, total-revenue (TR), average-revenue (AR), and marginal-revenue (MR) schedules.

TABLE 9-1: Hairever (Q, P, TR, AR, MR)				
1	**2**	**3**	**4**	**5**
Quantity (Q) of	Price (*P*)	Total Revenue (*TR =[P][Q]*)	Average Revenue (*AR = TR/Q*)	Marginal Revenue (*MR = ΔTR/ΔQ*)
0	$11	$0	$0*	
1	$10	$10	$10	$10
2	$9	$18	$9	$8
3	$8	$24	$8	$6
4	$7	$28	$7	$4
5	$6	$30	$6	$2
6	$5	$30	$5	$0
7	$4	$28	$4	-$2
8	$3	$24	$3	-$4
9	$2	$18	$2	-$6
10	$1	$10	$1	-$8
*0/0 mathematically is known as an indeterminate form, but here we will treat $0/0 as just $0 of average revenue.				

Let's deconstruct TABLE 9-1 column by column. Columns 1 and 2 display TriPharma's demand schedule for HairEver—the demand schedule should be a familiar concept to the reader from previous chapters. Next is column 3, total revenue (TR), which should be familiar as well: price (P) multiplied by quantity (Q) or (P)(Q). Remember that average revenue (AR) is total revenue (TR) divided by quantity (Q) or TR/Q, which is always equal to price (P):

$$Average\ Revenue\ (AR) = \frac{TR}{Q}$$

And since TR = (P)(Q),

$$AR = \frac{(P)(Q)}{Q} = \frac{(P)(\cancel{Q})}{\cancel{Q}} = P$$

Hence, columns 2 and 4 (with the only exception at Quantity [Q] = 0) of TABLE 9-1 are identical. Recall from chapter 8 that in addition to average revenue (AR) always being equal to price (P) under uniform competition or monopoly, average revenue (AR), when drawn as a curve, is identical to the demand curve. This is why the average-revenue (AR) curve is another name for the demand curve. Column 5 is marginal revenue (MR), the change in total revenue caused by the sale of another unit of the product. This is one of the greatest contrasts to uniform competition. Uniformly competitive firms can sell as much as they can in their market and always get the market-determined price, which they don't control because they are price takers. Monopolies have to reduce their price to sell another unit; this means not just reducing the price on the next unit sold, but also all units sold. For example, as can be seen in TABLE 9-1, for TriPharma to go from selling 5 units to 6 units, price has to fall *on all units* from $6 each to $5 each. Thus, a 6th unit gets sold, however, a dollar is lost on the other 5 units sold. Five dollars were gained on the sale of the 6th unit but \$5 were lost on the other 5 units. How did this affect revenue? It didn't: as can be seen in TABLE 9-1, total revenue (TR) was \$30 at 5 units and is now \$30 at 6 units. In other words, marginal revenue (MR) at 6 units equals \$0. However, something interesting happens when we move from 6 units sold to 7 units sold. Total revenue (TR) was \$30 at 6 units sold and is now \$28 at 7 units sold. In other words, marginal revenue (MR) at 7 units sold equals -\$2, or total revenue (TR) fell by \$2.

This brings us to another relationship:

$$MR < P$$

As can be seen in columns 2 and 5, price (P) and marginal revenue (MR) respectively, the two variables begin equal in value (\$10) at a quantity (Q) of 1, then price (P) declines at a slope of -1 while marginal revenue (MR) falls at a slope of -2.[39] In FIGURE 9-4, both curves can be seen diverging quickly from a single point on the Price/Revenue axis and moving in different directions based on their different slopes.[40]

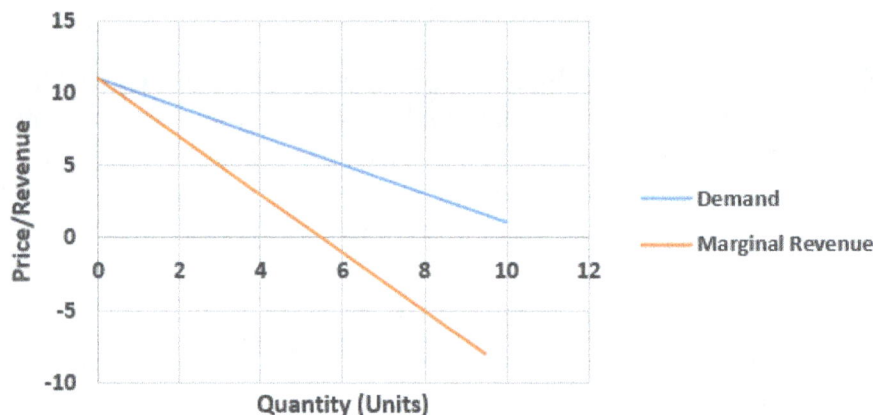

FIGURE 9-4: Demand and Marginal-Revenue Curves for a Monopoly

---

[39] Although it would be more accurate to state that MR ≤ P, this is only true at a quantity of zero, which is a very unique and rare situation for a monopoly.

[40] The marginal revenue (MR) curve in FIGURE 9-4 does not align with the data in TABLE 9-1 because discrete marginal values actually fall in between each unit of product if replication of realistic continuity is the goal. In other words, in the graphing of the marginal-revenue (MR) curve, the first observation of \$10 truly corresponds to a quantity of 0.5 units, \$8 corresponds to 1.5 units, \$6 corresponds to 2.5 units, etc. Because fractional units are unrealistic—How many consumers would enthusiastically purchase 1.5 loaves of bread or bags of pretzels?--they are treated as whole units in the table for simplicity.

In TABLE 9-1, why does total revenue (TR) steadily increase, reach a maximum at 5 and 6 units ($30) and then begin falling? Total revenue (TR) = (P)(Q), so there are price and quantity effects occurring:

price effect: when a fall in price causes a firm's total revenue to fall.

output effect: when an increase in quantity sold causes a firm's total revenue to rise.

Clearly the output effect dominates through 5 units (as TR increases to a maximum of $30) while the price effect starts dominating at 7 to 10 units (and TR starts falling steadily from its maximum value). This state of affairs is clearly different from uniform competition because under uniform competition there is no rise or fall in price, therefore there is no price effect, only an output effect.

9.3 Profit-Maximizing Output for a Monopoly

As previously stated, the profit-maximizing output for any firm, regardless of market structure, is where marginal cost is equal to marginal revenue or MC = MR. As with competition, so with monopoly and everything else in between. So far, we have seen the demand and marginal-revenue curves for a monopoly graphed in FIGURE 9-4. What we are missing are the cost curves relevant to monopoly, namely the average-total-cost (ATC) and marginal-cost (MC) curves. The average-total-cost curve should look at least similar to that of a competitive firm. In other words, U-shaped; i.e., as output rises from zero, the curve will fall before crossing an inflection point (slope = 0) at which the curve stops falling, average-total cost hits its lowest point, and after which average-total cost rises as output continues to rise. The marginal-cost curve should look at least similar to that of a competitive firm. In other words, it should appear as an upward-sloping curve where, as output rises from zero, the curve rises as output steadily rises). FIGURE 9-5 is a model of the process at which a profit-maximizing output and price per unit of output is arrived at for a monopoly; it includes the ATC and MC curves.

FIGURE 9-5: Finding Profit-Maximizing Output and Price for a Monopoly

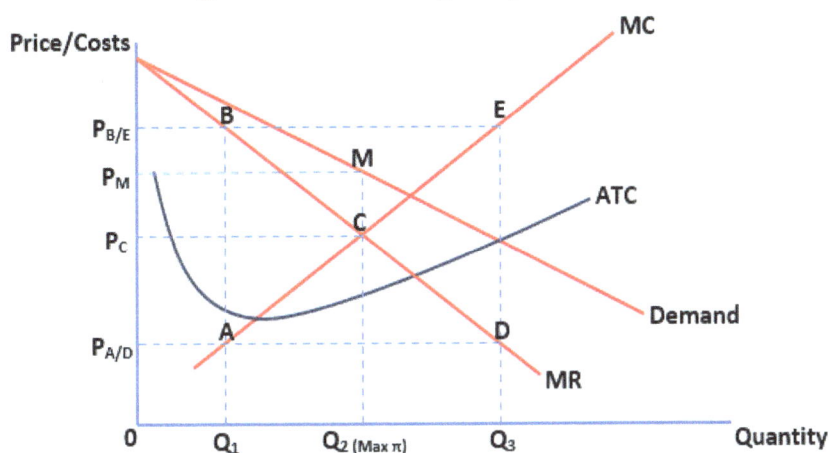

As previously noted, the profit-maximizing level of output for a monopoly is the level of output where marginal cost (MC) is equal to marginal revenue (MR). In FIGURE 9-5, MC = MR at point C. If we follow the dashed line downward from point C to the quantity axis, we can see that the profit-maximizing level of output for a monopoly is $Q_{2\ (Max\ \pi)}$. We know that $Q_{2\ (Max\ \pi)}$ is the profit-maximizing level of output because at Q_1, marginal cost (MC) at point A is less than marginal revenue (MR) at point B. Because we're adding more to revenue than costs at output levels $Q_1 < Q_{2\ (Max\ \pi)}$, to maximize profit we have to increase production as long as revenue exceeds cost, which is all the way up to $Q_{2\ (Max\ \pi)}$. At output level Q_3, it's the opposite story. Marginal revenue (MR) at point D is less than marginal cost (MC) at point E. Because we're adding more to cost than revenue at output levels $Q_{2\ (Max\ \pi)} < Q_3$, to maximize profit we have to decrease production as long as cost exceeds revenue, which is all the way down to $Q_{2(Max\ \pi)}$.

So now that we know the level of output that a monopoly produces, what about price? We already know that for a monopoly, marginal revenue (MR) is less than price (P), or MR < P. So obviously P ≠ MR = MC, but rather P > MR = MC (compared to P = MR = MC under uniform competition). So price under monopoly is not where MR = MC (point C, where price would be at the level of P_C). Instead, we have to travel upward along the dashed line above point C to point M on the demand curve, then turn left and travel along the dashed line to the price/cost axis to price P_M, or the price that a monopoly charges for $Q_{2\ (Max\ \pi)}$ output. So, to recap, as illustrated in FIGURE 9-5, *a monopoly maximizes profit by producing where MC = MR at $Q_{2\ (Max\ \pi)}$ and charges a price of P_M per unit produced.* The uncluttered results are displayed in FIGURE 9-6:

FIGURE 9-6: The Monopoly Firm

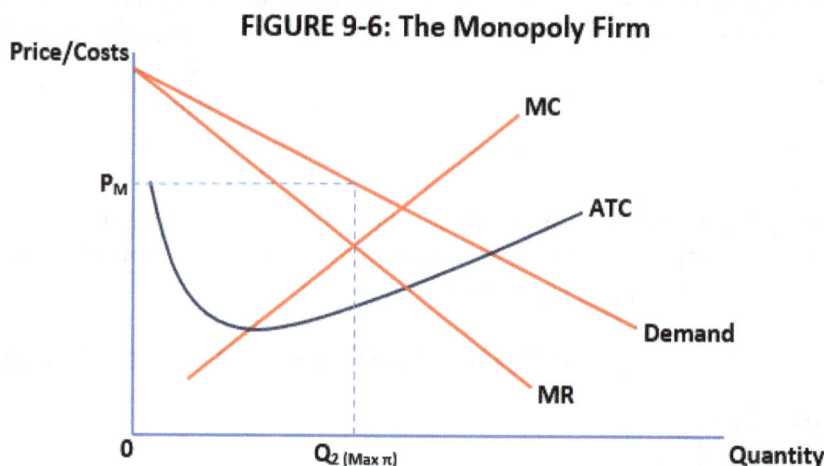

9.4 Monopoly Profits

The first step in determining profits for a monopoly is to resurrect the profit equation:

$$profit\ (\pi) = TR - TC$$

where TR = total revenue and
TC = total costs.

Next, we multiply both sides of the profit equation by 1 or Q/Q:

$$\frac{Q}{Q}\pi = \frac{Q}{Q}(TR - TC).$$

On the left side of the equals sign, we will revert $\frac{Q}{Q}$ back to 1 while on the right side of the equals sign we will separate the top Q (numerator) from the bottom Q (denominator):

$$\pi = \frac{Q}{1}\frac{1}{Q}(TR - TC).$$

We will then keep the top Q where it is and multiply the bottom Q into the parenthetical expression (TR – TC):

$$\pi = Q(\frac{TR}{Q} - \frac{TC}{Q}).$$

This last equation further reduces to:

$$\pi = Q(AR - ATC),$$

where AR = average revenue and ATC = average-total cost. Since we already know from our analysis of uniform competition and our discussion of TABLE 9-1 that average revenue (AR) is equal to price (P), we then get

$$\pi = Q(P - ATC),$$

or, moving output (Q) to the back of the parenthetical expression, as is customary,

$$\pi = (P - ATC)Q,$$

which is true for uniform competition or monopoly.

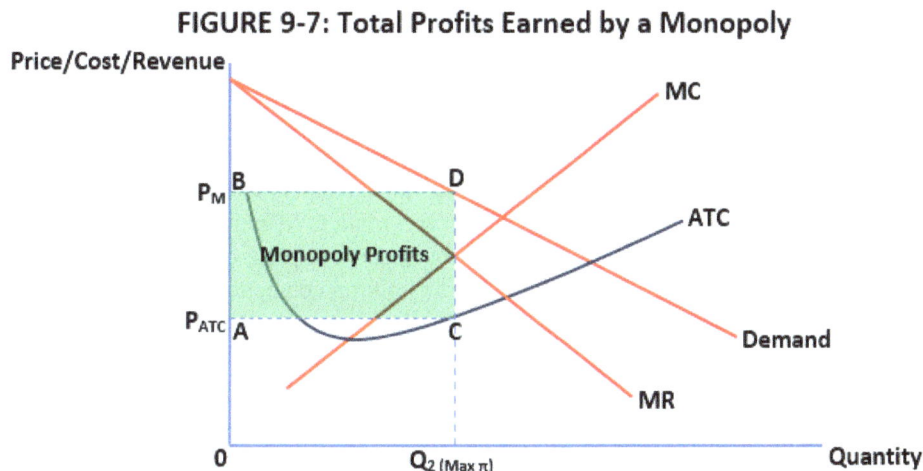

FIGURE 9-7: Total Profits Earned by a Monopoly

In light of the last version of the profit equation above [π = (P-ATC)Q], one can see the total profits earned by a monopoly as displayed in FIGURE 9-7. (Notice that FIGURE 9-7 is identical to FIGURE 9-6, except with economic profits highlighted in the green box.) The monopoly maximizes profit by producing where MC = MR at $Q_{2\ (Max\ \pi)}$ and charges a price of P_M per unit produced. The green profits box in FIGURE 9-7 is defined by the four corners of A, B, C, and D. Point B is at the same level as P_M, or price per unit. The same goes for point D, where the price line extending from P_M/B intersects the demand curve. If we follow the dashed line straight down from point D toward $Q_{2\ (Max\ \pi)}$, we intersect the average-total cost (ATC) curve at point C. Point C is at the same level on the price axis as P_{ATC} and point A on the profits box. Back to our equation $[\pi = (P\text{-}ATC)Q]$, the term $(P - ATC)$ refers to monopoly price minus ATC at monopoly output, or point D – point C (the right side of the monopoly-profits box, or the height of the profit rectangle). The variable Q just refers to monopoly output $[Q_{2\ (Max\ \pi)}]$ or point C – point A (the bottom side of the monopoly-profits box, or the length of the profit rectangle). *Ergo*, the height of the profits box $(D - C)$ multiplied by the length of the profits box $(C - A)$ equals the total profits earned by the monopoly firm.

9.5 Five Steps for Analyzing Monopolies

1. From market demand, estimate what marginal revenue (MR) is for different levels of output (Q).
2. From total costs (TC), estimate what marginal cost (MC) is for different levels of output (Q).
3. Estimate the level of output (Q) where marginal revenue (MR) is equal to marginal cost (MC).
4. From market demand, estimate the price (P) at which consumers will purchase each unit of output (Q).
5. If price (P) at the profit-maximizing output (Q) exceeds average-total cost (ATC) at the profit-maximizing output [i.e., P > ATC at Q], then the monopoly is earning a (positive) economic profit.

ECONOMIC CONTROVERSIES: Monopolies Don't Have Supply Curves? Why N. Gregory Mankiw Is Wrong

Some microeconomics textbooks (ahem, N. Gregory Mankiw's) assert that monopolies do not have supply curves (p. 297, 9th edition). The reasoning is as follows: Monopolies choose to produce the profit-maximizing output where marginal cost (MC) is equal to marginal revenue (MR). They then find the price their customers will be willing to pay for the product from market demand, as the monopoly is the supplier of the entire market in its industry. So far, so good. However, monopolies (at least according to Mankiw) allegedly don't have supply curves because rising or falling firm demand doesn't trace out a curve of price-quantity points that exactly matches the firm's marginal-cost (MC) curve as it does under uniform competition.

Mankiw's reasoning initially seems plausible until you actually consider market dynamics in a monopoly. FIGURE 9-8 represents a new patented drug, Bezempic, that comes to market by Pharmagic, Incorporated. Pharmagic produces the drug at a rate of Q_1 output per day and prices the drug at the level of P_{M1}. Point A in FIGURE 9-8 is the point of intersection of the dashed price and quantity lines. The drug was designed to control blood pressure and it is effective in that capacity. However, later studies show that the drug helps patients lose a substantial amount of weight.

With an advertising blitz on television, Pharmagic is able to significantly increase the demand for Bezempic by playing up the drug's ability to help consumers shed lots of pounds. The demand for Bezempic shifts from *Demand$_1$* to *Demand$_2$* and thus so does marginal revenue from *MR$_1$* to *MR$_2$*. As a result, Pharmagic now produces the drug at a rate of Q_2 output per day (where MC = MR for the new MR curve) and prices the drug at the level of P_{M2} (per the new demand curve). Thus, the quantity and price of the drug are now both higher. Point *B* in FIGURE 9-8 is the new point of intersection of the dashed price and quantity lines.

Now, there's no question that the old and new quantities and prices of Bezempic do not fall along the marginal-cost (MC) curve as they would under competition so that a supply curve for the firm is traced out. However, that does not at all mean that there's no supply curve for Pharmagic. A supply curve consists of a range of price-quantity points representing a firm's supply decisions in a market that is traced out by a shifting demand curve. FIGURE 9-9 shows just such a curve.

FIGURE 9-8: the Monopoly Firm with Increasing Demand

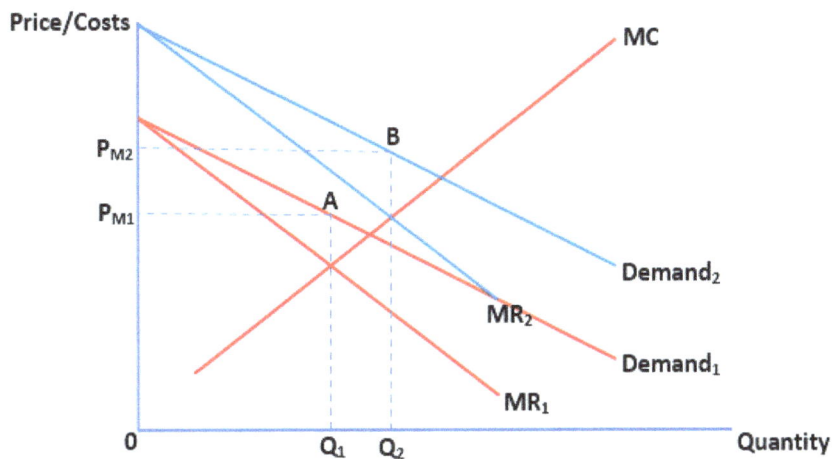

FIGURE 9-9: the Supply Curve for a Monopoly

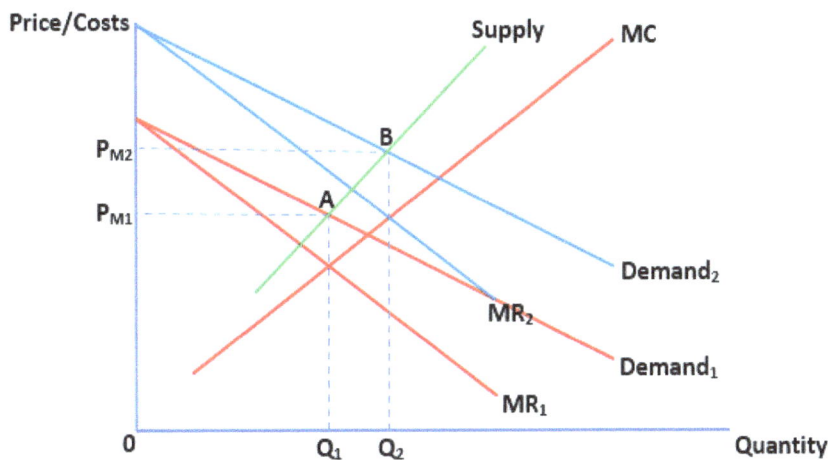

FIGURE 9-9 is identical to FIGURE 9-8 before it with the exception that it has the monopoly's supply curve drawn in through the market-equilibrium points *A* and *B*. So, monopolies definitely have supply curves, however, they are not like those of uniformly competitive firms. The supply curve of a uniformly competitive firm is the same as its marginal-cost (MC) curve because, as we showed in FIGURE 8-11 in chapter 8, when market demand (D) increases, firm demand (d) increases. Firm output (q) and firm price (p) rise to a higher level along the firm's marginal-cost curve because profit maximization requires a level of output (q) where MC = MR, and under uniform competition, MC = MR = P. Therefore, firm output (q) changes in response to firm price (p) along the

MC curve.

In contrast, monopolies have supply curves but they do not run along their marginal-cost curves. This is only because MR rotates downward away from demand (D) under monopoly. Profit-maximization requires a level of Q where MC = MR, but price follows market demand, which makes it greater than MR (i.e., P > MR). Therefore, when the market demand shifts, market equilibrium moves from point A to point B in FIGURE 9-9 (and not from where MC = MR for Q_1 to where MC = MR for Q_2, which *would* be along the monopoly's MC curve).

ECONOMICS IN ACTION: Why Don't Some Brand-Name Products Lose All of Their Market Power after Their Patent Expires?

brand-name product - a product that sells under a well-known and usually trademarked name and logo that serves as a guarantee of quality.

trademark - a legally registered unique word, phrase, character, or logo representing a business firm that gives the firm legal protection against unauthorized use of its name or logo.

A **brand-name product** is a product that sells under a well-known and usually trademarked name and logo that serves as a guarantee of quality. (A **trademark** is a legally registered unique word, phrase, character, or logo representing a business firm that gives the firm legal protection against unauthorized use of its name or logo.) The pharmaceutical industry sells many products under famous brand names: Tylenol, Zoloft, Lipitor, Zantac, Proair, Synthroid, Norvasc, Prilosec, and Vicodin, to name a few. Drugs receive twenty years of patent protection, however, since it often takes about a decade to get the average prescription drug to market, they realistically only receive about a decade of monopoly patent pricing.

So, after a decade of monopoly profits are over for a pharmaceutical company, what happens? Firms manufacturing generic competitors enter the market of the brand-name drug to grab a piece of the former monopoly's profits. Pressure is exerted on doctors (by patients and insurance companies) to prescribe the new, lower-cost generic alternatives. Does this mean that the former monopoly has to now price its formerly patented product at the same level as its new generic competitors? No, and FIGURE 9-10 shows why.

FIGURE 9-10: The Market for Drugs (Monopoly Versus Competition)

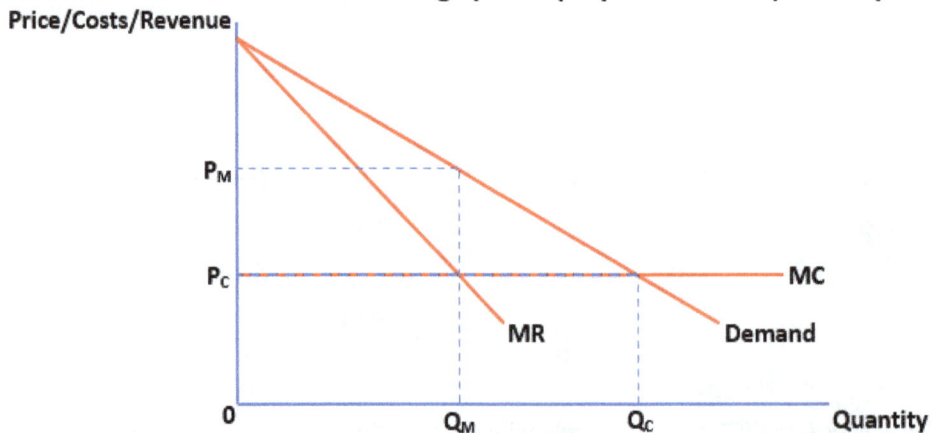

In FIGURE 9-10, the patented drug is produced by the monopoly at the rate of Q_M per week and priced at the level of P_M. After the patent expires the monopolist soon loses all of its market power. Lower-priced generic competitors storm the market and thus industry output rises to the level of Q_C per week with all units (brand name and generic) now selling at the competitive price of P_C. This is at least what could reasonably be predicted from theory.

So what happens in the real world? There is a substantial movement away from most brand-name drugs toward lower-priced generic drugs, as patients and insurance providers pressure physicians to prescribe the new lower-priced generic drugs. However, the no-longer-patented drug does not see all of its market power eroded by the new competitors. While most of the new generic competitors are, chemically, close to the brand-name drug, they aren't entirely identical. This doesn't sit well with some drug consumers who want the assurance of a brand name.

Take Xalatan, for example, a drug that reduces eye pressure in glaucoma patients and can be priced at $125 for a tiny 2.5 mL bottle. Without this drug, glaucoma patients begin to experience vision loss and eventual blindness. Xalatan's generic competitor (latanoprost) is far cheaper than Xalatan, usually under $10 per 2.5 mL bottle. Why do some patients insist on purchasing the much-more-expensive Xalatan? Fear that the generic drug is not of the same level of quality as the name-brand drug and that the use of the generic drug could jeopardize their priceless eyesight. Not surprisingly, this is a fear that, while largely unfounded, is not something that the maker of Xalatan is quick to disabuse its customers of! It's understandable that it wants to maintain as much market power as it can after the expiration of its coveted patent. It's also possible that some eye patients are sensitive to the difference in the chemical composition of the two products and these patients tolerate Xalatan better. This is probably not a large number of patients, but, along with the first group that fears that generic drugs are lower in quality and effectiveness, enough of a market to explain the continued difference in price between the two products.

9.6 The Social Effects of Monopolies (Part I): Deadweight Loss

In chapter 6 the concepts of consumer surplus, producer surplus, and total surplus were first introduced. If those concepts remain foggy, here they are again: **consumer surplus** (CS) is the value of a product to a consumer (as measured by the maximum willingness to pay) minus the price paid for the product. **Producer surplus** (PS) is the price paid for a producer's product minus the minimum cost of bringing the producer's product to the market. **Total surplus** (TS) is consumer surplus (CS) plus producer surplus (PS) OR the value of the product minus the cost of the product.

consumer surplus (CS) - the value of a product to a consumer (as measured by the maximum willingness to pay) minus the price paid for the product.

producer surplus (PS) - the price paid for a producer's product minus the minimum cost of bringing the producer's product to the market.

total surplus (TS) - consumer surplus (CS) plus producer surplus (PS) OR the value of the product minus the cost of the product.

FIGURE 9-11: Social Efficiency in a Competitive Market

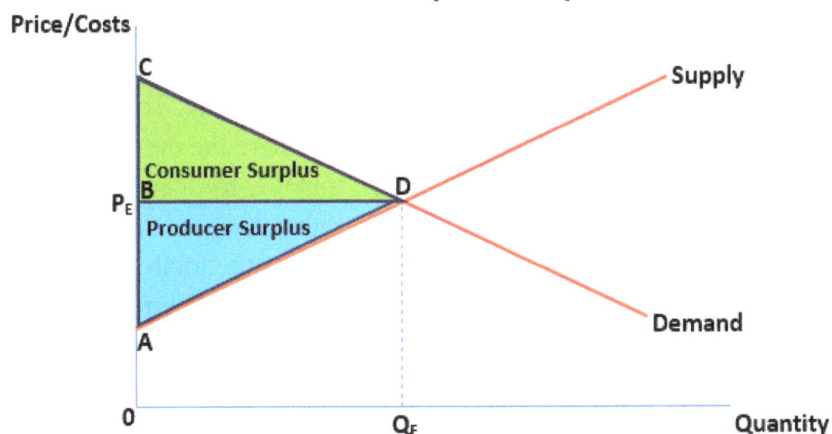

FIGURE 9-11 illustrates these concepts geometrically. The demand curve, by definition represents what consumers are willing and able to pay for a product. The market price P_E is what consumers in fact pay for a product. The difference between the demand curve and the market price (line segment $\overline{BD}$ in FIGURE 9-11) is the green triangle (BCD), consumer surplus. The area of any triangle is one half multiplied by the triangle's base mutliplied by the triangle's height or:

$$\left(\frac{1}{2}\right)(base)(height)$$

In the case of FIGURE 9-11, consumer surpus (CS) = (1/2)(C-B)(D). For P_E = $100, C = $125, and Q_E = 1,000, consumer surplus (CS) = (1/2)($25)(1,000) = $12,500.

The difference between the market price (line segment $\overline{BD}$ in FIGURE 9-11) and the supply curve is the blue triangle (ABD), producer surplus (PS). In the case of FIGURE 9-11, producer surpus (PS) = (1/2)(B-A)(D). For P_E = $100, A = $75, and Q_E = 1,000, producer surplus = (1/2)($25)(1,000) = $12,500 PS.

Total surplus (consumer surplus + producer surplus) = $12,500 CS + $12,500 PS = $25,000 TS.

FIGURE 9-12: Social Efficiency in a Monopoly Market

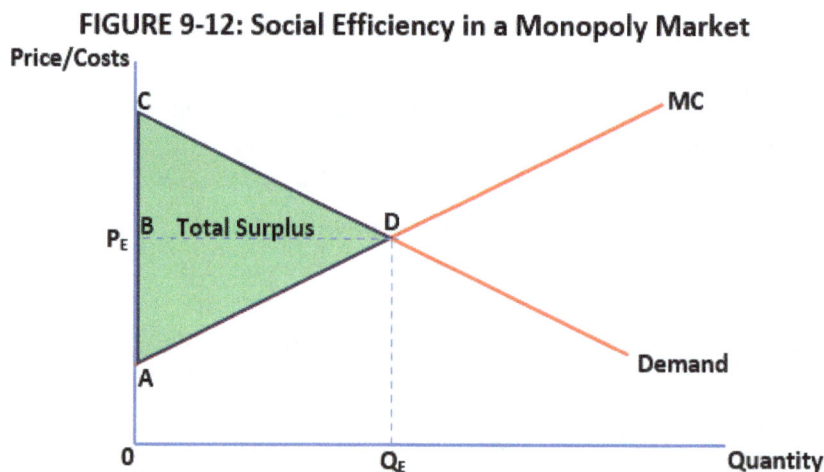

Now we subtly transition to monopoly. FIGURE 9-12 replaces market supply with marginal cost to illustrate monopoly. Consumer and producer surplus (CS + PS) are replaced with total surplus (TS, the bright-green triangle ABCD) to illustrate the latter concept geometrically. Total surplus is also maximum social well-being under a monopoly when price is set where the demand and marginal-cost curves intersect (point D) as in FIGURE 9-12. In fact, this is a competitive result rather than a monopoly result (where price is set on the demand curve above where marginal revenue equals marginal cost [MR = MC]). To directly calculate the area of the total-surplus triangle (instead of going the long way by calculating consumer surplus, calculating producer surplus, and then summing the two), we use the same formula for the area of a triangle:

$$\left(\frac{1}{2}\right)(base)(height)$$

Keeping the same numbers (A = \$75, B/P$_E$ = \$100, C = \$125, Q$_E$ = 1,000), gives us: (1/2)(C−A)(1,000) = (1/2)(\$50)(1,000) = \$25,000 (the same answer you arrive at for CS + PS). Having moved from competition to monopoly, now all we do is add marginal revenue (MR) to get FIGURE 9-13:

FIGURE 9-13: Monopoly Inefficiency

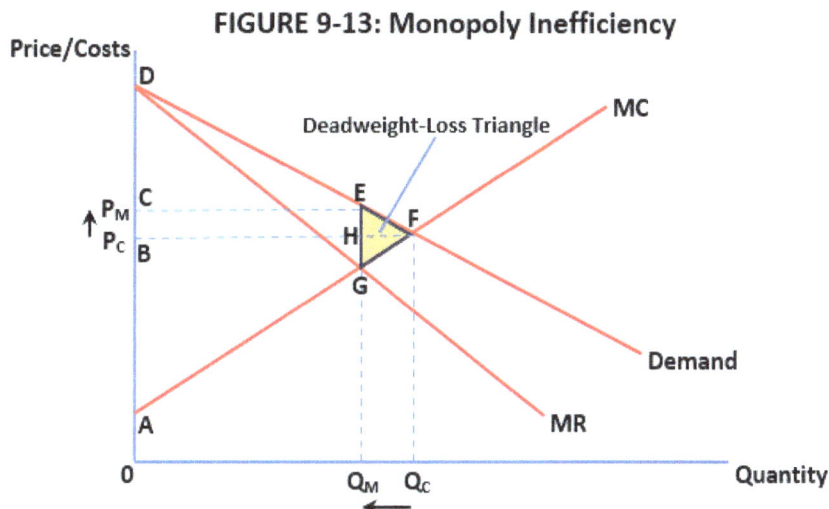

FIGURE 9-13 completes our comparison of competition and monopoly, as it allows us to see both results. We move away from the higher output (Q$_C$) and lower price (P$_C$) of competition to the lower monopoly output of Q$_M$ (where MC = MR) and higher monopoly price (on the demand curve) at P$_M$/point C.

This action reduces consumer surplus to a new and smaller triangle (CDE) from the old larger triangle (BDF). Producer surplus is altered as well, going from old triangle BFA to new four-sided polygon area ACEG. Producers lose small triangle GHF but gain rectangle BCEH. What results is a social inefficiency known as **deadweight loss** (triangle EFG), the loss to society from the reduced quantity of a good or service provided to a market by a monopoly. (Also: deadweight loss is the decline in total surplus [loss to demanders and suppliers] in a market caused by the imposition of a tax or control. See chapter 6.) Consumers willing to pay downward-sloping line segment $\overline{EF}$ for the good or service (above both MC and competitive price) are prevented from doing so. Geometrically, it is the tip of the bright-green-total-surplus triangle we saw in FIGURE 9-12.

deadweight loss - the loss to society from the reduced quantity of a good or service provided to a market by a monopoly. Also: the decline in total surplus (loss to demanders and suppliers) in a market caused by the imposition of a tax or control. See chapter 6.

One more note: if deadweight loss rings a bell, that's no accident. We first saw this concept in chapter 6. When a tax is imposed on a competitive market, there will be a loss of efficiency in that market from the imposition of a wedge between demand and supply. The wedge imposed by a monopoly can be seen in FIGURE 9-13: line segment $\overline{EG}$, or the base of the entire orange deadweight-loss triangle.

9.7 The Social Effects of Monopolies (Part II): Profit

In popular media and culture, there is much focus on the supposed "evils" of profits. The U.S. health-care system is denounced as focusing on profits over illness or the well-being of people. (No doubt U.S. health care has clear affordability and access problems, but they have nothing to with profits *per se* as we'll see in chapter 11.) Under an extant monopoly, price is greater than MC and for consumers who still demand the product, paying $1 more per unit of the product means the consumer is less well off by $1 and the firm's profits grow by $1. Current total surplus, however, remains the same. The problem is that the current total surplus, because of the deadweight loss, is not at a maximum (the bright-green triangle in FIGURE 9-12) because it has had a portion of it lopped off (deadweight loss, as in the orange triangle in FIGURE 9-13). Restoring this lost portion would maximize social efficiency. Also, deadweight loss is certainly not the end of the story in terms of lost social efficiency if the firm has to pay a portion of its producer surplus to the government to maintain its monopoly status. That loss does not show up in any graphs but is still a reality nonetheless.

9.8 Price Differentiation

price differentiation - the sale of the same product at two or more prices, usually to two or more different groups of consumers not based on different costs.

Price differentiation is the sale of the same product at two or more prices, usually to two or more different groups of consumers not based on different costs. That definition sounds distressingly complicated and unclear, so let's quickly cut to an example: it's a Friday and a movie that really interests you is released tonight.

1. You can go to see the movie at the theater tonight at its first showing at 7 p.m. and you'll pay $20 per ticket ($40 total for you and your date).
2. You can wait until the Saturday 1 p.m. matinee (daytime showing) and pay $10 per ticket ($20 total for you and your date).
3. You can wait six months until the movie appears on Netflix. This is $6.99 (pre-tax) if you are not a subscriber. Total: $6.99.

These three different viewing options define three different groups of consumers. Hardcore fans are at the first showing. More lukewarm fans buy matinee tickets. The more indifferent viewers wait for the movie to appear on Netflix. This isn't just the pattern for new movies, but new novels from James Patterson, and even the newest iPhone or Apple watch. Hardcore devotees camp out the night or nights before the sale to be the first in line. The rest wait a little longer or up to months or years.

What we're also seeing here is some degree of market power. This doesn't happen under uniform competition because firms that are uniformly competitive are price takers: if they raise their price above the market's, they lose just about all of their sales. There's no incentive to lower price because they can sell all they want at the current market price. Price differentiation requires market power.

9.8a What Drives Price Differentiation?

Why would it occur to a firm to create two different markets for the same product? Paramount Pictures is considering a new *Mission: Impossible* movie with Tom Cruise (again) playing the lead character, Ethan Hunt. The movie will appeal to two groups of consumers. The first is two million hardcore Tom-Cruise and *Mission: Impossible* franchise fans who will eagerly pay $20 per ticket at the movie theater to see the movie. The second group of consumers is general action-movie fans (4 million in number) who will pay $7 to see the movie streaming on demand. All production costs for the movie are $20 million.

If Paramount goes with just a single price, it can either earn [($20)(2 million) = $40 million revenue - $20 million costs =] $20 million profit catering to hardcore fans or earn [($7)(4 million) = $28 million revenue - $20 million costs =] $8 million profit catering to general action-movie fans. Given these numbers it's easy to see how, if forced to only charge a single price, Paramount would cater only to hardcore fans and earn $20 million profit.

The problem, though, is that we have lost $8 million of total surplus by not serving 4 million customers (at a marginal cost of just about $0 in providing the movie to streaming platforms). Therefore, Paramount decides to charge two prices, serve two markets, and maximize its profit at a total of [$20 million + $8 million =] $28 million.

What drives price differentiation? Maximizing profit and total surplus.

9.9 Two Conclusions About Price Differentiation

1. Price differentiation maximizes profit for the firm but also social welfare. While the gain in total surplus only accrues to the firm, also maximized is customers served and market efficiency.

2. Price differentiation requires two other conditions. First, it requires the ability to establish different sets of consumers based on their different willingness to pay (i.e., different demands). Second, it requires little to no arbitrage (buying the product in the lower-priced market and reselling it in the higher-priced market). For our movie example above, buying the movie in the $7 streaming market and reselling it in the $20 theater market is impossible.

9.10 Total Surplus and Profit Under Uniform and Differentiated Prices

Perfect price differentiation is the ability of a supplier to know and charge the maximum price each consumer is willing to pay for a product. A firm practicing such a selling policy would earn all market surplus in every transaction: all surplus would go to producers and none to consumers.

perfect price differentiation - the ability of a supplier to know and charge the maximum price each consumer is willing to pay for a product.

FIGURE 9-14: Standard versus Price-Differentiating Monopoly

Graph A: Standard Monopoly (Single Price)   Graph B: Perfectly Price-Differentiating Monopoly (Multiple Prices)

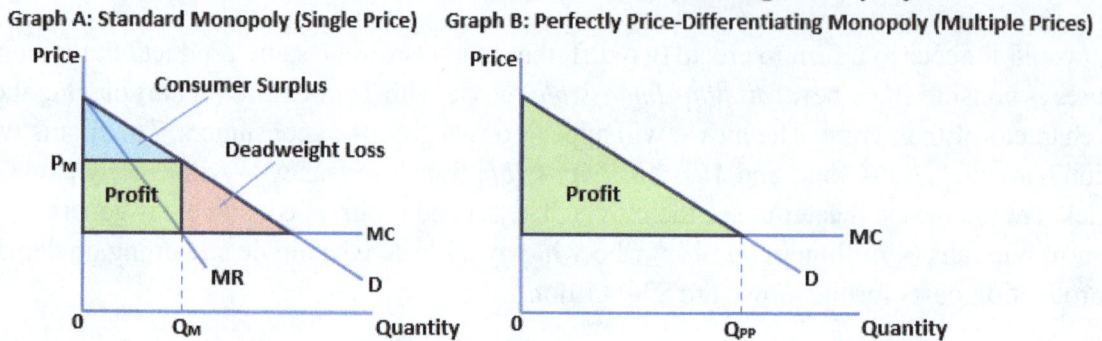

Although such an ability is impossible, FIGURE 9-14 nonetheless illustrates it. Assuming constant and equal marginal cost (MC) and average-total cost (ATC), the firm illustrated in Graph A of FIGURE 9-14 produces an output of Q_M and charges a single price above marginal cost, P_M. What results is a consumer surplus (blue right triangle), a profit (green rectangle), and a deadweight loss to society (red right triangle) from the market being underserved. Graph B in FIGURE 9-14 illustrates a firm with market power that is able to perfectly guess the maximum price each consumer in the market is willing to pay for its product and charge that exact same price accordingly. Output increases from Q_M (in Graph A where MC = MR) to the much higher Q_{PPD} (PPD = perfect price differentiation) in Graph B where demand (D) and marginal revenue (MR) intersect. With different prices for each customer, profit grows from a small green rectangle in Graph A of FIGURE 9-14 to a large green triangle in Graph B of FIGURE 9-14.

The impossibility of implementing such a price scheme (even *via* artificial intelligence [AI]) is beside the point. The true point is that price differentiation boosts profit, lessens deadweight loss, improves market efficiency, and serves consumers that value the product enough that it improves their well-being without having to be hardcore fans or customers.

9.11 Examples of Price Differentiation in the Real World

1. **Movies and documentaries.** Readers of this book received a preview of this in section 9.8a in the example about Paramount Pictures and *Mission: Impossible*. While a particular movie may have millions of potential buyers, the buyers certainly do not all have the same willingness and ability to pay for a viewing. These different demands by format (theater versus streaming) and time of viewing (evening versus afternoon) translate into different groups of customers that are charged different prices. Opening night seats in a theater will tend to carry a substantially higher price than online streaming months to years after first release.

2. **Airfares.** It is well known that airfares can vary significantly depending on the time of booking and the section of the plane the booking passenger chooses to be seated in. Wealthier and well-planning passengers with high opportunity costs tend to book early and first or business class. Less wealthy and more budget-minded consumers will choose coach or airlines such as Spirit that offer a completely no-frills flight where there is even a charge for light snacks and Wi-Fi service.

3. **Educational scholarships and grants.** These disbursements of funds are directed primarily at students from lower-income, less wealthy families. These individuals and their families have different demands for college or university education because of their different willingness and ability to play from that of wealthier individuals and families. Again, like all types of price differentiation, this type facilitates the maximization of profits for colleges and universities.

4. **Bulk or quantity discounts.** Ever notice that at Walmart, Target, or your usual grocery store, when you purchase a bigger size or quantity of a good, the price per item or price per weight declines? If you buy a five-pack of toothbrushes, you pay $1 each ($5 total), but if you purchase a ten-pack, each toothbrush is only $0.75 each ($7.50 total). The effect is even more pronounced at Costco, Sam's Club, and other warehouse stores where the deals are good (laundry detergent, baby products, meat) and hence appeal to low-income individuals or households and large families who don't mind paying more up-front per package in order to get a lower per-unit price of a good. For example, paying $25 to get 50 diapers at $0.50 each rather than paying $15 to get 15 diapers at $1 each.

5. **Coupons.** Whether they arrive in the Sunday editions of newspapers, bulk mail, or online, these discount certificates appeal to lower-income or low-opportunity-cost-of-time younger couples or seniors. They don't appeal much to high-income surgeons with a high opportunity cost of time who seldom use their valuable hours of the day clipping, printing, and collecting coupons.

9.12 Solutions to the Monopoly Problem

What is to be done about monopoly pricing above marginal cost and deadweight loss in certain industries? There are usually four solutions proposed to fix the problem.

1. Antitrust laws and enforcement.
2. Regulation.
3. Expropriation/nationalization.
4. Laissez-faire.

1. Antitrust laws and enforcement are laws and legal actions based on them designed to maintain competition in industries or limit the market power of firms. The approach of antitrust laws and enforcement began with the Sherman Antitrust Act of 1890 which was followed by the Clayton Antitrust Act of 1914. These two laws were supposedly designed to reduce the market power of monopolies by increasing competition in three ways: forbid mergers that would significantly limit competition, prevent firms from engaging in **collusion** (coordination among firms in an industry to keep prices relatively high and output relatively low by limiting competition), and finally, in the most extreme cases, dissolve a large firm into two or more smaller competing firms. What could possibly go wrong in any of these actions?

antitrust laws and enforcement – laws and legal actions based on them designed to maintain competition in industries or limit the market power of firms.

collusion – coordination among firms in an industry to keep prices relatively high and output relatively low by limiting competition.

The issue with antitrust laws is that politicians, regulators, and judges usually do not have enough information or expertise to accurately predict industry conditions before versus after a merger and many predictions have been wrong. An industry can go from three firms to two, which may substantially change its performance. It may no longer keep costs down as well as it once did and this can attract an efficient domestic or foreign competitor which sees the opportunity to earn substantial profits. Second, all firms in an industry may raise the price of their products, but that is not necessarily evidence of collusion. A crucial input used to manufacture an industry's product may be in reduced supply, which raises the price of that input, and therefore raises the price of the industry's final product from *all* suppliers. If the price of oil, a critical input in the supply of gasoline, rises, then the price of gasoline will rise at every firm that sells gasoline.

Lastly, there's no evidence that breakups necessarily make industries more competitive. The component firm that retains the managerial talent that brought it to the top of its industry can not only survive, but thrive, while its newly separated competitor barely survives or fails. This would have almost certainly been the fate of Microsoft had it been broken up into two firms (one that sold the Windows operating system [OS] and another that sold other non-OS apps) in the year 2000. Especially arbitrary was the government's position that it should be legal for certain apps to be included in an operating system (e.g., basic word processors such as WordPad) but illegal for other apps to be included (e.g., an Internet browser such as Internet Explorer). Many economists asked, "Why should politicians and judges be in charge of defining the features of computer operating systems rather than software developers and consumers?"

regulation - the government setting the price, output level, or other aspects of the operations of a firm.

2. Regulation is the government setting the price, output level, or other aspects of the operations of a firm. Under this solution, regulators require a monopoly to price its product at marginal cost (MC) to replicate the results of a competitive market. First, the most successful implementation of this option has been for industries thought to fit the structure of a natural monpoly (a notion controversial in and of itself as we saw in section 9.1). For example: local water and electric utilities. As a solution, it has a number of problems as illustrated in FIGURE 9-15.

FIGURE 9-15: Regulated Pricing Under Natural Monopoly

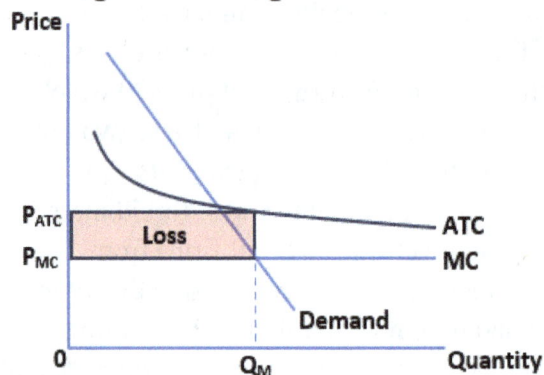

In the natural monopoly illustrated in FIGURE 9-15, state regulators fix the regulated price (P_{MC}) of the product equal to MC with output being produced at the level of Q_M. For a natural monopoly, though, this is a problem because average-total cost (ATC) steadily declines from low levels of output to higher levels of output. Marginal cost (MC), as it does under competition, lies below falling average-total costs (ATC). Thus, this pricing scheme imposes a loss on the firm (illustrated by the total area of the red loss rectangle in FIGURE 9-15), which causes it to exit the industry in the long run.

To prevent exit, regulators can pursue one of two remedies. One, they can levy a tax to generate revenue that compensates the firm for its continuous losses, but the tax itself will generate a deadweight loss, which we were already trying to avoid by setting price (P) equal to marginal cost (MC). The second option is to allow the firm to price at P_{ATC} and avoid losses, but again, any pricing above MC gets us right back to the problems of monopoly (P > MC) and deadweight loss.

Regardless of whether prices are set at MC or ATC, monopolies that have regulators who protect them from competition have no incentive to be more efficient and keep costs down. If MC or ATC fall, then so does price (P), hence there is little incentive to increase efficiency and reduce costs. Hence public utility performance has not been impressive. A recent investigation into severe forest fires in California found that Pacific Gas & Electric Company (PG&E)'s work on its infrastructure was the root cause of the fires. Ditto for the 2023 fires in Hawaii started by downed power lines owned by Hawaii Electric.

3. Expropriation/nationalization is the seizing of ownership of a private firm, usually without compensation to its owners or investors, by a government to either end its operation or continue its operation under a government board or bureaucracy. This happened to farms under Vladimir Lenin and Joseph Stalin in the Soviet Union, to Cuban industries under Fidel Castro, and Venezuelan industries under Hugo Chavez, to name just a few.

expropriation/nationalization – the seizing of ownership of a private firm, usually without compensation to its owners or investors, by a government to either end its operation or continue its operation under a government board or bureaucracy.

The first problem is any lack of incentive to control costs and maintain quality. Firms in industries that resemble either uniform competition or differentiated competition (see chapter 10) always have the incentive to reduce costs because it increases profits (which go to management in the form of bonuses and stockholders in the form of dividends) and benefits consumers with lower-priced products. Collective ownership does not have these incentives; hence, it's no accident that the lowest quality, least reliable automobile ever made was the East German Trabant (1957-1991).

234

A Trabant on the Streets of Dresden, Germany in 1961 (Deutsche Fotothek, CC BY-SA 3.0 DE)

The second problem is that in the wake of nationalization, the industry becomes protectionist and static. Any innovation or technology that represents a competitive threat to the nationalized industry gets outlawed because governments (monopolies in and of themselves) tend to eliminate all competition to protect their bureaucracies, which become a special interest that lobby against all competition. Consumers, faced with poor service, have no recourse to punish the firm in terms of switching to a competing product. The only hope of captive customers is to vote in better politicians who will reform the industry bureaucracy. Under one-party totalitarian states (Cuba, North Korea, Venezuela), this process is slim to rare and slight improvements may arrive only after decades, if at all.

laissez-faire – letting markets work with a minimum of interference from the government beyond enforcement of private-property rights (including protecting consumers from fraud, theft, and physical injury).

4. Laissez-faire in French literally translates to "let it happen" and means letting markets work with a minimum of interference from the government beyond enforcement of private-property rights (including protecting consumers from fraud, theft, and physical injury). The thinking here is that intervention unleashes secondary effects that generate costs that almost always end up exceeding those caused by the initial problem. One of the first economists to argue this was Ludwig von Mises (1881-1973).[41] A single producer of a unique good or service with few substitutes earns abnormally high profits for a good priced above marginal cost. This will continually provide an incentive for inventors, innovators, and

creative destruction – the process by which a new and more efficient technology replaces an old one.

entrepreneurs to invent and develop new technologies and goods that substitute for and compete against the incumbent firm to drain away its abnormally high profits. This process was named **creative destruction** by economist Joseph Schumpeter (1883-1950). Creative destruction is the process by which a new and more efficient technology replaces an old one. This is not a costless process, as workers, managers, and owners at firms in the old industry have to adapt as their work and capital get replaced by the new industry. An example is the pony express being replaced by the telegraph which was replaced by the landline telephone which has largely been replaced by the cellular smartphone, a small and advanced computer.

9.13 Conclusion

This chapter analyzed the behavior of firms with substantial market power, otherwise known as monopolies. Monopoly power is at its strongest at the level of government. Firms that manufacture goods and services that are genuine monopolies are usually holders of patents, copyrights, or have some barrier or barriers to entry to their industry provided by the government (e.g., salt in the ancient world to NASDAQ in the modern world). Overall, these types of firms

---

[41] Mises, Ludwig von. "Middle of the Road Policy Leads to Socialism." *Commercial and Financial Chronicle*. 4 May 1950.

are rare. Much more common than monopolies are firms with some degree of market power, but not as much market power as true monopolies. These types of firms will be examined in detail in the next chapter on differentiated competition. We will close this chapter with TABLE 9-2, which summarizes the differences between uniform competition and monopoly.

TABLE 9-2: Uniform Competition *Versus* Monopoly		
	Uniform Competition	**Monopoly**
Product	Uniform	Highly differentiated
Number of firms	Many	One
Number of consumers	Many	Many
Free entry?	Yes	No
Output Decision	MC = MR	MC = MR
Pricing Decision	P = MC = MR = Demand	P > MC where MC = MR
Maximizes total surplus?	Yes	No
Creates deadweight loss?	No	Yes
Has barriers to entry directly or indirectly rooted in government restrictions?	Has no barriers to entry at all	Yes

9.14 Chapter Concepts

monopoly
price maker
market power
economies of scale
natural monopoly
club good
excludability
rivalry
government
charter
patent
copyright
price taker
price effect
output effect
brand-name product
trademark
consumer surplus (CS)
producer surplus (PS)
total surplus (TS)
deadweight loss
price differentiation
perfect price differentiation
antitrust laws and enforcement
collusion

regulation
expropriation/nationalization
laissez-faire
creative destruction

9.15 Problems, Questions, and Discussion Topics (Items Requiring Examples are Marked with an Asterisk [*])

1. price maker (define, then provide a real-life example)*

2. Can monopolies really price a good or service "as high as they want?" Or is this an exaggeration and why?

3. three types of barriers to entry (name and define each, then provide an example of only one)*

4. On the three types of barriers to entry,

    A. Which does current thinking emphasize?

    B. Why?

5. *charter* versus *patent* versus *copyright* (define all three, then provide an example of only one)*

6. *Today, _____ (rather than _____ or _____) is now considered the most effective guarantor of a long-term monopoly.*

    A. Fill in the blanks: _____, _____, _____.

    B. Explain:

7. Three characteristics of a monopoly (name and define each, then provide an example of only one)*

8. Below in FIGURE 9-16 are the demand curves of two distinctly different market structures.

FIGURE 9-16

Graph A

Graph B

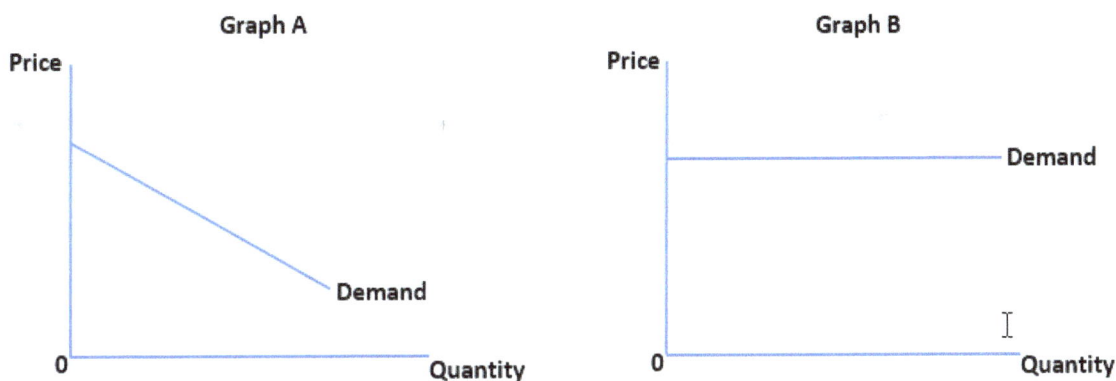

A. Which is that of a price taker? Why?

B. Which is that of a price maker? Why?

9. *price effect* versus *output effect* (define both, then provide a quantitative example of only one)*

10. Based on FIGURE 9-17 below,

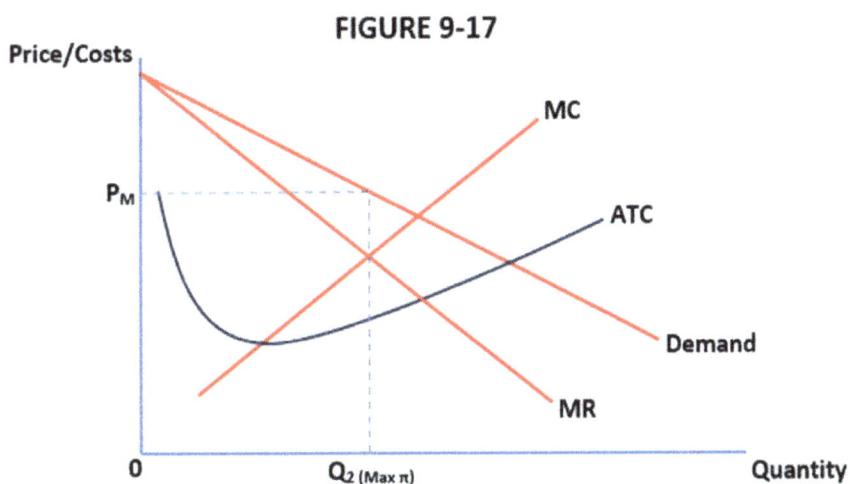

FIGURE 9-17

...*a monopoly maximizes profit by producing where* _____ = _____ *at* _____ *and charges a price of* _____ *per unit produced.*

A. Fill in the blanks: _____, _____, _____, _____.

B. Explain:

11. Based on FIGURE 9-18 below,

FIGURE 9-18

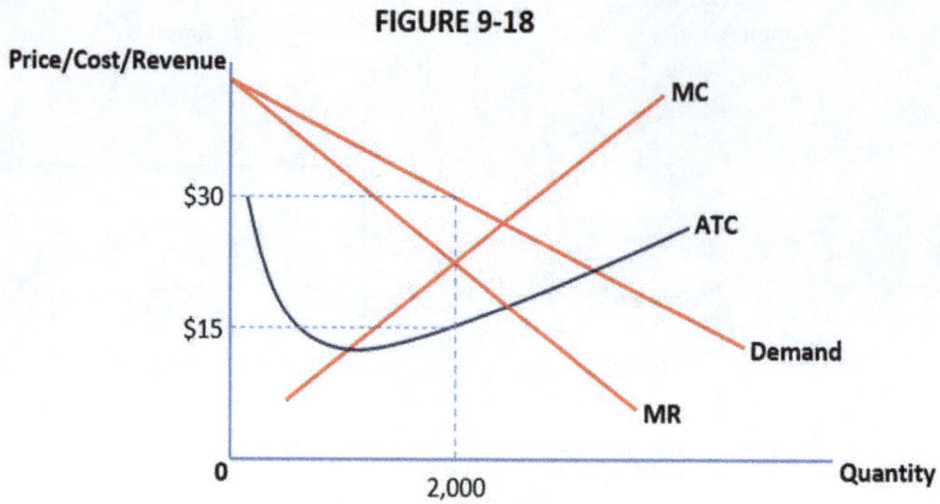

A. Calculate per-unit profit or loss. Show all the steps used to arrive at your final answer.

B. Calculate total profit or loss. Show all the steps used to arrive at your final answer.

12. What is the controversy over whether monopolies (in theory) have supply curves?

13. *brand-name product* vs. *trademark* (define both, then provide an example of only one)*

14. Why don't some brand-name products lose all of their market power after their patents expire?

15. Based on FIGURE 9-19:

FIGURE 9-19

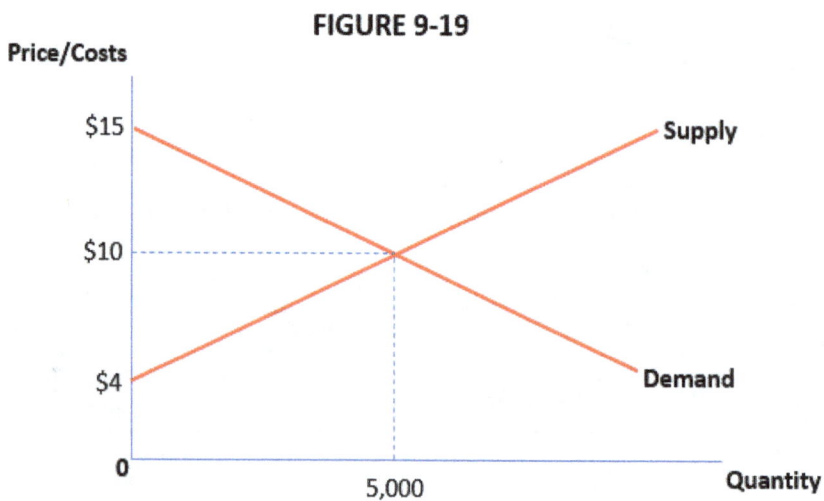

A. Calculate consumer surplus (CS). Show all of the steps used to arrive at your final answer.

B. Calculate producer surplus (PS). Show all of the steps used to arrive at your final answer.

C. Calculate total surplus (TS). Show all of the steps used to arrive at your final answer.

16. Based on FIGURE 9-20,

FIGURE 9-20

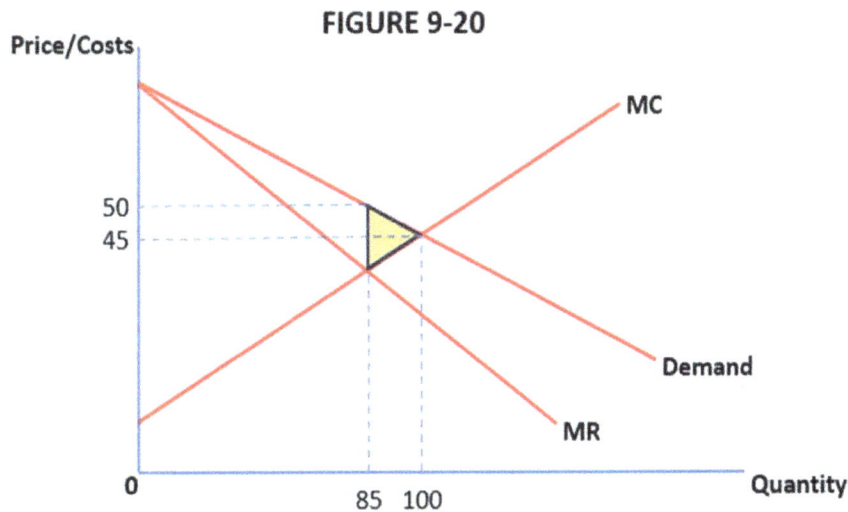

A. Calculate total deadweight loss. Show all of the steps used to arrive at your final answer.

B. Calculate total consumer loss (hint: total consumer loss = old consumer surplus – new consumer surplus). Show all of the steps used to arrive at your final answer.

17. price differentiation (define, then provide a quantitative example)*

18. *What drives price differentiation?* _____ *and* _____.

A. Fill in the blanks: _____, _____.

B. Explain:

19. perfect price differentiation (define, then provide an example)*

20. For FIGURE 9-21:

FIGURE 9-21

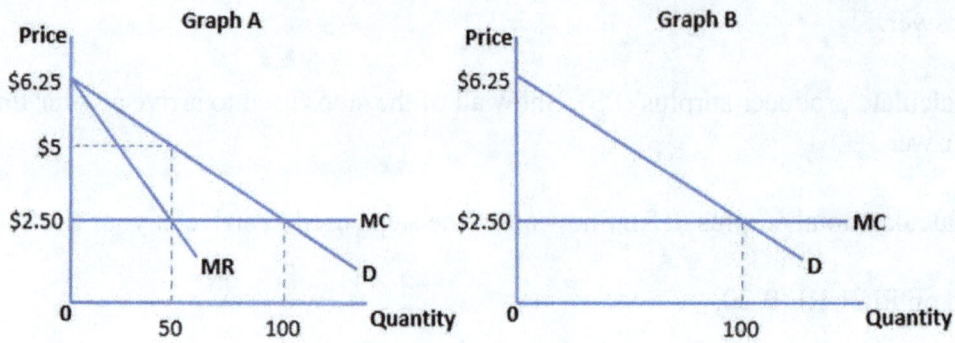

A. Calculate the profit of the standard monopoly depicted in Graph A. Show all of the steps used to arrive at your final answer.

B. Calculate the profit of the perfect price differentiator in Graph B. Show all of the steps used to arrive at your final answer.

C. Which is greater and why?

21. four solutions to the monopoly problem (name and define all four, then provide an example of only one)*

22. creative destruction (define, then provide an example in the area of transportation)*

Chapter 10: Differentiated Competition

10.0 Introduction

A. In chapter 8, we analyzed uniform competition, a market structure with three main features:
1. Many buyers and sellers such that not a single buyer or seller (price taker) can move the market's price either up or down.
2. A product that is uniform (nearly or exactly the same from seller to seller). Examples: 87-octane gasoline, No. 2 pencils, 8.5-inch x 11-inch photocopier or computer printer paper.
3. Individual sellers or firms are able to enter or exit the market at a low cost.

B. In chapter 9, we analyzed monopoly, a market structure with three main features:
1. Many buyers but one seller (a firm or government).
2. A highly differentiated product with no close substitutes, which means that each firm has substantial market power. Examples: electricity, water, and trash collection.
3. Barriers to entry in the short run and long run that include government charters, patents, and copyrights.

C. In this chapter, we analyze a market type that has a mix of features of the previous two that we will call **differentiated competition**.[42] It has the following features:
1. Many buyers and sellers.
2. Differentiated products with close substitutes, which means that each firm has some degree of market power. Example (fast-food pizza): Domino's vs. Papa Johns vs. Pizza Hut vs. Little Caesars.
3. Firms are able to enter or exit the market at a low cost.

> **differentiated competition –** an industry characterized by many buyers and sellers, differentiated products with close substitutes (i.e., each firm has some degree of market power), and firms able to enter or exit the market at a low cost.

Like uniform competition (under which uniform products are sold), differentiated competition is named after the type of differentiated products sold by the firms in the industry.

10.1 Differentiated Competition in the Short Run

Accepting the three assumptions about differentiated competition specified above, we arrive at FIGURE 10-1, which displays two differentiated competitors in the short run, the first one (Graph A) earning a profit and the second one (Graph B) incurring a loss.

---

[42] Other economics literature and books call it "monopolistic competition," which is another old term and misnomer. Among other problems, it confuses many students because it sounds like a contradiction in terms. *Differentiated competition* is a clearer term because it first emphasizes the type of products sold (differentiated) and then highlights competition--many firms that, at a relatively low cost, can enter or exit the market (like uniform competition).

FIGURE 10-1: Differentiated Competition in the Short Run (Profit and Loss)

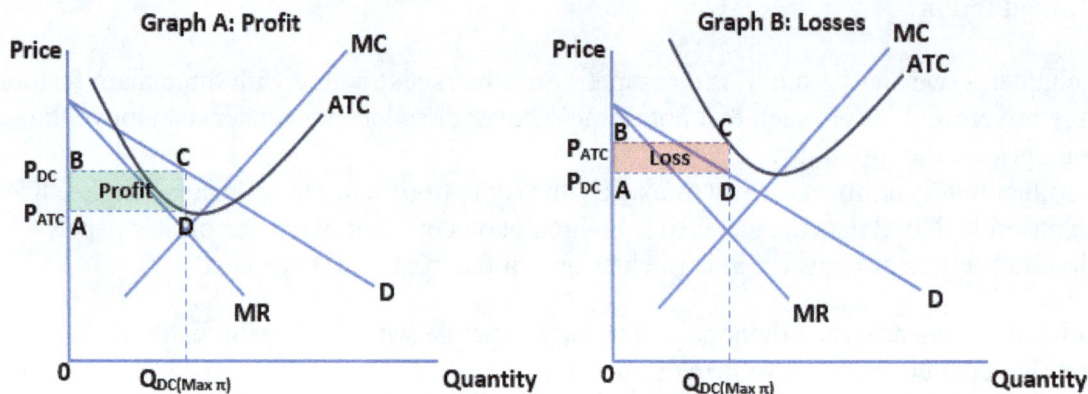

Graph A: Profit

Graph B: Losses

Graph A in FIGURE 10-1 represents a differentiated competitor earning a short-run profit. Like a uniform competitor and monopoly, its profit-maximizing output $Q_{DC(Max\ \pi)}$ (the profit-maximizing output for a differentiated competitor) is where marginal cost (MC) equals marginal revenue (MR). However, like a monopoly, it prices on the demand curve above its profit-maximizing output at P_{DC} (the price charged by a differentiated competitor).

Now that we have the price and quantity of a differentiated competitor, the next item of significance is the firm's profit, per unit and total. Per-unit profit is the vertical difference between price and average-total cost at the profit-maximizing level of output. That distance is represented by line segment $\overline{CD}$ in Graph A of FIGURE 10-1. Total profit is represented by the area of the green profit rectangle, which is height multiplied by length, or line segment $\overline{CD}$ times line segment $\overline{BC}$. (Alternatively, one could multiply line segment $\overline{CD}$ times line segment $\overline{AD}$ or just $Q_{DC(Max\ \pi)}$, as all three represent the length of the profit rectangle just as line segment $\overline{CD}$, line segment $\overline{AB}$, and the vertical distance between P_{DC} and P_{ATC} [P_{DC} - P_{ATC}] represent the height of the profit box.) Keep in mind that a profit, per-unit and total (as represented by the green profit rectangle), can appear in the short run, but it will never last into the long run as, unlike monopoly, entry can and does happen under differentiated competition just like it does under uniform competition.

Graph B in FIGURE 10-1 represents a differentiated competitor earning a short-run loss. Per-unit loss is the vertical difference between average-total cost and price. That distance is represented by line segment $\overline{CD}$ in Graph B of FIGURE 10-1 (or the difference between P_{ATC} and P_{DC}). The total loss is represented by the area of the red loss rectangle, which is height multiplied by length, or line segment $\overline{CD}$ times line segment $\overline{BC}$. (Alternatively, one could multiply line segment $\overline{CD}$ times line segment $\overline{AD}$ or just $Q_{DC(Max\ \pi)}$, as all three represent the length of the profit box just as line segment $\overline{CD}$, line segment $\overline{AB}$, and the vertical distance between P_{ATC} and P_{DC} [P_{ATC} - P_{DC}] represent the height of the profit rectangle.) As with a profit, keep in mind that a loss, per-unit and total (as represented by the red loss rectangle), can appear in the short run, but it will never last into the long run as the most marginal firms will exit the industry by the arrival of the long run.

Regardless of these differences between short-run profit and loss, differentiated competition in which a profit is earned over the short run (Graph A of FIGURE 10-1) and monopoly over the short run are analytically identical. It is the long run that separates the two, and we will discuss this distinction in the next section.

10.2 Differentiated Competition in the Long Run

From FIGURE 10-1's scenarios of profit and loss in the short run, we now move to the long run. Here, assumption three of this market structure (see section 10.0) is key: "Firms are able to enter or exit the market at a relatively low cost." As under uniform competition, this assumption affects firms earning a profit or loss. If the differentiated competitor resembles the firm in Graph A of FIGURE 10-1 (profit), as under uniform competition, new firms begin to be attracted to the industry to grab a portion of its profit. As firms enter the industry, incumbent firms each see the demand for their product fall (i.e., their demand and marginal revenue curves shift leftward. As this leftward shift continues, positive economic profit declines more and more until it reaches zero. As economic profit for the industry reaches zero, the entry of new firms into the industry ends and each firm in the industry looks like the firm illustrated in FIGURE 10-2.

If the differentiated competitor resembles the firm in Graph B of FIGURE 10-1 (loss), as under uniform competition, marginal incumbent firms begin to exit the industry to escape its negative profit (loss). As marginal firms exit the market, incumbent firms each see the demand for their product rise (i.e., their demand and marginal revenue curves shift rightward). As this rightward shift continues, economic loss declines more and more until it reaches zero. As negative economic profit for the industry rises to zero economic profit, firms stop exiting the industry and each firm looks like the firm illustrated in FIGURE 10-2.

FIGURE 10-2: Differentiated Competition in the Long Run (Zero Economic Profit)

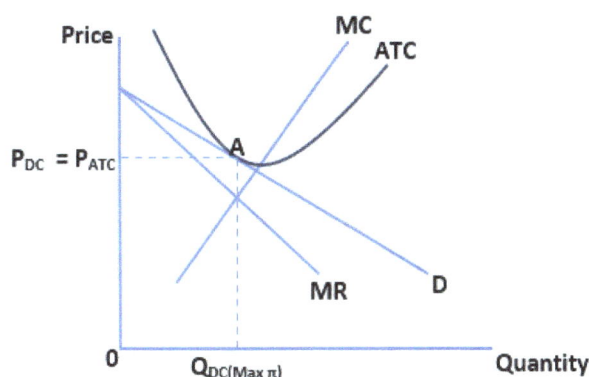

Notice a couple of aspects of FIGURE 10-2 *per se*: now that entry or exit are complete, the ATC curve and the demand curve (D) are tangent (i.e., they touch each other without crossing) at point *A*. This tendency is absolutely necessary for there to be zero economic profit in the industry. Notice that it also occurs, if you look down the dashed line toward the Quantity axis where MC = MR. This is because the differentiated competitor is producing a quantity that maximizes profit and is pricing on the demand curve above the profit-maximizing output.

Two concluding points about differentiated competition in the long run:

1. P > MC as it is under a monopoly. This occurs because, as with a monopoly, the firm has some degree of market power. This degree of market power causes the demand curve to slope downward, which in turn causes the marginal-revenue curve to slope downward as well, but at a steeper slope than the demand curve. The profit-maximizing firm (no matter the market structure) will produce output where MC = MR, and because market power allows firms to price on the demand curve, P > MR = MC, or just P > MC for short.

2. P = ATC as it is under uniform competition. This occurs because, just like a uniform competitor, entry and exit in this market can be accomplished at a relatively low cost. If there is an economic profit in the short run, firms will enter the industry and this entry will drive demand down for each firm's product until firm demand falls to the level of where it is tangent to the ATC curve, where economic profit equals zero. If there is an economic loss in the short run, firms will exit the industry and this exit will increase demand for each firm's product until firm demand rises to the level of where it is tangent to the ATC curve, where economic profit equals zero.

10.3 The Two Competitions Compared

FIGURE 10-3 is a comparison between uniform competition, which we analyzed in detail in chapter 8 and the differentiated competition that we are analyzing in this chapter. In Graph A of FIGURE 10-3, we see that under uniform competition, profit maximization leads the uniform competitor to produce the level of output where MC = MR at quantity Q_{UC} and charge price P_{UC} at the lowest point of ATC (known as efficient scale, a concept we encountered in chapter 8).

In Graph B of FIGURE 10-3, we see that under differentiated competition, profit maximization leads the firm to produce the level of output where MC = MR at quantity Q_{DC} and charge price P_{DC} at the point of tangency between the demand curve (D) and ATC curve (point A). Point A represents output Q_{DC}, which is below the level of output represented by point B (Q_{ES}), which lies at efficient scale. The difference between Q_{ES} and Q_{DC} (Q_{ES} - Q_{DC}) is known as **excess capacity**, the difference between the level of output that a differentiated competitor would produce at efficient scale and the level of output that a differentiated competitor actually produces.

excess capacity – the difference between the level of output that a differentiated competitor would produce at efficient scale and the level of output that a differentiated competitor actually produces.

FIGURE 10-3: Uniform Versus Differentiated Competition in the Long Run (Zero Economic Profit)

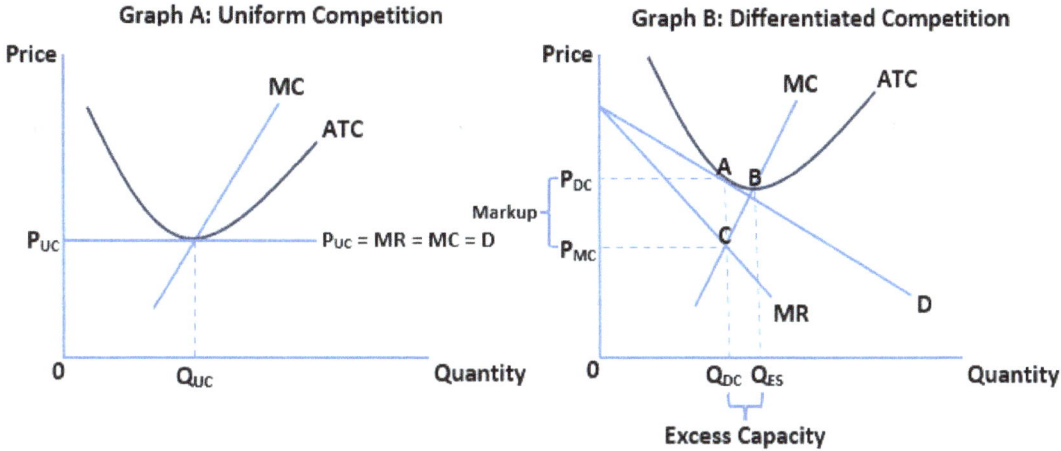

Graph A: Uniform Competition

Graph B: Differentiated Competition

In Graph A of FIGURE 10-3, we see that under uniform competition, P_{UC} = MC while in Graph B, for the differentiated competitor, P_{DC} > MC (or equivalently, P_{DC} > P_{MC}). The differentiated competitor sells its product at a **markup** (P_{DC} - P_{MC}, or line segment $\overline{AC}$), or the difference between the price a differentiated competitor charges and where price is equal to

markup – the difference between the price a differentiated competitor charges and where price is equal to marginal cost for a differentiated competitor.

marginal cost for a differentiated competitor. After all entry or exit of firms into or out of a differentially competitive industry is completed in the short run, demand adjusts so that ATC is just tangent to demand. While entry and exit at relatively low cost forced P to equal ATC, it does not (in the presence of market power) force P to equal MC.

10.4 Differentiated Competition versus Monopoly

FIGURE 10-4: Monopoly Versus Differentiated Competition in the Long Run (Positive versus Zero Economic Profit)

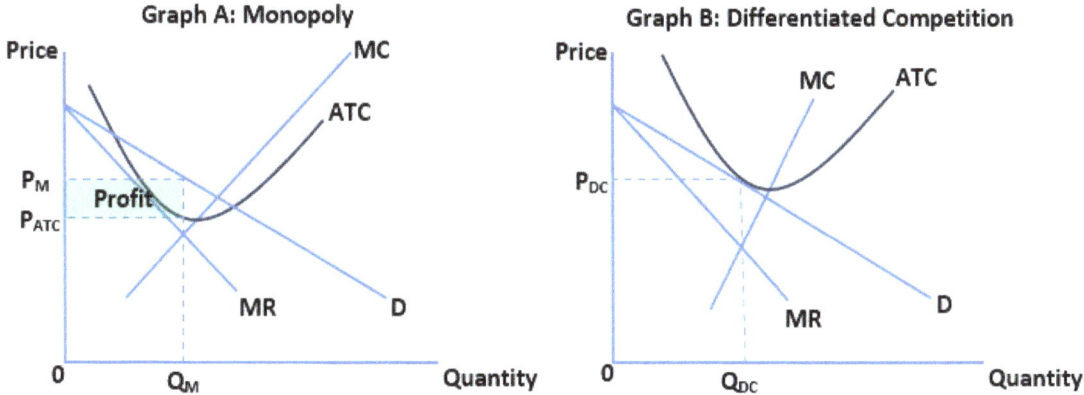

Graph A: Monopoly

Graph B: Differentiated Competition

To close out our market-structure comparisons, FIGURE 10-4 compares a monopoly to a differentiated competitor in the long run. The most obvious difference is the existence of per-unit and total profit in the long run for the monopoly (see green profit box in Graph A of FIGURE 10-4) but not a differentiated competitor. This state of affairs exists because a differentiated competitor is threatened with entry by new firms if profit exists in its industry in the short run, whereas a monopoly is shielded from entry in both the short run and long run, thus its profit exists in the long run.

10.5 Differentiated Competition and Social Welfare

While a uniformly competitive industry produces a socially efficient market outcome and monopolies create deadweight losses, what is the verdict on differentiated competition? First, because it prices above marginal cost (P > MC), and consumers who want to purchase the product at or above marginal cost but not at the level of price will go without the product, differentiated competition creates deadweight loss. Politicians could create laws that would force differentiated competitors to sell their products at marginal cost, but because differentiated products are so common this would be prohibitively costly. Taxes would have to be substantially raised and new taxes implemented to pay for the large bureaucracy that would be tasked with enforcing this likely impossible mandate would entail and increase deadweight loss as well.

Second, forcing prices to equal marginal cost returns us to the same problem created when natural monopolies (if they really exist) have their prices driven down to the level of marginal cost. If a monopolistic competitor is earning zero economic profit in the long run, then forcing it to price at the level of marginal cost forces it to earn economic losses. If the firm is not compensated for these losses, it will have no choice but to exit the industry. Taxes can be enacted or raised to generate subsidies given to the firm to cover its losses, but these create deadweight losses as well.

externality - a positive or negative effect a firm creates by its production that is external to that production and has a social cost or benefit.

product-variety externality - the positive benefit to consumers of having an additional product from which to choose as the result of a new firm in an industry.

business-stealing externality – in an industry, the movement of sales and market share away from incumbent firms to new entrants.

A possible **externality** is another consideration. An externality is a positive or negative effect a firm creates by its production that is external to that production and has a social cost or benefit. The first type of externality relevant to differentiated competition is what is known as the **product-variety externality**, the positive benefit to consumers of having an additional product from which to choose as the result of a new firm in an industry. The second type of externality is the **business-stealing externality**, or in an industry, the movement of sales and market share away from incumbent firms to new entrants. According to some economists, under differentiated competition an industry can have too many or too few firms depending on which of these two types of externalities is larger. If the business-stealing externality outweighs the product-variety externality, then the market has too many firms. If the product-variety externality outweighs the business-stealing externality, then the market has too few firms.

First, even if it were straightforward as how to measure the size of these externalities, how would the supposed problem they create even begin to be remedied? Second, it is far from crystal clear that excess capacity and markups are a problem to begin with. They only appear as alleged shortcomings in comparison to uniformly competitive markets (markets in generic goods). Consumers consistently prefer differentiated products to generic ones. If not, there would consistently be no difference in quality between store brands and name brands. While that is sometimes the case, at many other times it is certainly not. It all depends on…the product! Excess capacity and markups could be the tradeoff or cost of greater product variety. As long as consumers have a choice between differentiated products and generic products and between name brands and store brands, they will be better off choosing one or the other on a product-by-product basis.

What is clear is that under differentiated competition, where there is a markup (P_{DC} - P_{MC}; see FIGURE 10-3, Graph B), customer service is better. The additional customer in the shop who pays the full price for a differentiated product adds to the firm's profit (since P > MC) and hence is a valued customer. Under uniform competition (where P = MC), the next customer in the farmers' market who pays the market price for a sack of potatoes adds nothing to marginal economic profit, and thus is not appreciated much by the firm.

10.6 Advertising: Socially Beneficial or Wasteful?

As discussed at the end of the previous section, because under differentiated competition P > MC and this generates marginal profits for the firm, new customers are valued. **Advertising** is information about a product or a person running for political office. For firms producing products, advertising is an important means for generating new customers. Throughout the history of economics, there have been divergent views on the benefits versus costs of advertising.

advertising - information about a product or a person running for political office.

Con. The anti-advertising view, more prevalent among economists of the past than now, is that advertising only works to manipulate preferences toward a certain product rather than convey a true difference in quality or price. For example, television commercials for beer, run typically on Fall Sundays during NFL games, will show something like a man alone in his home watching television. After he opens a can of a particular brand (say, Old Milwaukee), bikini-clad women burst into his home and carry him off into the sunset. This is misleading entertainment at best that does not increase the well-being of the consumer, it just gives consumers a more positive view of a particular brand that is usually completely unmerited *vis-à-vis* competing brands. Further, continuing with our current example, Old Milwaukee's advertising encourages competing brands to retaliate by each advertising their own brands' illusory superiority over their competitors. This is misleading and wasteful because beer is beer and there are few real differences between brands. Thus, advertising does little more than decrease the price-sensitivity of demand for certain brands and products and boost firm profits with little in return to consumers.

Economists who have a more favorable view of advertising argue that, first, advertising depends on the product. Consumer goods are advertised far more than producer goods (restaurant supplies to heavy machinery) with the only exception being the type of goods sold under uniform competition such as flour, salt, sugar, and corn. Second, in terms of waste, firms selling products that are heavily advertised such as personal care (shampoos to deodorants to cosmetics), movies, automobiles, and prescription pharmaceuticals, on average spend approximately 15% of their revenue on advertisements. In terms of the entire U.S. economy, only about 2% of the revenue earned by all firms is spent on advertisements of all kinds (television, Internet, highway billboards, e-mail, and postal mail).

Pro.

1. Information. Yes, some advertisements are meant to entertain or exaggerate product differences, but many also provide valuable information: new products that are better than current products, the existence of new technologies, and the arrival of new drugs that are superior to all the old options. Local advertising via radio, television, and direct mail alerts residents to new stores in town that can serve their needs (gasoline to groceries to clothes tailoring) better than previous alternatives. What advertising can do for consumers it can also do for entrepreneurs and firms: alert them to better suppliers, software that can automate their customer billing and supplier payments.

2. Facilitating competition. Advertising has either two effects:

A. It makes consumers view products as much more distinct from one another than consumers would otherwise view them. This in turn makes the demand for advertised products more price insensitive and this in turn raises the prices and profits earned on advertised products.

B. Or…advertising provides more information to consumers that allows them to more quickly discover firms offering the products they want at the lowest prices. Competitive forces cause consumer demands to be more price sensitive and prices and profits to fall.

So which effect have economists found? Evidence favoring the second effect was provided by a study published in 1972 conducted by economist Lee Benham. Benham noticed that some states prohibited optometrists from advertising their services of eye exams and glasses fittings while other states allowed it. At the end of his study, what Benham found was that in states where advertising of optometric services was forbidden, prices were approximately 27% higher on average than they were in states that allowed advertising.

Jeffrey Milyo and Joel Waldfogel undertook a similar study to that of Benham's but of liquor stores in the state of Rhode Island, which were allowed to advertise their services after 1996 compared to those in the state of Massachusetts, which were forbidden to advertise. Not only did prices in Rhode Island drop more than 20% after advertising began, but the stores that advertised attracted far more customers, which lends support to the informational view of advertising.

These studies and more over the last 50 years have led to the gradual repeals of laws in certain states forbidding advertising among certain occupations (e.g., physicians, surgeons, attorneys, and pharmacists). Legislatures and judges came to discover that bans on advertising among older members of these professional groups had the actual intent of decreasing competition and protecting established firms from aggressive new entrants.

The informational aspects of advertising do not apply to just consumers. Entrepreneurs and marketing departments at different firms carefully monitor the advertisements created by their competitors. This gives them important information about competitor strategy and thus facilitates a response whereby they can respond to their competitor on the basis of lower price, higher quality, superior features, superior customer service, or a new and improved product line.

3. Signal of quality. What has also been found is the counterintuitive view that advertising serves as a signal of product quality, even if the information value in the ad is low and the ad is little more than a humorous skit with a celebrity endorsing the product.

Let's say that both Krispy Kreme and Dunkin' have plans to introduce a new flavor of doughnut to the national market. The new doughnuts will sell at $15 per dozen with a marginal cost of only $5, therefore profit will end up being $10 per dozen. The marketing departments at both firms project that $20 million in advertising will get one million dozen doughnuts sold initially, and if consumers like the product, one million dozen sold each month for five more months. In other words, if the product is a hit, the firm earns $60 million in profit. If the product is a bomb (i.e., consumers only purchase the new product once), the firm only earns $10 million in profit.

In test markets, Krispy Kreme discovers that consumers are very indifferent about its new flavor of doughnut. While it's not bad, it is also not anything that is as attractive as its current most popular flavors. Does Krispy Kreme decide to release the new doughnut anyway? No, because it would be spending $20 million on advertising to only earn $10 million in profit. On the other hand, at Dunkin', not only do market tests reveal that consumers are absolutely wild about its new doughnut flavor but they can barely wait for its national release. Dunkin releases the new doughnut, spends $20 million on advertising featuring professional-basketball star LeBron James endorsing the new doughnut, and earns $60 million profit.

What this parable about two rival doughnut sellers reveals is that advertising can have little informational value about the price, ingredients, or calorie counts of each doughnut. It can be nothing but an entertaining clip of LeBron James eating a doughnut, giving a thumbs up sign, and dunking a basketball. However, the expense behind the ad can convey to consumers that Dunkin' is making a serious investment that it would never undertake unless it was very sure that it would recover its expenditure plus a profit. Dunkin' cannot do that pushing a substandard or untested product. This is why products advertised in expensive time slots (prime-time network shows with high ratings, professional sports games, the NFL Super Bowl, etc.) tend to be products of high quality in the markets in which they sell. Advertising is an investment and firms that don't consistently recover their investments with high-quality products don't stay in business long.

4. Brand-name products. What can be established through advertising is a brand-name product, a product that (as we first saw in chapter 9) sells under a well-known and usually trademarked name and logo that serves as a guarantee of higher quality. As with advertising, the thinking on brand names has become more positive as more data and studies of them have been developed. Early on, some economists such as Edward Chamberlin (1899-1967) were opposed to brand name-products because they thought that brand-name products provided no higher value to consumers than generic or store-brand products. Consumers only perceived a higher value because of advertising and therefore paid higher prices for brand-name products.

More recently, economists see brand names as serving the dual roles of signaling quality and second, creating a business reputation that firms have an incentive to defend by maintaining quality. When a firm loses its reputation because it has let quality slip, it loses its business because consumers no longer see it as a reliable provider of quality goods or services. The tarnished firm's products are no longer perceived as worth their higher price in comparison to generic or lower-quality goods, and the firm's profits decline.

A very good example of a firm that started out well but suffered a blow to its reputation is Chipotle Mexican Grill. Between 2012 and 2015, the firm received good ratings from consumers for fresh, high-quality food, and good value.[43] Then a string of unfortunate incidents struck the firm that hasn't really let up until perhaps recently. Beginning in July 2015, a store in Seattle disseminated E. coli tainted food that sickened five customers. The next month (August 2015) a store in Simi Valley, California spread norovirus that sickened at least 234 customers. That same month and the next (September 2015), tomatoes at a location in Minnesota spread salmonella that sickened 64 customers. Then came two back-to-back E. coli outbreaks, the first and larger one running through eleven states from October to December 2015 that sickened 55 patrons and the second and smaller one in three states from November to December 2015 that sickened five people. As if that weren't bad enough, in December 2015 and March 2016, norovirus spread through two Massachusetts locations. As late as July 2024, the company was hit with another scandal: accusations that some locations were serving portion sizes smaller than stated on menus and advertisements.

In stark contrast is Chick-fil-A. Whether it is at a stand-alone store near a mall or in an airport, the experience is just about the same regardless of city or state. The only scandal that has touched the chain was in 2012 when there were news reports that the firm donated to anti-LGBT groups and its CEO Dan Cathy stated that he opposed gay marriage. Despite there being no serious ramifications to the scandal in terms of lost sales and profits, there has been no scandal since then that has affected the company. Only minor frustration from some customers that its stores are not open on Sundays.

Consumer behavior suggests that brand names are a market creation themselves that are a symbol of quality. Besides this apparent reality being confirmed by numerous studies, if brand names consistently failed to offer a difference in quality over generic or store-brand goods, they would quickly disappear as consumers would automatically gravitate toward lower-priced goods or services without fear of receiving lower quality. Yes, lower prices can sometimes signal a desire to reduce inventory (see our previous discussion of BOGOF sales in chapter 1) and good value. But as well-experienced shoppers also know, they can also signal a lower-quality good. It is an economic principle that you tend to get what you pay for ["There ain't no such thing as a free lunch," principle 1 in chapter 1 of this book, a.k.a., Every action has a cost (tradeoff)] and a suspiciously low price is sometimes a circumstance of "too good to be true."

10.7 Conclusion

This chapter began with a comparison between uniform competition, monopoly, and differentiated competition. We then examined differentiated competition, the subject of this chapter, in the short run and long run. Then, after graphically comparing uniform competition and monopoly to differentiated competition, we discussed differentiated competition and its implications for societal well-being. After this, the pros and cons of advertising were discussed as well as brand names. Since the chapter began with a verbal comparison of the three different

[43] Goldstein, Li. "When Did We Fall Out of Love With Chipotle?" *Bon Appetit*. 30 November 2023. <https://archive.ph/mZXRm#selection-2587.128-2587.143>

types of market structure that have been discussed so far in this book, it only seems fitting to end this chapter with a comparison in tabular form of uniform competition, monopoly, and differentiated competition.

TABLE 10-1: Summary of Market Structures (Uniform Competition, Monopoly, and Differentiated Competition)			
	Uniform Competition	**Monopoly**	**Differentiated Competition**
Product	Uniform	Differentiated	Differentiated
Quantity of firms	Many	One	Many
Firm Goal	Maximize profits	Maximize profits	Maximize profits
Output Level	MC = MR	MC = MR	MC = MR
Some Degree of Market Power Present?	No	Yes	Yes
Relation of price to MC	P = MC	P > MC	P > MC
Deadweight loss present?	No	Yes	Yes
Economic profit is possible in the short run?	Yes	Yes	Yes
Economic profit is possible in the long run?	No	Yes	No
Advertise?	No	Little to none.	A lot.

10.8 Chapter Concepts

differentiated competition
excess capacity
markup
externality
product-variety externality
business-stealing externality
advertising

10.9 Problems, Questions, and Discussion Topics (Items Requiring Examples are Marked with an Asterisk [*])

1. Three characteristics of differentiated competition (name and define all three, then provide a real-world example not found in the chapter)*

2. Why do economic profits disappear for differentiated competitors by the long run?

3. Differentiated competition shares some features with uniform competition. What are they? Explain each in detail.

4. Based on FIGURE 10-5 below,

FIGURE 10-5

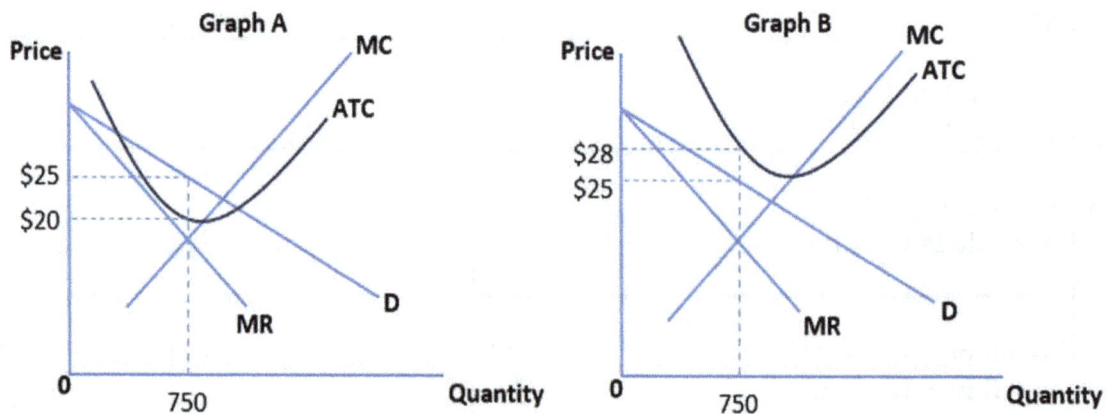

A. Calculate short-run profit. Show all of the steps used to arrive at your final answer.

B. Calculate the short-run loss. Show all of the steps used to arrive at your final answer.

5. Based on FIGURE 10-6 below,

FIGURE 10-6

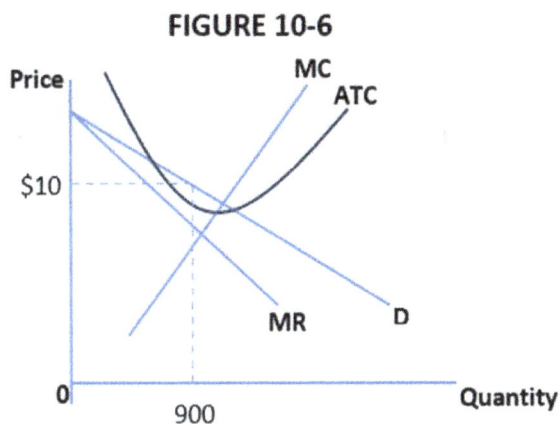

A. Calculate long-run total revenue. Show all of the steps used to arrive at your final answer.

B. Calculate profit or loss. Show all of the steps used to arrive at your final answer.

6. excess capacity (define, then provide a quantitative example)*

7. markup (define, then provide a quantitative example)*

8. Differentiated competition shares some features with monopoly. What are they? Explain each in detail.

9. *product-variety externality* versus *business-stealing externality*

   A. While some economists may look at these two concepts as a guide to determining an industry's optimal size, what is a potential problem with that approach?

   B. While some economists may look at excess capacity and markups as a sign of too few firms in an industry, what is a potential problem with that approach?

10. Regarding advertising,

    A. What is the "socially wasteful" argument against advertising?

    B. What are the four "socially beneficial" arguments for advertising?

11. Regarding advertising,

A. In what way has it been misleading to you (don't forget to include political campaigns, job resumes, and online dating profiles).

B. In what way has it been beneficial to you (don't forget ads for new products, help wanted ads, and online dating profiles that were actually honest).

12. What did economist Lee Benham find with respect to prices in states that allowed optometrists to advertise their services versus prices in states that forbid optometrists to advertise?

13. What did Jeffrey Milyo and Joel Waldfogel find with respect to liquor prices in Rhode Island, which allowed liquor stores to advertise, versus liquor prices in Massachusetts, which banned liquor stores from advertising?

14. How can advertising serve as a signal of quality?

15. *More recently, economists see _____ as serving the dual roles of _____ and second, creating a _____ that firms have an incentive to defend by maintaining quality.*

A. Fill in the blanks: _____, _____, _____.

B. Explain:

Chapter 11: Duopoly, Oligopoly, Cartels, Game Theory, and Antitrust Policy

11.0 Introduction

A. In chapter 8, we analyzed uniform competition, a market structure with three main features:
1. Many buyers and sellers such that not a single buyer or seller (price taker) can move the market's price either up or down.
2. A product that is uniform (nearly or exactly the same from seller to seller). Examples: 87-octane gasoline, No. 2 pencils, 8.5-inch x 11-inch photocopier or computer printer paper.
3. Individual sellers or firms are able to enter or exit the market at a low cost.

Uniform competition is named after the uniform products sold by the firms in the industry. It is also known elsewhere as "perfect" competition.

B. In chapter 9, we analyzed monopoly, a market structure with three main features:
1. Many buyers but one seller (a firm or government).
2. A highly differentiated product with no close substitutes, which means that each firm has substantial market power. Examples: electricity, water, and trash collection.
3. Barriers to entry in the short run and long run that include government charters, patents, and copyrights.

C. In chapter 10, we analyzed differentiated competition, a market structure with three main features:
1. Many buyers and sellers.
2. Differentiated products with close substitutes, which means that each firm has some degree of market power. For example, in fast-food pizza: Domino's, Papa Johns, Pizza Hut, Little Caesars, Marco's, Hunt Brothers.
3. Firms are able to enter or exit the market at a low cost.

Like uniform competition (under which uniform products are sold), differentiated competition is named after the type of differentiated products sold by the firms in the industry. It is known elsewhere as "monopolistic" competition.

D. In this chapter, we analyze three overlapping market types known as duopoly, cartel, and oligopoly. Because firms can exhibit interdependence and strategic choice in these market structures, we also introduce the topic of game theory.

A **duopoly** is an industry in which two firms produce and sell uniform to similar products. An **oligopoly** is an industry in which two to several firms produce and sell uniform to similar products. A **cartel** is an industry of two to several firms that behaves like a monopoly through either **government protection** (government laws or regulations that ban the entry of new firms into an industry) or **collusion** (voluntary close coordination of production and pricing decisions among an industry's members).

duopoly - an industry in which two firms produce and sell uniform to similar products.

oligopoly - an industry in which two to several firms produce and sell uniform to similar products.

cartel - an industry of two to several firms that behaves like a monopoly through either government protection or industry collusion.

government protection - government laws or regulations that ban the entry of new firms into an industry.

collusion - voluntary close coordination of production and pricing decisions among an industry's members.

ECONOMICS IN ACTION: the Two Most Dangerous Cartels?

I. Democratic-Republican-Party Cartel (Horizontal, Government-Protected Cartel)

Both parties currently control about 99 percent of elective party offices in the U.S. and have openly colluded over decades to cement their dominance over potential competitors by giving each other at least the following barriers to entry:

1. **Ballot-access laws** – laws requiring a minimum number of citizen signatures for a candidate's name to be on a ballot. *Per se*, there is nothing wrong with such laws (there is only such much room on a ballot) except that potential competitors have complained that the number of signatures required in many states is onerous and the amount of time to require them is purposefully inadequate.
2. **Front-loaded primaries** – primaries or caucuses held earlier and earlier in the election season to favor incumbents or party-establishment connected candidates with high name recognition provided by legacy mainstream corporate news and social media.
3. **Proportional allocation of party delegates** – the awarding of delegates in primaries by declining portions from winner on down (e.g., winner gets 60 percent of delegates, second place gets 30 percent, third place gets 5 percent, etc.). This barrier serves two purposes: first, it favors establishment-connected candidates and second, it makes a comeback against an opponent with a lead more difficult.
4. **Superdelegates (Democratic party only)** - created in 1984, these are party politicians currently holding office or party employees whose function is to block "unacceptable" candidates from becoming the party's nominee. They are authorized to publicly endorse candidates early in the primary season to tip the scale and media coverage toward establishment-favored candidates.
5. **Massive multi-state primary contests such as Super Tuesday and Super Tuesday 2** – these are multi-state primaries that overwhelmingly favor high-name-recognition, establishment-connected candidates. Outsider candidates have just about zero chance of winning these.
6. **Early voting** – voting weeks to months before election day favors incumbents and establishment-connected candidates with high name recognition and favorable mainstream-corporate-legacy-news and social-media coverage.
7. **Collusion is promoted, competition denigrated** – calls for "bipartisanship," "unity," and "compromise to get things done" aim to preserve the status quo as much as bludgeons of "grandstanding," "rogue behavior," and "brinkmanship."

All of these aforementioned actions are illegal under various state and federal antitrust laws, starting with The Sherman Antitrust Act of 1890. Further, this cartel more than any other is completely immune to prosecution by the vertically integrated Antitrust Division of the U.S. Department of Justice (DOJ) controlled and staffed by the Democratic-Republican cartel.

Dangerous because: It possesses the launch codes to 5,044 nuclear warheads[1] that could end human civilization, has run up a current national debt of $37 trillion[2] with no realistic plan to control its current rate of growth and avert national bankruptcy, and has actively cemented its dominance as a cartel by harnessing the power of government to create laws and regulations that exclude effective competitors.

II. U.S. Health-Care Industry [American Medical Association (AMA)-American Hospital Association (AHA) Cartel] (Vertical, Government-Protected Cartel)

AMA (physicians): The AMA half of the cartel was formed in 1910 in the wake of the Flexner Report, part of AMA's vision to create a monopoly of allopathic (M.D.) medical-school accreditation and limit entrance to substantially increase physician incomes and prestige as an occupational and social class. In 1910 there were 166 schools, by 1940 only 77 (54% reduction) with most rural schools closed and all black schools closed except two.

Pharmacists, who competed with physicians were banned from making diagnoses, writing prescriptions, and writing prescription refills. Midwives, who assisted women in childbirth and who women preferred, were highly restricted to banned depending on the state. Medical charity (*pro bono* physician and hospital services) was substantially restricted.

In 1910-1963, the U.S. population more than doubled from 92 to 189 million. Yet in 1963 the number of physicians *per capita* in the U.S. stood at 146/100,000, the same level as 1910 and lower than 1860 = 175/100,000. Of the approximately 375,000 physicians in practice in 1977, only about 6,300 or 1.7% were black.

AHA (hospitals): founded in 1898. At the time of the Flexner Report (1910), about 60% of hospitals were for-profit institutions but by 1968, only 11% were (82% reduction). For-profit medical schools and hospitals had owners and shareholders focused on minimizing cost and unnecessary waste to maximize profit. In contrast, AMA (through AHA) favored nonprofit medical schools and hospitals, which were much more agreeable to implementing much longer and costlier M.D. programs because they were a more effective barrier to entry to the profession. Later, medical residencies began to be funded through Medicare as another brilliant barrier to entry.

Health "Insurance:" for-profit hospital insurance began in the timber and mining industries of Oregon and Washington. In these plans, adjusters closely monitored tests, procedures, and hospital stays. Physician groups rejected these in favor of Blue Shield (1939), created by physicians, and Blue Cross (1929), created by hospitals, which had little adjuster oversight and cost control (a pseudo-insurance rather than genuine insurance). AMA lobbying created many government advantages for the Blues including but not limited to: no or low premium taxes, sometimes no property taxes, no minimum benefit to premium ratios, and no or low required reserves. In 1982, Blue Cross and Blue Shield merged with no antitrust challenge to the merger.

Dangerous because: It routinely limits access to lifesaving medical treatments through artificial scarcity of physicians, surgeons, hospitals, lifesaving drugs, and cadaveric transplant organs to maintain cartel profit. Studies estimate that there are 250,000 to 440,000 total[3,4] or, on average, 685 to 1,205 unnecessary deaths in U.S. hospitals *per day*. This makes preventable medical error the third leading cause of death in the U.S.[5] For a measure of comparison, the largest passenger airplane in the world, the Airbus A380, carries 525 passengers on an average flight. An A380 crash every day with no survivors for a year (191,625 deaths) would not equal the most conservative estimate of how many of its customers the U.S. medical cartel negligently kills every year (250,000), which is also more than four times the number of U.S. military casualties 58,220[6] in the 20-year Vietnam war (1955-1975).

References
1 Federation of American Scientists (FAS). "America's Nuclear Weapons Arsenal 2024: Annual Overview Released by the Federation of American Scientists." 7 May 2024. <https://fas.org/publication/nuclear-weapons-2024/>
2 U.S. Treasury. "What is the National Debt?" *FiscalData*. <https://fiscaldata.treasury.gov/americas-finance-guide/national-debt/>
3 Makary, Martin and Michael Daniel. "Medical Error—the Third Leading Cause of Death in the U.S." *TheBMJ*. 03 May 2016. <https://www.bmj.com/content/353/bmj.i2139>
4 James, John T. "A New, Evidence-based Estimate of Patient Harms Associated with Hospital Care." *Journal of Patient Safety*. September 2013. <https://journals.lww.com/journalpatientsafety/Fulltext/2013/09000/A_New,_Evidence_based_Estimate_of_Patient_Harms.2.aspx>
5 Sipherd, Ray. "The Third-Leading Cause of Death in U.S. Most Doctors Don't Want You to Know About." *CNBC*. 22 February 2018. https://www.cnbc.com/2018/02/22/medical-errors-third-leading-cause-of-death-in-america.html
6 U.S. National Archives and Records Administration. "Vietnam War U.S. Military Fatal Casualty Statistics." https://www.archives.gov/research/military/vietnam-war/casualty-statistics

11.1 Cartelization and its Discontents

A **government-protected cartel** is an industry of two to several firms that behaves like a monopoly because of government protection from outside competition. The production and pricing decisions of government-protected cartels are similar to those of

government-protected cartel
- an industry of two to several firms that behaves like a monopoly because of government protection from outside competition.

government-chartered monopolies. This makes sense since a government-chartered monopoly is a single firm protected from competition by law while a government-protected cartel is two or more firms protected from competition by law. In the United States, the two most prominent and powerful government-protected cartels are the political industry (Democratic-Republican-party cartel) and the health-care industry [American Medical Association (AMA)-American Hospital Association (AHA) cartel].

The Democrats and Republicans over time have given themselves a host of legal advantages that allow them control of about 99 percent of elective political offices in the U.S. (see the boxed exhibit above for further details). The American Medical Association (AMA)-American Hospital Association (AHA) have, using state and federal laws since 1910, greatly restricted the supply of licensed medical schools, doctors, and hospitals to greatly increase physician incomes and hospital profits (again, see the boxed exhibit above for further details).

horizontal cartel – a cartel composed of two or more of the same type of firm.

vertical cartel - a cartel composed of two or more different types of firms.

While both of these cartels are government protected, they differ in composition. The Democrats and Republicans are an example of a **horizontal cartel**. A horizontal cartel is one that is composed of two or more of the same type of firm. The Democrats and Republicans are both political parties. The U.S. health-care industry is an example of a **vertical cartel**. A vertical cartel is one that is composed of two or more different types of firms. The American Medical Association (AMA) represents physician interests while the American Hospital Association (AHA) represents hospital interests.

non-government-protected cartel - an industry of two to several firms that behaves like a monopoly because of collusion.

A **non-government-protected cartel** is an industry of two to several firms that behaves like a monopoly because of collusion. For duopolies, oligopolies, or cartels that are not government protected, because there are two to several (but not many) firms in an industry, each firm is interdependent on the other firms in the industry. Each firm, in contemplating its actions, must take into account how the other firm(s) in the industry will respond. This will eventually bring us to game theory later in this chapter.

Oligopolies (including duopolies) are best off when colluding to form a cartel. The ideal would be to produce the total output that a monopoly would (evenly divided between or among the firms in the industry) and charge the monopoly price. The problem is that there are strong incentives for each individual member of a cartel to undermine the cartel.

For many years, American Machine and Foundry (AMF) and Brunswick were the two major manufacturers of bowling balls in the U.S. Columns 1 and 2 of TABLE 11-1 contain the demand schedule for bowling balls in a U.S. state for a week's time. Columns 3 and 4 contain the total revenue (TR) and marginal cost (MC) at different quantities of bowling balls produced, respectively. While unrealistic, MC is assumed to be $0 at all levels of production for simplicity. With MC = $0, total revenue = profit (TR = π) since

$$profit\ (\pi) = TR - TC,$$

and if for all output levels MC = 0, then TC = 0 and

$$\pi = TR.$$

	TABLE 11-1: The Market for Bowling Balls		
1	2	3	4
Quantity (Q) of balls	Price (P) per ball in $	Total Revenue (TR) in $	Marginal Cost (MC) in $
0	100	0	0
10	90	900	0
20	80	1,600	0
30	70	2,100	0
40	60	2,400	0
50	50	2,500	0
60	40	2,400	0
70	30	2,100	0
80	20	1,600	0
90	10	900	0
100	0	0	0

If the market were uniformly competitive, with just boring generic black bowling balls produced, price would be equal to marginal cost (P = MC) and 100 balls would be produced with $0 revenue and hence $0 profit. While there are no costs, there is no revenue and hence no profit, an economic break-even situation. A monopoly can do far better by maximizing TR (and hence π) by producing 50 balls and selling them for $50 each to earn a maximum TR or π of $2,500 (see column 3 of TABLE 11-1).

If AMF and Brunswick both want to produce and sell in this market, their best course of action is to collude and perform jointly just like a monopoly: AMF would produce 25 balls, Brunswick would produce 25 balls, and each firm would earn ($2,500 ÷ 2 =) $1,250 TR and profit if the balls were priced at $50 each. What follows from this is, despite the fact that this industry is truly comprised of two firms, they are in effect operating as a monopoly and all the adverse social-welfare effects of monopoly we discussed in chapter 9 apply: underproduction, P > MC pricing, and deadweight loss.

Old AMF Advertisement Emphasizing the Potential Appeal of Bowling to Women (AMF, Fair Use)

An AMF Coca-Cola Bowling Ball for Sale on eBay (Unknown, Fair Use)

Collusion to create a cartel might seem an optimal solution for two or more firms in an industry. What the reader may have noticed already is that while it may seem intuitive at first to divide up the market output evenly between or among the firms in an industry, it's not necessarily a *fait accompli* (done deal). AMF would make more profit (total: $1,750) if its agreement with Brunswick were that it would produce 35 balls while Brunswick produced 15 ($750 total profit) at a price of $50 per ball. Brunswick would make more profit if its agreement with AMF were reversed (it produced 35 balls while AMF produced 15 at $50 each).

Cheating. Another development that can and has happened in the real world is that firms can enter into a cartel agreement and then cheat on it because maximizing profit gives a firm an incentive to do so. AMF and Brunswick could enter into their agreement to each produce 25 balls and sell each bowling ball for $50 for a total profit of $1,250 per firm. But AMF can make more profit if it produces 25 balls that Brunswick knows about and then an extra 10 *on the sly* (in secret) that it clandestinely sells to a bowling alley for $40 each. This earns AMF its usual cartel cut of $1,250 plus an additional profit of [($40)(10 balls) =] $400 from its secret production and sale of 10 extra balls for a total profit of ($1,250 + $400 =) $1,650.

11.2 Nash Equilibrium

In the event that there is no agreement (explicit or secret) between AMF and Brunswick, each firm following its own individual profit-maximizing interest, will end up at an output level where boosting production to earn more profit is no longer possible. Where is this level?

For the figures in TABLE 11-1, it would not be at the successful cartel total output of 50 balls sold for $50 each for a maximum industry profit of $2,500. Instead, we could start at the monopoly result with AMF deciding that it could increase its profit by producing 35 balls while Brunswick still produces 25. With a total of 60 balls on the market selling at $40 each for a total profit of $2,400, AMF earns a $1,400 slice of the profit pie while Brunswick earns $1,000. AMF is now earning $150 more in profit, but Brunswick lost $250. This is unacceptable to Brunswick, so Brunswick decides to produce 35 balls while AMF stays at the production level of 35. This brings 70 balls to the market at a price of $30 each for a total joint profit of $2,100, or $1,050 for each firm. Brunswick is now earning $50 more in profit but AMF is now earning $350 less. AMF is understandably upset about this. AMF, in response, boosts its production to 45 while Brunswick continues to produce 35. This brings 80 balls total to the market at a price of $20 each for a total joint profit of $1,600, or $900 for AMF and $700 for Brunswick. At 80 total balls of output, both firms are now worse off as AMF is now earning $150 less profit and Brunswick is now earning $350 less.

Both firms pull back to bringing 70 balls to market with each firm now producing 35 balls, charging $30 each, and earning $2,100 total profit, or $1,050 profit per firm. This output level is known as a **Nash equilibrium**, i.e., a price and output that maximize the profits of an industry given the actions of the other firm(s) or the best choice given the choice(s) of the other actor(s).

This is the paradox of oligopoly: both firms would each earn $200 more if they would just secretly cooperate and produce 10 fewer balls each. For less work they would each get more money. Yet in each trying to get more profit at the expense of the other, they both end up at the Nash equilibrium where they each do more work for less money. However, they don't end up at the uniformly competitive outcome (P = MC) where they produce a total of 100 balls for a price, total revenue, and profit all equal to $0. Profit maximization prevents this.

> **Nash equilibrium** - a price and output that maximize the profits of an industry given the actions of the other firm(s) or the best choice given the choice(s) of the other actor(s).

Key lesson: *Oligopolies not engaged in collusion will produce a higher level of output and lower price than monopolies but a lower level of output and higher price than uniform competitors. Profit maximation by each firm ensures this.*

11.3 How the Number of Firms Affects Price and Quantity

Now let's say that three more firms move into the market: We have the two incumbents, AMF and Brunswick, and then add Hammer, Storm, and MOTIV. For the maximum total profit for the industry, the ideal would be for all the firms to collude and produce the monopoly output (50 balls), charge the monopoly price ($50 per ball), and earn the monopoly total profit ($2,500). This would mean that each of the five firms would produce 10 balls each at a price of $50 per ball, with each firm earning $500 profit. Given the powerful incentives for firms to cheat on the agreement to increase their individual profit, such a collusion by all five firms to achieve the monopoly result seems impossible.

Step 1. Let's say that Hammer increases its production to 20 balls while the other four firms still produce just 10. This action raises industry production to 60 balls and drives the price per ball down to $40. Hammer earns [(20 balls)($40) =] $800 profit, $300 more than it did previously, but all the other firms each earn just [(10 balls)($40) =] $400, or $100 less than each did previously.

Step 2. Storm then increases its production to 20 balls while AMF, Brunswick, and MOTIV still produce just 10 and Hammer still produces 20. This raises industry production to 70 balls and drives the price per ball down to $30. Storm now earns [(20 balls)($30) =] $600 profit, $200 more than it did previously but with AMF, Brunswick, and MOTIV earning just [(10 balls)($30) =] $300, or $100 less than each did previously while Hammer now earns [(20 balls)($30) =] $600, or $200 less than it did previously.

Step 3. MOTIV now gets into the action by producing 20 balls while AMF and Brunswick still produce just 10 and Hammer and Storm still produce 20. This raises industry production to 80 balls and drives the price per ball down to $20. MOTIV now earns [(20 balls)($20) =] $400 profit, $100 more than it did previously but with AMF and Brunswick now earning just [(10 balls)($20) =] $200, or $100 less than it did previously while Hammer now earns [(20 balls)($20) =] $400, or $200 less than it did previously and Storm now earns [(20 balls)($20) =] $400, or $200 less than it did previously.

Step 4. AMF then decides to make a move by producing 20 balls while Brunswick still produces just 10 but Hammer, Storm, and MOTIV hold at 20. This raises industry production to 90 balls and drives the price per ball down to $10. AMF now earns [(20 balls)($10) =] $200 profit, the same as previously but with Brunswick now earning [(10 balls)($10) =] $100, or $100 less than it did previously while Hammer now earns [(20 balls)($10) =] $200, or $200 less than it did previously, Storm now earns [(20 balls)($10) =] $200, or $200 less than it did previously, and MOTIV now earns [(20 balls)($10) =] $200, or $200 less than it did previously.

Step 5. Finally, Brunswick gets in on the action by increasing its production to 20 balls while Hammer, Storm, MOTIV, and AMF hold at 20 balls each. This raises industry production to 100 balls and drives the price per ball down to $0. Brunswick now earns [(20 balls)($0) =] $0 profit, or $100 less than it did previously. Hammer now earns [(20 balls)($0) =] $0 profit, or $200 less than it did previously, Storm now earns [(20 balls)($0) =] $0 profit, or $200 less than it did previously, MOTIV now earns [(20 balls)($0) =] $0 profit, or $200 less than it did previously, and lastly, AMF now earns [(20 balls)($0) =] $0 profit, or $200 less than it did previously.

Now the industry has converged on the uniformly competitive result (P = MC). While revenue and profits are $0, costs are also $0. This will never do because the firms, with each constantly being tempted away from collusion by the prospect of higher individual profits, are all worse off at the uniformly competitive outcome (P = MC). In this chain of events, the industry was best off at 80 balls, because at 90 balls, AMF was earning $200 producing 20 balls, the same as it was earning at 80 balls while only having to produce 10 balls. The industry thus backs up to 80 balls (step 3), 10 greater than the Nash equilibrium of 70 when there were only two firms in the industry.

What we see going on in this movement toward non-collusive oligopolies with more than two firms but fewer than many firms are two effects in the dynamics:

> **price effect** (non-collusive oligopolies) - output increases but price and total profit decline.
>
> **output effect** (non-collusive oligopolies) - selling an additional unit increases profit when price is greater than marginal cost (P > MC).

price effect – output increases but price and total profit decline.

output effect – selling an additional unit increases profit when price is greater than marginal cost (P > MC).

What happened in our five-firm-bowling-ball-oligopoly example is that the output effect was greater than the price effect until step 4. At step 4, AMF raised production from 10 to 20 units (did more work) but profit held steady at $200. At step 4, the price effect began dominating the output effect and increased production does nothing for the firm (AMF) seeking to add to its individual profits.

Two key lessons:
1. *An increase in the number of firms in an oligopoly will push the industry past the old Nash equilibrium and more toward a uniformly competitive result (P = MC) with production higher, price lower, and the market outcome closer to social efficiency.*

2. *Adding competitors to an oligopoly through international trade is a way to get closer to a more socially beneficial outcome with output higher and price closer to marginal cost.*

11.4 Game Theory

Game theory is the study of strategic choice. **Strategy** is a plan to achieve a goal. A **dilemma** is a forced choice between two or more undesirable alternatives.

The **prisoners' dilemma** is a dilemma experienced by two or more suspects of a crime over whether to cooperate or not cooperate with law-enforcement authorities in the solving of said crime. The dilemma resides in the fact that cooperation and non-cooperation by a suspect can both be undesirable choices given the choices made by the other suspect(s).

The prisoners' dilemma is a strategic game known well by police detectives and teaches detective trainees that collusion among multiple captured suspects can be very fragile, even when the results of collusion are clearly in their best collective interest.

Example: the Menéndez brothers, Erik and Lyle, while driving, are pulled over for having an expired license plate. During the traffic stop, an officer discovers a sawed-off shotgun in the brothers' vehicle. However, the police are unable to tie the gun to the murder of the brothers' two parents, José and Kitty Menéndez, as ballistics tests do not work on shotguns.

The police interrogate Erik and Lyle in separate rooms. Erik is told that for possession of the illegal shotgun, he will receive a prison sentence of three years. However, if Erik confesses to the murder of his parents and testifies against Lyle, he will receive immunity from prosecution and be freed that day while Lyle will receive 30 years in prison. If both brothers confess to the murders, a costly trial will be unnecessary and each will receive a reduced sentence of 15 years in prison. Lyle is offered the same deal if he cooperates with the police against his brother Erik. What likely happens? FIGURE 11-1 is the decision matrix (a rectangular diagram used to analyze the choices made in a two-person game) for both brothers.

game theory - the study of strategic choice.

strategy - a plan to achieve a goal.

dilemma - a forced choice between two or more undesirable alternatives.

prisoners' dilemma – a dilemma experienced by two or more suspects of a crime over whether to cooperate or not cooperate with law-enforcement authorities in the solving of said crime. The dilemma resides in the fact that cooperation and non-cooperation by a suspect can both be undesirable choices given the choices made by the other suspect(s).

FIGURE 11-1: Decision Matrix for the Prisoners' Dilemma

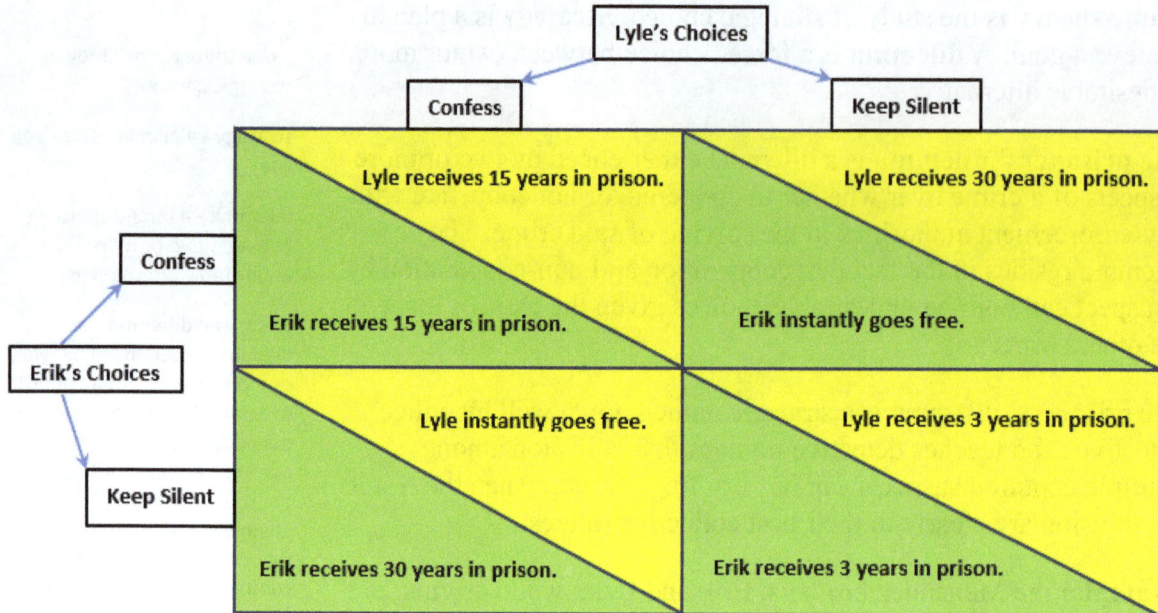

On the matrix, let's start with Erik on the left side. If Erik decides to confess and Lyle decides to confess, they each receive 15 years in prison. If Erik decides to keep silent and Lyle confesses, Erik receives 30 years in prison while Lyle instantly goes free. Now let's go up to Lyle at the top of the matrix. As we saw previously, if Lyle confesses and Erik confesses, they each receive 15 years in prison. If Lyle keeps silent but Erik confesses, Lyle receives 30 years in prison while Erik instantly goes free. Then finally, if both Lyle and Erik remain silent, each receives three years in prison.

Lyle (Left) and Erik Menéndez, When Each was Serving a Life Sentence Without Parole in the Richard J. Donovan Correctional Facility in San Diego, California

Many readers may assume that since Erik and Lyle are brothers, cooperation would be an easy and agreed-upon strategy if they ever fell into the hands of the law. And indeed, this could be the case. If both brothers persevere through a long interrogation and maintain their silence, they end up at the optimal solution of three years in prison for each brother, given the tough circumstances they are in. However, just like two people who are not related, brothers can often not see eye to eye and have sibling jealousies, resentments, and mutual distrust.

In this latter case of sibling distrust, Erik may not at all be confident that Lyle will hold his ground and stay silent. If Erik confesses but Lyle does not, Erik goes free while Lyle serves 30 years in prison. However, if both confess, Erik gets 15 years (as does Lyle), which is awful but better than 30 years. If Erik is **risk averse** (disliking negative outcomes more than liking positive outcomes of a similar nature), he likely confesses and so does Lyle when faced with the same set of potential costs and benefits. This brings us to the concept of the **dominant strategy**, the best choice for an actor regardless of the choice(s) made by the other actor(s). In the case of Erik, it is to confess and accept either zero or 15 years in prison. The same goes for Lyle, for whom confessing is the dominant strategy as well.

risk averse – disliking negative outcomes more than liking positive outcomes of a similar nature.

dominant strategy - the best choice for an actor regardless of the choice(s) made by the other actor(s).

In an interesting twist, let's say that Erik (the younger brother) was always a favorite of his parents and Lyle resented that. Thus, Lyle confesses hoping that Erik may not. Erik, aware of Lyle's resentment toward him, confesses as well because he fears Lyle could rat him out for instant freedom. In this way, both end up confessing, getting 15 years in prison, and ending up at the Nash equilibrium of the game (upper-left box of the matrix in FIGURE 11-1), the best choice given the choice(s) of the other actor(s). It is also the worst outcome for both of the brothers and it is achieved because they each followed their own individual perceived best interest. Had they successfully cooperated they would have received not a good result but a much better one than they actually both got.

11.5 The Decision Matrix Applied to Economics

We've just seen the decision dynamics of two criminal suspects, but how does game theory apply to the decisions of firms? FIGURE 11-2 is the decision matrix as applied to our example about the decision making and market outcomes of AMF and Brunswick.

FIGURE 11-2: Decision Matrix for the AMF-Brunswick Duopoly

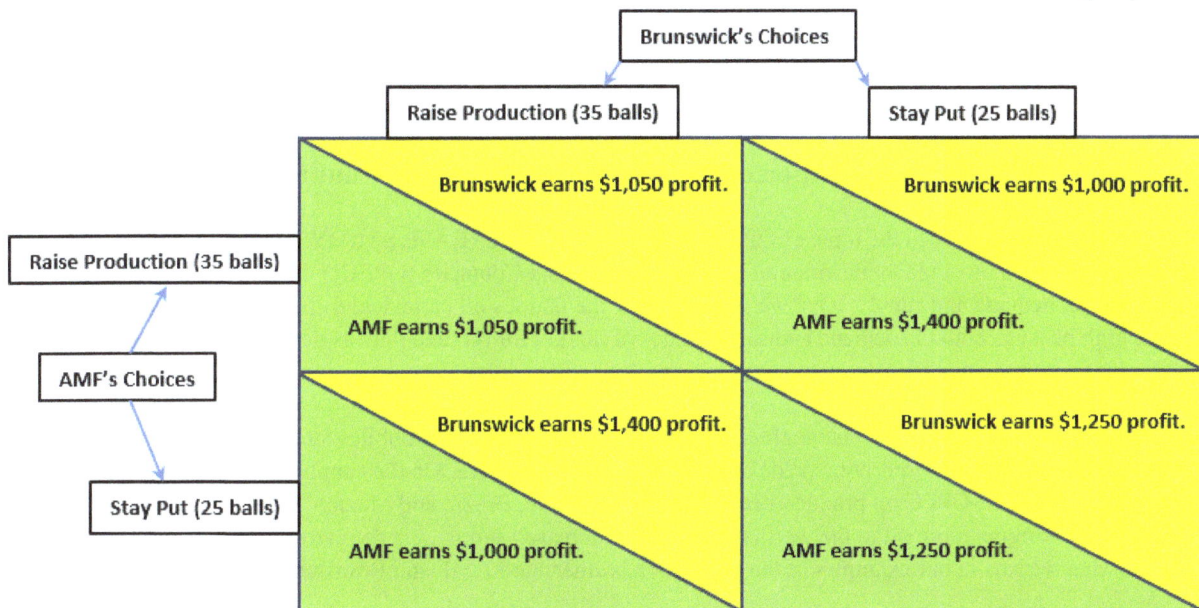

	Brunswick's Choices	
	Raise Production (35 balls)	**Stay Put (25 balls)**
Raise Production (35 balls)	Brunswick earns $1,050 profit. / AMF earns $1,050 profit.	Brunswick earns $1,000 profit. / AMF earns $1,400 profit.
Stay Put (25 balls)	Brunswick earns $1,400 profit. / AMF earns $1,000 profit.	Brunswick earns $1,250 profit. / AMF earns $1,250 profit.

(AMF's Choices shown at left)

Let's start with AMF and Brunswick agreeing to produce 25 balls each and selling each ball for $50. Total industry profit is $2,500, with each firm raking in $1,250 profit. The industry is a cartel (by collusion) so far and that puts us in the lower right square of the matrix. From that square, the cartel can break down to a Nash equilibrium in two ways.

First, AMF can raise production (from 25 balls to 35) while Brunswick stays put at 25 balls. Total industry production is now at (35 + 25 =) 60 balls selling at $40 each with total industry profit now at $2,400 and AMF earning $1,400 profit and Brunswick earning $1,000 profit. We have now moved to the top right square of the matrix. Brunswick, seeing the price of bowling balls drop $10, senses that something is amiss and that AMF has underhandedly boosted production. In response, Brunswick boosts its own production by 10 balls and now both AMF and Brunswick are producing 35 balls each with a total industry output of 70 balls selling for $30 each. Total industry profit is now $2,100 with each firm earning $1,050 each. This puts us at the Nash equilibrium we first encountered in section 11.4 which, in FIGURE 11-2 (like FIGURE 11-1) lies in the upper-left box of the matrix.

The other way to get to the Nash equilibrium box of the matrix is if we begin at the cartel box (lower right box of the matrix) as before and Brunswick is the first to raise production (from 25 to 35 balls) while AMF stays put at 25 balls. Total industry production is now at (35 + 25 =) 60 balls selling at $40 each and total industry profit is $2,400 with Brunswick earning [(35 balls)($40) =] $1,400 profit and AMF earning [(25 balls)($40) =] $1,000 profit. We have now moved to the lower-left square of the matrix. AMF, seeing the price of bowling balls drop $10 senses that Brunswick is cheating on the cartel agreement. AMF, in response, boosts its production by 10 balls and now Brunswick and AMF are producing 35 balls each with a total industry output of 70 balls selling for $30 each. Total industry profit is $2,100 with each firm earning $1,050 profit. This again puts us at the Nash equilibrium, the upper left box of the matrix in FIGURE 11-2.

Further, producing 35 balls each for a price of $30 for a profit of $1,050 each is the dominant strategy for each firm. Each firm could be making $200 more in profit, but short-term self-interest leads them away from that better result.

CASE STUDY: the Organization of the Petroleum Exporting Countries (OPEC), Part II

The last time that we visited the topic of OPEC was in chapter 5 (see "CASE STUDY: How Time and Technology Overthrew the Organization of Petroleum Exporting Countries [OPEC]). In chapter 5, on the price sensitivity of demand and supply, what we saw was how the famous oil cartel had difficulty keeping world oil prices high because both the demand and supply sides of market for oil (and thus its derivative, gasoline) became more price sensitive over time and this joint action pushed prices down.

On the demand side, a surge of reliable, fuel-efficient Japanese import automobiles into the U.S. lowered demand and consumer alternatives to driving made demand more price sensitive. On the supply side, the higher world oil prices motivated non-OPEC oil producers (e.g., the Soviet Union, Brazil, and Mexico) to increase exploration, drilling, and bringing more oil to the world market. This increased supply, but the cartel over time performed as well as what we saw in our examples of the Menéndez brothers and AMF and Brunswick.

The oil cartel formed in September of 1960 with Iran, Iraq, Kuwait, Saudi Arabia, and Venezuela as members.

By 1973, the beginning of the embargo, seven more countries had joined, in chronological order those seven were: Qatar, Indonesia, Libya, the United Arab Emirates, Algeria, Nigeria, and Ecuador. By 1985, as the cartel's heydays were coming to an end, only one more member had joined (Gabon), bringing the cartel to 13 members. It's no wonder that OPEC's power came to an end when it did. If a small cartel spread around the world (with more than 7,000 miles between Venezuela and Saudi Arabia) is difficult to monitor, how could a strict agreement between 13 firms be rigidly enforced?

As of May 2025, OPEC had twelve members. In an age of widespread fracking and electric vehicles, OPEC's glory days look long gone and likely never to return.

11.6 Game Theory Part II: Common Resources and Arms Races

The U.S.-versus-Russia Arms Race. From the Truman Doctrine on March 12, 1947 to the fall of the Soviet Union on December 26, 1991 was the era of the Cold War. The U.S. had nuclear weapons beginning on July 16, 1945. During this period, the government of the Soviet Union sought to catch up to the U.S. in terms of the technological level of its weapons and acquired its first nuclear weapon on August 29, 1949. After this, there was a continual arms race between the two countries for decades. But there was also an attempt to reduce tensions between the two countries, reduce the stockpile of nuclear weapons, and hence reduce the probability of nuclear annihilation of both countries. While the Soviet Union was dissolved on December 26, 1991, its former most-powerful nation, Russia, still has a large stockpile of nuclear weapons as does the U.S.

FIGURE 11-3 is the decision matrix for the two countries with regard to arms control. If the U.S. and Russia decide to cooperate and by treaty eliminate all nuclear weapons and return to just conventional weapons, the prospect of nuclear annihilation is gone and both countries are in the lower right square of the matrix in FIGURE 11-3. This brings peace and tranquility to both countries not seen since 1949. Each country can then put massive amounts of resources into internal improvements, infrastructure, etc.

However, if the U.S. cheats on the treaty and decides to begin secretly stockpiling nuclear weapons, the U.S. is safe from nuclear annihilation but Russian is in danger of it. When Russia discovers that the U.S. has cheated on the arms-control treaty, Russian immediately begins rebuilding its nuclear-weapons stockpile. This moves both countries to the upper-left square of FIGURE 11-3 (Nash equilibrium). Both countries are now worse off than when they both had completely eliminated nuclear weapons.

Of course, if Russia cheats on the treaty first, that triggers a clockwise movement around the matrix from the lower-right square to the upper-left square. Russia cheats by rebuilding its nuclear stockpile while the U.S. remains without any nuclear weapons. This moves the two countries from the lower-right square of the matrix to the lower-left square of the matrix where Russia is safer but the U.S. is in danger. After the U.S. discovers that Russia has cheated on the treaty, it starts rebuilding its nuclear stockpile and both nations move to the upper-left square in FIGURE 11-3 (Nash equilibrium), where both countries are armed with nuclear weapons.

Regardless of how Nash equilibrium is reached, both countries end up in an inferior position to disarmament because now they have to build and stockpile costly nuclear-weapons inventories instead of spending money on internal improvements, making the citizenries of both nations worse off.

FIGURE 11-3: Decision Matrix for the U.S.-Russia Arms Race

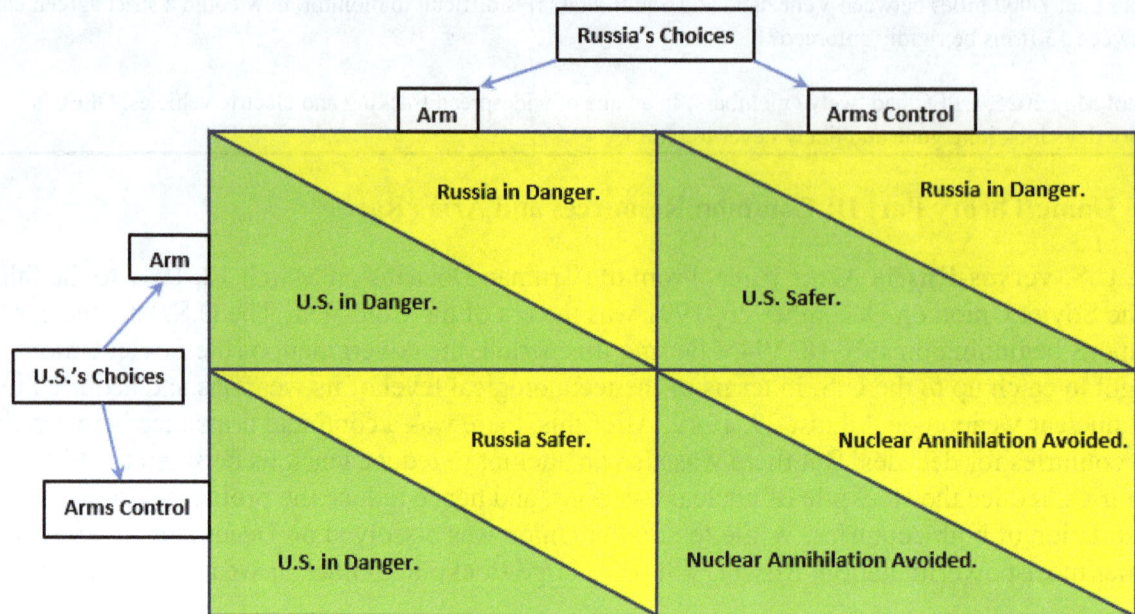

The U.S.-Russian arms race demonstrates how entire societies, millions of people, can be adversely affected by a failure to negotiate by individual governments to put two or more societies in an inferior position.

Commercial Fishing in British Columbia, Canada. In the Pacific Ocean west of British Columbia, Canada is an archipelago known as Haida Gwaii. In the archipelago there is Masset Inlet, where two fishing firms, Lockeport and Moresby (named after their owners Joe Lockeport vs. Aaron Moresby), are allowed to fish for salmon and halibut. Overfishing is not a great concern because the inlet is always restocked naturally by the Pacific Ocean after fishing season ends. The two firms are restricted to the inlet. Suitable commercial fishing vessels in the used boat market are priced at $250,000 each (including crew, fuel, and maintenance). A season's worth of salmon and halibut in the inlet is worth $3 million. The director of British Columbia's Department of the Interior recommends that each firm use just one boat to keep its costs down to maximize profit but can use as many boats as it wishes as long as it doesn't leave the inlet.

If each firm uses 1 boat, each firm catches half the fish and earns $1.5 million revenue minus $250,000 cost or $1,250,000 profit. If one firm uses 2 boats, it can catch 75 percent of the fish and earn $2,250,000 revenue minus $500,000 cost or $1,750,000 profit while the other firm using only one boat earns $750,000 revenue minus $250,000 cost or $500,000 profit. If both firms utilize two boats, they each get half the fish and earn a revenue of $1,500,000 each minus costs of $500,000 each which equals $1 million profit for each firm. So, what happens? The decision matrix in FIGURE 11-4 tells the story.

FIGURE 11-4: Lockeport Versus Moresby

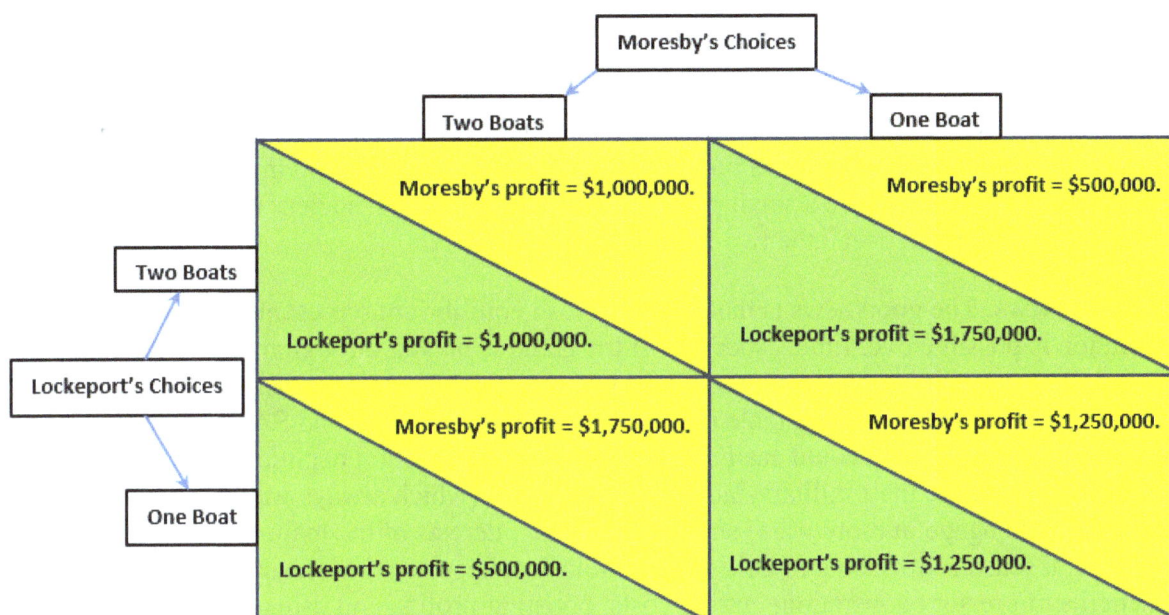

Assuming no inflation in the economy, Lockeport and Moresby each start out using one boat to catch fish. In the first season, each firm took the advice of the Department of the Interior and used one boat each to earn $1,250,000 profit, putting both firms in the lower-right square of the matrix. In the second season, Lockeport decided to use a second boat and earn a whopping $1,750,000 profit while Moresby only earned $500,000, which put both firms in the upper-right square of the matrix. In the third season, each firm fished the inlet with two boats and earned $1,000,000 profit each, which put both firms in the upper-left square of the matrix (Nash equilibrium).

Exercise for the Reader: proceed through the three-season cycle again in detail, but this time have Moresby be the first firm to "cheat" on the implicit agreement to use just one boat to fish the inlet. Show, step by step, how both firms end up at the Nash equilibrium.

Regardless of which firm ends up cheating on the agreement first, the two firms move from their best position on the matrix (the lower-right square) to the worst position on the matrix (the upper-left square, or Nash equilibrium). Clearly the best situation would be for the two firms to equally divide up the inlet and use just one boat to fish each firm's half. That strategy would yield the maximum profit for the least amount of work. However, paranoia and greed can lead to both firms doing more work to earn less profit…

11.7 …But, Cooperation is Possible Over Time

The Bad News. Now that we have seen several different scenarios of cooperation versus noncooperation and Nash equilibrium, we can now see that, from the standpoint of society, cooperation is not necessarily good and Nash equilibrium is not necessarily bad. In the case of AMF and Brunswick, a lack of cooperation was bad for the two firms in terms of earning lower profits but good for consumers in terms of getting more bowling balls brought to market at a lower price. In the case of the Menéndez brothers, a lack of cooperation between the two brothers brought longer prison sentences for both of them. In the case of the U.S.-Russia arms race, a lack of cooperation increases the chances of nuclear annihilation for both societies--both sides now have to build up and maintain costly nuclear-weapons arsenals that take money away from other pressing societal desires and needs. The Nash equilibrium outcome makes both societies poorer as a result. As for Lockeport and Moresby, the two fishing firms competing in British Columbia, the use of an extra boat by both firms eats up $500,000 in profit across both firms. Although both firms are a small part of society, nevertheless, society is worse off because of the noncooperation between the two fishing firms.

The Good News. The good news is that where a Nash equilibrium represents a bad outcome, cooperation is possible over time, especially if the game is played through multiple rounds. The U.S. and the Soviet Union over time each built up a formidable nuclear arsenal, but also returned to the arms-reduction negotiating table multiple times in the SALT-1 and SALT-2 treaties. Today, the U.S. and Russia could easily return to the arms-reduction negotiating table if they each decided to ignore their military-industrial complexes (which always want to manufacture more arms and engage in more wars) and seek the best interests of the majority of their citizens. After several seasons of fishing in British Columbia, Lockeport and Moresby can eventually see the benefits of greater cooperation: cutting costs, boosting profits, and using less resources.

Where a Nash equilibrium represents a good outcome (e.g., AMF and Brunswick), society benefits. Output is higher, prices are lower, and consumers and the broader society are better off. Adam Smith's invisible hand is at its peak performance. Less cooperation means more competition.

However, as with socially bad Nash equilibria, socially good Nash equilibria can be escaped as well. This can happen if all of the individuals and firms involved have a long-term commitment to their industries. AMF can cheat on Brunswick and temporarily boost its profits by ($1,400 profit - $1,250 profit =) $150. However, this breach of trust will trigger Brunswick to produce more, with both firms now looking at a lifetime of $1,050 profits each round, forgoing a lifetime of $1,250 profits each period. Over a lifetime, $200 extra per round is a substantial difference. This is why over repeated games, the incentive to cooperate grows.

In contrast, it is just the opposite with fly-by-night firms. Unlike AMF and Brunswick, Joe's Bowling Equipment is a fly-by-night firm. It is owned by house-painting contractor Joe Doe and friends who just want to compete for a round in the bowling-equipment industry and then return to their usual job of painting houses. Only in the industry for one round, it is easy to see why Joe's has an incentive to not cooperate with a competitor. To be exact, it is ($1,400 - $1,250 =) $150, or the amount Joe's would boost its profit by not cooperating. Whether Joe's cheats AMF or Brunswick, the firm feels no shame as it is exiting the industry after the round is over and will never see its competitor again.

tit-for-tat – cooperating with your opponent in the first round and then mimicking your opponent's moves in all successive rounds.

For the record, a study by Robert Axelrod revealed that the most successful strategy was one of **tit-for-tat**, or cooperating with your opponent in the first round and then mimicking your opponent's moves in all successive rounds. This was found to be the most successful strategy because while it immediately punished cheaters, it also immediately forgave them once they learned the error of their ways and resumed cooperation. The tit-for-tat strategy ended up being the one that outperformed all others in prisoners' dilemma tournaments.

Finally, more good news. Just because two or more firms have reached close cooperation after a few rounds of production decisions and obtained the monopoly result (as could happen with AMF and Brunswick over repeated rounds), it is not the end of the story unless the government blocks further entry. Without barriers to entry, if output falls, then prices and profits will rise and thus new firms (domestic or foreign) will get attracted to the industry. New entry forces the industry more toward permanent competition, which is what we see with OPEC. Five firms became 12 and cooperation went from challenging to impossible. While OPEC still exists, it's hard to know what purpose it's currently serving, certainly not to fulfill its original function of a price-boosting, output-stifling cartel.

ECONOMICS IN ACTION: Why Do Divorces Peak in March and August?

Every year there are two months in which divorces spike above all the others: March and August. Insights from game theory and incentive analysis can shed some light as to why divorces may follow a seasonal pattern. Examining divorce data from the state of Washington from 2001-2015, University of Washington researchers Brian Serafini and Julie Brines came to some interesting possible explanations.[44]

Divorce Filings by Month

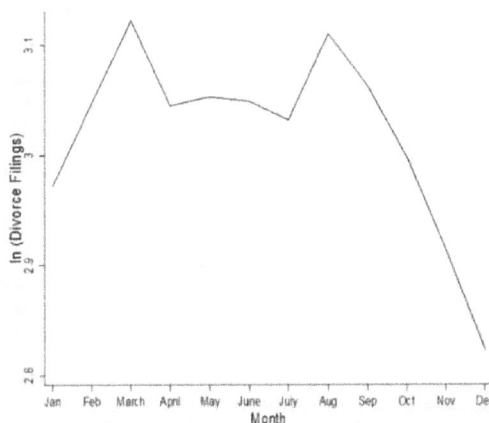

Data from Washington state, Nov. 2001 - Dec. 2015 (Serafini and Brines)

For the month of March, one line of thinking is that some couples take advantage of the time off from work during the Christmas-to-New-Year's holidays to attempt to settle their differences, but fail. March is two months after the winter holidays, so the winter holidays alone seem to be limited in terms of explanatory power. However, March comes right on the heels of Saint Valentine's Day—the love holiday—on February 14. Couples whose relationships are rocky or seemingly-forever-stuck-in-neutral could be observing the new beginnings of other couples and perceiving high enough marginal benefits (over costs) to make them decide to end their bad or stale relationships.

What about the month of August? This pattern could be driven by higher perceived marginal benefits as well. The high point of summer vacationing is in July. A number of couples whose relationships have grown strained or distant may decide to go on vacation or use some mid-summer time off from work to give their pairing one more try. If it doesn't work, they then spend the next few weeks planning for a divorce by the end of summer to be ready for a new beginning in autumn. Plus the school year begins in August, the kids won't be home as much, and the divorcing partners will have more time to find a new mate.

None of this is to put a positive spin on divorce. To begin with the obvious: Perceptions rule but don't always reflect reality. The same goes for perceived marginal costs versus perceived marginal benefits. As we noted with football in chapter 1 (see the section on principle number 3, *Rational economic decisions are made at the margin*), rational strategies can fail. Second, divorce has myriad explicit and implicit costs that vary from person

---

[44] Khazan, Olga. "Why Divorce Spikes in August and March: Bad holidays with a Spouse Can Start to Feel Like a Broken Promise." The Atlantic. 23 August 2016. < https://archive.ph/TTRkB>

to person. These certainly include the heavy emotional toll divorce so often takes on family members, friends, and children.

11.8 Public Policy

antitrust laws and enforcement – laws and legal actions based on them designed to maintain competition in industries or limit the market power of firms.

merger – the combining of two or more firms into one firm.

The public policy for dealing with cooperation among firms includes **antitrust laws and enforcement** (which we first discussed in chapter 9), laws and legal actions based on them designed to maintain competition in industries or limit the market power of firms. The two most prominent antitrust laws are the Sherman Antitrust Act of 1890 and the Clayton Act of 1914. The Sherman Act forbids monopolies and the Clayton Act forbids a **merger** (the combining of two or more firms into one firm) in industries where competition would substantially decline and allows a party harmed by restrained trade to sue and collect damages. The U.S. Department of Justice (DOJ), individuals, and firms have the ability to bring lawsuits for the purpose of enforcing antitrust laws. As the reader may guessed, actions taken under antitrust enforcement have never been free of controversy and may have become more controversial over time.

price fixing – the act of two or more firms colluding to set the prices of their products at the same level.

The Intersection of the Southwest Freeway and Weslayan Street in Houston, Texas (Google, Fair Use)

A. Price fixing is the act of two or more firms colluding to set the prices of their products at the same level. But how do we know when this occurs in a market? At the intersection of the Southwest Freeway and Weslayan Street in Houston, Texas sits three gas stations (Exxon, Shell, and Chevron). What's the problem? The price of 87-octane gasoline at all of the three stations is exactly the same. Why? It could very well be that all three gas-station owners secretly met and agreed upon a price for gasoline. That indeed would be price fixing, but in no way could one conclude that because all three stations sell gasoline for the same price that price fixing must be going on. First, given how quickly and frequently the demand for and supply of gasoline change, each change would require a new meeting of the station owners to fix a new price. Second, if just one of the three stations were selling gasoline at a price substantially higher than those of the other two, it would easily lose most of its business to the other two, especially if its convenience store was not substantially different from those of the other two.

The bottom line on price fixing: *Equal or close prices can be just as symptomatic of fierce competition as alleged price fixing. By themselves they prove nothing.*

predatory pricing – the act of pricing below cost the same product sold by a competitor for the purpose of driving said competitor out of business.

B. Predatory pricing is the act of pricing below cost the same product sold by a competitor for the purpose of driving said competitor out of business. For example, John's Crab Shack has a 65 percent share of the seafood-restaurant market in Niceville, Florida. The Crab Bucket is the new restaurant in town that has taken up the rest of the market (35 percent). John's decides to engage in predatory pricing by buying crabs at $10.00 per pound and selling them for $5.00 per pound to drive its new competitor out of business.

As a business strategy, any experienced entrepreneur could see the recklessness of this. First, the 50 percent cut in price, by the law of demand, is going to bring in more customers, in fact, a whole lot more because restaurant meals have a high price sensitivity of demand. This could push up John's market share to say, 90 percent, especially if The Crab Bucket doesn't match John's new price. This means that John's is taking 50 percent losses on 90 percent of the seafood-restaurant sales in town. Yikes. Even though The Crab Bucket's market share has been temporarily driven down to 10 percent, it ends up in far better shape than John's after John's is forced to return to market prices. While it may not have engaged in predatory pricing, Red Lobster learned the perils of pricing restaurant meals too low in the wake of its Endless Shrimp special that bankrupted the restaurant chain.

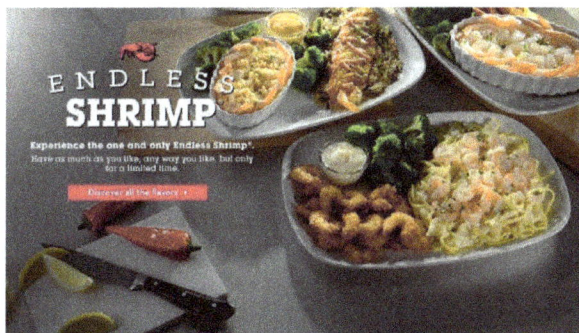

An Advertisement for the Notorious Endless Shrimp Campaign That Helped Push the Red Lobster Seafood Restaurant Chain into Bankruptcy (Red Lobster, Fair Use)

C. Resale price maintenance is the act of a manufacturer requiring authorized retailers to resell its product at a certain price. For example, let's say that Samsung requires all of its authorized retailers to sell one of its newest 85-inch OLED smart televisions for not lower than $1,800. Going from Best Buy to Kohl's to Walmart to Target and seeing all four stores price the same television at $1,800 may lead some consumers to believe that the four retail outlets are engaged in anticompetitive price fixing. However, this makes no sense. If Samsung wants to raise the price of its television above the competitive level, it can raise the price that all retailers pay for it. That would be the more direct and sensible way. What Samsung may desire is that the higher-than-market price going to its chosen retailers will help fund a better showroom or electronics department and more knowledgeable sales staff. This would prevent "showrooming," where consumers visit a full-service retail store to research an electronic good and get recommendations from knowledgeable sales staff, and then purchase that same good from a discount or online retailer with a much lower price but little customer service and helpful sales staff. In other words, the practice of resale price maintenance, just like dealer authorization, can be another way to ensure that a manufacturer's customers get better service at the retail level and discount retailers aren't able to free ride off of full-service physical stores.

> resale price maintenance – the act of a manufacturer requiring authorized retailers to resell its product at a certain price.

D. Tying is the selling of two or more products together. It can be anything from Dove including a free trial-size bottle of its new shampoo packaged with its standard four-pack of soap for the purpose of promoting its new shampoo to the more controversial (at least at the time) act of Microsoft making its Internet browser a part of its Windows operating system (more on this later).

> tying - the selling of two or more products together.

First, there is a good reason that the shampoo packaged together with the four-pack of Dove soap bars is free. If Dove's loyal customers are willing to pay a maximum of $6 for the four bars of soap and nothing for the trial-size bottle of unfamiliar new shampoo, then the maximum they will pay for the combined product is also $6 and not a penny more, the exact same price they were planning to pay for just the soap. Forcing Dove's loyal customers to accept a shampoo they may or may not like does nothing to boost the price of the combined product and certainly does nothing to increase Dove's market power in soap. Companies give out free samples because customers like them and acquire a positive view of the firm even if they don't end up using and continually purchasing the new shampoo. The case of Microsoft is more complicated and explored further below.

horizontal merger - the combining of two or more firms in the same industry into one firm.

vertical merger - the combining of two or more firms from different industries into one firm.

E. A horizontal merger is the combining of two or more firms in the same industry into one firm while a **vertical merger** is the combining of two or more firms from different industries into one firm. Antitrust authorities (often attorneys by training and trade) have traditionally brought cases against and been much more concerned about the anti-competitive effects of horizontal mergers than vertical mergers. But as we saw above, one of the most potentially dangerous cartels in the U.S. (health care) is a vertically integrated cartel. Second, enforcement, even for horizontal mergers, has been highly selective, even nonsensical. If there was one merger that (in the interest of consistency) should have been of concern to antitrust authorities, it should have been the proposed merger of Blue Cross and Blue Shield. Yet, the firms were allowed to merge in 1982 with not even a hint of protest from antitrust authorities. This is in stark contrast to the proposed merger of jetBlue airlines and Spirit Airlines in 2024, which was hardly a threat to competition in air travel but was nevertheless blocked by a judge in January 2024.

Government-Protected Cartels. In the interest of consistency, these should have been targeted by antitrust enforcement long ago. Most antitrust authorities are either Democrats or Republicans or appointed by Democratic or Republican politicians who are hardly enthusiastic about reducing the dominance of the two-party political cartel and making campaigns for elective offices more competitive. As for health care, the AMA-AHA medical cartel is one of the top-five wealthiest and most powerful lobbies in the U.S. that has repeatedly lobbied its way out of antitrust enforcement.

CASE STUDY: U.S. v. Microsoft Corporation

This case relates to accusations of tying, and as such a number of economists thought it was a very costly much ado about nothing. With the release of its Windows 98 operating system in May 1998, Microsoft made its Internet Explorer (IE) Internet browser a part of its Windows operating system. The U.S. government accused the company of tying its browser to its operating system to increase its market power in browsers and discourage other firms from competing with it in the browser market. Microsoft's response was that it was only trying to add a feature to its operating system to improve it. While the company held an approximate 80% market share in operating systems, it still had competition from Apple and Linux. In the browser market, Microsoft's main competitor was Netscape Navigator. Microsoft had also invested millions of dollars in Apple because a substantial number of Apple customers used Microsoft's Office software. While Microsoft's Windows operating system came preloaded on most new computers, it only represented approximately 3% (on average) of the price of the computers.

In November of 1999, Microsoft lost in court. In June of 2000, a federal judge ordered that the company be broken up into two separate companies: one that created and sold the Windows operating system, and another one that sold other non-operating system software applications. In June of 2001, a Federal Appellate Court overturned the breakup ruling and sent the case to a new judge. In September 2001, under a more business-friendly George W. Bush administration, the U.S. Dept of Justice agreed to settle the case. In November 2002 a settlement was agreed upon whereby windows would keep its browser and Microsoft would change some of the ways it did business.

In the 20/20 vision of hindsight, the government couldn't have been more wrong about the supposed threat of Microsoft integrating its browser into its Windows-98 operating system. Today, there are number of non-Microsoft alternatives on the market: Firefox, Chrome, DuckDuckGo, Brave, and Opera are just a few of the many out there. More than a couple are at least equal to if not clearly superior in performance and features to the current Microsoft Windows browser, Microsoft Edge.

11.9 Conclusion

This chapter closes out this book's unit on industrial organization. This chapter began with oligopoly and moved through cartels (protected and unprotected) to game theory to antitrust and antitrust controversies. Throughout the discussion of oligopoly, cartels, and game theory we examined the difference in market outcomes and social well-being between more competitive industries on the one hand versus government protection or voluntary collusion on the other hand.

In FIGURE 11-5 is what is known as the market-structure tree. It is a rough guide to classifying the market structure of industries according to the four market structures of industrial organization that we studied in chapters 8 (uniform competition), 9 (monopoly), 10 (differentiated competition), and this chapter, 11 (duopoly, oligopoly, and cartels). In determining market structure, the first issue that must be answered about an industry is the number of firms. If an industry is composed of just one protected firm, it is a monopoly. If it is composed of two to several firms, it is a duopoly, oligopoly, or cartel. If the industry is comprised of many firms, then it is competitive in either a uniform or differentiated sense.

FIGURE 11-5: The Market-Structure Tree

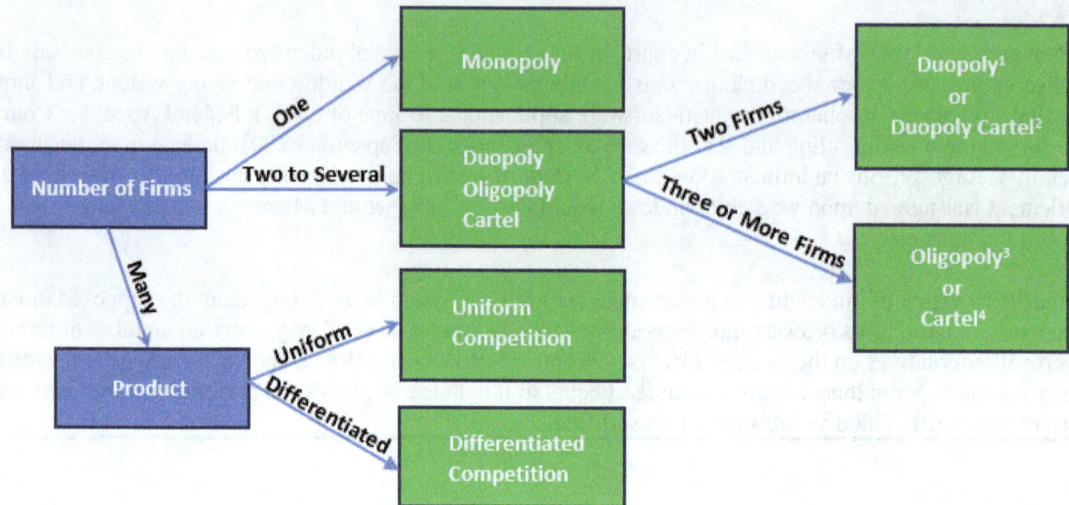

Notes:
[1] Duopoly with no apparent collusion.
[2] Duopoly cartel characterized by either willful collusion or government protection.
[3] Oligopoly with no apparent collusion.
[4] Cartel of three or more firms characterized by either willful collusion or government protection.

TABLE 11-2 summarizes all of the types of market structures that we have studied, from uniform competition to oligopoly.

TABLE 11-2: Summary of Market Structures (Uniform Competition, Monopoly, Differentiated Competition, and Oligopoly)				
	Uniform Competition	**Monopoly**	**Differentiated Competition**	**Oligopoly**
Product	Uniform	Differentiated	Differentiated	Uniform to some differentiation
Quantity of firms	Many	One	Many	Two to several
Firm Goal	Maximize profits	Maximize profits	Maximize profits	Maximize profits
Output Level	MC = MR	MC = MR	MC = MR	MC = MR
Some Degree of Market Power Present?	No	Yes	Yes	Yes
Price in relation to MC?	P = MC	P > MC	P > MC	P > MC
Deadweight loss present?	No	Yes	Yes	Yes
Profits are possible in the short run?	Yes	Yes	Yes	Yes
Profits are possible in the long run?	No	Yes	No	Yes
Advertise?	No	Little to none.	A lot.	Little to more.

11.10 Chapter Concepts

duopoly
oligopoly
cartel
government protection
collusion
government-protected cartel
horizontal cartel
vertical cartel
non-government-protected cartel
Nash equilibrium
price effect
output effect
game theory
strategy
dilemma
prisoners' dilemma
risk averse
dominant strategy
tit-for-tat
antitrust laws and enforcement
merger
price fixing
predatory pricing
resale price maintenance
tying
horizontal merger
vertical merger

11.11 Problems, Questions, and Discussion Topics (Items Requiring Examples are Marked with an Asterisk [*])

1. *duopoly* versus *oligopoly* versus *cartel* (define each industry, then provide an example of only one)

2. With respect to the two potentially most dangerous cartels,

   A. name and define each cartel.

   B. For each one, what is the alleged source of their danger?

3. *horizontal cartel* versus *vertical cartel* (define both, then provide an example of only one not found in this book)*

4. Nash equilibrium (define, then provide a quantitative example)*

5. *Oligopolies not engaged in collusion will produce a higher level of _____ and lower _____ than monopolies but a lower level of _____ and higher _____ than uniform competitors. _____ by each firm ensures this.*

    A. Fill in the blanks: _____, _____, _____, _____, _____.

    B. Explain:

6. *price effect* versus *output effect* (define both, then provide a quantitative example of only one)*

7. *An increase in the number of firms in an oligopoly will push the industry past the old Nash equilibrium and more toward _____ with production _____, price _____, and the market outcome closer to social efficiency.*

    A. Fill in the blanks: _____, _____, _____.

    B. Explain:

8. *Adding competitors to an oligopoly through _____ is a way to get closer to a more socially beneficial outcome with _____ higher and price closer to _____.*

    A. Fill in the blanks: _____, _____, _____.

    B. Explain:

9. FIGURE 11-1 (reproduced below for convenience) is the decision matrix for the Menendez brothers.

FIGURE 11-1: Decision Matrix for the Prisoners' Dilemma

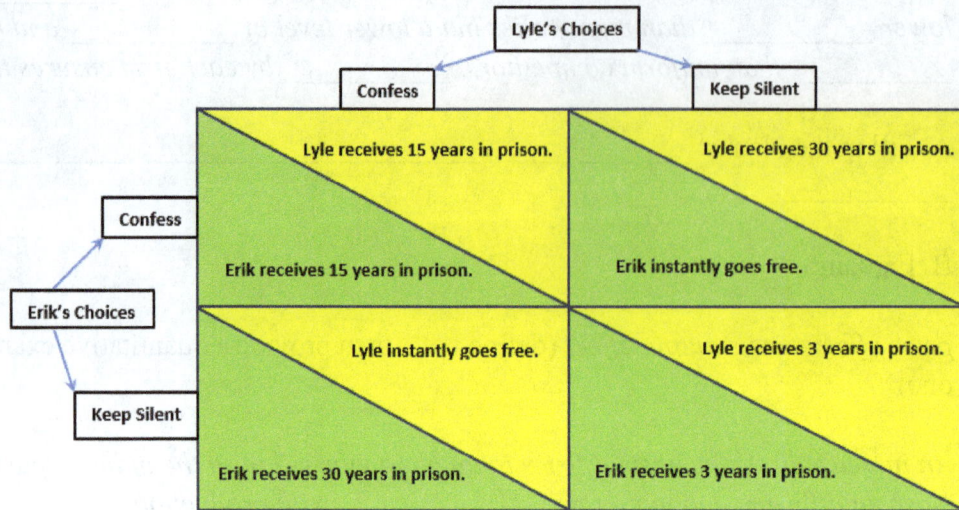

		Lyle's Choices	
		Confess	Keep Silent
Erik's Choices	Confess	Lyle receives 15 years in prison. / Erik receives 15 years in prison.	Lyle receives 30 years in prison. / Erik instantly goes free.
	Keep Silent	Lyle instantly goes free. / Erik receives 30 years in prison.	Lyle receives 3 years in prison. / Erik receives 3 years in prison.

A. Although they are brothers, what circumstances could make it difficult for Erik and Lyle to collude to ensure that they end up at the best possible outcome in the matrix?

B. Assuming that each brother is risk averse and follows a dominant strategy, how could they end up at the worse possible outcome for both brothers? Explain each step.

10. FIGURE 11-2 (reproduced below for convenience) is the decision matrix for AMF and Brunswick.

FIGURE 11-2: Decision Matrix for the AMF-Brunswick Duopoly

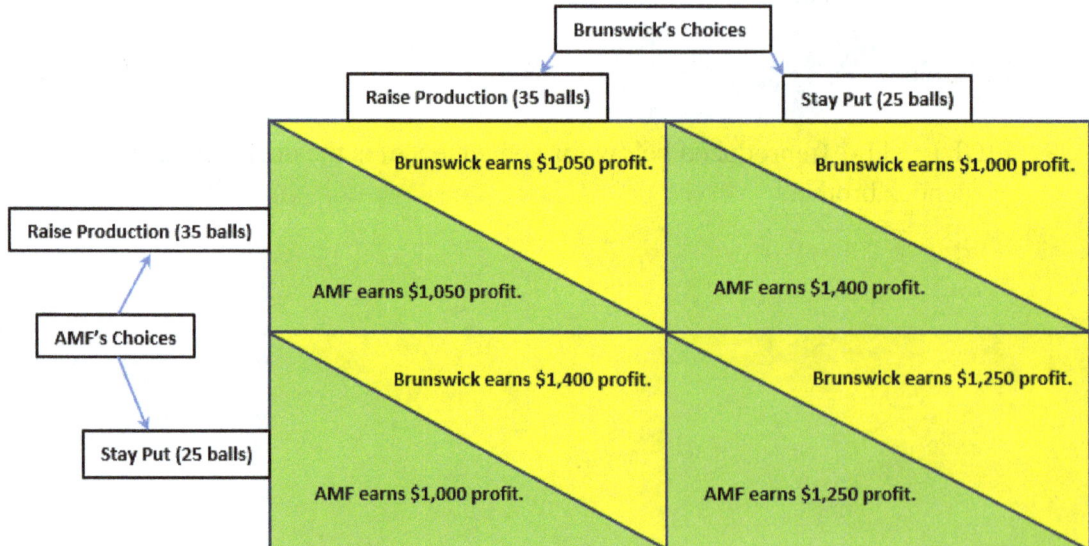

		Brunswick's Choices	
		Raise Production (35 balls)	Stay Put (25 balls)
AMF's Choices	Raise Production (35 balls)	Brunswick earns $1,050 profit. / AMF earns $1,050 profit.	Brunswick earns $1,000 profit. / AMF earns $1,400 profit.
	Stay Put (25 balls)	Brunswick earns $1,400 profit. / AMF earns $1,000 profit.	Brunswick earns $1,250 profit. / AMF earns $1,250 profit.

A. Although it would maximize their collective benefit, what circumstances could make it difficult for AMF and Brunswick to collude so that they end up at the best possible outcome in the matrix?

B. Assuming that each firm is risk averse and follows a dominant strategy, how could they end up at the worse possible outcome for both firms? Explain each step.

11. Regarding the Organization of the Petroleum Exporting Countries (OPEC) cartel,

A. From 1973 to 1985, as its membership grew, did control of the cartel and enforcement of its rules become easier or more difficult?

B. After 1985, what two technological developments further undermined the economic power of the OPEC cartel?

12. FIGURE 11-3 (reproduced below for convenience) is the decision matrix for the U.S. and U.S.S.R.

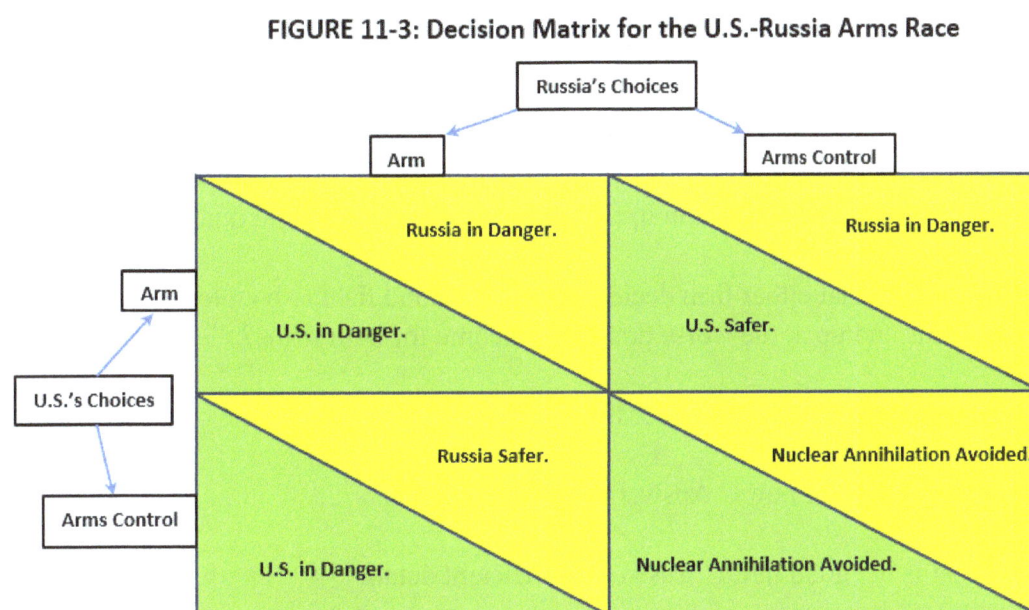

FIGURE 11-3: Decision Matrix for the U.S.-Russia Arms Race

Russia's Choices

Arm | Arms Control

Russia in Danger. | Russia in Danger.

Arm

U.S. in Danger. | U.S. Safer.

U.S.'s Choices

Russia Safer. | Nuclear Annihilation Avoided.

Arms Control

U.S. in Danger. | Nuclear Annihilation Avoided.

A. Although they are better off mutually agreeing to arms control, what circumstances could make it difficult for the U.S. and U.S.S.R. to continue to hold their position at the best possible outcome (lower right box) in the matrix?

B. Assuming that each follows a dominant strategy, how do they end up at the worse possible outcome for both countries?

13. FIGURE 11-4 (reproduced below for convenience) is the decision matrix for Lockeport and Moresby.

FIGURE 11-4: Lockeport Versus Moresby

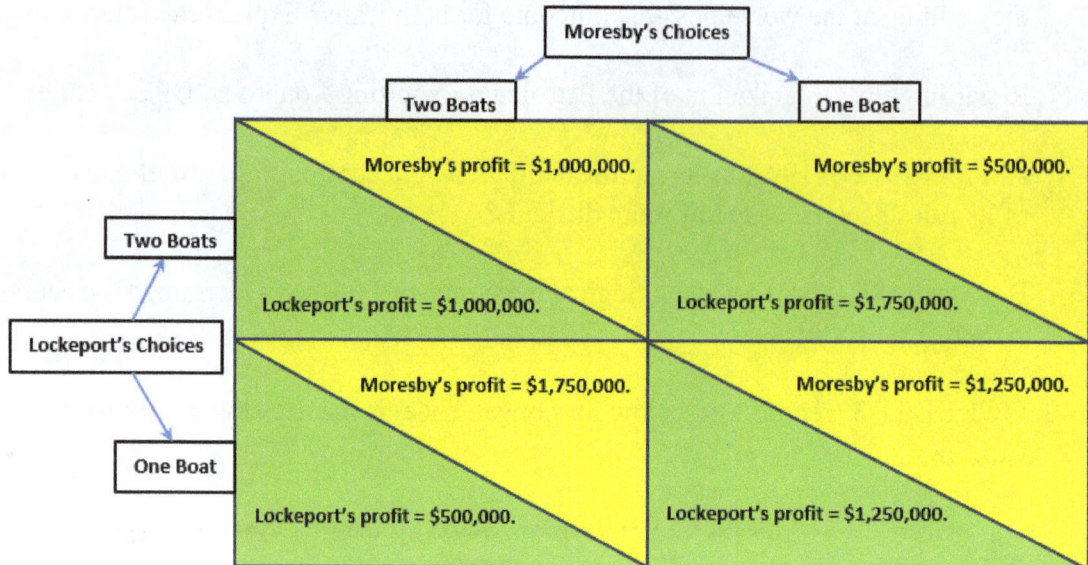

	Moresby's Choices	
	Two Boats	**One Boat**
Two Boats	Moresby's profit = $1,000,000. Lockeport's profit = $1,000,000.	Moresby's profit = $500,000. Lockeport's profit = $1,750,000.
One Boat	Moresby's profit = $1,750,000. Lockeport's profit = $500,000.	Moresby's profit = $1,250,000. Lockeport's profit = $1,250,000.

(Lockeport's Choices shown on left axis)

A. Although they are better off mutually agreeing to control costs through the use of one fishing boat, what circumstances could make it difficult for Lockeport and Moresby to continue to hold their position in the matrix at the best possible outcome for both firms?

B. Assuming that either firm decides to use a second fishing boat to catch fish, how could both firms end up at the worse possible outcome for both firms?

14. With respect to cooperation over time,

   A. What is the bad news? Answer in sufficient detail.

   B. What is the good news? Answer in sufficient detail.

15. With respect to cooperation over time,

   A. What is tit-for-tat?

   B. What did Robert Axelrod's study discover about the tit-for-tat strategy?

16. What did Brian Serafini and Julie Brines discover about the different reasons why divorces likely rise

   A. in March?

   B. In August?

17. *Equal or close prices can be just as symptomatic of _____ as _____. By themselves they prove nothing.*

    A. Fill in the blanks: _____, _____.

    B. Explain:

18. Although predatory pricing is an oft-alleged practice, what is one peril that a firm, especially one with a product having a high price sensitivity of demand, could encounter?

19. Although resale price maintenance could create the appearance of price collusion among some retailers, what purpose could it serve in terms of creating better customer service for a manufacturer?

20. What inconsistency has been repeatedly been observed in the difference of antitrust enforcement against

    A. vertical mergers as opposed to horizontal mergers?

    B. Government-protected cartels versus non-government-protected cartels?

21. Concerning the case of *U.S. v. Microsoft Corporation,*

    A. of what anticompetitive practice was Microsoft Corporation accused of committing?

    B. In June of 2000, what was the original sentence that Microsoft was given after losing the first round of the lawsuit?

    C. After winning its appeal of the initial verdict, what did Microsoft agree to in its final settlement with the U.S. Department of Justice in November 2002?

Index of Key Concepts, Names, and Firms

288